Urban
Europe's Challenges

Sabine Urban (Ed.)

Europe's Challenges

Economic Efficiency and Social Solidarity

With the contributions of:

Hanns A. Abele, Jürgen G. Backhaus, Adamantios Diamantopoulos & Heidi Winklhofer, Peter Eichhorn, Marc Gaudry & Ulrich Blum & John McCallum, Lewis D. Johnson, William Kingston, Wim Kösters, Giovanni Palmerio, Marina Ricciardelli, Youri Roubinski, Waldfried Schliesser, Peter Standish, Horst Steinmann & Albert Löhr, Jim Stewart

GABLER

Sabine Urban is a Professor at Strasbourg University (Robert Schuman) and heads the CESAG (Centre of Managerial Research)/I.E.C.S. which is affiliated to it. She teaches international economics and corporate strategies in several universities both in France and abroad, and is in charge of the International Commerce degree at the I.E.C.S.-European Management School. She sits on the board of several industrial and financial firms. Her main research fields are International Business and European economy.

Acknowledgement
The editor is grateful to the Société des Amis des Universités de l'Académie de Strasbourg and to the Conseil Général du Bas-Rhin for their financial support.

Die Deutsche Bibliothek - CIP-Einheitsaufnahme

Europe's challenges : economic efficiency and social solidarity / Sabine Urban (ed.). With the contributions of: Hanns Abele ... - Wiesbaden : Gabler, 1996

NE: Urban, Sabine [Hrsg.]; Abele, Hanns

ISBN 978-3-409-13246-6 ISBN 978-3-663-13432-9 (eBook)
DOI 10.1007/978-3-663-13432-9

Publishing editors: Barbara Roscher/Annegret Heckmann

Preface

The current work is the third volume in the series "Europe's Economic Future", edited by Strasbourg's Robert Schuman University, under the direction of Professor Sabine Urban, head of the CESAG-IECS research center. This series intends to analyze the European situation - not through idealized models of operation or abstract schemas - rather based on concrete observations, equally close to the actions and the life of the European citizen as of Europe's corporations and institutions. The studies that are presented here are not, however, simply descriptions; they refer to precise conceptual frameworks and nourish a long-term reflection.

This volume, like its predecessors, reflects the diversity which characterizes Europe, rich and stimulating but, at the same time, difficult to manage. Spectacular advances are followed by moments of hesitation. With European construction, new processes of adaptation and new competitive strategies must be implemented by businesses. Public authorities must respect the convergence constraints imposed by the European Union (Maastricht I) and imagine a modified institutional framework for the European Intergovernmental Conference of 1996 (Maastricht II). The citizens of the fifteen countries involved need themselves to be enlightened about the future, to understand how - between independent markets and coordinated policies - a desirable economic and social cohesion in the European area will be realized. Furthermore, the area itself is not fixed; it is evolving between the strengthening of links and the opening of new horizons.

In this evolution, political will is certainly fundamental, but it is largely supported by material or immaterial investments made by each of the actors. This infinity of decisions on every level makes the Europeanization process irreversible, even if the challenges which must be overcome remain numerous. The accounts presented here are the contributions of fifteen professors invited by Robert Schuman University (IECS) during the 1994-95 academic year; they come from diverse horizons (university professor, expert, or diplomat) and from eight different countries. This collective and international work intends both to enlighten and encourage; with concern for the intellectual honesty characteristic of scientists, it will not mask the difficulties inherent to a complex reality.

Sabine URBAN

Contents

List of Contributors 9

1. Introduction
Sabine Urban 15

2. A Republican Concept of Corporate Ethics
Horst Steinmann and Albert Löhr 21

3. Performance Centers in Public Administration
Peter Eichhorn 61

4. Economic and Monetary Union: Between Solidarity and Efficiency
Marina Ricciardelli 81

5. The Drift of the Public Debt: Threat for Europe? The Italian Case
Giovanni Palmerio 107

6. Stability Culture as a Precondition for the Sustainability of the European Monetary Union (EMU)
Wim Kösters 137

7. Financial Governance in the New Europe
Lewis D. Johnson 159

8. Core-Periphery Interactions in European Stock Markets
Jim Stewart 183

9. What Kind of Patent System Does Europe Need?
William Kingston 211

10. The Impact of European Policies Towards Science and Technology on the European Research Landscape
Jürgen G. Backhaus 247

11. The Technology of Communication and the Reshaping of the European Broadcasting Industry
Hanns A. Abele 291

12. The European Union and Russia
Youri Roubinski 331

13. Consolidation and Expansion of the European Single Insurance Market
Waldfried Schliesser 363

14. Differences in the Export Profiles Among Users of Export Marketing Research: Evidence from Two European Countries
Adamantios Diamantopoulos and Heidi Winklhofer 395

15. Accounting Codification: Experience and Prospects in the European Context
Peter Standish 419

16. A First Gross Measure of Unexploited Single Market Integration Potential
Marc Gaudry and Ulrich Blum and John McCallum 449

Contributors

Hanns A. Abele received a Doctor's Degree in Law from the University of Vienna in 1963 and moved on to Habilitation (economics) there in 1972. He was appointed full professor (economics) at the University of Fribourg, Switzerland in 1973. Currently he is full professor (political economy) at the University of Economics and Business Administration Vienna. He taught at various academic institutions and was a Fulbright Scholar in 1987/88. Being a member of a number of scientific organizations he was elected president of the Fribourg Working Group for Broadcasting Economics in 1992. Among his fields of interest are money and credit, finance, theory of economic policy, cultural economics, and media economics. In these areas he published books and articles in journals. Besides his interests in theoretical economics he has been active in computer based instruction for more than a decade.

Jürgen G. Backhaus has been the professor of Public Economics at the University of Limburg at Maastricht (The Netherlands) since 1986. He holds doctorates in Law and Economics from the University of Konstanz (1976 and 1985 respectively). His research emphasizes all fields of applied public finance taxation, including public accountability, public enterprise economics, environmental economics, health economics and the history of public economics. In his work he emphasizes a law and economics approach. In 1993, he founded (with Frank Stephen) the *European Journal of Law and Economics*, which is published with Kluwer Academic Publishers.

Adamantios Diamantopoulos holds the Chair in International Marketing at the European Business Management School, University of Wales, Swansea. His research interests are in pricing, sales forecasting, marketing research, and international marketing and he is the author of some 100 publications in these areas. He is a founding member of the Consortium for International Marketing Research (CIMaR), the Academy of Marketing Science Country Representative for the UK, associated editor of the International Journal of Research in Marketing, and a member of the Editorial Review Boards of several academic journals.

Heidi Winklhofer is a Research Assistant in International Marketing at the European Business Management School, University of Wales, Swansea. Currently a doctoral candidate under the joint supervision of Professor A. Diamantopoulos and Professor S.F. Witt (Tourism), her research interests are in business forecasting and export marketing. Her work has appeared in the International Journal of Forecasting, in the proceedings of the Academy of International Business (UK) and the European Marketing Academy.

Peter Eichhorn is the head of the chair of Public Management in the Faculty of Business Administration at Mannheim University. His main fields of research are public administration, public enterprises, especially hospitals, and institutions of public enterprises (f.i. non-profit organisations).

Marc Gaudry is professor of Economics at Université de Montréal (Département de sciences économiques et Centre de recherche sur les transports, CRT) and Associate Researcher at Université Louis-Pasteur (Bureau d'économie théorique et apppliquée, BETA), Strasbourg. He obtained his Ph. D. from Princeton University. His research pertains to applied econometrics, often in the area of transportation. He was awarded a number of research prizes, including a 1990 Alexander von Humboldt Research Award.

Ulrich Blum is professor of Economics at the Technical University of Dresden. He obtained his Ph. D. from the University of Karlsruhe. His fields of research pertain mostly to spatial economics. He was awarded the August Lòsch Prize and is a member of the Bavaria-Saxony Commission on the future.

John McCallum is Senior Vice President and Chief Economist with Royal Bank of Canada, Toronto. Prior to that, he was professor of Economics at McGill University, as well as Dean of the Faculty of Arts. He holds a Ph. D. from McGill University. His research interests include macroeconomic analysis, Canadian constitutional issues and regional trade integration.

Lewis D. Johnson is a Professor of Finance at the School of Business, Queen's University, Kingston, Canada, and is also Academic Director and Dean of Studies at the International Study Centre, Herstmonceux Castle, East Sussex, UK. He has authored or co-authored more than sixty academic papers and books in the field of finance, particularly in the areas of stock and bond valuation, portfolio strategy, and corporate governance. He is an independent director of a venture capital company listed on three exchanges. His PhD was conferred by the University of Toronto.

William Kingston has taught Innovation in Trinity College, Dublin, since 1969. His books include "The Political Economy of Innovation (1984)" and "Innovation, Creativity and Law (1990)" In 1987, he edited "Direct Protection of Innovation", a study of possible reforms of the Patent system, for the European Commission. He is currently directing research into the phenomenon of simultaneous invention, which is being carried on in several European countries as well as in the United States.

Wim Kösters holds a chair for Economic Theory (monetary economics and business cycle theory) and the Jean Monnet chair for European economics as well as the position of the managing director of the Institute for the European Economy in the Faculty of Economics and Business Administration of the Ruhr-University of Bochum. His main fields of research are monetary economics (including European monetary integration), international economics (especially trade policy) as well as economics of employment and labor market performance.

Giovanni Palmerio is Full Professor of Economics at Luiss University (Rome) and President of ISCO (National Institute for Economic Forecasts). He is the author of many books and articles on cycles, growth and development theory, public finance and inflation.

Marina Ricciardelli is a Senior Lecturer in Economics at "La Sapienza" University of Rome and a supply Professor at University of l'Aquila (Italy). She is a member of ETUC (European Trade Union Confederation) representing Italy in the Economic Policy Committee (Brussels), an expert on fiscal problems on the Economic and Social Committee of the European Communities.

Youri Roubinski graduate of the Moscow Institute of International Relations (1953), doctorate of history, head of department of the Institute of World Economy and International Affairs of the Russian Academy of Sciences (1956-1977, 1986-1987), first Counsellor of the Ambassy of Russian Federation in France (1978-1985, 1987-1993). Visiting professor in French University - Aix-en-Provence (1969), Strasbourg (1992), Tours (1993-1995). Author of several monographies and articles on the contemporary French economy and politics as well on the international subjects, especially european integration.

Waldfried Schliesser born in Baden-Baden in 1932, and a graduate of Humboldt University, is Professor of Economics. After his viva, he became accredited fellow at the Faculty of Economics, Berlin, where he was awarded a tenure as Professor in 1965, a position he occupied until 1991. Since 1992 he has been a visiting Professor at the Institute of Insurance Economics of the University of Economics, Vienna

Peter Standish Professor of European Accounting, Nottingham-Trent University. Visiting Professor, Université de Paris-Dauphine. Honorary Member, Conseil National de la Comptabilité, Paris. Primary research interest in comparative international accounting and auditing, particularly between in Britain and France.

Horst Steinmann born 1934, holds a Chair in Business Administration and Management at the University of Erlangen-Nürnberg. For more than 25 years his research has centred on the philosophical foundation of management theory. He is Chairman of the "Deutsches Netzwerk Wirtschaftsethik", established in 1993 a national branch of the European Business Ethics Network, where he served on the Executive Committee for 8 years. He is also a member of several editorial and advisory boards of business ethics journals (Journal of Business Ethics, Revue Ethique des Affaires, Business Ethics: A European Review) and of a book series (Kluwer Issues in Business Ethics). His numerous publications focus on issues in Strategic Management, Corporate Governance, and Business Ethics. Recent book publications as author or co-author include: Grundlagen der Unternehmensethik; Unternehmensethik; Lexikon der Wirtschaftsethik; European Casebook on Business Ethics.

Albert Löhr born 1955, is Assistant at the Chair for Business Administration and Management, University of Erlangen-Nürnberg. He is a member of the Executive Committee of the European Business Ethics Network EBEN, and chairs the Programme Committee of the 9th annual conference of EBEN in 1996. He is also a member of the editorial board of Business Ethics: A European Review, and serves as a member of the adjudicating panel of the European Business Ethics Essay Prize of the London Business School. Many of his publications are on business ethics, including his dissertation, for which he was awarded the "Max-Weber-Preis für Wirtschaftsethik 1992".

Jim Stewart is a lecturer in Finance at Trinity College, Dublin. He has written a book and several articles on corporate finance and taxation and the financial behaviour of multinational companies. His current research interests relate to the effects of taxation on corporate financing, capital markets and economic development and pension funds and capital markets.

Sabine Urban is a Professor at Strasburg University (Robert Schuman) and heads the CESAG (Centre of Managerial Research)/IECS Strasbourg which is affiliated to it. She teaches international economics and corporate strategies in several universities both in France and abroad, and is in charge of the International Commerce degree at the IECS Strasbourg. She sits on the board of several industrial and financial firms. Her main research fields are International Business and the European economy; she is author and co-author of numerous publications in these fields.

Introduction

Europe is shaken. Deep-reaching changes are occurring, stimulating the resistance of some and the hope of others. Demand for efficiency is reinforced. Challenges to civilization and social well-being must be overcome. Important questions remain unanswered.

In a very uncertain global environment, Europe has the ambition of remaining a pole of strong development where quantitative and qualitative preoccupations are joined. Confidence in the future will probably require the mastery of unfolding technologies but also the efficiency of organizational management methods and the respect of fundamental principles regarding ethics, solidarity, and balance. The authors of the present volume look at these problems from different points of view.

The functioning of a society according to the ancient concept of "res publica" continues, beyond the debates of political philosophy, to prove extremely delicate. Could social stability be a myth after all? **Horst Steinmann** and **Albert Löhr** ask the question and argue the debate from a multidisciplinary angle, including economic, political, and managerial considerations, as well as philosophical and theological concerns. In the current confusion of a society lacking references and values, subjected to violent tensions and obvious malfunctioning, it is extremely important to question the interaction between private interests and social solidarity, the role of corporate profit and the societal responsibility of business. German schools of politico-philosophical thought (Habermas in Frankfurt, Lorenzen in Erlangen) have animated this debate. Is it appropriate to prefer the principle of consensus or the principle of compromise? Which will best guarantee the most valuable asset, i.e., social peace achieved through a process of free determination of the parties involved? How can we overcome the conflict between utopia and violence illustrated by Karl Popper, and more generally between social stability and individual profit?

We can admit that considerations of entrepreneurial ethics must be evaluated in the context of a capitalistic market economy which imposes its own constraints of efficiency. The system, which is defensible both from an ethical and an economic point of view, supposes in any case a stated and lived responsibility of the different actors involved. Europe will have to implement this concept at every level of subisiarity.

The question of the responsibility of the various actors is also addressed by **Peter Eichhorn** who analyzes management constraints in the public sector. The subject is of current interest everywhere in Europe! The fact that the missions of public organizations are defined by Political Authority, with respect to general interests, cannot justify that these entities may not be managed and controlled in a rigorous and rational manner. Peter Eichhorn - relying on cost/opportunity methods of evaluation, on results obtained in relation to expectations, and on the means required in relation to the pursued goals - demonstrates that the needs for economic efficiency and common interest are not antinomic. The author provides here a framework for reflection and action which should be taken into account in all countries. Social dialogue and public efficiency would hence be consolidated for the good of all.

1996, with the meeting of the European Intergovernmental Conference, will bring out these combined demands for efficiency and rigor in the social organization. This theme is developed by **Marina Ricciardelli** who titles her analysis "The Economic and Monetary Union, between Solidarity and Efficiency". The 1996 deadline gives us the opportunity to reflect on the past development of the European Union and on the validity of the theoretical model which underlies its functioning. We must, indeed, confront the expected results of this model (with respect to given conditions) with the observable socio-economic reality, particularly with regard to employment, distribution of wealth, social solidarity, and growth. The stakes are high, and the credibility of the procedures used for European construction is at issue.

The text of Marina Ricciardelli recalls first of all the paradigm of the European Union and examines the theoretical elements as well as the institutional procedures which characterize this Union. The problem of employment retains particular attention; it leads to a critical analysis of the model and to constructive propositions which consider the demands of defending a democratic society and fostering social equilibrium, combined demands which are not automatically assured by production growth. From this point of view, the European institutions (with independent resources) have an important role to reconsider.

The rule of convergence, admitted as an evident necessity with regard to the principles of European integration, does not of course in any way resolve the risks of conflict nor reduce the difficulties of adjustment imposed on all the actors concerned, public or private.

Giovanni Palmerio addresses the problem of convergence/conflict from the angle of public finance. Based on the case of Italy, can the slide of the public debt be considered a menace to European construction? The author sustains his argument by relying on contributions from economic theory and by commenting on real economic evolution as it may be interpreted in terms of growth, monetary stability (or instability), and social equilibrium. The situation of Italy is rather heterodox when compared to the dominant Anglo-Saxon and German models; its situation is all the more interesting because Italy, since 1950, has continued to surprise: discretely it has become the fifth economic power in the world. Can this development be considered thus solid and lasting? A hesitation in the response may be entertained.

Obviously, no simple affirmation can reflect the complexity of reality: objective data and psycho-sociological reactions, technical arguments and political visions, are strongly mingled. **Wim Kösters** demonstrates this by affirming that the "culture of (monetary) stability" is a prerequisite for an enduring European monetary union. This point of view is shared by the Central Bank of Germany;

however, the bank acts within an institutional framework of solidarity among the "Länder" ("Finanzaugleich" recognized by the constitutional basic law) which is far from existing at the level of the European Union. The union has an even greater need for a strong political will and for public confidence, created by dialogue and earned by actions.

We cannot, however, under-estimate the market mechanisms. Notably as far as finance is concerned, market mechanisms play a formidable role in the allocation of resources and in the division of power. **Lewis D. Johnson** demonstrates this while at the same time insisting on the difficulty in harmonizing financial structures, presently in place in Europe, which are very different in their conception. **Jim Stewart** also wonders about the possibility of homogenizing the European financial arena in a forseeable lapse of time. For the moment, the national institutional systems and the reality of distinct monetary blocks explain the numerous divergences which are reflected notably in:

- the relative importance of financial markets in terms of market capitalization and of the number of companies listed,
- the share of domestic and international companies listed in the various stock markets,
- modes of stock evaluation and exchange,
- the role of banks in financing business,
- the nature of active stockholders (pension funds, insurance companies, banks, individuals),
- more or less restrictive regulations,
- transaction costs,
- the impact of capital tax, clearly far from being neutral.

It seems that the opposition between an Anglo-American model, animated by a short-term profit rationale, and a continental European model, more concerned with long-term economic efficiency, will endure.

The European long term also depends to a very large extent on the entrepreneurial initiatives of the Europeans and on the technological mastery which this geo-political European area will have managed to achieve faced with North America and Japan. **William Kingston** defends the idea that, in this perspective, Europe, grappling with reinforced worldwide competition, has a particular need for new policies to protect industrial property. **Jürgen G. Backhaus** looks into the impact of European-level policies concerning science and technology. In the different European countries, research conducted in specialized institutions is organized in a manner which is not homogeneous, relative to specific objectives and communication forms. What will change the scientific policies which are in place on the European level? The analyses presented by the author are enriched by the theoretical reflections of Eucken (Freiburg school of thought), largely unknown outside of Germany, regarding the concept of order underlying economic processes. **Hanns A. Abele** analyzes the evolution of a technological sector of particular importance, that of information and communication. This evolution brings with it considerable consequences: new markets, new actors, new products, increasing value of equipment, financing of heavy investments, modifications of power, increased incertitude due to globalization of markets, necessity of concluding strategic alliances, etc.

The eastern border of the European Union (EU) raises great political debates addressing the appropriateness and modalities of the EU's opening to eastern countries, and in this case the enlargement of the integrated zone. Further, Russia, while close in many regards, cannot help but raise worries and hopes. Is it not an area so different from that of Asia's western cape, yet so complementary? **Youri Roubinski** presents historical and cultural elements and details the economic links which unite the zone of the EU and that of Russia. The "Expanded Europe" whose two pillars could be the EU and Russia is not, however, an immediate reality.

The markets of central and eastern Europe are, on the contrary, very promising in the short run. **Waldfried Schliesser** demonstrates this based on the case of the insurance sector, a business sector which is relatively unknown despite its financial and social weight. The strategies for developing European insurance companies must today, and after all in a quite brutal manner, consider at the same time the constraints of a necessary harmonization among the current member states of the European Union and the opportunities for considerable expansion in the East where socialized insurance systems are on the decline. The playing field is immense because of the current under-development of the market system.

The powerful insurance sector is clearly not the only one at issue when it comes to adapting to the European New Deal. **Adamantios Diamantopoulos**, presenting methods of international marketing used by international companies, and **Peter Standish**, presenting methods of accounting management and evaluation, attest to this fact. Lastly, **Marc Gaudry** offers a model, applied to the inter-regional commercial flows, which enables the definition of a measure of the potential for integration of the single market which remains unexploited. The future does not cease to invent itself.

Horst Steinmann
and Albert Löhr

A Republican Concept of Corporate Ethics

1. Introduction
   A. The german discussion on business ethics
   B. Three basic questions
2. A general framework for business ethics
   A. The good reason approach
   B. A six level framework to locate corporate ethics
3. The philosophical foundation of corporate ethics
   A. The problem of justification
   B. The content approach
   C. The process approach of the Erlangen School
   D. Conclusion: the philosophical starting point
4. Corporate ethics in a capitalist market economy
   A. Alternative approaches
   B. Legitimacy of profit seeking
   C. Corporate ethics as self-imposed restriction
   D. Corporate ethics as a republican approach

We would like to thank Mike Dowling from the University of Georgia for all his comments and help to bring the manuscript into its final form.

1. Introduction

A. The german discussion on business ethics

The *German debate* on business ethics has often been estimated to be at least 10 years behind the state of the art in the United States. One may point to the recent developments and initiatives in the American business world, e.g. the remarkable idea of Federal Sentencing Guidelines (Nagel & Swenson - 1993), or the incorporation of business ethics as a subject of research and teaching in the academic field of business administration (DeGeorge - 1991, Dunfee & Robertson - 1988, Piper, Gentile & Parks - 1993). Generally speaking, one may be properly impressed by the successful institutionalization of business ethics in the U.S. and the ongoing practical efforts in the field.

However, there is also a growing literature on the topic of business ethics in Europe that American scholars should consider. Especially in Germany, there has been a *flood of publications* since the late 1980s, which has led to a very distinctive discussion of ethics, economics, and business (for an overview see for instance Dahm - 1989, Enderle et al. - 1993, Forum für Philosophie - 1994, Homann & Blome-Drees - 1995, Koslowski - 1985, Steinmann & Löhr - 1991; bibliographies are provided by Forum wirtschaftsethik 3 (1995)/Special Issue 1, Müller & Diefenbacher - 1992, Siefkes - 1993). This literature is actually built on a long term tradition of research in the field of ethics and business in Germany throughout the whole of this century. And although it was primarily a subject of moral philosophy and economics in the past, it also came up in cycles in business administration under various labels and circumstances, e.g. as a background for the debate on co-determination (Steinmann & Gerum - 1978). Even the *roots of business administration* as an academic discipline were strongly influenced during the 1920s by public interest oriented normative approaches (Löhr - 1991, pp. 75 ff.). As a tragedy in history, these normative approaches were abused by the Nazi regime for their ideological purposes (Hundt - 1977), and so the business ethics debate is viewed with suspicion by its critics even today (e.g. Schneider - 1990, p. 889). Furthermore, since the modern main stream of philosophy in Germany has been telling the same story as elsewhere about the impossibility of a reasonable foundation of norms and values (Popper - 1945, Albert - 1980), the upcoming debate on business ethics was widely estimated as a hopeless venture until the 1990s, particularly in the academic world of business administration.

Thus one cannot help but wonder that the international discussion on business ethics and its German protagonists are already noted, particularly in the business community, but they meet only an *ambiguous response* throughout the academic disciplines. German business faculties are apparently reluctant, while other social sciences and the considerable disciplines, like philosophy and economics, often disqualified the international (and mainly U.S.) debate as theoretically poor and merely instrumental (e.g. Schneider - 1990, p. 883). Some sociologists even called the whole endeavour nonsense (Luhmann - 1993). As a matter of fact, the challenge to talk on ethics in Germany is probably harder than in other countries, with respect to the outstanding philosophical traditions one never should ignore, and with respect to traditional borderlines between those academic disciplines which treat the problems of business, economics and ethics under their very subtle and specific perspectives.

This institutional segmentation of the debate has also led to the fact that the discussion of the field in Germany doesn't strictly correspond to the international term *"business ethics"*. For a long time the subject was split into analyses at the *macro level* with a particular focus on the legitimacy of market institutions, and research on the *micro level* about the role of individual ethics for a proper functioning of the market. Thus, on the one hand, there emerged an ongoing and widely differentiated debate on rather general ethical issues on the macro level ("system ethics") by philosophers and economists, which have been treated with high theoretical power and with reference to the entire tradition of the ethics & philosophy discussion (see, for instance, the discussions of the committee "Wirtschaftswissenschaft und Ethik of the "Verein für Socialpolitik", Enderle - 1985, Hesse - 1988, Homann - 1994b).

On the other hand, the contributions to the field of moral philosophers from theology often stress predominantly the importance of individual ethics as an indispensable counterpart to institutional arrangements, but without distinctive focus on corporate actors as social entities (Lefringhausen - 1988, Kerber - 1988, Rich - 1990/1991, Kirchenamt der ekd - 1992, Konsultationspapier - 1994; with reference to the corporate level Hengsbach - 1991, Furger - 1994; see also Steinmann & Zerfass - 1996). Of course these normative discussions about individual ethics are constantly influenced by new empirical research on the moral development of managers and students (Kaufmann, Kerber & Zulehner - 1986, Ulrich & Thielemann - 1992, Löhr & Kilian - 1993).

Obviously this *bipolar focus* on macro and micro level issues promoted a certain tendency to disregard the role of corporations as important intermediate institutions (e.g. Homann et al. - 1988). Therefore *corporate phenomena* of ethics in particular businesses ("corporate ethics" as a special aspect of business ethics), which are also prominent in the U.S. dicussion besides the individual ethics, remained quite underdeveloped in the German arena, although many business people show serious interest in that field. In other words: business administration as an academic discipline primarily concerned with the *"meso level"* (Enderle - 1991, p. 180) has put the ethics theme on its agenda too late, while other disciplines have been setting high theoretical standards for the discussion one cannot simply ignore.

Considering this background, one has to undertake a very *thorough reasoning* in Germany to develop a modern concept of corporate ethics as a special approach to business ethics. From the perspective of business administration, one has to take into account the elaborated positions of present moral philosophers and economists, basically refer to the outstanding tradition of philosophy in Germany, find arguments against the widely shared idea of value-free social sciences, and after all one should not expect too much support from the business faculty colleagues. Under these circumstances we published the first of a series of articles on corporate ethics in 1985, discussing the philosophical and economic presuppositions underlying the claim for corporate ethics (Steinmann & Oppenrieder - 1985). Since then quite a few academics from different disciplines have contributed to the discussion, and we have steadily tried to develop our integrative concept of business ethics according to their arguments (Steinmann & Löhr - 1988, 1991, 1994a, 1994b, 1995, Löhr - 1991).

B. Three basic questions

Nevertheless, a final consensus on the basic problems has not been reached. There are mainly *three questions of disagreement:*

1. In general, what is a reasonable *notion of corporate ethics?* Obviously a comprehensive answer to this question can only be found as the result of an interdisciplinary discussion about the modern role of the corporation in state, society and economy. Thus, the following two questions are a kind of a subset to that general first question.

2. On the one hand, there is the *economical challenge* for corporate ethics: is there room at all in a market economy for an ethical orientation of corporate strategies beyond profit maximization? Or, in other words: is the level of the corporation a proper place at all for addressing ethical claims? Or isn't it strictly the level of the national economic system and the law, i.e. the level where the rules of a market competition are established, and restrictions for corporate actions are set by law? Especially in Germany many economists defend this latter view when they refer to the neo-classical approach of economics and its basic message: you can't afford anything but increasing profits, so ethics is luxury (see particularly Homann - 1994a).

3. On the other hand, there is the *philosophical challenge* of corporate ethics: how can we establish an ethical concept for business and corporate ethics, against the prevailing view that value judgements are simply arbitrary personal opinions, and therefore business or corporate ethics should not be discussed as an academic discipline (Popper - 1945)? In other words: how can business ethics become a recognized academic discipline in our times of scepticism? This third question also closely relates, of course, to the philosophy of constitutional law.

In this paper, we would like to present our approach to business ethics with special regard to the last two questions. As far as the reader may get the impression that our approach is rather *theoretical* as compared to the more *pragmatic* approaches to business ethics in the international discussion, he or she should keep in mind that our perspective reflects the very distinctive German situation we briefly sketched above. But, before we turn to our fundamental questions in more detail we shall try to locate them in a general framework (exhibit 1). This may be a helpful guide to understand the following discussion of our concept.

2. A general framework for business ethics

A. The good reason approach

Very generally speaking corporate ethics (as a subset of business ethics) deals with the question: what can and must be done on the corporate level to establish and continuously maintain the *legitimacy of corporate actions?* Our suggestion is to qualify corporate actions as legitimate and therefore ethical to the extent that questions about why management is entitled to take those specific actions can be answered sufficiently by *good reasons*, which means to get to an overall consensus by forceless insight. We shall turn later to this problem in more detail (in section III). For the moment one should simply note that this "good reasons approach" as our point of departure will lead us to a formal and *procedural notion* of corporate ethics, i.e. a manifestation of *"discoursive ethics"* as developed in Germany by Jürgen Habermas of the "Frankfurt School" (Habermas - 1984, 1987, 1989, Rehg - 1994) and by the mathematician Paul Lorenzen of the so called constructivist "Erlangen School" (Lorenzen - 1984, 1987, 1991, Kamlah & Lorenzen - 1984, Butts & Brown - 1989), where it is called *"dialogue ethics"*. An open dialogue should therefore lead us to the free consensus, which is simply another notion of the overall ethical goal, *peace in society* (Lorenzen - 1987, pp. 228 ff.).

Figure 1: A General Framework for Business Ethics

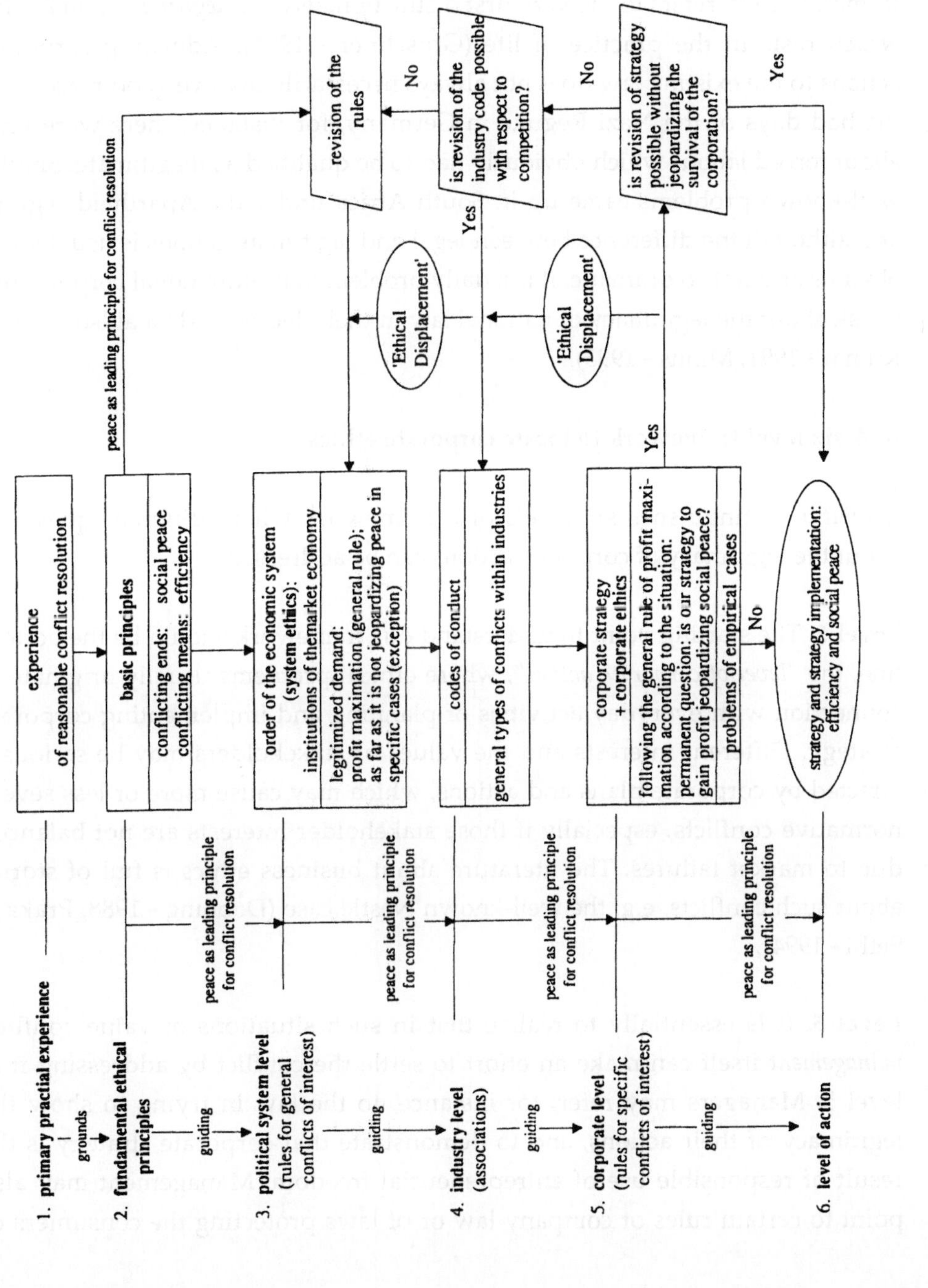

One should not overlook the fact that this quest for legitimacy, though quite formal, already refers to the very first distinction between *legitimacy* and *legality* which rests in the practice of life (Gröschner - 1991). Adjusting corporate actions to the existing law does not always necessarily involve good reasons. In the bad days of the Nazi Regime in Germany, for instance, there were laws about forced labour which obviously had to be qualified as illegitimate. Similar well-known problems came up in South Africa under the Apartheid regime; and although the difference between legal and legitimate actions is usually less obvious and not so dramatic, it is a daily problem in multinational corporations to ask about the legitimacy of national law in their decisions (Donaldson - 1989, Kumar - 1991, Minus - 1993).

B. A six level framework to locate corporate ethics

Exhibit 1 distinguishes six levels of a framework where different questions about the legitimacy of corporate actions can be addressed.

Level 6. The starting point to understand our framework should be the bottom line, the *"level of corporate action"*, where ethical problems usually originate in connection with everyday activities of planning and implementing corporate strategy. Different interests and the values of stakeholders may be seriously affected by corporate plans and actions, which may cause more or less severe normative conflicts, especially if those stakeholder interests are not balanced due to market failures. The literature about business ethics is full of stories about such conflicts, e.g. the well-known Nestlé case (Dobbing - 1988, Prakash Sethi - 1994).

Level 5. It is essentially to realize that in such situations of value conflict, *management* itself can make an effort to settle the conflict by addressing it at level 5. Managers may refer, for instance, to the law in trying to show the legitimacy of their actions, and to demonstrate that corporate strategy is the result of responsible use of entrepreneurial freedom. Management may also point to certain rules of company law or of laws protecting the consumers or other stakeholders. If such - or other substantial - arguments are finally accepted as good reasons by *all parties involved* in the conflict, i.e. if the conflict is settled *peacefully* with all concerned, the legitimacy of corporate action can already be achieved by the general rules of law. Furthermore, if a reference to law is not enough, management itself may also revise their strategy in accordance with reasonable demands of concerned stakeholders. Obviously those good reasons have to be developed through an open dialogue as the basis for that revision.

Levels 4 and 3. But, a revision of corporate strategy or action on level 5 is only possible if it is - according to the best judgement of management - compatible with the *competitive situation* in a free or social market economy, namely the economic imperative to gain sufficient profits for the company to survive. If this is not the case in a certain ethical conflict, a higher level of conflict resolution in the economic system than the corporation must be sought, which provides a chance to strive for legitimacy and does not put the company into a serious competitive disadvantage. In other words, according to the principle of *subsidiarity* (see Roos - 1993) the problem of conflict resolution must be addressed at the appropriate level. But if the conflict is so difficult that the corporation cannot handle it alone, the resolution must be addressed by "ethical displacement" (DeGeorge - 1990) to the *industry level* (level 4) or, of course, up to the *political level* (level 3). As far as the actors on either of these levels succeed in modifying and enforcing the rules of the game for all companies concerned, there is a good chance that conflicts with stakeholders can be avoided or solved peacefully in the future, thus a new source to legitimate corporate action is established. The new rules of the game can then function as good reasons to justify corporate actions.

In this sense, for instance, the chemical industry has initiated a well-known world-wide program called *"Responsible Care"* to improve environmental protection, health conditions for the local community, and consumers and safety conditions for the workers (Cefic - 1993). Similarly, the German law on *co-determination*, which specifies that half of the supervisory board seats be reserved for labour representatives, may be understood as an endeavour on the political level to improve the conditions for peaceful conflict resolution between capital and labour, thereby strengthening the legitimate basis of both corporate actions and of the market economy as a whole (Steinmann & Gerum - 1992).

Levels 2 and 1. At a first glance it seems that the political level is the end of the "stairway to ethical heaven". In a democracy it appears that there are no higher sources than legislation and the constitution to clarify questions about the legitimacy of corporate actions, or any other institution - even democracy itself. Thus, even liberal economists notice a certain kind of a gap in the foundation of democratic theory (Homann - 1993), which gives us reason to add two more levels in exhibit 1.

These two levels refer to the intricate *methodological question* of a proper beginning of the case for corporate ethics, namely to the foundation of ethics principles, which has given rise to so many philosophical disputes in Germany and elsewhere. *What are* the highest principles or values on which we should all ground our common life and should hence also guide our ideas of corporate ethics (level 2)? And still more profound: *where do these values come from?* Is it reason? Is it religion? Or is it - as many modern philosophers hold - simply arbitrary decisions or an act of faith by which values are brought into the world? These fundamental questions about the source of ethics principles are referred to on level 1.

Answers to these questions are obviously of the utmost importance today in our *post-traditional societies,* where most traditional and religious values are no longer automatically regarded as valid by a majority of people, but are steadily eroding as the common ground for social rules. Traditional values as such, without any further legitimation, are no longer able to integrate the modern society with its pluralism of interests, different conceptions of living and happiness, and its variety of personal opinions. From where, we must ask, should we obtain an ethical orientation in this situation, since this is obviously necessary for common action and social peace?

Before examining this problem and suggesting a methodological solution, we want to point to the fact that the three basic questions about corporate ethics we raised in section I can be addressed now in our framework, regardless of the different answers which give rise to so many disputes. Obviously, level 1 and 2 are related to the third, the *philosophical* question, which asked for a solid foundation of an ethics principle. Levels 3 and 4 refer to the second, the *economic* question, which is centred on a proper understanding of the economic system and its legitimacy, i.e. of capitalism and market competition, the role of federations of industry, and, above all, the intended role of the corporation in the system. Finally, levels 5 and 6 refer to the first question of a reasonable *notion of corporate ethics*.

3. The philosophical foundation of corporate ethics

The *philosophical challenge* in developing a conceptual foundation of corporate ethics comes from the question of what legitimacy of corporate action really means, and how it can be established. In general, we hold that the "good reason approach" laid down in the idea of "discoursive ethics" would be a proper solution to this problem. In order to defend this general assertion more specifically, one should present a clear idea of what the "philosophical problem" of ethics is all about. Otherwise, and this is actually a common deficiency in the hugh body of literature on business ethics, one would only talk in a simple manner about the application level, without reflection on the unsafe ground. Strangely enough, talking that superficially without explicit foundation is less often attacked by critics than by researchers who emphasize their philosophical background.

A. The problem of justification

Infinite regression. When we went through the six levels of our framework we implicitly referred already to a *hierarchical order* of reasoning in the following sense:

1. To justify demands for individual actions on the corporate level we must refer to *reasonable ends,* for which the individual actions could be understood as *rational means.* It is familiar to us as management theorists that these ends are *corporate strategies* as points of reference for all individual actions.

2. But, to justify these strategies one has to seek another end, for which a certain strategy can be regarded as a rational means. From an economist's point of view, strategic actions may be justified to the extent that they are really rational means for *profit maximization,* or at least profit making, in the world of a competitive market economy. Furthermore, it is clear that profit seeking must stay within the *limits of the law,* i.e. norms which must be considered as a reasonable condition for economic actions of all companies, at least within an industry (see even Friedman - 1970).

3. Now, of course, if these norms are not simply *put into being* by legislative power, but can claim to be universally *justified,* one again has to give good reasons for these norms. Why, for instance, can the core norm of the marketplace be called justified and therefore ethical: "maximize your profit!"

One quickly realizes that whatever level we may reach, there always remains the possibility to ask another "Why"-question. There seems to be no reasonable end to reasoning: this is what philosophers call the "regressus ad infinitum" or *"infinite regression",* which is the central problem of this type of moral reasoning, in contrast to empirical assertions testing (Popper - 1959). In the latter case you have - roughly speaking - *empirical reality* as an "authority" against which to judge whether a hypothesis is falsified or not. But what authority do you have in ethics? An ethical claim cannot be falsified with reference to the facts of real life, e.g. nobody would remove murder as a crime from our penal codes just because there is actually a high rate of murder.

The discussion on this central philosophical problem of moral reasoning is highly controversial in Germany and elsewhere. Actually, it is the ever-lasting basic question of the occidential practical philosophy since the ancient Greek discovery of reasoning, and it would need encyclopedias to treat it regarding all approaches and positions which have been developed so far (see the splendid work of Becker/Becker - 1992). Apparently such a treatise would be far beyond our aim to provide a fundamental introduction to the field. Thus, asking only *fundamentally*, what are the possibilities of tackling the problem of justification? Logically speaking there are obviously only two general types of answers, namely the "content approach" and the "process approach" to ethics.

B. The content approach

Dogmatism. Within the *content approach* one has to look for highest *substantial values* or principles as an Archimedical anchor from which to derive and justify all other norms and ends. Such values, if they are to fulfill their role at all, must be unquestionable: no "Why"-questions are allowed any more with respect to these highest values. In order to stop reasoning at such a point we usually find *dogmatic solutions* to avoid the "infinite regression problem" (Albert - 1980, pp. 14f.). The reasoning must find its end by revelation or determination, where one may point, for instance, to infallible authorities as a source of highest values. Christian ethics are often criticized as approaches in this sense (see the overview of Gustafson - 1992).

Decisionism. Although the dogmatic approach may be convincing for certain groups of people, it is definitely not an enlightening solution of the ethics problem for an entire *pluralistic society*, in which coherent values are not shared by definition. Therefore, another group of philosophers in Germany and elsewhere simply suggest that there is *no* solution to the problem of infinite regression at all (usually with reference to Popper - 1945; see particularly Albert - 1980). Highest substantial values, they say, are subject to *private decisions* or confession, and cannot be grounded on good reasons, or any other intersubjectively binding method. Furthermore, since norms cannot be derived from facts, ethics as a normativistic endeavour cannot be qualified as scientific discipline at all (Albert - 1975).

At first glance, this critical rejection of moral philosophy as a rational endeavour is obviously in danger of total relativism, where absolutely nothing can be said about what is right and wrong. To avoid this disastrous consequence for humanity, modern approaches try to combine decisionism with a criterion of rationality (Albert - 1980, Lübbe - 1971), so that they can no longer be compromised like the traditional decisionism (Schmitt - 1932). But, as long as they understand rationality exclusively as a matter of *empirical* theory building, they still imply the same fatal consequences for the rational foundation of a moral orientation. All attempts to justify a *normative* approach to ethics beyond empirical facts remain *irrational,* because these empirical facts are the only authority to judge what is right and wrong. Therefore academics who understand themselves as critical rationalists are only entitled to rationalize means for whatever (irrational) ends, and leave the decisions on the ends to private interests.

Moreover, it is a commom understanding that all these private interests and claims in society compete with one another without a reasonable preference for anything, balanced only by a *"marketplace for ethics"* (a vicious circle, obviously), or, more likely, as a matter of *micropolitics,* where it is only a question of power which interest will set the normative agenda. Consequently, one should understand society as a permanent battlefield of interest groups striving for a change of the existing power structure through micropolitics and "majority seeking". In sum, there would be no hope for a stable peace.

C. The process approach of the Erlangen School

Against deduction. The Erlangen School of philosophy does not accept these consequences. They claim that the problem of the "infinite regression" only persists if we restrict the good reason approach to *deductive reasoning,* figuratively said if we want to deduct ethics principles from the stairway to heaven (Lorenzen - 1987, Gethmann - 1987, Kambartel - 1989, Mittelstrass - 1989, Lueken - 1992). It is clear that this deductive approach needs a *substantial starting point* with a true and highest value, because only then it becomes possible to transfer the truth of this value from one level to another by the logical operation of deduction. But, since this position would assume a metaphysical idea of true values, it is to be rejected. From an inner world view of philosophy there are no pre-exisiting values which have to be detected (eventually by professional philosophers). Consequently deductive ethicists would run into a logical failure by assuming pre-existing moral values: out of nothing, nothing follows.

The only way out of this deductive dilemma is to turn to a *procedural understanding* of moral reasoning. We must not ask: "*what* are the highest values?"; but: "*how* can we achieve a reasonable foundation of highest values?" Of course, this *process-approach* can only be accepted if it itself can be set up in a non-arbitrary manner; otherwise there would be no good reason to prefer it to the content approach.

The methodological starting point: practice of life. Right here the concept of the *methodological constructivist philosophy* in the sense of the Erlangen School wants to give an orientation (for an overview, see recently Scherer & Dowling - 1995; see also Sagal - 1987, Butts & Brown - 1989). Unfortunately the term "constructivist" is already used in the English-language literature by researchers with a very different meaning which some have held as essentially almost the same as relativism (e.g. Berger & Luckmann - 1966, Schuetz - 1967, Coulter - 1979). Completely to the contrary, the Erlangen School is definitely non relativist. Furthermore, the Erlangen School constructivism must not be misunderstood in the sense of the *radical constructivist approach*, which has been developed through combining traditional constructivism with the basic idea of "autopoiesis" by Chilean cognition biologists (Maturana - 1980, Maturana & Varela - 1980, Varela - 1979), and which has become very popular in Germany over the last decade (Glasersfeld - 1981, Gumich & Mohler - 1985, Schmidt - 1987; for a comparison with the Erlangen School, see Janich - 1992).

Methodological constructivism can be traced back to pragmatism (Peirce - 1931/1958, Dewey - 1976, Dingler - 1964) and the linguistic turn of philosophy (Hall - 1952). The basic idea is to turn the intricate problem of moral reasoning upside down: instead of starting with and looking for highest values in the "heaven of ideas" the suggestion is to begin "on earth" in our own *practice of life* and to derive from there, from our everyday experience of the basic difference between successful and unsuccessful ways of problem solving (Kamlah & Lorenzen - 1984). Based on these distinctive everday experiences in life further theoretical endeavors of science and arts can be built up to concepts, ideas, and theories for improvement of our future life (Lorenzen - 1987). Constructivist philosophers and management theorists thus regard the basic practical experience of life, what they call the *"primary praxis"*, as the highest resort which is prior to any theory and scientific effort, which they call *"theoretical praxis"* (Kambartel - 1989, Inhetveen - 1983, Löhr - 1991, Lueken - 1992, Scherer & Dowling - 1995). *Theory follows practice,* one may call the basic idea, so theory must get its basic orientation out of life, or, as Sagal (1987, p. 176) explained it: "theory arises out of practice, and the first theoretical steps must be rooted in practice". As well as saying that all the *technical* disciplines did not invent the criterion of technical efficiency by themselves, but found it as a demand of practice, we can also say that the *political* disciplines must seek their right orientation in practical experience (Lorenzen - 1987, p. 239). Since theory in general, and ethics in particular, cannot deduce their principles from anywhere, they should give up their search to find an orientation for such theoretical reasons. They should start in practice.

Consensus through dialogue. But how can an ethics principle be found in a non-arbitrary manner if we start in real life? Isn't that a traditional positivistic, or simply inductive approach? Not at all, because our experiences in life are only a *starting point* for further reflection, and are not taken as merely empirical facts. From our everyday practice of life each of us can tell and understand examples and counter examples of conflict resolution, e.g. within the family, the firm, or any other realm. If we then start to reflect on the *categorial difference* between conflict resolutions which we have experienced as successful and more desirable, and those which we think less favorable, we can begin to articulate our practical experience as a difference in terms and put it into words. Since we can all do so - and actually always did so - prior to all scientific theory building, in a pre-theoretical and ordinary language so to speak, we basically don't need a theoretical approach which deduces ethical orientations out of the heaven of nothing. It is just the other way round. We ourselves as participants of life are already able to distinguish categories of experience, specify them in ideal terms, name them with significant words, and set priorities, which in turn should give a normative orientation for all theoretical activities, which ought to be understood as contributions to a better life. After all it is only this ability to name things and phenomena via the operation of linguistically establishing differences, that makes the world accessible and understandable to us. This is the basic insight we owe to the linguistic turn in philosophy which has been coming up since the Fifties (for Germany see Apel - 1973).

This basic consideration becomes relevant here in our field of ethics with respect to the difference between experienced conflict resolutions resting on *dialogical argumentation,* and those which rest on a *power structure.* Translated literally we use the words "consensus" versus "compromise" to mark this categorial difference in conflict resolution - a terminology which may be easily misunderstood in the sense that "arguing" and "consent" are tainted with counter connotations like individual advantage calculating (Buchanan & Tullock - 1962). But, as a matter of course, we can explain our catchwords on the language level more precisely, because the difference in experience might be available to all of us.

A *free consensus* means an agreement or assent by all concerned on the basis of a free and enlightened insight in the better argument or line of reasoning. It is the "peculiar, forceless force of a better argument", as Habermas (1971, p. 137) has put it, which effects consensus here. To *argue* means to put forward reasons for an assertion or for a claim, so that all others concerned can understand, scrutinize, and evaluate it, and in turn can bring into the dialogue their own assertions, claims and arguments (see also Kambartel - 1974, Habermas - 1989,

Schneider - 1994). Therefore we should strive for the *ideal "benchmark"* of an unrestricted free discourse or dialogue between all persons concerned from their own participator perspective, to find out what will finally be accepted in practice as a good reason in a specific situation. Only an orientation towards this *ideal procedure of discourse* will guide us to a stable peace. No external moral expert can give enlightened individuals insight but only themselves. This is the reason why post-traditional ethics must necessarily be conceptualized as formal process rules against all substantive prescriptions. The free and open discourse as a duty of practical life in situations of moral conflicts is an indispensable part of the good reason approach, and it is at the heart of discoursive ethics (i.e. the term of the Frankfurt school) or dialogical ethics (i.e. the term of Erlangen).

The decisive difference between "consensus" and "compromise" is, thus, that the use or abuse of *power* in any form must be abandoned in a consensual process, including either physical force or subtle strategies of manipulation, such as the socio-technical approaches to effective negotiation. Only in the absence of power we can speak of a *free consensus* (Lorenzen - 1987, pp. 228 ff.). And it should be clear by now that what is meant here by "free" must not be confused with the "arbitrariness" or "discretion" of the so-called "free will" of an individual. This would make the concept of consensus meaningless.

Motivation for consensus. One may ask now, why should we recognize discourse and consensus as a binding procedure for conflict resolutions at all. Why shouldn't we insist on our own personal "free will"? Of course, one cannot physically be forced into dialogue, but the question would obviously mean to neglect our starting point in a more or less arbitrary manner. One would fall back behind his or her own practical experience of better conflict resolution. In other words: one simply cannot reasonably ask for another reason to assure the practically based insight to what is right (for details see Lueken - 1992, pp. 354 ff.). This would actually mean to ask for a compelling *theoretical solution* for the *practical problem* of ethics. Thus, the sceptic's question only tackles the practical heart of the ethical challenge: the one and only conclusion we can draw from our insight without self-denial is to act ethically, based on a self commitment to what is right.

Finally, with respect to the probability of ethical behavior becoming prevalent in the entire society, the key to improvement lies obviously in the *culture* in which we live and in which we are brought up, and which enables us (or not) to learn from experience about the peaceful way to shape our life. Culture leads us to a judgement whether to regard reason and consensus as the highest values, or whether irrationality and power are the dominant ways of conflict resolution. But fortunately, the given culture of a society is not an unchangeable fact of life, change is always possible, and it starts with proper education.

The highest ethical value: peace. Now, having introduced the distinction between "consensus" and "compromise" in a methodological and - what is important - in an inter-subjectively understandable manner we can go on and introduce the central notion of the process approach, namely *peace in society.* We propose to use the word "peace" in the sense of a *general free consensus* between all parties concerned. Which of these parties should be involved in the dialogue, depends, of course, on the specific conflict in a specific situation, which cannot be theoretically pre-determined by philosophers or whoever, but only found out in the real life of conflicts. Right here, in the practice of life, it is important for a proper understanding of social peace that we must strive for transcending merely *particularistic* solutions of a conflict, i.e. solutions which we only prefer at the moment to find a compromise which fosters private interests. In contrast, striving for consensus may require, where necessary, sacrificing one's private self-interest in order to have peace.

Accordingly the basic principle for peace is: *"transcend your subjectivity!"* (Lorenzen - 1984, p. 82). Peace as free consensus based on transcended subjectivities of all concerned with respect to the better argument is thus, in principle, the highest ethical value we are looking for; it is the essence of the *public interest.* And this means more than the absence of war.

What is required then for peace, are proper institutions at all levels of society, which by their very construction promote conflict resolutions through arguing and consensus. Such institutions can be called *"democratic"*, if democracy is more than merely an exercise of the majority rule, which as such means simply the use of *power* of the majority over the minority. From the perspective of "consensus" and peace something different is necessary, namely a process of serious *argumentation* which *precedes voting,* in an effort to reach consensus, pragmatically of course as much consensus as possible. From this perspective, the majority rule must be understood as a pragmatic rule to stop arguing, i.e. when the minority has not yet been able to provide *good enough reasons* to convince the majority, and when - because of the necessity to act - not enough time is left to gather further arguments (Habermas - 1992, pp. 612 ff., referring to the social democrat Julius Froebel - 1847). The consequences for political disciplines are obviously that their task should be not only research about the power structure in political processes. This is merely the *empirical* side of the problem. Equally important is the *normative* challenge we are discussing here, namely to develop and design social institutions which make peace more stable in our societies (Lorenzen - 1987, pp. 228 ff.).

D. Conclusion: the philosophical starting point

The discussion about corporate ethics in this sense can be understood as a contribution of business administration as an academic discipline to social peace. Therefore the philosophical starting point to develop a reasonable concept of corporate ethics can be summarized as follows:

(1) Corporate ethics must be understood primarily as a *procedural concept,* not as an a priori *substantial content approach* to normative orientations of management.

(2) Corporate ethics must be understood as a discoursive or *dialogical concept;* thus it has to be distinguished carefully from all *monological* concepts in the field. Such a monological concept is, for instance, the traditional idea of corporate responsibility of management, which was proclaimed during the early 1970s (Steinmann - 1973).

But one should also clearly mention that peace as the highest ethical principle must be understood as a *"regulative idea"* for action in the sense of Kant, which on the practical level has to be implemented in a given *historical situation*, i.e. it has to be contextualized (see the integrative model of business ethics by Donaldson & Dunfee - 1994). This means that there are empirical conditions for ethical demands one has to take into account with respect to a *non-utopian concept* of corporate ethics (see Apel - 1988). Neglecting these situative conditions by demanding, for instance, that all institutions in our society should be strictly organized on the basis of the consensus principle, would only lead to *utopian solutions*. And as we know, and Karl Popper has pointed out over and over again: utopia and violence have always occured closely together in history (Popper - 1965).

Accordingly, a *realistic notion* of corporate ethics has necessarily to take into consideration that it must be implemented in a capitalist market economy as historical condition, with competition, individual freedom of choice, and profit maximization as its central elements. The next question therefore is unavoidable: how is the relationship betwen "peace" and "profit" to be seen? This is our second question stated at the beginning; it has also been - and still is - the subject of extensive debate in Germany.

4. Corporate ethics in a capitalist market economy

A. Alternative approaches

Straight economical and ethical positions. In the debate in Germany, two answers to our second opening question about the room for corporate ethics in a market economy are quite prominent. First, many economists claim strongly that on the level of the corporation the one and only goal for decisions should be to maximize profits. Accordingly, the responsibility for social peace should be addressed exclusively at the *political level*, where the rules of the competitive market game are set (Homann & Blome-Drees - 1992). This claim is in the line with the libertarian view, which regards the corporation as a strictly *private sphere* and plays down the role of corporate ethics. Milton Friedman (1970) has put this idea into the well-known formula: the social responsibility of business is to increase its profits (but within the rules of the game, an amendment which is quite often overlooked).

Second, some critics of libertarians point to the ubiquity of *externalities* in modern market economies; they are thus highly sceptical about the role of profits as an indicator of allocative efficiency in the market economy. They propose looking at the big corporation as a *quasi-public* institution (Ulrich - 1977) which should not simply strive for profits, but contribute substantially to social peace through ethical performance (Ulrich - 1993). Against Friedman they would hold that the social responsibility of business should be to increase the ethical performance of the corporation in order to incorporate externalities. As a consequence, corporate ethics is shifted to the centre of this concept instead of left to the political level.

Double responsibility of management. Our own position is somewhere in between, stressing both the political and the managerial level with their responsibility for peace. Focusing on the corporate level, we suggest a *double role* of management in competitive market economies, namely:

(1) on the one hand, management should be held responsible for the survival of the corporation in the market economy, where in the *end* ***profit*** is the indicator of whether this economic role has been fulfilled more or less successfully; and

(2) on the other hand, management should also be held responsible for contributing to ***peace*** in society by designing and implementing adequate corporate strategies, which are in fact the concrete *means* to gain profits.

By differentiating in this sense between corporate ends (profit) and corporate means (corporate strategy) the conceptual relation between the profit goal and corporate ethics becomes more clear. Obviously corporate ethics is to be understood as a *self-imposed restriction.* It reduces the set of strategic means, the set of feasible solutions, which are available for a moral management to maximize the profits. In this sense one can say that corporate ethics should *dominate* the options to act with profit motivation. But on the other hand, it should be clear that corporate ethics cannot ignore or change the general profit goal, nor can it repeal all the other legal restrictions which are set on the political level as the rules of the game for all competitors in a market economy. In other words, according to the very purpose of the corporation in a market economy, it should be understood primarily as an *economic institution* ("working shop"). To function properly as such an economic institution the corporation cannot be primarily interpreted as an *ethical institution* ("talking shop"), with a general ethical responsibility to resolve social problems.

In order to argue for this position, we must show how the general goal of profit seeking can be justified. Next we have to show why the social responsibility of business is not described sufficiently with profit seeking, but it is still necessary for management to set their own ethical restrictions on their strategic choices, in order to establish thorough peace in society.

B. Legitimacy of profit seeking

So what about the *legitimacy of profit*? With respect to our philosophical foundation of ethics it becomes immediately clear that the market itself cannot be regarded as an genuine source of its own legitimacy. According to our distinction between "consensus" and "compromise" the market has to be classified as a political instrument to establish *compromise,* not consensus, with money and purchasing power as the means to pursue one's own private interests. To legitimate the market and its profit motive we must, instead, look at the higher ethico-political level which owes its legitimating force - as explained in detail above - to the democratic procedure of a free consensus; a procedure by which the required *unity* of society and individual freedom can be reconciled and peace assured. This *prerogative of a moral concept,* the priority of reason to rationality as a means was also emphasized by Rawls (1985) against misunderstandings of his critics, which try to read his "Theory of Justice" merely as a rational-choice approach (see an enlightening discussion of these misunderstandings by Barry - 1995, pp. 52 ff.).

But, if ethics should methodologically dominate over economics, one could ask why we don't simply use democratic procedures everywhere to coordinate the economic plans of individuals. Wouldn't this be an immediate and direct way of legitimation? Putting the question in such a radical manner already paves the way for an appropriate answer: because consensual procedures are unable to cope with all the *complexity* of the economic coordination problem in highly developed societies. We know about this fact from the convincing empirical evidence of the failure of all centrally planned economies in East Europe. The market and the price system have empirically proven to be more efficient in solving the problem of coordinating individual economic actions.

The reason for this superiority is that in a market economy individual actions are no longer coordinated via the moral *intentions* of the actors, but via the *consequences* of their acts (Homann & Blome-Drees - 1992, pp. 47 ff.). Individuals are free to follow their own objectives and interests in setting up and carrying out their economic plans, and it is left to the market to coordinate the individual plans and to figure out ex post the economic consequences (profit or loss) for each actor. It was Adam Smith (1776) who stressed this point in his famous statement that we should not expect to get our food because of the benevolence of the butcher, the brewer and the baker, but due to their self-interests. Within our framework this change of the coordination mechanism from "intentions" to "consequences" can be understood as a waiver of argumentation in the context of economic transactions in the market place; in other words, as a *transition* from ex ante consensus building for each and every action, to compromising with ex post coordination through the results (profit or loss).

We propose to legitimate this transition by pointing to the overwhelming *empirical evidence* of higher efficiency of market economies as compared to central planning economies, even though Hayek (1976), Polanyi (1951), Shackle (1972), and others have tried to prove the advantage of a decentralized economy *theoretically* by pointing to the overall detection of "tacit knowledge" (Gray - 1992, pp. 5 ff.). We understand these considerations as a very helpful explanation of market efficiency, but in our view the legitimacy of competition and the market economy cannot be proved with theoretical conclusions. Their arguments must be accepted *practically* with respect to the purposes of life. Only there in life we can see that scarcity and poverty are really a permanent source of conflict in societies, as we know from our East European neighbours. And on the other hand, we also learned from empirical experience (not logical models!) that market efficiency really helps to remove those scarcities of goods and poverty. Thus the market is obviously a better means for securing peace in society than central planning.

This empirical and comparative strategy of legitimation has some important implications. Because we refer to the status of the market as a means to an end (and not as an end in itself), it is clear that we can only provide a *weak legitimation* in our approach, in the sense that whenever better means are found in the future it may be necessary to replace the market by these more efficient coordination mechanisms. But at the moment, of course, no such better means are in sight.

Furthermore, our approach rejects the *axiomatic-theoretical* foundation and reasoning about Pareto-optimal solutions in welfare economics (agreeing with Ulrich - 1993, pp. 173 ff.). But from our methodological perspective, the observation of "ubiquitous external effects" must not be understood as a theoretical argument against the axiomatic theory of welfare economics, which leads necessarily to a complete destruction of the legitimacy of the profit principle. In contrast, externalities should be understood as empirical phenomena, which don't need to be resolved through a general *alternative conception* of the market mechanism, which obviously has to be established on the political level. Accordingly we suggest that externalities should, prior to a system redesign and all political level solutions, be treated on the corporate level by decentralized initiatives within the market, right there where they arise as specific conflicts. Life itself may show whether these subsidiary efforts can help to resolve ethical problems, not axiomatic theory.

In summary, a key address to resolve conflicts around external effects is the level of the *corporation* itself, where particular corporate means are developed to generate profits. After all, it is only on this level that externalities may arise and cause conflicts with the stakeholders of the corporation. The reason behind that fact is, that on the corporate level, the mere *formal* principle of profit maximization is turned into concrete *substantial* economic choices in terms of strategy (product-market-concepts). And only these specific actions can affect stakeholder interests besides the market mechanism as external effects.

C. Corporate ethics as self-imposed restriction

The corporate ethics principle. This line of reasoning brings us back to the question: why is it reasonable for management to *self-impose restrictions* on their strategic choices? A reasonable call for corporate ethics would require to show that it is a necessary means for the end of a peaceful coordination of economic activities and thus for social peace at all. If this can be proved successfully it will have, of course, repercussions for our understanding of the profit principle and its legitimacy. It would imply that the profit principle cannot simply be understood as an *unconditional* request to pursue one's own private interests in business. Instead, it must be understood as conditioned by a *proviso for peace.* The double function of the corporation must then read as follows: *"Maximize your profits as far as this is in accordance with peace in society".*

From this perspective, profit maximization would then have to be regarded as a *necessary,* but not concurrently *sufficient* condition for social peace. It would become a necessary *and* sufficient condition only in conjunction with ethical provisions for peace concerning corporate strategy. In other words: the competitive market forces can only generate *some* ethical results, but the institutionalization of utilitarianism through the market system leaves many questions open for further ethical treatment. We suggest that the corporation should be held responsible for these ethical demands, as well as every other actor in society.

Two assumptions underly this claim for corporate ethics. (1) One has to show that the ethical proviso is indeed necessary. (2) One has to show that peace cannot be provided for fully and sufficiently at the political level of the state, the legislator, and the law. Otherwise there would be no need for ethical reasoning at the corporate level.

The necessity of a proviso for peace. As for the first part of the proof, we hold against all strictly *libertarian positions* that the freedom of the individual cannot be regarded as the highest value of society per se, but only in conjunction with the social end of unity. To avoid a most common misunderstanding, this is certainly not a plea for socialism according to the traditional contradictory "freedom *or* unity", but an approach to combine "freedom *and* unity" together as an expression of the public interest, which is reflected in the notion of peace as "free consensus". The principle of peace, thus, implies by definition that *freedom* must be seen as inseperately intertwined with the *responsibility* for unity. And responsibility for unity is to be understood as the responsibility to contribute to consensual conflict resolution in society.

It is, in short, the formula: "no freedom without responsibility!", which is *universally* valid and as such applicable to the design of *all* institutions in society, including economic institutions as, for instance, the private corporation. And the reason for the claim that it is necessary for any private corporation to add an ethical proviso to the profit goal soon becomes evident through the argument of the *ubiquity* of external effects.

Law and self-commitment. Of course, nothing has been said as yet about how the proviso for peace should be imposed on managerial action: should it be imposed by law at the political level? Or should it be self-imposed by management? Our assertion here is that *legal provisions* for conflict resolution at the company level are also necessary, but not sufficient for peace in society. To support this argument one normally points to the limitations of the law, e.g. implementation problems, time lag of legislation, etc. (Stone - 1975).

These well-known ideas about "where the law ends" can be systematically put forward by the fundamental difference between "structural" conflicts (which occur in general) and "specific" conflicts (which occur ad hoc).

Structural conflicts in market economies arise when there are structural, not accidental, inequalities in the power distribution between the parties, for instance between capital and labour. For such conflicts, because they can be anticipated and analyzed ex ante, general legal provisions for a peaceful conflict resolution are possible and make sense. As an important consequence, rules for *corporate governance* are established (Steinmann & Gerum - 1992).

On the other hand, specific questions of corporate ethics arise when there occur *"ad-hoc-conflicts"*, i.e. ethical conflicts with stakeholders which are affected by specific features of the individual corporate strategy, as, for instance, in the Nestlé-case (Dobbing - 1988, Prakash Sethi - 1994). Such conflicts cannot be anticipated on the level of legislation since they arise as a consequence of creative acts of corporate strategies, or even as unintended side-effects of it. In the competitive world of a market driven economy, the decentralized activities are permanently creating new ideas which may cause conflicts, thus law must systematically fall short. With respect to this shortcoming of regulations for ad-hoc-conflicts an ethical proviso seems to be conceptually necessary also on the corporate level to assure that corporate strategy is not only profitable, but contributes at the same time to a peaceful coordination of economic activities. Furthermore we have seen that such a proviso can only be a *self-commitment* of the corporate actors, and it must necessarily be *procedural* not substantial in order to find a peaceful solution to the very special conflicts by dialogue.

Consequently corporate ethics must be regarded as an integral, indispensable, and important part of all endeavors to provide for peace in society. Acting ethically therefore is, of course, not at the *discretion* of corporate managers at all; this follows from the principle that the *responsibility* to contribute to peace in society does by necessity correspond to the idea of managerial *freedom*. Corporate ethics in this sense is reflecting on the public aspect of the role of corporations in a market economy, and it shows that without this role the entire system is in danger of collapsing with regard to the misguiding idea of an unconditioned freedom.

D. Corporate ethics as a republican approach

Thus, in short, we claim a double responsibility of corporate actions for both economics *and* ethics, and we understand this double role of corporations as an expression of the general call in society for a free commitment of personal interests to the public interest ("res publica"). Therefore, according to a suggestion of Lorenzen (1991, p. 50) we want to call this approach *"republican ethics"* (see also Ulrich & Thielemann - 1992, pp. 161 ff.; Koslowski - 1994, pp. 87 ff.; Münkler - 1991a; Schachtschneider - 1994).

We are very well aware of the problem that this term may lead to some confusion if not *misunderstandings* because of the political connotation coming into mind with respect to republican parties. This problem is even more serious in Germany, where a small radical nationalist party calls themselves "republicans". So why "republican ethics"? In short, using this term deliberately we want to suggest a revitalization of the traditional republican political philosophy, which has its historical roots in the Greek influence on the Roman republic, which was the guideline for the French philosophers in the beginning of the age of the European Enlightenment, and which was still the starting point for the political philosophy of Kant, (Schachtschneider - 1995, Münkler - 1991b). Thus the revitalized meaning of the republican concept in our sense must not be mixed up with the misguiding labels of some modern parties. Moreover, the republican concept certainly not a new invention; it has only been forgotten in the libertarian age, and it is still waiting for a proper rediscovery under the conditions of the modern world.

Obviously, this means a conceptual approach beyond the strictly *libertarian* position, which refers basically to the merely private interest, and it is also clearly beyond the historically collapsed *socialistic* point of view, which only referred to the public interest. Ethics, in contrast, means a voluntary commitment to general norms, and the republican approach is the only one which takes this double aspect seriously. As a consequence, we think that a proper notion of *corporate ethics,* as it was asked for in our first opening question, must be summarized as follows (Steinmann & Löhr - 1994, p. 106 ff.):

> *Corporate ethics* should be understood as a *discoursive* ethics procedure directed towards a *consensus* about *good reasons* for the *peaceful* resolution of ad-hoc-conflicts with the (internal and external) stakeholders of the corporation. Corporate ethics should be concerned with conflicts, which are caused by the mere economic focus on *profit maximization* through profitable *corporate strategies* (product-market-concepts) and the management of their *implementation* (means of getting things done), and should lead to *self-imposed* commitments which supplement existing law to assure the *legitimacy* of corporate action.

There are, of course, many further details concerning those problems which are related more to the *practical side* of implementing this idea of corporate ethics. These include: codes of conduct, ethical displacement, implications of corporate ethics for planning and controlling, the ethically sensitive organization, the moral development of human resources, leadership styles, ethics in the corporate functions (Production, Marketing, Finance), and so forth. But that discussion is clearly beyond the scope of this conceptual groundwork paper (Steinmann & Löhr - 1994, pp. 144 ff.). In general, our basic idea is to redefine the role of the corporation from the strictly libertarian approach to the *republican concept,* from the mere economic definition of the corporation to a double responsibility for ethics *and* economics. This republican approach should guide all considerations about the implementation of corporate ethics, as well as the reconstruction of the entire system of the competitive market economy, in order to establish peace through *subsidiary ethical responsibility.*

Finally, we probably have to mention that this reconceptualization does not simply imply an automatic change of business, which could be achieved through theory or order. The business world itself as well as all the other parties in society must take the initiative, in order to contribute their part to the overall peace of society.

Résumé

Un concept "républicain" de l'éthique d'entreprise

Le libellé, peut-être étonnant au premier abord, se réfère au terme latin de "res publica" et suggère la revitalisation d'un concept antique de philosophie politique pour l'adapter au mode de fonctionnement de la société contemporaine.

Dans le désarroi actuel d'une société en mal de références et de valeurs, soumise à des tensions violentes ainsi qu'à des dysfonctionnements évidents, le débat pluri-disciplinaire (englobant des considérations économiques, politiques, managériales aussi bien que philosophiques et théologiques) sur l'interaction entre les intérêts privés et la paix sociale, sur le rôle du profit des entreprises et leur implication sociétale, est d'une brûlante actualité.

Les auteurs présentent tout d'abord les fondements philosophiques de ce débat en mettant l'accent sur les apports des écoles de Francfort (Habermas) et de Erlangen (Lorenzen). Convient-il de mettre en avant le principe du consensus ou celui d'un compromis ? Quel est celui qui garantira le mieux le bien le plus précieux, à savoir la paix sociale acquise à travers un processus de libre détermination des parties ? Comment dépasser le conflit illustré par Karl Popper entre utopie et violence, et par delà entre paix sociale et profit individuel ?

Les considérations d'éthique entrepreneuriale doivent être faites dans le contexte d'une économie de marché capitaliste, qui impose ses propres contraintes d'efficience. Le système défendable à la fois du point de vue éthique et du point de vue économique suppose une responsabilité affirmée et vécue des différents acteurs impliqués.

Zusammenfassung

Unternehmensethik als "republikanisches Konzept"

Die Diskussion um Wirtschafts- und Unternehmensethik (Business Ethics) ist in Deutschland bislang weniger von betriebswirtschaftlichen Konzepten oder Management-Ansätzen beeinflußt, sondern eher von den differenziert ausgearbeiteten Theorien der Philosophen und Nationalökonomen. Unter Berücksichtigung dieses recht abstrakten Focus der Diskussion, der eigentlich nicht genau diejenigen Sachverhalte trifft, die mit dem international üblichen Terminus "Business Ethics" angesprochen werden, entwickeln wir ein integratives Rahmenkonzept. Dadurch soll die vielschichtige Debatte um Wirtschafts- und Unternehmensethik systematisch geordnet werden und das Problem ethischer Verantwortung auf der Unternehmensebene klarer hervortreten.

Innerhalb dieses Rahmenkonzepts wird unser Begriff von Unternehmensethik näher präzisiert. Wir nehmen dabei Bezug auf die konstruktive Philosophie der Erlanger Schule, deren Prinzip der Dialogethik besagt, daß zur Sicherung des sozialen Friedens in Konfliktfällen um das unternehmerische Handeln nach einem freien Konsens auf der Grundlage rationaler Argumente gestrebt werden soll. Dieses allgemeine Prinzip begründet eine doppelte Verantwortung des Managements in der Marktwirtschaft: es geht zugleich um profitables und ethisch verantwortliches unternehmerisches Handeln zur Sicherung des sozialen Friedens. Da dieser Ansatz eine fundamentale Alternative zum üblicherweise liberalen Verständnis der unternehmerischen Verantwortung darstellt, möchten wir ihn - im Anschluß an eine fast vergessene europäische Richtung der politischen Philosophie - als "republikanisches Konzept" kennzeichnen.

References

ALBERT, H. (1975): Transzendentale Träumereien. Karl-Otto Apels Sprachspiele und sein hermeneutischer Gott. Hamburg. Hoffmann und Campe.

ALBERT, H. (1980): Traktat über kritische Vernunft. 4th ed. Tübingen. J.C.B. Mohr (Paul Siebeck).

APEL, K.-O. (1973): Transformation der Philosophie. 2 Vol. Frankfurt/M. Suhrkamp.

APEL, K.-O. (1988): Diskurs und Verantwortung. Das Problem des Übergangs zur postkonventionellen Moral. Frankfurt/M. Suhrkamp.

BARRY, B. (1995): Justice as Impartiality. Oxford. Clarendon Press.

BECKER, L.C./BECKER, Ch.B. (Eds.) (1992): Encyclopedia of Ethics. 2 Vol. New York/London. Garland.

BERGER, P.L./LUCKMANN, Th. (1966): The Social Construction of Reality. New York. Doubleday.

BUCHANAN, J./TULLOCK, G. (1962): The Calculus of Consent. Logical Foundations of Constitutional Democracy. Ann Arbor. University of Michigan Press.

BUTTS, R.E./BROWN, J.R. (Eds.) (1989): Constructivism and Science. Essays in Recent German Philosophy. Dordrecht. Kluwer.

COULTER, J. (1979): The Social Construction of the Mind. New York. MacMillan.

CEFIC EUROPEAN CHEMICAL INDUSTRY COUNCIL (1993): Responsible Care: A Chemical Industry Commitment to Improve Performance in Health, Safety, and the Environment. Brussels.

DAHM, K.-W. (1989): Unternehmensbezogene Ethikvermittlung. Literaturbericht: Zur neueren Entwicklung der Wirtschaftsethik. Zeitschrift für Evangelische Ethik, 33. 121-147.

DEWEY, J. (1976): The Moral Writings of John Dewey, ed. by James Gouinlock. New York. Hafner Press.

DINGLER, H. (1964): Aufbau der exakten Fundamentalwissenschaft. hrsg. von Paul Lorenzen. München. Eidos Verlag.

DOBBING, J. (Ed.) (1988): Infant Feeding. Anatomy of a Controversy 1973-1984. London et al. Springer.

DONALDSON, Th. (1989): The Ethics of International Business. New York/Oxford. Oxford University Press.

DONALDSON, Th./DUNFEE, Th. (1994): Toward a Unified Conception of Business Ethics: Integrative Social Contracts Theory. Academy of Management Review, 19. 252-284.

DUNFEE, Th./ROBERTSON, D. (1988): Integrating Ethics into the Business School Curriculum. Journal of Business Ethics, 7. 847-859.

ENDERLE, G. (Ed.) (1985): Ethik und Wirtschaftswissenschaft. Berlin. Duncker & Humblot.
ENDERLE, G. (1991): Zum Zusammenhang von Wirtschaftsethik, Unternehmensethik und Führungsethik. In Steinmann, H. & Löhr, A. (Eds.). Unternehmensethik (2nd Ed.). 173-188. Stuttgart. C.E. Poeschel.
ENDERLE, G./HOMANN, K./HONECKER, M./KERBER, W./STEINMANN, H. (Eds.) (1993): Lexikon der Wirtschaftsethik. Freiburg/Br. Herder.
FORUM FÜR PHILOSOPHIE BAD HOMBURG (Ed.) (1994): Markt und Moral. Die Diskussion um die Unternehmensethik. Bern/Stuttgart. Haupt.
FORUM WIRTSCHAFTSETHIK, hrsg. VOM DEUTSCHEN NETZWERK WIRTSCHAFTSETHIK - EBEN DEUTSCHLAND E.V., Vol. 3 (1995): Sonderheft 1. Wirtschaftsethische Literatur.
FRIEDMAN, M. (1970): The Social Responsibility of Business Is to Increase Its Profits. New York Times Magazine, 13. September 1970. pp. 32-33. cont'd pp. 122-126.
FRÖBEL, J. (1975): System der sozialen Politik. Teil 2. Neudruck der Ausgabe Mannheim 1847. Aalen. Scientia Verlag.
FURGER, F. (1994): Sozialethik und Ökonomik. (Ethik und Wirtschaft im Dialog, Bd. 5). Münster/Hamburg. Aschendorff.
GETHMANN, C.F. (1987): Letztbegründung vs. lebensweltliche Fundierung des Wissens und Handelns. In Forum für Philosophie Bad Homburg (Ed.). Philosophie und Begründung. 268-302. Frankfurt/M.. Suhrkamp.
GLASERSFELD, E. von (1981): Einführung in den radikalen Konstruktivismus. In Watzlawick, P. (Ed.). Die erfundene Wirklichkeit. 16-38. München. Piper.
GRAY, J. (1992): The Moral Foundations of Market Institutions. London. IEA Health and Welfare Unit.
GRÖSCHNER, R. (1991): Zur rechtsphilosophischen Fundierung einer Unternehmensethik. In Steinmann, H. & Löhr, A. (Eds.). Unternehmensethik (2nd Ed.). 103-123. Stuttgart. C.E. Poeschel.
GUMICH, H./MOHLER, A. (Eds.) (1985): Einführung in den Konstruktivismus. München. Piper.
GUSTAFSON, J.M. (1992): Christian Ethics. In Becker, L.C. & Becker, Ch.B. (eds.). Encyclopedia of Ethics. Vol. 1. 151-157. New York/London. Garland.
HABERMAS, J. (1971): Vorbereitende Bemerkungen zu einer Theorie der kommunkativen Kompetenz. In Habermas, J. & Luhmann, N. Theorie der Gesellschaft oder Sozialtechnologie - was leistet die Systemforschung? 101-141. Frankfurt/M. Suhrkamp.
HABERMAS, J. (1984, 1987): The Theory of Communicative Action. Translated by Th. McCarthy. 2 Vol. Boston/MA. Beacon Press.
HABERMAS, J. (1989): Moral Consciousness and Communicative Action. Translated by C. Lenhardt and S. Nicholsen. Cambridge UK. Polity Press.
HABERMAS, J. (1992): Faktizität und Geltung. Frankfurt/M. Suhrkamp.

HALL, E. (1952): What is Value? An Essay in Philosophical Analysis. London. Routledge and Kegan Paul.

HAYEK, F.A. von (1976): Individualism and Economic Order. London et al. Routledge.

HENGSBACH, F. (1991): Wirtschaftsethik. Freiburg/Br. Herder.

HESSE, H. (Ed.) (1988): Wirtschaftswissenschaft und Ethik. Berlin. Duncker & Humblot.

HOMANN, K. (1993): Demokratie. In Enderle, G. et al. (Eds.). Lexikon der Wirtschaftsethik. 186-197. Freiburg/Br. Herder.

HOMANN, K. (1994a): Marktwirtschaft und Unternehmensethik. In Forum für Philosophie Bad Homburg (Ed.). Markt und Moral. Die Diskussion um die Unternehmensethik. 109-130. Bern/Stuttgart. Haupt.

HOMANN, K. (Ed.) (1994b): Wirtschaftsethische Perspektiven I. Theorie, Ordnungsfragen, Internationale Institutionen. Berlin. Duncker & Humblot.

HOMANN, K. & AL. (1988): (Ausschuß "Wirtschaftswissenschaft und Ethik" des Vereins für Socialpolitik). Wirtschaftswissenschaft und Ethik. In Hesse, H. (Ed.). Wirtschaftswissenschaft und Ethik. 9-33. Berlin. Duncker & Humblot.

HOMANN, K./BLOME-DREES, F. (1992): Wirtschafts- und Unternehmensethik. Göttingen. Vandenhoeck & Ruprecht.

HOMANN, K./BLOME-DREES, F. (1995): Sammelrezension: Unternehmensethik - Managementethik. Die Betriebswirtschaft, 55. 95-114.

HUNDT, S. (1977): Zur Theoriegeschichte der Betriebswirtschaftlehre. Köln. Bund-Verlag.

INHETVEEN, R. (1983): Konstruktive Geometrie. Eine formentheoretische Begründung der euklidischen Geometrie. Mannheim/Wien/Zürich. Bibliographisches Institut.

JANICH, P. (1992): Die methodische Ordnung von Konstruktionen. Der radikale Konstruktivismus aus der Sicht des Erlanger Konstruktivismus. In Schmidt, S.J. (Ed.). Kognition und Gesellschaft. 24-41. Frankfurt/M. Suhrkamp.

KAMBARTEL, F. (1974): Moralisches Argumentieren - Methodische Analysen zur Ethik. In Kambartel, F. (Ed.). Praktische Philosophie und Konstruktive Wissenschaftstheorie. 54-72. Frankfurt/M. Suhrkamp.

KAMBARTEL, F. (1989): Philosophie der humanen Welt. Frankfurt/M. Suhrkamp.

KAMLAH, W./LORENZEN, P. (1984): Logical Propaedeutic. Pre-School of Reasonable Discourse. Translated by H. Robinson. Lanham/MD. University Press of America.

KAUFMANN, F.X./KERBER, W./ZULEHNER, P.M. (1986): Ethos und Religion bei Führungskräften. München. Kindt Verlag.

KERBER, W. (1988): Sittlich handeln unter dem Druck ökonomischer Sachzwänge. In Hesse, H. (Ed.). Wirtschaftswissenschaft und Ethik. 241-258. Berlin. Duncker & Humblot.

KIRCHENAMT DER EKD (Ed.) (1992): Gemeinwohl und Eigennutz. Wirtschaftliches Handeln in Verantwortung für die Zukunft. Eine Denkschrift der Evangelischen Kirche in Deutschland (2nd Ed.). Gütersloh.

KONSULTATIONSPAPIER (1994): Zur wirtschaftlichen und sozialen Lage in Deutschland. Diskussionsgrundlage für den Konsultationsprozaß über ein gemeinsames Wort der Kirchen. hrsg. vom Kirchenamt der Evangelischen Kirche in Deutschland und vom Sekretariat der Deutschen Bischofskonferenz. November 1994.

KOSLOWSKI, P. (Ed.) (1985): Economics and Philosophy. Tübingen. J.C.B. Mohr (Paul Siebeck).

KOSLOWSKI, P. (1994): Ethik und Politik bei Aristoteles. Tübingen. J.C.B. Mohr (Paul Siebeck).

KUMAR, B.N. (1991): Unternehmensethik im Kontext internationaler Unternehmensführung. In Steinmann, H. & Löhr, A. (Eds.). Unternehmensethik (2nd ed.). 225-241. Stuttgart. C.E. Poeschel.

LEFRINGHAUSEN, K. (1988): Wirtschaftsethik im Dialog. Stuttgart. Radius-Verlag.

LÖHR, A. (1991): Unternehmensethik und Betriebswirtschaftslehre. Stuttgart. Metzler-Poeschel.

LÖHR, A./KILIAN, S. (1993): Die moralische Urteilskraft von Wirtschaftsstudenten. Ein Diagnoseversuch anhand des empirischen Forschungsstandes. Diskussionsbeitrag Nr. 73 des Lehrstuhls für Allgemeine Betriebswirtschaftslehre und Unternehmensführung. Nürnberg.

LORENZEN, P. (1984): Normative Logic and Ethics (2nd ed.). Mannheim/Wien/Zürich. Bibliographisches Institut.

LORENZEN, P. (1987): Lehrbuch der konstruktiven Wissenschaftstheorie. Mannheim/Wien/Zürich. Bibliographisches Institut.

LORENZEN, P. (1991): Philosophische Fundierungsprobleme einer Wirtschafts- und Unternehmensethik. In Steinmann, H. & Löhr, A. (Eds.). Unternehmensethik (2nd Ed.). 35-67. Stuttgart: C.E. Poeschel.

LÜBBE, H. (1971): Theorie und Entscheidung. Freiburg/Br. Rombach.

LUEKEN, G.-L. (1992): Inkommensurabilität als Problem rationalen Argumentierens. Stuttgart-Bad Cannstatt. Frommann-Holzboog.

LUHMANN, N. (1993): Wirtschaftsethik - als Ethik?. In Wieland, J. (Ed.). Wirtschaftsethik und Theorie der Gesellschaft. 134-147. Frankfurt/M. Suhrkamp.

MATURANA, H.R. (1980): Autopoiesis. Reproduction, Heredity and Evolution. In Zeleny, M. (Ed.). Autopoiesis, Dissipative Structures, and Spontaneous Social Orders. pp. 45-79. Boulder/Col. Westview Press.

MATURANA, H.R./VARELA, F. (1980): Autopoiesis and Cognition. Dordrecht. Reidel.
MINUS, P. (Ed.) (1993): The Ethics of Business in a Global Economy. Boston/Dordrecht/London. Kluwer.
MITTELSTRAß, J. (1989): Der Flug der Eule. Von der Vernunft der Wissenschaft und der Aufgabe der Philosophie. Frankfurt/M. Suhrkamp.
MÜLLER, E./DIEFENBACHER, H. (Eds.) (1992): Wirtschaft und Ethik. Eine kommentierte Bibliographie (Texte und Materialien der Forschungsstätte der Evangelischen Studiengemeinschaft Reihe A, Bd. 39). Heidelberg. Forschungsstätte der Evangelischen Studiengemeinschaft.
MÜNKLER, H. (1991a): Wieviel Tugend braucht die Demokratie? Die neue Gesellschaft / Frankfurter Hefte, 38. 612-617.
MÜNKLER, H. (1991b): Die Idee der Tugend. Ein politischer Leitbegriff im vorrevolutionären Europa. Archiv für Kulturgeschichte, 73. 379-403.
NAGEL, I.H./SWENSON, W.M. (1993): The Federal Sentencing Guidelines for Corporations: Their Development, Theoretical Underpinnings, and Some Thoughts About Their Future. Washington University Law Quarterly, 71. 205-259.
PEIRCE, C.S. (1931-1958): Collected Papers. 8 Vols. Cambridge/Mass. Belknap Press. Harvard University Press.
PIPER, T.R./GENTILE, M.C./PARKS, S.D. (1993): Can Ethics Be Taught? Perspectives, Challenges, and Approaches at Harvard Business School. Boston. Harvard Business School.
POLANYI, M. (1951): The Logic of Liberty. Chicago. University of Chicago Press.
POPPER, K. (1945): The Open Society and its Enemies. London. Routledge & Kegan Paul.
POPPER, K. (1959): The Logic of Scientific Discovery. London. Hutchinson.
POPPER, K. (1965): Utopia and Violence. In Conjectures and Refutations. The Growth of Scientific Knowlegde (2nd ed.). 355-363. London. Routledge & Kegan Paul.
PRAKASH SETHI, S. (1994): Multinational Corporations and the Impact of Public Advocacy on Corporate Strategy. Nestle and the Infant Formula Controversy. Boston/Dordrecht/London. Kluwer.
RAWLS, J. (1985): Justice as Fairness: Political not Metaphysical. Philosophy & Public Affairs, 14. 223-251.
REHG, W. (1994): Insight and Solidarity. A Study in the Discourse Ethics of Jürgen Habermas. Berkeley/Los Angeles/London. University of California Press.
RICH, A. (1990): Wirtschaftsethik, Bd. 2: Marktwirtschaft, Planwirtschaft, Weltwirtschaft aus sozialethischer Sicht. Gütersloh. Verlagshaus Mohn.
RICH, A. (1991): Wirtschaftsethik, Bd. 1: Grundlagen in theologischer Perspektive (4th ed.). Gütersloh. Verlagshaus Mohn.

ROOS, L. (1993): Subsidiarität. In Enderle, G. et al. (Eds.). Lexikon der Wirtschaftsethik. 1045-1049. Freiburg/Br. Herder.

SAGAL, P.T. (1987): Paul Lorenzen's Constructivism and the Recovery of Philosophy. Synthesis Philosophica, 3. 173-178.

SCHACHTSCHNEIDER, K.A. (1994): Res publica res populi. Berlin. Duncker & Humblot.

SCHACHTSCHNEIDER, K.A. (1995): Vom liberalistischen zum republikanischen Freiheitsbegriff. In Wirtschaft, Gesellschaft und Staat im Umbruch, Festschrift zur 75-Jahr-Feier der Wirtschafts- und Sozialwissenschaftlichen Fakultät der Friedrich-Alexander-Universität Erlangen-Nürnberg. 418-449. Berlin. Duncker & Humblot.

SCHERER, A.G./DOWLING, M. (1995): Towards a Reconciliation of the Theory Pluralism in Strategic Management - Incommensurability and the Constructivist Approach of the Erlangen School. Advances in Strategic Management. ed. by Shrivastava, P. & Stubbart, Ch. 12A. 195-248.

SCHMIDT, S.J. (Ed.) (1987): Der Diskurs des Radikalen Konstruktivismus. Frankfurt/M. Suhrkamp.

SCHMITT, C. (1932): Der Begriff des Politischen. Berlin. Duncker & Humblot.

SCHNEIDER, D. (1990): Unternehmensethik und Gewinnprinzip in der Betriebswirtschaftslehre. Zeitschrift für betriebswirtschaftliche Forschung, 42. 869-891.

SCHNEIDER, J. (1994): Ethisches Argumentieren. In Hastedt, H. & Martens, E. (Eds.). Ethik. Ein Grundkurs. 13-47. Reinbek. Rowohlt.

SCHUETZ, A. (1967): Collected Papers. The Hague. Nijhoff.

SHACKLE, G.L.S. (1972): Epistemics and Economics: A Critique of Econiomic Doctrine. Cambridge. Cambridge University Press.

SIEFKES, F. (1993): Ethics and Economics - Bibliography on Economics and Business Ethics (Ethik und Wirtschaftswissenschaften - Bibliographie zur Wirtschafts- und Unternehmensethik). Kleine Bibliographien zu aktuellen ökonomischen Themen des Weltwirtschaftsinstituts Kiel. Bd. 11. Kiel.

SMITH, A. (1776): An Inquiry into the Nature and Causes of the Wealth of Nations. London (Strahan & Cadell).

SOCIETY FOR BUSINESS ETHICS NEWSLETTER. Vol. 1. 1989 ff.

STEINMANN, H. (1973): Zur Lehre von der "Gesellschaftlichen Verantwortung der Unternehmensführung" - zugleich eine Kritik des Davoser Manifests. Wirtschaftswissenschaftliches Studium, 2. 467-473.

STEINMANN, H./GERUM, E. (1978): Reform der Unternehmensverfassung. Köln et al. Carl Heymanns Verlag.

STEINMANN, H./GERUM, E. (1992): Unternehmensordnung. In Bea, F.X., Dichtl, E. & Schweitzer, M. (Eds.). Allgemeine Betriebswirtschaftslehre, Bd. 1. Grundfragen (6th ed.). 216-307. Stuttgart/Jena. Gustav Fischer Verlag.

STEINMANN, H./LÖHR, A. (1988): Unternehmensethik - eine "realistische Idee" Zeitschrift für betriebswirtschaftliche Forschung, 40. 299-317.

STEINMANN, H./LÖHR, A. (Eds.) (1991): Unternehmensethik (2nd ed.). Stuttgart. C.E. Poeschel.

STEINMANN, H./LÖHR, A. (1994a): Grundlagen der Unternehmensethik (2nd ed.). Stuttgart. C.E. Poeschel.

STEINMANN, H./LÖHR, A. (1994b): Unternehmensethik - ein republikanisches Programm in der Kritik. In Forum für Philosophie Bad Homburg (Ed.). Markt und Moral. Die Diskussion um die Unternehmensethik. 145-180. Bern/Stuttgart. Haupt.

STEINMANN, H./LÖHR, A. (1995): Unternehmensethik als Ordnungselement in der Marktwirtschaft. Zeitschrift für betriebswirtschaftliche Forschung, 47. 143-174.

STEINMANN, H./OPPENRIEDER, B. (1985): Brauchen wir eine Unternehmensethik? Ein thesenartiger Aufriß einzulösender Argumentationspflichten. Die Betriebswirtschaft, 45. 170-183.

STEINMANN, H./ZERFAß, A. (1996): Republikanische Unternehmensethik und katholische Soziallehre. In Brieskorn, N. (Ed.). Gerechtigkeit und Soziale Ordnung. Festschrift für Prof. Dr. Walter Kerber SJ. Freiburg et al. Herder (in preparation).

STONE, Ch. (1975): Where the Law Ends. New York et al. Harper & Row.

ULRICH, P. (1977): Die Großunternehmung als quasi-öffentliche Institution. Eine politische Theorie der Unternehmung. Stuttgart. C.E. Poeschel.

ULRICH, P. (1993): Transformation der ökonomischen Vernunft (3rd. ed.). Bern/Stuttgart. Haupt.

ULRICH, P./THIELEMANN, U. (1992): Ethik und Erfolg. Unternehmensethische Denkmuster von Führungskräften - eine empirische Studie. Bern/Stuttgart. Haupt.

VARELA, F. (1979): Principles of Biological Autonomy. New York/Oxford. Oxford University Press.

Peter Eichhorn

Performance Centers in Public Administration

1. Institutional point of view
2. Social wants and public goods
3. Public tasks and institutions
4. The performance of public tasks
5. Entrepreneurial administration
6. Managerial autonomy above all
7. An appropriate accountability
8. Summary and conclusions

1. Institutional point of view

Public administration is mostly analysed by political and administrative scientists, jurists, sociologists and economists. Meanwhile there exists worldwide a growing interest of scientists of Business Administration in investigating this field. The latter classify public administration as economic unities on the national, regional or municipal level which make decisions and act conclusively within a specific framework. These entities differ from other participants of the market economy in three ways: first, there are specific legal and factual requirements for public purchasing and resourcing of labour (recruitment) and capital (borrowing); second, the organizational structures, processes and behaviour patterns of the public service follow their own legal and factual conditions; third, -and this is most essential- the administrative output follows political goals and consists of "public goods" such as promotion and regulation of industry or a particular service-delivery.

In this contribution I try to understand public administration from an institutional point of view. This approach offers alternative performance and will help to answer the question either of a more bureaucratic or more business-oriented fulfillment of public tasks by public administration or even a privately-owned undertaking.

I am not going into theoretical problems of the criteria of public goods. Given a set of social wants provided by public administration I try to examine different organizational solutions and different operating methods such as are suggested from the point of view of business management. Perhaps this business-oriented inquiry shows that public administration is not only a powerful executive governmental organism but an organ to provide services for the public in a market economy.

2. Social wants and public goods

In contrast to the market where market prices regulate the input of factors production, the State produces public goods to satisfy social wants in circumstances in which either market forces fail totally (so-called public goods proper) or the outcome of the free exercise of market forces would be either excess demand or supply (merit goods). Where the market fails the State itself can produce and provide public goods based on policies of either deficit-spending, cost-covering or profit-making. It can also induce private behaviour by regulations, incentives or disincentives towards the expected efficient direction.

The State, conceived as unitary or as a corporate body comprising central, regional and local government and the associated administrative units is motivated by a blend of commercial and non-commercial considerations. In other words, the State acts by either self-production and service-delivery or promotion and regulation.

Within the first the dominating medium is primarily money or cost while the latter is dominated by law and political supervision although there exist numerous interdependences. For example publicly produced goods (such as postal delivery) supplied either above or below market values (via user fees or administrative charges) are priced by legal or political processes; on the other hand regulative authorities (such as the Department of Energy) charged with specific functions in the public (for instance national) interest can levy certain contributions. These media of money and law are complementary. What is of interest is the extent to which social wants can be satisfied in an entrepreneurial way by payment rather than by bureaucratic or law-oriented means.

The following survey shows some examples (the broken line stands for transitions).

Table 1: Money and law as media of public tasks

media \ tasks	self-production and service-delivery	promotion and regulation
money (user fees and grants)	postal system, local transport, waterways, airports, forestry, waste disposal	subsidizing of rents, public purchasing, supporting of research
law (statutes and ordinances)	police, levy of taxes, defence, libraries, fire protection	mining and natural resources, urban development, environmental protection

It is possible to go into further detail. For instance one can introduce the instruments of planning and control.

Table 2: Money and law as media and planning and control as instruments of public tasks

media	instruments \ tasks	self-production and service-delivery	promotion and regulation
money	planning	budgeting, cash limits, medium-range financial planning	(ex-ante) cost-benefit analyses, evaluation of research projects
money	control	public accounting, appropriation accounts, income statements, programme evaluation	national accounting, (ex-post) cost-benefit analyses
law	planning	personnel planning, planning of ambulatory service, highway planning	devising agricultural improvements, development planning, civil defence planning
law	control	state school supervision, local government supervision	building code supervision, food inspection, supervision of working conditions

The economic theory of public goods does not give a sufficient answer to who ought to be responsible for the fulfillment of these tasks. It explains public goods as goods with certain qualities like nonexclusion, nonrivalness, indivisibility, nonstorage life, externalities and so forth. It is accepted that all of them are contentious. Which goods ought to be public ones depends on the place and the period, in other words: on the situation and on decision-making processes. It could be a help for decision makers or decision-making bodies, however, to pay more attention to comparative analyses of institutional alternatives. Provided certain social wants exist or are defined as those from the political point of view one has to decide to what extent, in which quality and by whom they have to be satisfied. This includes the question of which are the best media of performance and who is most economical, efficient and effective in producing and supplying public goods.

3. Public tasks and institutions

In all bureaucratic (public and private) organizations one can identify the same trend towards an autonomous task fulfillment becoming an end in itself. There is a tendency for the status quo to be accepted uncritically, in which circumstances radical assessment or wider objectives or alternative means might be done.

One has to keep in mind that public functions are not determined once and for all but may alter, namely when political objectives change, new insights are made, innovations are introduced or cost consciousness becomes stronger. Each generation has to reflect which significant public task they have inherited, which should be retained so far, which changed or abolished. Less important public tasks (in view of public interest) should be regularly revised. Even if the political-administrative system decides that a particular duty is public, the question remains, whether it should be performed and supplied by public administration, public enterprises or privately-owned companies or other conceivable institutions. In any case it is wrong to associate with any public responsibility any necessary means of fulfillment. In other words, the appropriate governing body is confronted with two questions: the identification of a function as public and the decision as to how it should be performed.

The institutional approach of understanding the peculiarities of planning, budgeting, controlling, organizing, co-ordinating, running, building, maintaining, accounting, purchasing, supplying, delivering, marketing, researching, in short, managing these public tasks, actually requires a clarification of economic units. In a market economy decentralized economic units plan autonomously and make their decisions within the legal framework and actual circumstances. In the following table I would like to differentiate four classes of economic institutions or units on the basis of criteria of their objectives and the means of finance.

Table 3: The four basic economic units

institutions / characteristics	private households	enterprises	associations	public administration
objectives	self-fulfillment	making of profits, cost coverage	supply of needs of groups	supply of needs of the public
financing	income	turnover (sales revenues)	membership dues	levies
examples	families, singles, consumers	industrial firms, banks, craft businesses	charity organizations, sporting clubs, trade unions	central govt. departments, county agencies, city offices

Needless to say the objectives of these institutions vary from principally self-determined personal aims in the case of households, to earnings-oriented entrepreneurial objectives in the case of business or to task-oriented public performances. In reality one also can recognize that boundaries between personal aims and organizational targets are indistinct.

Which kind of institution primarily exists depends on the main objectives and financing. Public transportation (railroads, undergrounds, buses) for example has to offer an optimal service for the public often as a subsidised service. Thus, the competent authority is a public administration. If recovery of costs or even a modest surplus is required the characteristics of a business become stronger and the transportation agency becomes a transportation enterprise. Such a public enterprise has a complex set of objectives: the supply of needs of the public with more or less market-conforming policies. In the past this development happened in Germany at first among municipal savings banks, and later on among the German Federal Railways (Deutsche Bundesbahn), the German Federal Post Office (Deutsche Bundespost), municipal transportation services, public building societies, airports, publicly-owned electricity, gas, district heating, and water supply. Meanwhile the tendency reached broadcasting, theatres, congress centres, port authorities, car parks, hospitals, old-age homes, adult evening classes, public baths, publicly-owned abattoirs, waste disposal, and water disposal. In these cases the public task is increasingly financed by charges on users as the proportion of public subsidy diminishes.

The question is still: how can the public tasks be performed in a more economic, efficient and effective way? That is to say: the superior public interests are taken into consideration and dominant political goals have to be achieved simultaneously by cost minimization of the undertaking relative to internal structures and processes and by the supply and delivery to the people. This means not only optimising inputs and outputs or costs and returns, but also the positive and negative outcome (quality, value) and impact (acceptance, satisfaction) of the activities on the users, consumers, or the public and the whole environment. Therefore the behaviour pattern of firms must be extended. One has to add to the business costs and proceeds, the social costs and benefits of the external effects - knowing that their physical and monetary evaluation generates great difficulties because of their lacking market prices. Law and money as the media of planning and controlling the public tasks must be laid down in a performance programme which incorporates political goals into relevant areas of activity.

4. The performance of public tasks

An essential part from the institutional point of view is a mixed top-down/bottom-up planning system for parliament, federal, state and local government and subordinated units on a feedback basis. On the side of "top-down" the public interests and political goals are identified as a whole to provide a framework for the preparation of performance programmes. Political objectives, consequences for other goals, priorities, minimum standards, resource allocation, jurisdiction or responsibility, impacts and the desired achievements of objectives should be declared. This, of course, cannot be done in detail: firstly, politicians are not willing or able, problems and practice are too complex, and operational scales often do not exist; secondly, institutions and managers involved in the fulfillment of public tasks need an area of discretion in decision-making and incentives for performance.

On the other side executive officers start "bottom-up" with concrete statements of production and supply of public goods, the relations to other services, the estimated business and social costs, the demand, the target group, the possible revenues, the grant required, the impact on the nations and citizens; in sum the degree of task performance. Subsequently this planning system with contributions by politicians and professionals[1] (that is to say by members of parliament, councils or districts and the officers on the central and local level) has to pass through legislation or governmental procedures. Wherever and

1 "Public policy-making is to a large degree a co-operative enterprise in which bureaucrats and politicians are joined. The authority of the politician now is greater than that of the bureaucrat... In contrast the bureaucrat generally has the advantages of longer tenure, more specialized knowledge and greater familiarity with the complexities of the administrative world". See Johnson, N. (1983, p. 205). This statement applies to the situation in Germany as well as in Great Britain.

however the defined goals and responsibilities may be expressed, for example in forms of statutes, amendments, ordinances, other legally binding formulae or simple letters of intent, one must be able to develop performance programmes of joint tasks. Sometimes one only delegates the public responsibility to the government concerned. This alternative seems attractive with respect to the public choice for self-administration or contracting with proprietary enterprises or private firms. In other words: there is a wide range of performance programming, starting from defined goals and tasks up to charging an institution performing public tasks with nationally, regionally or locally given minimum standards.

In any case performance programmes should evaluate both the input and the output as well as the outcome and the impact. The executive institutions need clearly defined performance indicators, a performance level, area and period of performance, target groups, and a performance budget, especially financing of capital expenditures by taxes, grants, and considerations for performance. This leads back to the question as to whether we should aim for a more bureaucratic (tax- and grant-oriented) or a more business (user charge- or price-oriented) method of fulfillment of public tasks.

5. Entrepreneurial administration

The management approach towards entrepreneurial fulfillment of public tasks continues by describing what is required for economic, efficient and effective performance. To begin with the definition of the terms on which these claims are based[2]: to describe performance of public tasks as "economic" implies some optimisation either of the ratio of output to input, of goods and services

2 These definitions seem to be suitable, since they complement those found in the White Papers of the House of Commons Treasury and Civil Service Committee (1982, p. IX): "By the effectiveness of a programme the Sub-Committee understands such matters as the definition of objectives, the measurement of progress towards achieving those objectives and the consideration of alternative means of achieving objectives. By efficiency the Sub-Committee understands, given the objectives and the means chosen to pursue the objectives, the minimising of inputs to the programme in relation to the outputs from it".

produced and delivered with respect to factor utilization or between a predicted and actual output also in physical or monetary terms. "Efficiency" and "effectiveness" are more general and imply consideration of means-end relations or target-performance comparisons besides economic effects. Highly efficient fulfillment of public tasks entails an optimal mix of both factors of economy of operation and the social outcome and impact on both the public and employees. A programme totally achieved with respect to underlying economic and non-economic objectives is called an effective one.

Entrepreneurship in the management of central, regional and local administration and affiliated organizations requires an institutional autonomy and a proper organization, appropriate levels of accountability and, last but not least, more or less self-contained finances. We call these units performance centres. Management means the authority to make decisions and to know how to run an administration (or an enterprise or an association) professionally. It is the level of executive action below the political (Parliament, Ministers, Councils, Councillors, Committees, etc.) at which certain management techniques should be acquired.

Performance centres have no end in themselves but are an instrument of government to fulfill public tasks within the legal framework. Therefore it is inaccurate of some organizational theorists to view public administration as organizations with the goal of self-preservation. Perhaps that would be the view of certain bureaucrats. But government and the administration are distinct entities.

Those public authorities which provide services for which the public pay a fee should be authorised distinctively. The idea is the same as in the case of business companies establishing profit-centres or cost-centres: the activities are focused on the customers (cost and performance), accountability and responsibility can be guaranteed, and the organizational unit may become a trading body.

6. Managerial autonomy above all

Managerial autonomy starts if "big government", or, more precisely, big administration is disaggregated. What does that mean? Disaggregation has four different characteristics.

In its political sense, disaggregation "means that local bodies, elected, or appointed in some other manner, by the local voters themselves, are competent to make a series of decisions as regards the legal precepts which the inhabitants of the area must conform to"[3].

The functional characteristic refers to a task-oriented deconcentration or delegation of administrative competence, mostly connected with a division of work and specialisation.

Institutionally considered disaggregation stands for debureaucratization by deregulation of legal provisions which are dispensable, seldom applied or expensive.

Finally: the geographical element of disaggregation covers decentralized administrations, that is to say the shifting of the primary competence from the centre down to an extensive deglomeration with branch offices.

Disaggregation should not "atomize" public administration since units which are too small generate problems of control, co-ordination and co-operation. One could state the principle of a balance between a managerially proper size of organizations and the span of control.

It is much more difficult to determine the optimal size of a public administrative unit than of a business enterprise. The latter compares, for instance, costs (of production and supervision) and proceeds of a large centralized firm with a structure of small decentralized branches.

3 See Meyer, P. (1957, p. 57).

A public organization, however, must take into account both the costs of the tasks performed (in physical or monetary terms) and the positive and negative external effects to the public caused by different distances, duration, convenience, and costs of a centralized or decentralized administration. Given a fixed level of performance of public tasks (i.e. the comprehensive delivery of services) that public administration shows the optimal size which minimizes the operating and capital costs and the costs of the customers (strictly speaking also the social costs of the employees).

The optimal organizational pattern for the performance of public responsibilities is a function of economy, efficiency and effectiveness as well as of political and public accountability. This includes the political decision as to which government, the federal, state or local one, should control the administration or administrative unit under consideration. From a national point of view one tends to favour the central government while the idea of citizen participation suggests rather an organization at local government level. A similar situation existed in the business world where in the Sixties and Seventies the maxim "the bigger the better" was valid with the consequence of huge conglomerates and so forth. Meanwhile a counter-movement with the motto "small is beautiful"[4] recognized the advantages of an accessible supply and flexible service close to customers.

In general the provision of (public or private) goods for the use of numerous customers needs dispersed institutions. They guarantee advice to customers, clarity of purpose, accountability, and cost-consciousness within the unit as well as strategic controlling from the top.

4 See Schumacher, E. F. (1974).

7. An appropriate accountability

Accountability is a tool for information-gathering, decision-making and securing responsibility. It has external and internal elements relative to the main target groups: in the case of public accountability the politicians as representatives of the public, and in that of administrative officers as agents for public task-performance. As is well known business accounting serves equivalent external and internal target groups: the shareholders and the interested public including banks, suppliers, competitors and trade unions on the one hand, the board of directors, other company managers and actually the employees on the other. But nevertheless there are differences in the accountability.

Public accountability gives information on estimated outflows (Financial Statement and Budget Report, Supply Estimates in the Public Expenditure Survey) and (tax and other) inflows (National Revenue) and the actual spending and income of public activities. Parliament, councils and governments are interested in the target-performance comparison in order to control budgeting and accounting. Primarily, accountability of firms involves expost control and justifying what profits have been made or to what extent costs have been recovered. Inside public administration accountability is basically used to check for regularity and legality of accounting, while business companies need it for the optimum combination of production factors.

They should learn from each other[5].

Management in governments and allied departments requires a long term planning, budgeting and accounting system which gives information about departmental expenditure and revenue (from taxes, customs and excise, duties,

5 This means that there should be a mutual exchange of knowledge and experience. It is often affirmed that there could only be a transfer of management techniques from business to government. Actually commercial firms can for internal purposes also learn from the approved target-performance comparisons of public budgeting and accounting. Corporate budgeted income statements and budgeted balance sheets show quod erat demonstrandum.

grants, interest payments and further miscellaneous receipts) as well as on costs and financing of the performance of public tasks. In particular cost and results budgeting and accounting of administrative units charged with given functions would satisfy the decision-makers' needs.

Without such an enlarged data base the challenge of economical, efficient and effective performance cannot be met.

Politicians and executives must know the administrative expenses (including depreciation, equity yield rate, overhead cost, and employers pension commitments) of putting acts, statutes and orders into effect before they decide and act, and whether and how far their assumptions and behaviour were right. It must be emphasized that this quasi-operating system is not a substitute for either the existing financial system or the proposed social cost-benefit analyses of programme-budgeting systems.

Administrative cost and results budgeting and accounting should serve as a supplementary tool of entrepreneurial thinking. Only knowledge of cost and attainment gives a glimpse into the resources used as "inputs which produce "outputs" expected to achieve or contribute to the fulfillment of the objective (the "outcome" measures the extent of the achievement)"[6]. After that strategies of cost reduction or scrutinies of objectives can follow; furthermore cost-benefit, voting, bargaining, or national criteria may be applied.

The idea of entrepreneurial accountability of public administration will be reinforced as far as the organizational units provide funds or receive grants dependent on performance or are allowed to levy public charges. It is essential that there exists a connection between the flow of goods and services and the flow of expenditure and receipts. As I argued above an administration is normally financed by taxes that is to say, by payments without direct equivalents. Enterprises differ since they sell their products "quid pro quo".

6 See Keeling (1972, p. 42).

Public administration becomes entrepreneurial as far as it exchanges performance against money. The money can be derived either commercially from customers: entailing a transition from public administration to public enterprise or partly from customers and partly from government or own funds on a more or less free market policy.

Mixed-financing occurs via three channels of subsidy: first, the performance centre responsible for the fulfillment of public tasks (for instance the promotion of housing) may dispose of equity capital (with fund budgeting and accounting) interest on which helps to produce and to offer administratively cheap goods and services. Second, the performance centre receives and spends governmental means for subsidizing objects (for example residential construction) and third, the performance centre subsidizes subjects (for example tenants or proprietors of owner-occupied homes) both by low interest loans, grants and other kinds of subsidies from public funds. In all cases the customers (for example building societies or private persons) pay prices below the market prices and the difference indicates the public task performed by public administration.

8. Summary and conclusions

There are three major theses which I want to repeat. In the first place, I wish to maintain the proposition that public tasks or the responsibilities of public administration are derived from political goals. Consequently, all discussion of introducing entrepreneurial elements into public administration has to begin with a clear understanding of its political context. Second, I want to suggest that performance of public administration must be understood in terms which reach beyond the administrative entity itself. An institutional point of view includes the purpose of the undertaking, namely the service for the public.

Therefore the internal inputs and outputs as well as the external outcome and impact on customers, citizens, community and the environment ought to be considered. Third, public administration can improve the fulfillment of public tasks if a management approach is introduced. This implies governmental authorization and control of performance centres, which possess managerial autonomy, proper organization, appropriate accountability, and self-contained finances within a politically given framework. Above all, these trading bodies of federal, state or local government in the form of a separate administrative unit, a semi-autonomous agency, an executive body with legal personality or a publicly-owned company can stimulate corporate identity for the public and motivation for the employees.

Résumé

Centres de performance au sein de l'administration publique

Les missions de service public se déduisent des objectifs politiques. C'est la tâche du parlement et du gouvernement, respectivement du conseil municipal et du maire, de les préciser tandis que leur réalisation incombe à l'administration publique. Cette dernière doit-elle se considérer et se comporter comme une entreprise prestataire de services ou bien comme un centre de performance orienté vers les clients ? Le management de ces centres est-il chargé de les gérer de manière économique (au regard de la relation prestations-coûts), efficiente (au regard de la relation but-moyens) et effective (au regard de la relation objectif prévu-résultats) ? Les conditions préalables de respect de ces exigences comprennent un certain pouvoir décisionnel (dans le cadre des missions prescrites), une dotation financière propre ainsi qu'une gestion de moyens financiers indépendante et une comptabilité autonome. Il est alors possible de développer une "Corporate Identity" qui reflète une image claire de l'organisation aux yeux du public et qui représente un facteur stimulant pour les employés concernés. Peter EICHHORN démontre que missions de service public et rigueur de gestion ne sont pas antinomiques.

Zusammenfassung

Leistungszentren in der öffentlichen Verwaltung

Öffentliche Aufgaben leiten sich von politischen Zielen ab. Zuständig für die Ziele sind Parlament und Regierung bzw. Stadtrat und Stadtvorstand, während die Wahrnehmung der öffentlichen Aufgaben bei den öffentlichen Verwaltungen liegt. Diese haben sich als kundenorientierte Dienstleistungsbetriebe bzw. Leistungszentren zu verstehen. Ihr Management muß wirtschaftlich (i.S.v. Leistungs-Kosten-Verhältnis), effizient (i.S.v. Zweck-Mittel-Verhältnis) und effektiv (i.S.v. Soll-Ist-Verhältnis) handeln. Voraussetzungen sind ein gewisser Grad an Selbständigkeit bei den Entscheidungen (im Rahmen vorgegebener Aufgaben), eine finanzielle Ausstattung sowie eine eigenverantwortliche Mittelbewirtschaftung und Rechnungslegung. Dann ist auch die motivierende Corporate Identity der Leistungszentren für Öffentlichkeit und Bedienstete sichergestellt.

References

BANNER, G . (1991): Von der Behörde zum Dienstleistungsunternehmen. In: Verwaltungsführung, Organisation, Personal (Zeitschrift). Vol. 13. pp. 6-11.

BOVAIRD, T. (1991): Performance assessment in leisure services. Working Paper No. 20. ed. by Public Sector Management Research Centre of the Aston Business School. Birmingham.

BRÄUNIG, D. (1994): Pretiale Steuerung von Kommunalverwaltungen. Nomos Vg. Baden-Baden.

COMMON, R./FLYNN, N./MELLON, E. (1992): Managing Public Services. Competition and decentralization. Butterworth-Heinemann. Oxford.

EICHHORN, P. (1979): Verwaltungshandeln und Verwaltungskosten. Nomos Vg. Baden-Baden.

EICHHORN, P. (1984): Leistungssteigerung in der öffentlichen Verwaltung. Forschungsbericht 37 der Konrad-Adenauer-Stiftung. Melle.

FLYNN, N. (1990): Public Sector Management. Harvester Wheatsheaf. New York.

HOUSE OF COMMONS (1982): Efficiency and Effectiveness in the Civil Service. Third Report from the Treasury and Civil Service Committee. Vol. I: Report. HMSO London.

JACKSON, P./PALMER, B. (1989): First Steps in Measuring Performance in the Public Sector. A Management Guide. Public Finance Foundation. London.

JOHNSON, N. (1983): State and Government in the Federal Republic of Germany. 2nd ed. (1st ed. 1973). Pergamon Press. Oxford.

KEELING, D. (1972): Management in Government. Allen and Unwin. London.

MEYER, P. (1957): Administrative Organization. Stevens. Copenhagen and London.

NOLTING, O. F. (1942): Management Methods in City Government. The International City Manager's Association. Chicago.

SCHUMACHER, E. F. (1974): Small is Beautiful. Abacus Edition. London.

Marina Ricciardelli

Economic and Monetary Union: Between Solidarity and Efficiency

1. Introduction

2. The EMU paradigm

3. Theoretical rationality and practical solutions

   A. Nominal convergences
   B. The equality criterion

4. Problems of the real economy: employment

5. Some observations

6. The Intergovernmental Conference: opportunity not to be missed

   A. An independent resource
   B. The principle of subsidiarity

1. Introduction

The work of the Intergovernmental Conference (IGC), due to start in 1996, will mark an important institutional commitment towards the creation of the EU. The IGC's agenda will include examining and redrafting certain provisions of the Maastricht Treaty on the subjects of foreign policy and joint security, justice and the relevant decision-making structures.
In our view the work of the IGC will also provide an opportunity to reflect on and elaborate practical proposals on how to adapt the methods and organizations behind the completion of Economic and Monetary Union or EMU. Along with the important progress it has made, EMU has also encountered various difficulties and setbacks. Hence the IGC has the opportunity to include on its agenda some of the problems linked specifically to the process of creating EMU, which is the subject of this paper.
These difficulties inevitably stem from the ambitious nature of the project which is obliged daily to take account of the dynamic events of reality. In our opinion, however, the lack of solutions provided by the politicians and institutions to the serious problems emerging is also partly to blame. What we are referring to are topics concerning the real economy and society, such as the problem of unemployment, the constant debilitation of the welfare state, the growing number of poor people and those who are isolated from society. The result of all this appears to be less support on the part of the general public for the completion of the European project, associated with the introduction of a single currency. In order to accept EMU in fact, people must be convinced that it can represent an element of stability and economic growth and therefore create prosperity for all. In other words EMU should be able to provide the answers to the problems listed above.

The general public's scepticism and indifference are worrying both for national governments, who are influenced directly, and also for the community institutions. To quote one of the most recent publications on this subject, the report presented by the Competitiveness Advisory Group in the summer of '95: "Dichotomies between individualism versus managed consensus, competition versus cooperation, free market versus social welfare policies, seem too simplistic. The need is to orchestrate broad consensus in favour of a European model, in which market mechanisms are promoted and, at the same time, are integrated by policies respecting the social dimension of all economic activity. The danger of a dual society, a widening gap between the very rich and the very poor, is real. On the whole, European countries have always attributed a high value to social cohesion and solidarity. This must remain our touchstone".

Considering the vast array of problems mentioned so far, it is worth remembering that significant progress has also been made which strengthens the credibility of the march towards EMU. The main examples of progress can be summarized as follows. Firstly the technical reports on changing over to a single currency and defining the types of coinage and banknotes have recently been made available. Two groups were at work on this aspect; one group was given a mandate by the Ecofin Council and the Commission, the other was a team from the European Monetary Institute (EMI). The results of the Expert Group, chaired by Mr. Cees Maas, are also complete. The following phrase taken from this technical document brings us back to the original subject of our paper: "A challenge will be set for citizens since the creation of the single currency can only succeed if there is broad popular support. The currency of the union cannot take off as an abstract means of payment".
This problem has acquired a new significance and urgency in the light of other events, four of which we will mention. The first is the likelihood that only some of the 15 member countries of the Community will be ready to enter phase three of the Union when it is launched; this is due to take place by January 1st 1999 at the latest. The existence of "differentiated integration" and the chance of resorting to the opting out clause (available to two of the member states) could make it difficult to achieve a shared train of thought and hence a common solution. The second event is the enlargement of the Union over the next 10-15 years to include a growing number of countries,

each with their own development problems. The third matter is linked to the fact that EMU is actually at a more advanced stage of development compared to the other aspects of European Union and for this reason it is considered the driving force behind the whole political project. Its role is not therefore a secondary one, indeed it poses a number of important questions; primarily as regards the significance of the role played by economic matters in the evolutionary pattern of the complex relations that exist between the European states. The fourth matter concerns the fact that economic and monetary union is part of a wider international context, for which the World Trade Organisation (GATT's successor) has partially attempted to draw up the framework and the steps forward. It is politically short-sighted to underestimate the solutions that EMU can provide both within the Union and beyond, considering the significance of its role in an international context.

This paper will deal briefly with the following subjects: the theoretical model behind EMU and its institutional procedures; problems of the real economy; possible institutional changes that could resolve some of the difficulties.

2. The EMU paradigm

As we have already mentioned, Europe's political and technical structures are committed to respecting the deadlines laid down in the Maastricht Treaty regarding specific practical matters, often of a technical nature. It does not therefore seem opportune for the Community organs to go over again the concepts and scientific hypotheses underlying the EMU project. Also during cultural and doctrinal debates, it is often underlined that before we begin to speculate about the validity of the chosen theoretical model, in keeping with the above, we must first face the numerous economic crises that the European Community has to cope with.

We believe, on the contrary, that the complex dynamics of the events and problems emerging make it both plausible and opportune to continue reflecting on the validity and completeness of the analytical model behind the project. Only by rereading and comparing the scheme with real events can we hope to formulate proposals for integrating the institutional procedures.

In short, one could argue that the scientific conjectures behind the EMU project confirme the validity of the fundamental hypotheses of the neoclassical theory. This theory is based on two main hypotheses: firstly that individual behaviour is based on rationality and hence on maximizing utility (or productivity) in a context of scarce resources and secondly on market equilibrium where price flexibility is one of the rules of business and where economic agents can freely express their preferences.

The first scientific elaboration of these hypotheses implies the existence of a simultaneous equilibrium, which results in a static system. When it is subsequently elaborated on a doctrinal level, an attempt is made to address the problem of time and the related phenomenon of the empirical economic cycle, thereby introducing the idea of rational expectations. We shall take a closer look at this latter element which affects the optimization processes of both the private sector economic agents as well as the relationship between the public economic agents and their private sector counterparts. When we talk about expectations we mean the forecasts made by economic agents. These expectations are defined as rational in so far as they are not based simply on a weighted average of past experiences. Using all the available information, they also take into account the various connections contained within the economic model in which they operate. By means of a learning process that is not foolproof but which does prevent systematic mistakes from occurring, the agents gradually develop the ability to make the best possible forecasts. This also allows for changes in behaviour aimed at exploiting all the available opportunities, including for example economic policy decisions and variations. The rational expectations theory brings about important consequences in terms of the economic laws governing private investments and the credibility of the forecasts on which the traditional normative prescription models are based; such models are fundamental for the public economic agent to play an active role in economic processes. The methodological doubts emerge on how plausible these models may be in practical terms, in so far as they could not embrace the decision-making problems and the possible future scenarios, mentioned earlier, which are used as points of reference by the private economic agents, above all entrepreneurs, in order to make investment decisions.

Decisions affecting capital formation and the consequent enlargement of the productive base create a link between micro and macroeconomic levels. In fact, while productivity and capital formation are considered part of the microeconomic approach and the performance of each production factor can be evaluated separately, the overall performance of all the resources put together gives rise to macroeconomic effects. Hence the conflict between micro and macroeconomic analysis disappears. What the economic agents need is the freedom to act and to choose which, in a context of factor mobility, thanks to the competition mechanism, ensures the efficient allocation of resources and general welfare creation.
According to the neoclassical model the concepts behind the function of investments, as described above, are in line with the basic model which they stem from; however more recent doctrinal debate emphasizes that these concepts are borne out by what happens in reality. It is in fact pointed out how such an analysis reinforces the conviction that controlling the supply through the level of aggregate demand has plunged the industrialized nations, over the past two decades, into a serious productivity crisis.

To round off our brief summary of the logical framework behind EMU, let us make a final reference to the "Economic Theory of Politics". Though influenced to some extent by the doctrinal principals mentioned so far, this latter elaboration is inspired by the fact that in all the industrialized capitalist systems public expenditure accounts for a significant part of all economic transactions. This gives rise to two problems: choosing the optimum price for collective goods and interpreting the reasons behind spending decisions. According to the model in question, by analysing the behaviour of those who govern and the political class in general it is possible to overcome the concept that public interest is a point of reference for government action. The principle of the "economic model of man" (Neumann 1991) maintains that public agents also act rationally and seek to maximise their own personal utility rather than pursue the objective of "social good": they do not base their decisions on specified aims or priorities but rather on their own fixed personal preferences, within a framework of variable institutional ties. The primary constraint is the problem of election or re-election which is regarded as the greatest single influence on how actions and decisions are taken and which ultimately can lead to a business cycle driven by politics.

3. Theoretical rationality and practical solutions

The theories referred to earlier provide a framework for the basic elements and institutional procedures behind the EMU project. As regards the former, in addition to believing in the benefits derived from increased trade in goods and services between countries resulting in sector specialization and economies of scale, great attention is also paid to real phenomena, which provide confirmation of the fact that economic power functions on a world-wide scale. For example, national governments can do nothing to prevent companies and capital from moving from one country to another. Given the entirely free movement of capital, a qualitative change is taking place in how national macroeconomic policy is operated. Such policies are now much more closely linked to what goes on in the rest of the world. Furthermore, in a common market, where a system of stable exchange rates is essential and the ultimate goal is to achieve a single currency, as is the case with the evolving European Community, national monetary policies no longer have any autonomy.

We need only think of the fact that once a single currency is in place, economic shocks on supply and demand can no longer be counteracted by resorting to devaluation or revaluation. National sovereignty is replaced by a form of supra-national control. The macroeconomic stability of EMU is therefore linked to a strong currency. Along with microeconomic efficiency and equality between countries and regions, a single currency also determines balanced development throughout the economic system.

A. Nominal convergences

A strong currency means keeping inflation under control. Along with stable exchange rates and equal interest rates, control of inflation is one of the key elements of the nominal convergence required by Maastricht and specified in the Treaty as necessary criteria for the Member States to be fully admitted to the EMU project. Control of inflation is the redeeming factor that links production costs to public spending, interest rates, financial capital markets and to the future expectations which in turn influence the economic plans of entrepreneurs.

That is why a supra-national monetary policy is needed to give lasting credibility to price stability. The task must be assigned to a central European bank that is allowed to act with complete autonomy. Since the bank is charged only with this single institutional objective, it can remain impartial in the trade off that inevitably occurs when there is a clash of opinions regarding a political decision. In fact, we should remember that the political self-interest drives governments to taking recourse to inflation since they believe in the existence of a Phillips curve which they can exploit; in other words, the possibility to reduce unemployment by resorting to inflation, increased public spending and lower taxes.

Given the crucial need for credibility during this transitional phase, the Bundesbank has emerged as a potential leader, not only because of Germany's economic importance but also because it has a history of independence as an institution. The transition period is important not only for each Member State individually but also because a central bank which may be influenced by national events could end up straying from the path of stability and thus jeopardize the whole EMU project. This may also be due to the fierce scepticism of those making predictions on which to base their future economic programmes.

Hence we could say that the theoretical models recognize a standard value in historical and real events. Even when these theoretical models take into account the behaviour of the public sector economic agents, they simply reinforce the idea that efficiency is inherent to microeconomic behaviour and it becomes all the more necessary for each country to stipulate maximum thresholds regarding public debt-to-GDP and deficit-to-GDP ratios. This sums up the criteria for admission to EMU, as specified by the Maastricht Treaty.

B. The equality criterion

Let us now briefly refer to the third guiding principle of the EMU project, namely equality between the regions. This criterion stems from the belief that where companies choose to locate and the economic sectors they operate in can help create an unequal distribution of economic wealth, generated by the opening up of markets. This in turn can aggravate territorial imbalances and cause short-term unemployment problems.

To help solve the problem, measures were introduced in the form of "structural funds". Currently in the second intervention cycle, which runs from 1994 to 1999, these funds are allocated according to decisions taken at the 1992 European Council Meeting in Edinburgh. Some 141 billion ECUs have been earmarked for the six-year period in question.

These funds, which take up 33% of the Common budget, therefore represent the privileged tool of the Community solidarity policy and currently benefit some 26.6% of the Community's population compared to 21.7% during the first intervention cycle. This percentage increase can be explained chiefly by the arrival of five new German Länder into the Community.

The Intergovernmental Conference will be launched during a period of economic recovery. Let us turn our attention to the most recent forecasts by the European Commission. The statistics confirm that the economic recovery, which began at the end of 1993 should continue throughout 1996 (Table 1). By 1996, production levels in the Community are expected to be 10% higher than they were in 1991. This growth is primarily due to increased exports, which are expected to continue, and also to investment spending.

Table 1: The Community economy: Use and supply of goods and services (annual real percentage change)

	1993	1994	1995	1996
Private consumption	-0.1	1.5	2.0	2.5
Government consumption	0.7	0.7	0.8	1.0
Gross fixed capital formation	-5.5	2.4	5.7	6.3
Domestic demand (incl. stocks)	-1.8	2.0	2.8	3.1
Exports of goods and services	7.5	10	7	6.7
Imports of goods and services	-0.5	4.5	6	6
Gross domestic product	-0.4	2.6	2.9	3.2

Source: European Commission, Annual Economic Report for 1995, *European Economy*, n°59.

The statistics on unemployment are much less reassuring. In the 1992-1994 period a Community-wide loss of 5.8 million jobs was recorded (a drop of 3.9%). For the sake of comparison, we can consider that between 1984 and 1990 some 9.3 million jobs were created throughout the EEC. During 1995 and 1996 an estimated 3 million jobs will be created in the Community. The dramatic nature of the employment figures hardly comes as a surprise. The reasons behind them reinforce the findings of the 1993 White Paper "Growth, Competitiveness, Employment" - the first publication to draw

Europe's attention to the problem. In the wake of this White Paper, the proposal was made at the European Council Meeting in Essen (December 1994) to adopt active policies to stimulate the job market [1].

The heterogeneous structure underlying the comprehensive 1994 unemployment figures, which the Commission discussed in a detailed report, is summarized as follows: in 1994 total unemployment accounted for approximately 11% of the active population (between 16.7 and 17.6 million depending on whether we consider a total of 12 or 15 Member States). The current economic recovery could solve the problem of cyclical unemployment, which represents 2% of the working population.
The remaining 9% is considered to be medium-term and is therefore tied to the priorities defined by the Essen Council Meeting. Almost half of the 9% category, also defined as "structural unemployment", is considered to be caused by the fact that the workforce does not correspond to the requirements of the evolving job market. The remaining portion, the so-called "classical" (or capacity-strained) unemployment is regarded as being tied to present levels of production capacity. It can therefore only be solved by the creation of new jobs (Table 2).

(1) These policies highlight the following priorities: promoting investment in training; adopting more flexible methods of organization at work and salary policies that do not take up the entire productivity increase; reducing indirect wage costs, especially those of unskilled workers; going beyond certain practices, in particular those related to income support, which can ultimately discourage individuals from continuing to look for a job

Table 2: Growth, wages, prices and productivity (EC, average annual rate of growth, in percent)

	1986-90	1991-95	1996-2000
Growth (real GDP)	3.3	1.5	3.4
Labour productivity (Real GDP per employee)	2.0	2.1	2.1
Nominal wage per employee	6.0	5.0	4.0
Real wage per employee*	1.2	1.2	1.4
GDP deflator	4.8	3.8	2.6
Private consumption price	4.1	4.0	2.6
Nominal unit labour costs	4.0	2.9	1.9
Real unit labour cost	-0.8	-0.9	-0.7
Capital profitability index**	84.8	90.7	101.6

* deflated by GDP deflator
** net operating surplus per unit of net capital stock, index 1961-73=100.

Source: European Commission, European Economy, Supplement A, n°1,1995.

Assuming that the Essen policies will be put into effect, the Commission has predicted that the unemployed will gradually be re-absorbed and that the rate of unemployment will settle at a level of 6.9% by the year 2000 (Table 3). This prediction is based on the continuation of the historic trend of productivity (at around 2%) and also continued GDP growth of between 3% and 3.5%. The Commission does warn however that such a path would be obstructed should the risk emerge of a conflict between the stability objective and budgetary and wage developments.

Table 3: Population, employment and unemployment, EUR 15 (harmonised data, in million people)

	1994	1995	1996	1997	1998	1999	2000
1. Tot. popul.	370.5	371.8	373.1	374.3	375.3	376.1	377.2
2. Act. rate (%)	66.2	66.2	66.3	66.5	66.7	66.9	67.1
3. Tot. employm.	146.3	147.5	149.2	150.9	153.1	155.4	157.6
4. Unemploym.	17.6	16.9	16.0	14.9	13.8	12.6	11.5
5. Unem. rate (%)	10.9	10.4	9.8	9.1	8.4	7.6	6.9

Source: Eurostat and Commission services, 1995.

The NAIRU concept (non accelerating inflation rate of unemployment) emerges again, even though the Commission underlines the fact that as an indicator it is difficult to measure on a practical level because it does not remain constant in time and should therefore be rejected because of its lack of practicality. The chance to lower it, in other words to control the inflationary tensions resulting from too high a rate of capacity utilization or wage slippage in the process of unemployment reduction is nevertheless suggested, linking it to the general framework which already contains such negative factors as less competitiveness in terms of prices and community exports on world markets and less stable exchange rates.

A detailed analysis of the above data would be beyond the scope of this concise paper; in fact we shall limit ourselves to making a few brief comments. If we examine the data relating to the most recent job losses, we can find confirmation of the "hysteresis" phenomenon, which tends to turn cyclical unemployment into long-term unemployment. In other words part of the diseconomies created during the recession were not recovered in the period that followed.

It must also be stressed that the more recent models of interpretation (Phelps 1994), which the Commission appears to have been at least partially referring to, tend to go beyond the previous arguments and attribute the systematic changes in the unemployment rate primarily to non-monetary factors (significant drop in production, market saturation for certain products, high level of productivity).

Consequently we can note that the EEC framework on labour market policies, by reinforcing the fundamental principles of its general design, increases the responsibilities of job supply behaviour with the aim of reabsorbing unemployment. The inelasticity of the labour demand is in fact influenced not only by the labour productivity curve but also by a series of other phenomena. As a result the job supply must also take account of the new ties linked to the international context: for example by moderating salaries (in relation to the dynamics of productivity) to tackle the increase tendency and also the high level of long-term interest rates which are another important factor affecting production costs.
Finally, increased productivity, which is essential for those sectors of economic activity which have to compete on an international level, should also allow for an increase in the relative importance of those sectors with high labour intensity (and low productivity growth). This in turn should help distribute the wealth created and hence prevent the increase in productivity being translated into a drop in the labour intensity of the growth process.

We are fully convinced that high unemployment is an extremely serious issue and that it is also a highly complex problem to solve. The observations that follow are not intended to be alternatives to the numerous evaluations of the official European documents mentioned previously. Rather they are meant to complement them, given the complexity and diversification of the causes behind the imbalance in the job market. In fact we believe that, though there is evidence of some quite fundamental changes to the economic context, the problems we are discussing and the difficulties in resolving them are still relevant to the EMU paradigm and some of its institutional choices. On the basis of this assumption, let us try to identify the analytical and practical steps that should be taken.

5. Some observations

Recent cultural debate has affirmed that the real economy is in serious crisis and that the problem is exacerbated by the crisis inherent in the theoretical analyses, in particular the contrast between models of general equilibrium and historical models (Davidson 1986).
The former are based on pre-established theories and have a tendency to replace reality with an abstraction rather than to simplify it. The latter do not observe the fundamental principle of rational behaviour, thereby removing all scientific content from the interpretive model. The framework of our essay, inspired by this diagnosis, is developed along the lines of two main principles: how comprehensive is the heuristic content of the theoretical model behind the completion of EMU (whether it is excessively inelastic or abstract) and how necessary it is for this model to complement the analytical models relating to other aspects of the real economy.

5.1. Regarding the first aspect, we shall consider just a few problems. The fundamental principles of the theoretical model, as described at the beginning of this paper, underline that the pursuit of an equilibrium, in other words a set of relative prices for all goods and services that creates a balance between the various markets, is based on the theory of automatic regulation that tends to push the system towards an unequivocal transformation. It would appear that the introduction of rational expectations does not alter, but rather reinforces the determinism and static nature of this logic. This idea of "unequivocal" transformation, in relation to the completion of the EMU project, should take account of the complex innovations of post-industrial society where the level of knowledge, scientific performance and the rate of technological progress all contribute to creating a particularly dynamic reality. If the equilibrium concept is the system's preferred benchmark, then the route adopted for achieving it should take account of existing imbalances and not ignore them simply because they are considered as short-term, or related to a period of time that is transient and considered to have no objectives of its own. This is all the more necessary since the vast array of elements that make up the economic system, each with their own individual dynamics, probably do not converge towards the unequivocal transformation, mentioned above. Price flexibility, which is regarded as a fundamental principle of economic equilibrium and efficient allocation of resources, does not allow for the fragmentation and specificity of the various markets (concerning speculation, raw materials and labour), each of which has its own rules of determination for which price signals do not represent effective regulatory mechanisms. It has been rightly argued that it is the stickiness of prices and nominal wages, guaranteed by the contract principle, that allows capitalist economies to become involved in lengthy production processes and the prices of goods to remain stable (Davidson 1986).

When the theoretical model is applied to reality, the idea of overcoming the conflict between micro and macroeconomic levels may suppress the scientific need to tackle head-on the behavioural standards of both multinational companies and financial brokers in a complex system of fixed and flexible exchange rates.
Another consequence of removing the conflict between micro and macroeconomic levels is that, by professing an absolute faith in the virtues of free enterprise, it links the dynamics of private investment solely to changes on a microeconomic level. However, if we underestimate the influence of macroeconomic policy on the microeconomic level, we effectively extract all content from the aim of competitiveness, especially when it refers to a large geographical area and is therefore tied to long-term expectations and not just to those of an individual firm. We must think about the effects, in terms of real growth, of considering even slight variations in the unemployment rate merely as an indicator of future inflation on a macroeconomic level. In order for the whole system to benefit, the need is stressed for improved microeconomic efficiency, associated with a higher rate of macroeconomic growth. In other words, all the resources created by rationalization should be effectively re-employed.

5.2. Let us turn our attention to the second aspect, namely the relationship between economic analyses and other types of analyses related to different aspects of human society. We can see that the contrast between "rationality and time" becomes heightened (Shackle 1973), with the latter introducing uncertainties and choices that are "not rational in economic terms". In other words, in the long run it is not the price system but rather society's scale of values, within which the economy operates, that is of significant importance for the economy.

If we expect the theoretical model to be of practical help in interpreting dynamic processes, it is essential for it also to be feasible, to overcome the principle of a deterministic "supernatural aim".
In order to regulate an economy between external and internal changes, the idea of a closed system for each branch of the social sciences must be overcome and a process of so-called reciprocal permeation should be achieved (Bartoli 1991).
It is the complementarity, or lack of autonomy of the various fields of analysis, that pushes every interpretation of a complex society in this direction. The importance of the role played by political and institutional factors, as well as the growing weight of social phenomena, when combined with the market's internal cohesions, can create new economic problems, for example in terms of distribution. The multiple dimensions of the real economy draw our attention again, in terms of analysis, to the possible tensions that may arise in the passage from the micro to the macroeconomic level.

By way of example we can consider the mobility factor connected to the idea of efficient allocation of resources. The four freedoms (movement of goods, services, labour and capital), one of the aims of the Treaty of Rome, were introduced with the completion of the single market. However, this does not mean that they were automatically put into effect, especially as regards the workforce, which is still burdened by numerous difficulties and sacrifices both on an individual and a social level.

We can therefore conclude our reflection with the rather concise affirmation that employment problems and the social questions they raise need a global political design and not a partial one. Let us recall what we said at the beginning about the validity and neutrality of the economic model and the dominance of its role (in terms of political philosophy) in the wider context of the European project.

6. The Intergovernmental Conference: opportunity not to be missed

On the basis of the arguments and phenomena outlined above we can say that employment growth and the defence of society's democratic institutions, are only partly linked to production growth.

Increasingly open markets and economic systems can multiply the risks of social fragmentation through a more marked separation between insiders and outsiders and the effects are aggravated by the weakening of social security systems. In order to keep these systems under control, a long-term social and macroeconomic framework is needed to coordinate all the relevant spheres of society. The problems to be tackled within the production system must be linked to the wider problems of society in general. The recommendations of the Essen Council should be integrated with a redistribution of labour not only to develop processes of economic solidarity but also to allow the welfare state's potential workers to assert themselves. For this to happen the quantitative, or market logic, must be accompanied by a logic that reconfirms an overall qualitative role. Given the way in which the process of European integration constricts national policies, this means that the macroeconomic and social framework, beginning with its affirmation on a political philosophy level, is defined and sustained also at a European level.

Arising from this are two initial subjects of an institutional nature which the IGC should tackle: providing the EEC budget with an independent resource and redefining the subsidiarity principle.

A. An independent resource

The Edinburgh summit established that the EU budget should reach 1.27% of GNP by 1999. The structural funds are amongst the budget's most controversial expenditure items because they are considered to be the primary reason for the existing imbalances between the various Member States' national budgets. We shall not dwell on this problem, which is nevertheless critical for the EU's future, but limit ourselves to recalling that the all-important solidarity principle requires resources of the EU budget to be doubled gradually in the years following 1999, given the increased distribution gap on a territorial level, caused by the predicted enlargement of the Community.

Let us return to the initial idea of the independent resource. With respect to budgetary equilibrium, this resource should represent an institutional and operational fly-wheel for assisting the European macroeconomic framework. The increasing need for coordination between national economic policies would have a practical point of reference and room for manoeuvre in adjusting the Union's budget, as regards expenditure that would no longer be pre-established on a long-term basis and more directly linked to economic changes.

In this way the conflict between compulsory and non-compulsory expenditure would be mitigated and greater interaction would be achieved between the Council and the Parliament (strengthening the latter's role) even in the presence of negative shocks which the same microeconomic rationalization processes can cause on a level of macroeconomic interdependence. The role of the EU in the macroeconomic stabilization policy is essential, given that the policy of investment concentrated on direct action by the Member States has been surpassed. However, the development of continuity, in other words the encouragement of long-term private investment and the introduction of new technology, can be defended provided that Europe as a whole is truly aiming at the effective relaunch of the total potential of each country's real economy. To underline the importance of these potentials we should bear in mind that more than 90% of European investments are covered by internal production. Coordination between the states in terms of development continuity would avoid the systematic restriction of domestic demand being translated into simple recourse to external demand. It is in this dynamic context that active job market policies could operate effectively, also to get rid of the dispersion and inefficiencies of certain transfer flows.

Defining an independent tax may not be an easy matter. On this subject it is worth paying greater attention to the somewhat neglected Commission proposal (1993) on linking it to currency issuing by the European Central Bank. A pollution tax is another valid alternative or additional means of raising resources.
Finally, we must underline that a Europe-wide taxable base can be brought back to the financial market transactions through the adoption of a simple coupon with sliding values within a fork mechanism (according to the characteristics of the operations: spot transactions, round trip speculation, etc.) the effects of which would be linked above all to the short term and therefore to those financial resources that are currently isolated from trade flows and real investment projects.

Finally, the opportunity should be weighed up, at least initially, of accompanying the introduction of the independent resource with a cut in national taxation, not so much in order to guarantee the fiscal neutrality of the Community, as to win public support for the new proposal.

B. The principle of subsidiarity

The subject of forms of taxation and how to coordinate them brings us to the second subject mentioned earlier, the principle of subsidiarity. According to this principle, tasks should be carried out at the most appropriate level of government. In other words, higher levels of government are called upon to intervene only when the lower levels are unable to act satisfactorily.

This principle, worth noting for its transparency and democratic legitimacy, is considered highly relevant to the subject of taxation, also because of its utility in planning a form of fiscal federalism.

On the contrary, we are of the belief that, also in terms of fiscal policy, the IGC needs to relaunch the idea of increased coordination to moderate the current emphasis on the advantages of decentralization. Not only because of what we said earlier on the subject of a European macroeconomic policy but also because of its links to the welfare state. The welfare state is no longer a choice that a single national system can continue to sustain in isolation. Fiscal competition between the European States, together with factor mobility, reduces the procurement of public services and therefore also the scale of redistribution, with significant regressive effects. This opens the door to problems of future instability: we need only think of the problem of old age pensions that are not based on available funds. It also encourages inefficiency in the system as a whole. This happens for two reasons: firstly because each country ignores the external effects that their domestic tax privileges may have on other States and secondly because the same categories of economic agents and incomes which currently benefit from fiscal privileges are set to benefit again in the future. Clearly, mobile factors exert considerable bargaining power in the tax field, but presumably greater harmonization and cooperation between States would create conditions of greater neutrality and hence this power could be kept under control and a balance could be achieved between cuts in public spending and the tax burden on less mobile factors and incomes.

Moreover, fiscal coordination and cooperation allow us to tackle other problems, some of which are particularly delicate and the control of which is crucial for the democratic growth of the system. By way of example we could mention the replacement of the special tax regimes applied to financial services centres linked to "off-shore" zones or the battle against tax fraud and money laundering. It is worth underlining that the inefficiencies and external effects do not involve only the level of taxation but also other important matters. For example maintaining a high level of environmental standards, a topic which is of growing importance, can also be pursued via the introduction of a common tax on pollution.

At the beginning of this paper we referred to the recommendations of the official documents on the need for widespread consensus for the European project. We would now like to finish the paper with another reference to one of these documents. The conclusions of the European Council Presidency at Cannes (June 1995) urged the IGC preparatory think tank to concentrate their proposals on certain priorities such as "consolidating public consensus for the European project, by responding to the need for a democracy that is closer to Europe's citizens, who are anxious about problems like employment and the environment". We remain optimistic that the concrete opportunities for dialogue that present themselves today will allow some of the above-mentioned themes to be analysed.

Résumé

L'Union Economique et Monétaire (UEM) : entre solidarité et efficience

1996 marque une étape importante dans l'évolution de l'Union européenne puisqu'une Conférence intergouvernementale va réexaminer le traîté de Maastricht entré en vigueur en 1993.

Cette échéance donne l'occasion de réfléchir au développement passé de l'Union européenne et à la validité du modèle théorique qui sous-tend son fonctionnement. Il s'agit en effet de confronter les résultats attendus de ce modèle (dans le respect de conditions données) avec la réalité socio-économique observable, plus particulièrement au niveau de l'emploi, de la distribution des richesses, de la solidarité sociale et de la croissance. Les enjeux sont considérables et la crédibilité des procédures de la construction européenne est en cause.

Le texte de Marina RICCIARDELLI rappelle tout d'abord le paradigme de l'Union européenne et examine les éléments théoriques ainsi que les procédures institutionnelles qui marquent de leur empreinte cette Union. Le problème de l'emploi retient une attention particulière ; il conduit à une analyse critique du modèle et à des propositions constructives qui tiennent compte des exigences de défense d'une société démocratique, et de respect de l'équilibre social, exigences combinées qui ne sont pas automatiquement assurées par la croissance de la production. Les institutions européennes (avec des ressources indépendantes) ont de ce point de vue un rôle important à repenser.

Zusammenfassung

Die Europäische Währungsunion (EWU) : zwischen Solidarität und Effizienz

1996 ist ein wichtiges Jahr in der Entwicklung der Europäischen Union: eine Regierungskonferenz ist damit beauftragt, den 1993 in Kraft getretenen Maastricht-Vertrag zu überprüfen.

Hierbei wird über die neuere Entwicklung der Europäischen Union und die Gültigkeit des ihr zugrunde-liegenden theoretischen Modells nachzudenken sein. In der Tat geht es darum, unter Beachtung der gegebenen Bedingungen und angesichts der sozio-ökonomischen Wirklichkeit, insbesondere des Arbeitsmarkts, der Verteilung der finanziellen Ressourcen, der sozialen Solidarität und des Wachstums die an das Modell gehegten Erwartungen zu überprüfen. Beträchtliches steht hierbei auf dem Spiel, und nicht zuletzt geht es um die Glaubwürdigkeit der europäischen Konstruktion selbst.

Der Text von Marina RICCIARDELLI erinnert zunächst an die Grundlagen der Europäischen Union und unterzieht dann die theoretischen Elemente sowie die institutionellen, die Union prägenden Verfahren einer Prüfung. Sie geht besonders auf das Problem der Arbeitslosigkeit ein, wobei sie das Modell der europäischen Integration einer kritischen Analyse unterzieht und konstruktive Handlungsalternativen aufzeigt, die den Erfordernissen einer demokratischen Gesellschaft und der Einhaltung des sozialen Gleichgewichts Rechnung tragen. Dies wird nicht automatisch durch das Produktionswachstum gesichert. Den europäischen Institutionen mit ihren eigenen Ressourcen kommt hierbei eine bedeutende, neu zu überdenkende Rolle zu.

References

ASSOCIATION FOR THE MONETARY UNION OF EUROPE (1994): Preparing the transition to the single currency. Paris. May.

BARTOLI, H. (1991): L'économie multidimensionelle. Economica. Lassay-Les Chateaux.

BELL, D. (1986): Les modèles et la réalité. Crise et renouveau de la théorie économique, Paris.

COMMISSION OF THE EUROPEAN COMMUNITIES (1993): Growth, competitiveness, employment - the challenges and ways forward into the 21st century. Luxembourg.

COMMISSION DES COMMUNAUTÉS EUROPÉENNES (1993): Fonds structurels communautaires 1994-1999. Textes règlementaires et commentaires. Bruxelles.

COMMISSION EUROPÉENNE (1995): Economie Européenne. Rapport économique annuel pour 1995. n°59.

COMMISSION OF THE EUROPEAN COMMUNITIES (1991): The Economics of EMU. European Economy. n°1. Brussels.

CEPR (1993): Making sense of subsidiarity: how much centralization for Europe?. London.

DAVIDSON, P. (1986): L'économie postkéynesienne, solution à la crise de la théorie économique. Crise et renouveau de la théorie économique. Paris.

EXPERT GROUP (mandate by European Commission) on the changeover to the single currency (1995): The preparation of the changeover to the single European currency. Brussels. January.

NEUMANN, M.J.M. (1991): Central bank independence as a prerequisite of price stability. The economics of EMU. European Economy. Brussels.

PHELPS, E.S. (1994) Structural slumps - the modern equilibrium theory of unemployment, interest and assets. Harvard University Press. Cambridge, MA.

SHACKLE, G.S.L. (1973): Epistemics and economics: a critique of economic doctrines. Cambridge University Press.

THE PHILIP MORRIS INSTITUTE FOR PUBLIC POLICY RESEARCH (1995): Au delà de Maastricht - Les enjeux de la CIG de 1996. Paris.

THE PHILIP MORRIS INSTITUTE FOR PUBLIC POLICY RESEARCH (1994): L'Unione Monetaria Europea è morta?. Bruxelles.

Giovanni Palmerio

The Drift of the Public Debt: Threat for Europe? The Italian Case

1. The evolution of public finance in the countries of the European Community (1960-1995)

   A. Phase of balanced expansion of the public sector

   B. Phase of strong deterioration in budget positions

   C. Phase of corrective intervention

2. The evolution of public finance in Italy in the period 1950-1970

3. Italian public finance during the seventies

4. Italian public finance during the eighties

5. The policies aimed at the reduction of the public debt in Italy during the nineties

6. The negative effects of the public debt and the perspectives for the Italian economy

1. The evolution of public finance in the countries of the European Community (1960-1995)

In the current debate on economic policy the main international institutions and numerous scholars maintain that the size of the public debt in many countries represents a threat to the economic stability of Europe, so that governments should adopt measures that rapidly reduce the public debt-GDP ratio.

As is known, the Maastricht Treaty (1991) underlines that, in order to create a European monetary union, it is necessary to keep the evolution of public finance under control. The fundamental need is to pursue sound budget policies, even if this does not mean systematically requiring identical results for all the parameters of public finance, such as the dimension of the public sector, the budget balance and the public debt.

In any event, a consensus has been reached about some principles and fundamental budget rules that would facilitate economic convergence and attainment of macroeconomic goals at the national and Community levels.

First of all, budget discipline is necessary, based mainly on the observation of three rules:

a) the absence of obligatory monetary financing of public deficits: there must be in force, therefore, a regime that divorces the Treasury from the central bank;
b) the absence of bailouts and the exclusion of guarantees of debt service;
c) the necessity of avoiding excessive budget deficits.

On this last point, the Treaty envisages that already in the second stage in the process of European monetary unification, the Commission will oversee the evolution of budget and public debt situations of member countries. In particular, budget discipline should respect three criteria:

a) the ratio between the public deficit and GDP should not exceed 3 %;
b) the ratio between the stock of public debt and GDP should not exceed 60 %;
c) the budget deficit should not exceed expenditures for investment; this is the so-called golden rule of public finance.

Because in several countries the values of the deficit-GDP and debt-GDP ratios are far greater than 3 % and 60 %, these countries are requested to adopt economic policies that result in a constant reduction in those ratios, at a satifactory rate.

The Maastricht Treaty also exhorts member states, in addition to reducing the deficit, to improve the revenue structure and overhaul public expenditure. These principles are intended essentially to increase the flexibility, efficiency and productivity of the economy and refer therefore to aspects of structural policies of the member states. In general, on more than one occasion, at meetings of the organs of the European Union, the necessity for member states to create an efficient public sector has been underlined.

The differences between member states' situations with respect to debt and deficit are still very great. In 1991 the public debt-GDP ratio had the highest value, of 130 %, in Belgium and the lowest value, of 37 %, in France. In 1994 it was 138.7 % in Belgium and 49.5 % in France.

With respect to Italy, in spite of the fact that the public spending/GDP ratio did not noticeably increase from 1985 to 1994 (going from 49.4 % to 52.4 %), the public debt/GDP ratio continued to increase measurably: it went from 66.4 % in 1982 to 100.9 % in 1990 to 124.7% in 1994. During the eighties, the average annual growth rate in the public debt/GDP ratio was greater than in the seventies. Breaking down the principal factors that caused the growth in this ratio into primary deficit and spending on interest, we see that during the eighties there was a gradual increase in the share of interest spending simultaneously with a decrease in the primary deficit, beginning in 1986.

Since 1992, Italy has experienced primary surpluses every year and in 1995, for the first time, a decrease in the public debt/GDP ratio is expected.

An important consideration regards the criteria for defining deficit and public debt in various countries. The general principle is to consider the state deficit and the consolidated gross debt of the state sector, but, obviously, discussion could be had about whether some items should be included or not, considering either the internal situation of a country, or comparing different countries. For example, in Italy some long term debt of the Treasury held by the Bank of Italy represents a component of debt, but certainly has no effect on the economic system. Analogously, the value of bonds acquired by the central bank, pursuant to which monetary base was issued, in some countries such as Italy enters into the definition of debt and in others does not; yet the burden and the implications for budget policies of this type of debt are very different from those of Treasury bonds issued to the general public.

These considerations are not irrelevant; they can cause substantial variations in the value of the debt/GDP ratio, so that a country like Italy, for example, could find itself in a clearly better situation, even though quite far from the ideal value of 60 %.

In this brief essay it is not possible for me to analyze the problem of the definition of deficit and debt, but I will cite an example, which certainly induces reflection. According to the German government, the deficit/GDP ratio in Germany in 1994, defined according to the criteria of Maastricht, was equal to 3 %, while according to other authoritative sources it was equal to 6 %, if the cost of reconstructing Eastern Germany is considered.

But let us see how we arrived at the current situation. During the last forty years the public finance of countries in the European Union has undergone considerable transformations, which essentially reflect the evolution of the economic context and continually changing views about budget policies. We can identify three rather clearly distinct phases:

A. Phase of balanced expansion of the public sector

An initial period, from 1960 until the early seventies, was characterized by a rapid growth in the share represented by public spending in economic activity. Since public receipts were advancing at an almost analogous rate, the budget remained for the most part in equilibrium. This balanced expansion of the public sector reflected the acceptance of its growing role and the faith in the efficiency of public intervention in the economy. These were the years in which state social services to citizens grew, for education, health care, pensions, etc. This was also made possible by the stability of the international economic context, characterized by the Bretton Woods system based on fixed exchange rates and the exceptionally rapid growth recorded by the European Community during the sixties.

B. Phase of strong deterioration in budget positions

The period 1970-1982 saw the emergence of considerable and strongly increasing budget deficits, which translated into a rapid growth in the ratio between public debt and GDP. The deterioration in the budget positions was due to an explosion in public spending, which, in contrast with the preceding phase, was not compensated for with a corresponding increase in taxes and social security contributions. The contraction in economic growth and a rise in unemployment, generated by oil shocks which characterized the period, contributed to aggravate the budget position. The contraction in economic growth caused a reduction in fiscal receipts, while the rise in unemployment caused an increase in public spending directed toward distributing subsidies and creating jobs in the public sector.

C. Phase of corrective intervention

Following a fundamental reorientation towards a policy of balancing public finance, the rate of expansion of public spending suffered a slowdown in the first half of the eighties, and the share of public spending out of GDP lessened, beginning in 1985, when recovery of economic growth was added to the measures taken to contain the expansion of the public sector. In spite of the fact that several countries effected a reduction in fiscal pressure, a significant improvement in budget positions occurred.

The rethinking of the role and the concept of budget policies was induced by many factors and was inspired, among other things, by growing worries about the negative economic effects that a public sector of excessive size could have on the growth of GDP and on employment and about the growing rigidity of budgets due to increasing expenditures for interest and current transfers.

If the general tendencies outlined above for the European Union taken together are also perceptible to a majority of member states, the convergence of budget positions has tended to be less emphatic at the end compared to the beginning of the period examined (1960-1995). This is mainly due to two factors: divergent reactions of the various countries of the Union to the two oil shocks of the seventies (for example some countries such as Italy recorded inflation rates in excess of 20 %, while others such as Germany contained the rate of inflation to below 6-7 %) and differences in the intensity and timing of balancing interventions effected in the eighties.

For example, while Denmark and Luxembourg were able to improve quickly to a significant degree their own budget positions, in most of the other countries, governments were able to reduce the budget imbalance only beginning in 1985, after the economic recovery.

These considerations explain therefore the actual degree of disparity existing in the budget positions between countries in the European Union.

Some authors maintain that a certain correlation seems to exist between budget positions and the capacity of the European monetary system to impose discipline; this is however a tenuous connection, in view of the fact that countries like Spain and the United Kingdon, which adhered later than other countries to the exchange rate mechanism, obtained better results than countries such as Belgium and Italy. Furthermore, after what has happened to the European monetary system in recent years, these considerations appear even more fragile.

After the prescriptions of the Maastricht Treaty, the Delors report also underlined the necessity for coordination between monetary policy and budget policy of member countries in order to attain the goals of economic growth and employment, without creating conflict with the goal of price stability, pursued by the central banks.

2. The evolution of public finance in Italy in the period 1950-1970

Italy, at the end of the Second World War, was an agricultural country, from which the population emigrated. During the fifties and sixties Italy experienced strong growth, based mainly on exports. The average annual growth rate of GDP from 1951 to 1972 was 5.1 %. In those years many small and medium sized firms were created and developed, mainly in the Centre-North, and a virtuous circle of this kind begins. The labour supply was almost unlimited due to the transfer of population from agriculture, where there was disguised unemployment, to industry, especially building, and the service sector. The percentage of the population employed in agriculture, which in 1951 was 43.9 %, in 1972 had become 17.6 %.

Wages remained low until the end of the sixties, while productivity grew rapidly. Profits to the firms therefore grew, which were reinvested. Prices of manufactured goods were stable or even declining and because the Bretton Woods system was in effect and exchange rates were fixed, Italian goods were competitive on international markets. The growth, driven mainly by exports, was also fueled by investments and by the expansion of consumption. In spite of the great increase in productivity, employment also grew, given the higher increments of GDP.

The increase in exports was strengthened with the progressive opening of the Italian economy to international exchanges and the joining of the European Economic Community in 1957. This policy represented a complete reversal of direction from the protectionist and autarchic policies that Italy had pursued during the thirties.

In this context, public spending which in 1951 was 25 % of GDP, became 31 % in 1960 and 35 % in 1970. Spending on education, health, retirement and welfare increased most, given that in the twenty years from 1950 to 1970 social services rendered by the state to citizens grew. Spending on public works also grew, while defense spending declined and spending on interest on the public debt remained low, representing less than 5 % of total public spending.

The increase in public spending during the period 1950-1970 was essentially financed by the growth in tax revenues. Current revenues, which in 1951 were 23 % of GDP, in 1970 were 33 %. The great increase in current revenues was caused by the rapid growth in tax revenues and social security contributions. The latter, which in 1951 were 23 % of the total current revenues, in 1971 constituted 35 %. Tax revenues in that period were supplied mainly by indirect taxes, while direct taxes constituted a fairly constant share of the current revenues of the public administration, equal to 18-19 %.

In the twenty years under examination, the public debt decreased. The public internal debt, which at the end of the Second World War had reached 120 % of GDP and was pulverized by inflation during the forties, in 1951 was equal to 26 % of GDP, declined to 24 % in 1961 and to 18 % in 1971. It is true that there were other forms of indebtedness of the state, such as the collection of savings by the Postal Administration, Treasury debt to the Bank of Italy and the foreign debt. Keeping all these elements in mind, the total debt of the public sector in 1971 was equal to 45.1 % of GDP, but foreign debt represented only a little more than 1 % of GDP. It was therefore a well balanced situation that did not give rise to any worry.

3. Italian public finance during the seventies

The situation changed radically during the seventies. The great social conflicts that occurred in firms and in the country already at the end of the sixties, and the two oil shocks of 1973 and 1978 caused a deep recession. The rate of growth in GDP suffered a drastic contraction and even became negative in one year (1975); unemployment grew. Public spending grew explosively, going from 35 % of GDP in 1970 to 42 % of GDP in 1980. A large part of the increse in spending occurred mainly from 1970 to 1975. Spending for welfare and interest grew most, going from 18 % of GDP in 1970 to 27 % of GDP in 1980. Welfare payments were made to families and to firms: these payments included social services such as unemployment benefits for workers temporarily unemployed and other forms of unemployment subsidies, pensions, payments to firms in difficulty, to firms investing in the Mezzogiorno, etc. The amount of interest increased due to the rapid growth of the public debt.

The increase in public revenues slowed down significantly during the seventies because of the contraction in GDP growth. Public revenues went from 30 % of GDP in 1970 to 33.7 % of GDP in 1980. After the tax reform of 1974 the weight of direct taxes increased significantly, while the weight of indirect taxes, both business taxes and consumption taxes, decreased.

The much faster increase in public spending than the increase in revenues during the seventies, caused a continuous growth of public deficits, so that the public debt went from 45.1 % of GDP in 1971 to 61.1 % in 1981 while foreign debt remained in 1981 slightly greater than 1 % of GDP.

During the seventies, therefore, the financing needs of the public deficit became more and more pressing. The high and variable inflation rates that occurred at the beginning of the period and the uncertainty regarding the future movements of the interest rates caused a sudden fall in the demand for bonds, just when the financing needs of the public sector were increasing.

The government decided to finance the growing public deficit to a great extent through the creation of monetary base. This was possible thanks to the institutional characteristics of the system. The Treasury, in fact, was able to obtain financing automatically, although within predetermined limits, through the credit line it had with the Bank of Italy; moreover it could issue bonds that were bought by the Central Bank; it could even issue bonds that banks, until 1975, could deposit as compulsory reserves at the central bank and that, therefore, were close substitutes for the monetary base.

The monetary financing of the public deficit induced high inflation, which in some years was greater than 20 %. The monetary authorities were able to keep interest rates under control. Nominal interest rates were often lower than the inflation rate and the real interest rates reached in some years the value of - 5 %. This was possible because it was prohibited to export capital abroad. Furthermore, interest rates were partly deprived of their natural function to ration and select the supply of loans through a policy of administrative controls on credit, effected through portfolio constraints, limits on credit expansion and an increase in the required reserve coefficient.

This explains why, even though fiscal policy was strongly expansionary during the seventies, the public debt - GDP ratio in 1981 was still 61.1 %.

During the seventies the Italian lira freely fluctuated in the exchange market. The high inflation rates of Italy relative to other industrialized countries such as Germany, in fact, caused a continuous devaluation of the exchange rate of the lira. We had, in this period, a spiral of inflation and devaluation. The lira, however, devaluated to a large extent against the D-mark and to a lesser extent against the U.S. dollar. Since international prices of raw materials are quoted in dollars, we did not experience a strong increase in the costs of Italian imports, while the devaluation with respect to the D-mark gave a strong competitive advantage to exports, and this made it possible to avoid a serious balance of payments crisis.

4. Italian public finance during the eighties

The situation described above changed radically during the eighties. During the seventies, in fact, mechanisms generating strong increaseases in public expenditure had been created; mechanisms that started producing their effects just at the beginning of the eighties. Also during the eighties, this process of expansion of public spending continued.

Expenditure for health services grew significantly because of the progressive extension of the number of beneficiaries and the increases in the quantity of services provided to each citizen. The expansionary effect on health spending, induced by the increase in the volume of services provided, was increased by demographic evolution and by the cost of services. The ageing of the population, in fact, represented a continuous stimulus toward the increase in spending, while the cost of services increased in an uneven way.

Retirement spending also increased for different reasons. In the first place, we had an increase in the number of disability pensions, which, to be obtained, it is sufficient that the worker has worked and paid contributions for only 5 years. A law at the end of the sixties required that they be given to invalids, not only taking into account their health situation, but also the social and economic situation of the area in which they lived, i.e. the possibility of finding a job in that area. This caused a strong increase in the number of disability pensions granted to people who lived in the Mezzogiorno. In the public sector it was also possible to retire after 15 years of work for women and 20 years of work for men, and in some cases these periods could be shortened. In 1969 the "social pension" was created, which is given to anyone who has reached the age of 65 and is in a situation of need, even though he has never worked and therefore has never paid contributions to any retirement fund.

Moreover, the dynamics of pensions, starting at the end of the sixties, was no longer linked to the payments made by the workers, but to wage dynamics. This is always faster since, because of the inflationary process, the indexation mechanisms linking wages to prices had been strengthened. In 1975 the agreement on the "scala mobile" between Confindustria and the trade unions was signed, which established a high indexation of industrial wages. In 1977 the mechanism of the "scala mobile" was extended to public employees.

Finally, the transfers to the Mezzogiorno increased: the transfers to households in the form of disability pensions, hiring in the public sector, etc.; tranfers to firms in the form of financial and tax incentives.

Revenues during the eighties did not increase sufficiently, even though there was an increase in the growth rates of GDP. Therefore the budget deficits continued to grow and the public debt - GDP ratio went from 61.1 % in 1981 to 100.9 % in 1990.

Since the beginning of the eighties, the guidelines of monetary policy have radically changed.

In July 1981 the "divorce" between the Treasury and the Bank of Italy was introduced. This means that the responsibility of financing the public deficit pertains to the Treasury, while the Central Bank can decide which part of the financing must take the form of monetary base. Before 1981 an excessive expansion of the public deficit in the short run caused an increase in Treasury bonds bought by the Bank of Italy and therefore did not cause any upward pressure on interest rates. After 1981 an increase in the deficit did not necessarily translate into an automatic increase in the portfolio of the Bank of Italy, and the Bank of Italy could decide whether and to what extent to buy Treasury bonds. The Bank of Italy decided the ceiling on the expansion of the monetary base and credit and consequently decided which part of the monetary base could finance the Treasury deficit. The monetary financing however, which occurred through the overdraft of the current account of the Treasury at the Bank of Italy, remained. The law stated that the Bank of Italy was obliged to finance the Treasury until the total overdraft of the current account of the Treasury reached 14 % of the spending envisaged by the State budget.

As a whole, however, the "divorce" was successful in placing a limit to the automatic monetary financing of the public sector. In 1983, moreover, direct credit controls were abolished. The Bank of Italy reacquired control over the monetary base, and the market for government bonds developed and became larger.

This policy, if it on the one side produced an increase in interest rates, on the other side caused a reduction in inflation, that during the eighties went down from 21.2 % in 1980 to 6.5 % in 1990. This was possible because, in the meanwhile, oil prices had stabilized and the cost of labour no longer underwent the increases of the seventies.

The new directions in monetary policy were also adopted because in 1979 Italy had joined the European Monetary System.

The exchange rate policy, therefore, changed radically. The entrance of Italy into the EMS, at the beginning with bands of fluctuation of 6 % for the lira and subsequently (1990) with margins of 2.25 %, and the gradual liberalization of capital movements, which had begun in the eighties and was completed in 1990, drastically reduced the possibility, for Italy, of pursuing an autonomous monetary policy. The need to finance the public sector deficit had generated high real interest rates.

In conclusion, during the eighties we observed a constantly expansionary fiscal policy with continuous increases in the budget deficit and a restrictive monetary policy, with high interest rates. It is no wonder that the public debt - GDP ratio in 1990 reached a value of 100.9 % and that the annual expenditure for interest payments was 22 % of the total public spending and 9.5 % of the public debt.

5. The policies aimed at the reduction of the public debt in Italy during the nineties

Since 1991 Italian interest rates have continued to grow. The complete liberalization of the capital movements, in effect, anchors Italian interest rates to the German ones. Moreover, since the beginning of the Italian political crisis (1992), which started with the corruption episodes known as "tangentopoli" but then spread to the entire system of political parties, the Italian interest rates, in order to avoid the outflow of capital, had to be higher than the German ones with a risk spread of 3 or 4 base points, which in the worst moments became greater than a 5 base points. This spread also includes the difference between the inflation rates of the two countries, which is very small.

As we know, Germany reached political unification in 1990 with an exchange rate of 1 western mark = 1 eastern mark. This choice in effect entailed the increase of wages of the former East Germany almost to the level of those of the former West Germany, while labour productivity of the industrial sector in the former remained at about one quarter of the productivity of the latter. The ultimate effect has been an increase in global monetary income and therefore in demand much greater than production, with inflationary pressures which alarmed the German authorities. These authorities neither increased taxes nor decreased public spending by such an amount as to reduce excess demand, but they have mainly relied on a restrictive monetary policy, which incidentally was enacted by the central bank, formally considered independent from the government.

The high German interest rates have implied a decrease in inflation, but also a strong slowdown in production activity and primarily an increase in unemployment. Moreover, they also caused a strong capital inflow to Germany, which was used mainly to finance industrial restructuring in the former East Germany and created difficulties in other European countries; in particular in those, like Italy, with a weak currency.

Several countries were not inclined to increase interest rates to the level of the German ones (in real terms) in order to avoid internal recessionary impulses and therefore underwent strong capital outflows and consequent downward pressures on the exchange rate. England and Italy in September 1992 "temporarily" left the EMS and other countries like Spain and Ireland adopted restrictive measures on capital movements. Exchange rates fluctuated much beyond the limit of 2.25 % above or below the central parities. In August 1993 all the countries decided to widen the fluctuation band from 2.25 % to 15 % with the only exception of the relationship between the D-mark and the Dutch florin.

In Italy capital outflow continued to occur even after this date, because of the political instability of the country, because of the doubts of the financial markets over the determination of Italian governments to reduce the public debt and because of the weakness of the dollar, due to the financial crisis of Mexico, which attracted speculation on the weakest currencies such as the lira. The Bank of Italy has continued to increase the official discount rate in the second half of 1994 and in the first half of 1995. The high interest rates have continuously induced an increase in the public debt, which in 1995 was estimated as 125 % of GDP.

Italy started reducing the budget deficit as of 1992. Before that date it had made only partial and temporary attempts. The governments that have followed from 1992 to 1995, instead, have proceeded with determination on the road towards the reduction of the deficit.

The government led by Amato in 1992 has engaged in an economic policy strategy based on two points: on the one hand it has devalued the exchange rate, taking the lira outside the European monetary system, and on the other hand it has drastically reduced internal demand. It has in fact arrested the growth of wages in the public sector, and also wages in the private sector have had only a moderate growth. Moreover, indirect taxes have increased and some extraordinary taxes have been imposed: one on luxury goods, such as cars and boats with an engine more powerful than a certain amount;

one on bank deposits; another one on the net assets of firms. This last tax has been renewed also by the successive governments. Finally, the Amato government also made meaningful cuts in public spending, especially in the area of pensions and health and has stopped recruitment in the public administration. The negative expectations generated by these measures have caused a reduction in private consumption and investment. Investment in construction and public works has fallen because of judicial investigations of the corruption phenomena diffused in the whole national territory. Moreover, contributions and incentives in the Mezzogiorno have been reduced, also because of the changed political situation. The Italian economy therefore in 1992 and 1993 underwent a recessionary phase, except for exports, which instead experienced an intense growth which still continues today (1995). The devaluation of the exchange rate, however, did not cause inflation since there are no internal stimuli both on the demand and on the cost side.

The subsequent governments continue with the policy of reduction of the deficit although with less drastic measures. They always adopt balancing manoeuvres of the public accounts, which cut spending and increase tax revenues.

The philosophy underlying these manoeuvres is always the following. The free circulation of short run capital cannot be discussed. On the contrary, the freedom of movement of currency inside the European Union must continue to exist. It is not even thinkable to reintroduce any form of the controls that existed until 1990. This causes the interest rates to be determined by financial markets and strongly influenced by the German central bank. In this situation it is not even thinkable to tax public debt bonds or their interest, because this would cause a great capital outflow. The only way to reduce the interest rates on the Italian public debt is by reducing their differential with German rates. This can only be done by aligning the Italian inflation rate with the German one and by providing confidence to the markets through an economic policy which shows a constant determination to reduce the deficit up to the point of reversing the growth of the public debt-GDP ratio.

In this situation an autonomous monetary policy in Italy is no longer possible nor is it thinkable for the deficit of the Treasury to be financed through money. As a matter of fact, in order to enact the Maastricht agreements, in 1993 the line of credit (i.e. the overdraft) of the current account of the Treasury was abolished.

The strategy therefore can only be the following: to reduce the stock of public debt (more precisely the debt-GDP ratio) through measures that affect current revenues and current expenditures. It is obviously a strategy that does not impose any sacrifice on the owners of public debt bonds, while it makes the weakest classes pay for the burden of overhauling public finance. Public spending cuts, in fact, hit the less wealthy social strata and also the same effect is produced by the increase in taxes, which pertain mainly to indirect taxes, since it is argued that the marginal rates of direct income taxes are too high and that the progressivity of taxes must be reduced and moreover that taxes on wealth must be excluded since they frighten savers and induce a capital flight.

The effects on income distribution are evident. It may be interesting to compare the current situation with that of the seventies. During the seventies real interest rates on government bonds were negative, in some cases they were also equal to - 5 %; inflation was very high (sometimes greater than 20 %), but wages were indexed. During the nineties real interest rates are positive, inflation is about 4 %, but the indexation mechanisms have been abolished and wages grow less than inflation.

Households that own government bonds are about 25 % of total households. The manoeuvres aimed at overhauling public finance, which increase indirect taxes such as the gasoline tax and VAT on widely consumed goods, hit more than 80 % of the population. Both the interest rates on government bonds and dividends (in almost all cases) are taxed in Italy with a withheld proportional tax at a rate of 12.5 % and therefore avoid the progressivity of the tax structure. Labour incomes, instead, are subject to a personal income tax which is highly progressive and whose maximum marginal rate is 51 %. Moreover, there is a tendency to increase indirect taxes on sales and consumption.

Another instrument adopted to reduce the public debt is represented by the privatization of public firms. This should have the twofold purpose of bringing back to the rules of the market some sectors in which public firms operate in a regime of monopoly or in a privileged situation and to raise revenues to the State to reduce the deficit. In the concrete Italian experience of the last years, however, privatizations, realized to a very limited extent, have resulted in the acquisition of public firms or public banks by Italian oligopolistic groups, and there has been neither an effective increase in competition nor a spreading of property to private shareholders.

6. The negative effects of the public debt and the perspectives for the Italian economy

The strategy of Italian governments during the nineties has aimed at eliminating the primary deficit, i.e. the deficit net of interest expenditures on the debt, and to convert it to a surplus in order gradually to reduce the total debt (in relation to GDP). From 1992 until today (1995) the government has succeeded in obtaining a primary surplus, but the public debt-GDP ratio has continued to grow and only in 1995 is an inversion of that tendency foreseen.

The operators in the financial markets wish to see an inversion of tendency, which continues over time. This is the main issue. But at this point it is legitimate to ask, beyond the effects on the financial markets, what is the damage to the economic system that derives from a high public debt?

On this issue there is a great deal of literature and I will limit myself only to some short considerations. As is well known, the Keynesian point of view according to which the budget deficit stimulates economic activity and induces an increase in income and employment had already undergone a revision during the seventies. The theory of crowding out states that public spending crowds out private spending and generates a reduction in the growth perspectives or inflation and deficit of the balance of payments.

These revisions reflect prevalently a short term view. For the long term the most frequently accepted idea is the following: public spending crowds out private spending; the former is mainly current spending, and in every case, has a lower productivity than the latter; therefore an excessive public deficit reduces the rate of growth of the economy. Moreover, the public deficit produces inflation; in order to fight inflation authorities must adopt restrictive monetary and fiscal measures which mainly hit private investment; the final result is a slowdown in economic activity, an increase in unemployment and a reduction in the growth rate of GDP.

These analyses aimed mainly at explaining the economic evolution of the seventies, when in the majority of industrialized countries there were high budget deficits, high inflation and low growth rates.

The experience of the eighties however has shown that, if monetary policies remain rigid, high public deficits do not produce inflation, but produce high interest rates.

Other authors have argued that the problem is not represented so much by the deficit as much as by the volume of public spending and by the tax burden. For supply side economists, for example, the only way to accelerate growth is to stimulate private investment which expands production capacity. In order to reach this aim, it is necessary to reduce public spending, taxes and the public regulation of private economic activities.

The underlying idea is that three elements (public spending, taxes, regulation) introduce distortions in the market mechanisms, reduce the incentive to risk and generate a reduction of investment, of productivity and of the growth rate. In this situation policies aimed at stimulating demand produce only inflation.

Thirty years ago the dominating opinion was that in industrialized countries an expansion of public deficits could accelerate the rate of growth of an economy. During the sixties the economic advisors of the President of the United States not only suggested expanding the deficit in order to reduce the gap between potential and effective output and therefore unemployment, but also suggested adopting a *constantly* expansionary fiscal policy. Today the contrary is claimed: an increase in the public deficit slows down or impedes the growth of the economy. It is true that the economic context has changed, and in particular the *dimension* of the public budgets and therefore of the deficits relative to GDP, but we cannot help remaining perplexed.

As a matter of fact, the manoeuvres adopted every year to reduce the budget deficit in Italy risk causing a gradual dismantling of the Welfare State (free or almost free health services, pensions, free education up to a certain level) and of the transfers to firms and households of the weakest areas of the Mezzogiorno. The result could be an increase in inequalities and poverty, a worsening of the regional gap between North and South and an increase in unemployment, especially in the weakest areas.

Moreover, in the Italian experience, there is no evidence of a negative correlation between public deficit and growth rate and between deficit and inflation and not even between public deficit and balance of payments deficit.

During the nineties we had in some years growth rates lower than 1 % and in other years rates greater than 3 %, in the presence of analogous situations of deficit and debt. The growth of exports seems linked to the level of the exchange rate and to internal demand, besides foreign demand. The growth of private consumption depends on disposable income and on expectations; the growth of investment is influenced by expectations, by income distribution and by a policy of public works.

Analogously, also in the presence of high deficits, inflation in Italy has touched low levels, lower than 4 %, because monetary policy remained rigid.

Nor there is evidence in Italy of a phenomenon like the twin deficit, that during the eighties several scholars have examined with reference to the United States, where there seems to be a positive link between the federal deficit and the deficit of the current account of the balance of payments. In Italy the current account has had a strong surplus since 1993 and the projections of the International Monetary Fund show that among the seven major industrialized countries only Japan and Italy will maintain the trade balance in surplus in the period 1995-1999.

The need to reduce the public debt - GDP ratio derives therefore essentially from the exigencies of financial markets. The operators in fact, if they lost confidence in our country, could start a mechanism of capital flight, a fall in the value of the lira and of government bonds and acceleration of prices. The example usually cited is the financial crisis of Mexico in 1995.

In the comparison between Italy and Mexico two main differences must be kept in mind. The public debt-GDP ratio in Mexico is about 55 %; in Italy it is about 125 %. But 92 % of the Italian public debt is owned by residents in Italy, mainly by families, and the holding is very fragmented, while 99 % of the Mexican debt is owned by big foreign corporations, mainly American.

As is known, according to authors like Keynes and Lerner, the public debt, if it is internal, does not represent a burden for future generations. If, in addition, the State has utilized the debt to finance public investment and has therefore increased income and employment, future generations will find themselves with a greater quantity of wealth.

Several authors, however, have questioned the Keynesian thesis according to which public debt does not produce negative effects on the economic system, insisting on the possibility that public indebtedness may have crowding out effects on private investment or that, when it goes beyond certain limits, it leads to monetization with inflationary consequences. In fact, a massive sale of bonds, generated by negative expectations in the markets, would cause a fall in prices and an increase in interest rates with recessionary consequences. In order to avoid this, the central bank could buy bonds in order to sustain their price, but in this way it would create money with inflationary consequences.

Moreover, if there are free capital movements across boundaries, the distinction between internal public debt and external debt loses a great part of its relevance, because if the residents who own government bonds lose confidence in the government of the country, they can sell them in order to acquire foreign bonds and this would produce a capital flight and a balance of payments crisis.

Until now, this phenomenon has not occurred in relevant proportions, and this may be due to various reasons, besides the fact that a massive confidence crisis did not occur. Even though there is freedom of short term capital movements, both through banks and by moving cash across borders (for this there is a limit for any single operation, but this does not represent a relevant obstacle), these capital movements have costs both in monetary terms (commissions paid to banks, payments to those who materially transfer currency beyond the border) and in psychological terms, because those who acquire foreign bonds are identified by the Tax Administration differently from those who only acquire Italian bonds. The Administration therefore will be able in the future to impose controls on the income tax returns of those who own foreign assets. Moreover, selling bonds at moments at which prices are low may cause big capital losses, and this is another element that slows down financial crises, known in the fifties as the Roosa effect. These considerations are particularly relevant for small savers, who prefer the stability of an investment in bonds, even in the presence of some differential in the real interest rate.

However, any Italian government, if it wants to maintain the freedom of capital movements, must proceed with determination on the road of the balancing of the public accounts, because the experience of the last years has shown that this is the only way to obtain the confidence of the financial markets. It is questionable, however, whether this can be achieved by destroying the Welfare State and by increasing indirect taxes. It is necessary to take into account the possibility of introducing a property tax or increasing the tax rates on dividends and interest, in order to make the owners of financial assets, and in particular the owners of government bonds, participate in the overhauling of the public accounts. Of course, in order to prevent this from causing a capital flight, it will be necessary to introduce currency controls, that limit the freedom of movement of currency across borders, without impeding citizens from buying foreign bonds through the banking system. In this way the government, if it decides to tax the interest or the principal of Italian bonds, could tax the foreign bonds owned by residents in Italy in the same way.

The freedom of short term capital movements must be allowed, but must not imply that financial wealth and rents can be exempted from the tax burden, especially at a moment at which it is necessary to distribute the costs of the financial overhaul between all the social groups and not only between the less wealthy classes.

This could easily be done if it does not represent only a unilateral initiative of the countries with a high public debt like Italy, but instead the appropriate measures, agreed upon among the members of the European Union, were to be adopted.

As a matter of fact, asearly as 1978 James Tobin had formulated the proposal of introducing a uniform world wide tax on spot transactions across currencies, in order to throw some sand in the superefficient wheels of the international financial vehicles. This would allow the restitution of a greater autonomy to national monetary policies.

This proposal, even though it is subject to criticisms and sceptical comments, seems highly appropriate at a moment at which financial markets, because of their dimension and the technological innovations adopted, seem to be able to determine exchange rates and interest rates even for long periods, in contrast with the values of the fundamental variables of the economy; while, at the same time, an effective intervention of governments and central banks does not seem possible.

Résumé

La dérive de la dette publique : une menace pour l'Europe ? Analyse du cas italien

Le débat relatif aux finances publiques est très vif à la fois en termes théoriques puisque diverses écoles de pensée s'affrontent sur ce thème, et au regard de l'évolution économique (stabilité de la monnaie, dynamique de la croissance, politique sociale).

L'entrée en vigueur du Traité de Maastricht a accentué les hésitations et interpelle les acteurs, hommes politiques et dirigeants d'institutions financières tout spécialement.

Giovanni PALMERIO éclaire le débat en analysant la réalité passée en Italie c'est-à-dire en présentant un cas un peu hétérodoxe par rapport aux modèles dominants anglo-saxon et allemand, et qui n'en est que plus intéressant puisque dans le même temps l'Italie est devenue la 5e puissance marchande du monde.

Au regard de l'histoire récente, Giovanni PALMERIO distingue quatre périodes de gestion de la dette et des budgets publics :

1. Les années 1950-1970 marquées par une croissance spectaculaire de l'économie italienne s'ouvrant sur le monde, et une expansion équilibrée du secteur public ;
2. Les années 70 avec une détérioration importante des comptes publics (déficits budgétaires, dette) ;
3. Les années 80 avec une accélération des déséquilibres publics et un changement de la politique monétaire conduisant à une hausse des taux d'intérêt et une diminutionn de l'inflation ;
4. Les années 90 marquées par une forte volonté de redressement largement influencée par les réactions des marchés financiers internationaux.

La dépendance croissante de l'Italie par rapport à ces marchés non contrôlés est analysée par l'auteur qui en décrypte les modalités et les effets. Doctrines fluctuantes selon que l'on se place du côté des théoriciens de l'offre ou de la demande, des monétaristes ou des néo-keynésiens, et réalités contraignantes conduisent à des réflexions essentielles sur l'équilibre socio-économique.

Zusammenfassung

Das Ausufern der Haushaltsdefizite: eine Gefahr für Europa? Die Analyse des italienischen Beispiels

Die Diskussion über die öffentlichen Finanzen wird sowohl in der Theorie - es stehen einander ja verschiedene Denkschulen gegenüber - als auch hinsichtlich der Wirtschaftsentwicklung (Währungsstabilität, Wachstumsdynamik, Sozialpolitik) sehr kontrovers geführt.

Das Inkrafttreten des Maastricht-Vertrages hat die Unsicherheiten noch verstärkt und fordert insbesondere die Entscheidungsträger, also die Politiker und Führungskräfte von Finanzinstituten, heraus.

Giovanni PALMERIO leistet einen wichtigen Beitrag zu dieser Debatte, indem er die Situation Italiens analysiert und dabei einen im Vergleich zum angelsächsichen und deutschen Modell atypischen Fall aufzeigt. Dieser gewinnt noch dadurch an Interesse, daß Italien gleichzeitig zur fünften Handelsnation aufgestiegen ist.

Giovanni PALMERIO unterscheidet im Falle Italiens in der jüngeren Geschichte hinsichtlich des Finanzgebarens der öffentlichen Hand vier Perioden:

1. Die Jahre 1950 - 1970 zeichneten sich aus durch ein spektakuläres Wachstum der sich zur Welt hin öffnenden italienischen Wirtschaft und durch eine ausgewogene Ausweitung des öffentlichen Sektors.
2. Die 70er Jahre waren durch eine nachhaltige Verschlechterung der öffentlichen Haushalte (Haushaltsdefizite, Staatsverschuldung) gekennzeichnet.
3. Die 80er Jahre erlebten eine immer raschere Zunahme der Defizite der öffentlichen Haushalte und einen Wechsel in der Währungspolitik, der zum Anstieg der Zinssätze und zur Reduzierung der Inflation führte.

4. Die 90er Jahre sind durch starke Bemühungen zur Stabilisierung geprägt, die weitgehend durch Reaktionen der internationalen Finanzmärkte beeinflußt wurden.

Der Autor analysiert die zunehmende Abhängigkeit Italiens von diesen unkontrollierten Märkten und entschlüsselt dabei deren Modalitäten und Auswirkungen. Er zeigt ferner die unterschiedlichen Lehrmeinungen der Angebotstheoretiker, der Nachfragetheoretiker, der Monetaristen oder der Neu-Keynesianer sowie die Sachzwänge auf, die zu grundlegenden Aussagen hinsichtlich des gesamtwirtschaftlichen Gleichgewichts führen.

References

ARTONI, R. (1986): Debito e squilibrio strutturale della finanza pubblica. in Ente Einaudi, Oltre la crisi. Il Mulino. Bologna.

BERNARDI, L. (1984): Linee per l'interpretazione della dinamica della finanza pubblica. in E. Gerelli e A. Majocchi eds.. Il deficit pubblico: origini e problemi. Angeli. Milan.

BROSIO, G./MARCHESE, C. (1986): Il potere di spendere. Economia e storia della spesa pubblica dall'unificazione ad oggi. Il Mulino. Bologna.

ENTE PER GLI STUDI MONETARI, BANCARI E FINANZIARI "Luigi Einaudi" (1992): Il disavanzo pubblico in Italia: natura strutturale e politiche di rientro. Il Mulino. Bologna.

FOSSATI, A. (1981): La spesa pubblica in Italia dal 1951 al 1980. in «Rivista di Diritto Finanziario e Scienza delle Finanze». September.

FRATIANNI, M./SPINELLI, F. (1982): The Growth of Government in Italy from 1861 to 1979. in «Public Choice», n. 39.

GIARDA, P. (1988): Una interpretazione della crescita della spesa pubblica in Italia. in «Rivista Bancaria», n. 11-12.

GRAZIANI, A. (ed.) (1988): La spirale del debito pubblico. Il Mulino. Bologna.

PEDONE, A. (1967): Il bilancio dello Stato e lo sviluppo economico italiano: 1861-1963. in «Rassegna Economica», n. 2.

SARCINELLI, M. (1990): Tendenze e squilibri nella finanza pubblica italiana. in «Economia Italiana», n. 2.

SPAVENTA, L./ARTONI, R./MORCALDO, G./ZANCHI, P. (1984): L'indebitamento pubblico in Italia: evoluzione, prospettive e problemi. Camera dei deputati. Rome.

SPAVENTA, L. (1987): The Growth of Public Debt. in «IMF Staff Papers». Vol. 34.

Wim Kösters

Stability Culture as a Precondition for the Sustainability of the European Monetary Union (EMU)

1. The state of preparations for the EMU

2. On some deficiencies of the present debate on the EMU

3. European monetary policy and the problem of accountability

4. On the necessity and feasibility of a european stability pact

5. Final remarks

1. The state of preparations for the EMU

The preparations for the European Monetary Union (EMU) are by now up to the schedule agreed upon in the Maastricht treaty. It started on July 1, 1990 with stage I in which mainly a free movement of capital within the EU as well as a closer cooperation on economic, fiscal, exchange-rate and monetary policies should have been realized. This was considered to be the case when entering stage II on January 1, 1994 in which the preparation for the final stage via economic convergence in the member states and the establishment of the European Monetary Institute (EMI) as forerunner of the European Central Bank (ECB) are most important. The main task of the EMI is the planning of instruments, strategies and technical regulations necessary for the conduct of the common monetary policy and making them ready for the use by the ECB in the third stage. Up to then the responsibility for monetary as well as exchange rate policy remains with the member states. Besides this the EMI has to strengthen the cooperation between the national central banks and the coordination of their monetary policy. In addition, it has to survey the convergence process and to supervise the functioning of the European Monetary System (EMS).

The start of the third and final stage of the EMU is possible at the earliest on January 1, 1997 if a majority of the member states then meet the convergence criteria. However, since presently only Germany and Luxembourg strictly fulfil these conditions most observers and even the members of the European Council (ECOFIN) do not expect that this will be the case. Therefore, the interest of policymakers is directed towards the next important date for a start of stage III, January 1, 1999. Then, all those member states meeting the convergence targets are supposed to join the monetary union. According to Art. 109 j, Para. 4 first, the European Commission and the EMI have to report to the European Council on the fulfilment of the convergence criteria and then a qualified majority of Council members[1] has to decide which countries will become members of the EMU.

---

1 Since 62 of 87 votes are necessary the blocking minority consists of 26 votes.

Since in the framework set by the Maastricht Treaty the emphasis is clearly put on policy integration the public discussion on the EMU centers upon the question which countries will manage to meet the convergence criteria just in time and thus can become members of the EMU in the first round. In addition, the European Commission's Green Paper on the Practical Arrangements for the Introduction of the Single Currency focuses on the more technical problems of transition and on how to make the process to the EMU irreversible as early as possible. Up to now the problems of sustainability and of acceptance by the people of the envisaged political solutions in the long run have played only a minor role, if any in the debate in spite of their importance.

Although it is often publicly declared, especially by German politicians, that a strict fulfilment of the convergence targets must be given top priority in comparison to the deadlines set in the Maastricht Treaty it has to be pointed out that the European Council composed of the heads of state and government will make the last decision with a qualified majority of its members. According to Art. 109 j, Para. 3 and 4 the Council has in the course of this only the legal obligation to take into account the reports of the Commission and the EMI so that some room is left for political considerations[2]. This is all the more valid considering that in the Council the approval is also required of those countries which will not be participating immediately. Therefore it can not be excluded that reaching an agreement will take more time than expected, will have to be payed for by the participating states giving transfers to those who do not participate, and/or countries will be allowed to join the EMU

2 This became obvious in the autumn of 1994 when the Council (ECOFIN) publicly certified that Ireland does not violate the debt to GDP target ratio. This was done in spite of the fact that this member state with its 90 % level exceeded by half the 60 % debt to GDP target ratio fixed in the Treaty. ECOFIN justified its decicion by the substantial reduction of the level reached in the last years. This shows that the regulations of the Treaty with respect to the debt criteria are ambiguous and therefore open to interpretation. This means that there is quite a large amount of scope left to give reasons for certain political decisions.

which do not meet all convergence targets strictly[3]. Though the German Constitutional Court erected a barrier to this. In its well known decision it allows the German government to join the EMU only if the convergence criteria are met strictly by the countries envisaged to participate and it can thus be expected that it will become a community of stability and not of inflation. In case the latter would be probable Germany has the right to opt out.

2. On some deficiencies of the present debate on the EMU

From the remarks made before it follows that the present public debate on the EMU has deficiencies because some very important problems are either not discussed at all or do not get the attention they deserve. Even if one disregards for a moment the question whether the Maastricht criteria are the right indicators to measure the convergence of an economy necessary for joining a monetary union a decision of the Council on membership made to a good extent on political and not on economic grounds would create problems for the sustainability of the EMU. For this would establish trouble spots. A common monetary policy striving for price level stability will then either not be accepted by all members and/or will cause demands for financial transfers by countries with deficiencies in economic convergence. This would mean that the aims set up for the EMU in the Maastricht Treaty could not be reached. Failing to achieve price level stability, however, would consume the economic advantages of the monetary union and soon overcompensate them. In this case the EMU would lower and not increase the welfare of Europeans and eventually would, therefore, be rejected by them (Kösters, 1993).

3 Because of their debt to GDP ratio by far exceeds the required threshold value of 60 %, even such countries as Italy (1994: 123.7 %) and Belgium (1994: 140.1 %) can hardly be admitted since a significant reduction, not to speak of a meeting of the target level, seems to be quite questionable. In this case, however, one would have to exclude two of the founding members of the European Economic Community (EEC) from joining the EMU in the first round. Can this be carried through politically? A first impression of the arising difficulties in this respect provoked the strong reactions in the countries concerned and in the financial markets when the German Minister of Finance on September 20, 1995 in a small committee allegedly said that Belgium and Italy probably could not participate in 1999 because of their high debt to GDP ratios.

The same could be true if transfers had to be made to countries with a deficient convergence. Those payments would on the one hand not necesserily solve the convergence problem in the member states concerned and would on the other hand create acceptance problems in the donor-countries. Therefore, only those states should become members of the EMU which meet the convergence targets strictly if one is interested in the sustainability and acceptance of the EMU in the longer run. It is, however, the question whether the Maastricht criteria adequately measure the required convergence. Without being able to discuss here the critical objections made in this respect[4] it has to be pointed out that the criteria at best only catch nominal but not real convergence. The latter is, however, important too for the sustainability of the EMU: "... convergence is more likely to be sustainable if further progress is made to improve the structural performance of labour and goods markets" (EMI, 1995, p. 58)[5].

Therefore, overall and permanent convergence is what matters with respect to the sustainability of the EMU. The impression one, however, gets from the public discussion is that it would be sufficient to meet the Maastricht criteria just in time and just for those (rather short) periods before the start of stage III that are prescribed by the Treaty. It seems that many politicians and other participants contributing to this impression forget a very fundamental truth: a monetary union cannot be established and made long-lasting by the political will and political plans alone even if they are agreed upon in international treaties. Although they are certainly important and necessary, the acceptance by the people of the union is decisive in the last instance. In a democracy this approval has not only to be met once but again and again. Since people act on markets, political solutions considered not to be workable and in their interests will cause reactions. These can also come from market participants outside the EU as especially financial markets are highly integrated on a worldwide scale.

4 See e.g. Kösters, W., Belke A. and Kruth, B.-J. (1992) and Ohr, R. (1955).

5 For a more vigorous and detailed argumentation in favour of real convergence criteria see Schmidt, Ch. and Straubhaar, Th. (1995).

What happens if it is attempted to maintain economically non-workable solutions for political reasons was shown by the reactions of foreign exchange markets in 1992 and 1993 to the political attempt to leave the exchange rates in the EMS unchanged. It was argued by the European Council and politicians on the national level that this would be justified by the relatively high degree of convergence they considered already to be reached among the member countries. As is known this political assessment was not found convincing by the markets and, therefore, some currencies had to leave the EMS and for the others the narrow band had to be given up in favour of a wide margin of +/- 15 percent which for nearly all practical purposes means flexible exchange rates.

This rather recent experience teaches again that in market economies with a democratic constitution political solutions, particularly fixing exchange rates and founding a monetary union cannot be introduced by decree. Instead, people as participants of markets and as voters have to be convinced again and again that this project is advantageous to them so that they accept it voluntarily and permanently. This is all the more true in the case of the EMU considering that the new currency has to become the generally accepted means of payment and a store of value. Only the confidence of the future demanders will decide if the new currency will serve these functions and will through this become money.

Therefore the most significant task to be performed in the EMU is to gain and maintain the confidence of money demanders for the new currency. Among others, this includes finding a widely accepted name for it and a design for the coins and notes, choosing an adequate, i.e. confidence-building, transition procedure and providing the instruments, operational targets, and strategies necessary for reaching price level stability as the final goal of the single European monetary policy. Most important in this respect is, however, the form and public approval of the future monetary order. The rules should be such that the ECB has an incentive to strive for price level stability and can trust in a broad public support for the pursuit of this goal and the monetary policy required for it. If this were the case an important precondition for the sustainability of the EMU in the longer run - what might be termed *stability culture* - would have been established.

3. European monetary policy and the problem of accountability

In the course of the debate on monetarism following M. Friedman a consensus among economists developed to the effect that inflation defined as *continuous* increase in the price level is a monetary phenomenon (see e..g. Mishkin (1992), pp. 554). It is, therefore, only consistent - as the Maastricht Treaty does - to make monetary policy in the first instance responsible for keeping the price level stable. Because of this clear assignment the success and failure of monetary policy should principally be judged by the level of inflation [6].

In the postwar period (1948-1990) Germany had on average one of the lowest annual inflation rates in the world (2.8 percent). The authors of the Maastricht Treaty, therefore, probably considered the German monetary order to be the best national answer in the EU to the problem of stability and tried to adopt its most important features for the future European monetary constitution. By "Europeanising" the German monetary order it is obviously expected that one ends up in the EMU with the same high degree of price level stability as in Germany in the past and can transfer some of the reputational capital of the Deutsche Bundesbank to the ECB.

For this purpose three features of the Bundesbank Act considered to be essential in this respect were transformed to the European level: the ECB will be obliged by the Treaty to pursue the goal of price level stability, will be independent, and will be not allowed to finance public deficits. The wording of setting price level stability as the primary objective for the ECB (Art. 105) is even more explicit and much clearer in the Treaty than the corresponding

6 Since there are some short term influences on the measured inflation rate (such as e.g. wage and import-price shocks) which cannot be controlled by monetary policy an average of the inflation rate over two to three years has to be taken.

wording in paragraph 3 Bundesbank Act [7]. The same is true regarding the prohibition of financing public deficits. According to the Treaty, to carry out overdraft and other facilities with the ECB or any other central bank of a member state is just as prohibited as acquisition of government bonds on the part of the ECB or national central banks (Art. 104). This is therefore an extended version of paragraph 20 of the Bundesbank Act. The latter had even to be cancelled resp. changed when stage II started on January 1, 1994 and Art. 104 came into force.

The Treaty regulations protecting the ECB's independence, that is ensuring that it is not subject to orders from national governments or from EU bodies (Art. 107) largely coincide with the regulations of paragraph 12 Bundesbank Act. This also applies to the organizational structure, since the federal shape as well as the managing bodies of the ECB are a copy of the Deutsche Bundesbank model. The most fundamental elements of the German monetary order therefore seem to be incorporated into the ECB statute. Due to the large number of similarities, the ECB has already been termed "Super-Bundesbank" and "made in Germany" [8].

The expectation that the future inflation rate in the EMU will be on average as low as the German one in the past would be well founded and realistic if by means of the Europeanisation of the three important features of the German monetary order mentioned before the complete German solution to the stability problem would have been transferred. Unfortunately, this is not the case since the latter is of a much more complex structure than was assumed by the authors of the Treaty on European Union. However it is important that the three essentials (independence of the central bank, its legal obligation to pursue price level stability, and no financing of public deficits) are embodied in a system of checks and balances termed stability culture before. A further most significant element of the German stability culture contributing to a large extent

7 For a comparison of the most important regulations concerning price level stability in the Treaty on European Union and the Bundesbank Act see the annex to this chapter.

8 See EMU Made in Germany, The Economist, November 2, 1991, p. 85.

to the low inflation rates in the past is the fact that the Bundesbank was monitored relatively efficiently by the German electorate. By this it is held accountable to the public. This important feature of the German monetary order is not laid down in the Bundesbank Act but did instead evolve spontaneously in the postwar period and can not be transferred directly to the European level. Let me briefly explain this argument [9].

Independence and legal obligation to pursue price level stability can only act as an efficient safeguard against heavy political pressure for a more accomodating monetary policy, if the present and all future members of the central bank council always act in the public and not in their private interest. Only then would monetary policy be strictly oriented towards price level stability, since this would maximise the welfare of a country.

For an efficient solution to the stability problem one cannot, however, rely simply on the assumption that this would occur. It would be irresponsible to assume that all people act in their own interest with the exception of politicans and central bankers who instead always act altruistically for the benefit of the general public. Taking into account the present state of research in this area, I consider it more adequate to assume that, in line with the theory of public choice and the theory of bureaucracy, *everybody* acts in his own interest [10]. This does not mean that I assume that indeed everybody does so or even should do so but instead that we must base our planning of institutions on this worst possible case and hold the central bank accountable to the public for price level stability.

The goals of bureaucrats - and central bankers have to be regarded as belonging to this group - are usually the preservation of their organisation, the enhancement of their prestige and a rise in their incomes [11]. The pursuit of these individual goals can be detrimental to the public goal of price level

---

9 For a more detailed explanation see Kösters (1991). For a different view see Neumann (1991).

10 For a survey of these approaches see e.g. Mueller (1989).

11 For this approach see e.g. Chant/Acheson (1972) and Toma/Toma (1986).

stability. This could for example be the case if the members of the central bank council support the government by permitting a more expansionary monetary policy, purely in the hope of being re-elected [12].

Since Germany has experienced two periods of hyperinflation within a single generation, there is a strong aversion to inflation amongst the German public. These strong public preferences had to be taken into account by German central bankers in the past and at present, should they wish to maximise their own private welfare. They can best serve their goals as outlined above, if they ensure price level stability. As a result their public prestige increases, the Bundesbank remains as an independent organisation and in addition this guarantees members of the central bank council that their high income does not diminish in the future. Therefore, there exist certain incentives for German central bankers to pursue the public goal of price level stability by looking after their own interests [13]. Thus, German central bankers have to take into account the strong basic consent with respect to the high priority of price level stability among the German public, i.e. voters, policymakers, trade unions etc. In turn, they can be sure that a monetary policy aiming at price level stability will find a broad public assent. By lucky chance this system of checks and balances evolved in the postwar period.

This element of the German monetary order will, however, be missing at the European level, since it is not taken into account in the Treaty on European Union. As the German experience with and aversion to inflation is not shared equally by all EU citizens it can not simply be expected that a system of checks and balances similar to that in Germany will develop spontaneously

12 Art 109a of the Maastricht Treaty determines that the term of office of the members of the Executive Board of the ECB shall be eight years and shall not be renewable. If however someone becomes appointed at the age of 45 and therefore has to leave at the age of 53 he or she might want to serve e.g. as a minister in the government of his or her country thereafter. In this case, he or she while being a member of the ECB- council could be inclined to vote in a way that is favourable to the personal aims of becoming a minister later on. This, however, might not necessarily be favourable to the goal of price level stability.

13 An incentive system for politicians like this, providing for a coincidence of private and public interests was demanded by Buchanan (1986).

in the EMU [14]. Since the latter is thus not transferable directly to the European level, an equivalent device would have to be found, if one is interested in transferring fully the German solution and reaching a degree of price level stability similar to that attained in postwar Germany [15]. A possible equivalent action could be a rule - similar to that in New Zeeland - that the members of the European central bank council would have to resign if the inflation rate exceeded a certain threshold. Another possible equivalent rule could be that the remunerations of the members of the central bank council are negatively linked to the inflation rate. An increase in the inflation or deflation rate would then lower their salary [16]. In this case there would exist a private incentive for central bankers to pursue the public objective of price level stability. They would be thus held accountable to the public for this goal. However, since in the Maastricht treaty this incentive is lacking, the future European inflation rate in the EMU may be higher than the one achieved in postwar Germany. Consequently, the actual result would now depend on the good (or bad) intentions of the European central bankers with respect to the goal of price level stability, despite the fact that research on public choice offers better and more efficient solutions [17].

In the interest of maintaining a low future inflation rate in the EMU it would therefore be highly recommendable to discuss this issue at the Intergovernmental Conference (Maastricht II) in 1996 and make an amendment to the Treaty along the lines proposed before. Unfortunately, however, the reflection group preparing the conference at present does not plan to have issues of the EMU on the agenda at all. Besides the problem of accountability of the central bank discussed before there are more features of a stability culture some of which will be dealt with in the following pages.

14 This has become clear in the last years when the Bundesbank has been heavily criticized for its too restrictive monetary policy.

15 Such an equivalent would have gradually to be found also in Germany, since it cannot neccessarily be expected that this aversion to inflation resulting from experience will remain among the population also in the distant future.

16 For these proposals see Buchanan (1986) and Vaubel (1990).

17 The incentive system for central bankers mentioned above could even make it unneccessary to announce money supply rules. See Buchanan (1986), p. 148.

4. On the necessity and feasibility of a european stability pact

As should be clear from the argumentation before, monetary policy is not made in a political vacuum. Instead, central bankers are again and again exposed to attempts by public authorities and private pressure groups on the national as well as on the international level aiming at influencing monetary policy to their own advantage. An important feature of stability culture is, however, the provision of checks and balances as safeguards against those partial influences endangering price level stability. Since on the European level - as shown before - accountability of the ECB to the voters comparable to that of the Bundesbank in Germany will most probably be missing it is all the more necessary to establish efficient protection in this respect. For it is known from experience that even the most independent central bank can hardly permanently withstand high pressures for a more expansionist policy. Besides many others there is one especially important source of them.

As can be observed from many instances in the past and present this pressure is regularly built up whenever an excessive public debt triggered hefty increases in interest and redemption payments. If there is no basic consensus in favour of price level stability among the electorate which controls the central bank efficiently this could result in a too expansionist monetary policy. Because of this danger the Maastricht treaty provides for the introduction of upper limits for the share of public budget deficits and public debt in relation to the gross domestic product serving in the second stage as convergence criteria and then in the final stage as permanent safeguards. According to this, the public budget deficits would not be allowed to exceed 3 per cent and the national debt would not be allowed to exceed 60 per cent of GDP (article 104 c, para. 2).

However, a functional asymmetry exists [18]. Before entering the third stage of the EMU meeting or not meeting the two criteria has in principle clear cut consequences for a country: participation or non-participation in monetary union. After having joined the EMU in the final stage meeting or not meeting

18 This is emphasized not only by academic economists but even by the Italian minister of the budget, Masera (1995).

the two criteria does not have these clear cut consequences any more because it is difficult to exclude a member state from the EMU particularly as there is no provision for this case in the Maastricht treaty. It is therefore argued that an amendment to the Maastricht treaty or a separate stability pact is necessary to guarantee sound public budget financing in the third stage by all member states of the EMU. In view of the assumed incentives for creating larger public deficits on the level of single member states, the regulations of article 104 c of the Maastricht treaty are by many economists and the German federal minister of finance considered to be too weak [19]. They point to the fact that financing public deficits becomes cheaper in a monetary union, because the increase in the interest rate induced by the additional indebtedness of a single member state is smaller than that on separated national capital markets. In addition, those member states would no longer be controlled by the disciplinary effects of exchange rate adjustments and therefore would not have to pay a risk premium on top of the normal interest rate. The latter would also be absent in another case: if it is assumed that there will be a bail out for those members of the EMU which become insolvent. Then differences in the financial standing of countries will show up less than now in the interest rate they have to pay for their loans.

There are, however, also counter-arguments put forward to this. In their view the member states of the EMU are confronted by even stronger budget restrictions which are created by the markets. It is argued that in the EMU the political independence of the ECB will have disciplinary influences and markets will supply even clearer warning signals since the interest rate differentials among public debtors due to their differing creditworthiness are not distorted any more by national monetary policies and inflationary expectations. Premiums on interest rates because of the insolvency risk could even be higher because in the EMU an escape via a monetization of the public debt is impossible.

---

19 See e.g. Heinemann (1994), Hasse (1995), Lehment and Scheide (1995), Gros (1995), Berthold (1995) and Waigel (1995).

The validity of this argumentation, however, depends critically on the assumption that no bail out will take place in the case of insolvency of a participating country. Although the Maastricht treaty contains a clear no bail out-clause (art. 104 b) it is highly questionable whether it would strictly be applied in practise. For this would mean that the EU-countries would allow a member state to go bankrupt. This is hardly imaginable. For the contingency of an insolvency of a country is not even mentioned in the Maastricht treaty leave alone taken care of by proper procedures to follow in this case. If by the inability to pay of one member state a systemic risk, i.e. a general banking crisis, would be triggered off the other countries whether they like it or not would come to its rescue. Therefore, all in all, a bail out is highly probable. This has not necessarily to happen directly but could also be managed indirectly via the structural and cohesion funds or in the framework of package deals e.g. on the occasion of the joining of new member states.

Consequently, the no bail out-clause of art. 104 b is not very credible. Binding rules for public debt and deficits thus seem to be very desirable. Some proposals with respect to the form of those rules and the sanctions which should become effective in case of their violation are discussed in public [20].

The legal requirements of art. 104 c aiming at the avoidance of excessive government deficits in the third stage of EMU are not really binding rules but more likely recommendations. Exceeding the limits of 3 per cent deficit and 60 per cent debt to GDP ratio does not mean automatically a violation of budgetary discipline. This rather has to be established by a decision of the Council with a qualified majority. In addition, the impending sanctions are not severe. The requirements in the Maastricht treaty first just provide for recommendations, then for a publication of these recommendations, and thereafter for a request of the Council for measures of deficit reduction. Only if all this does not remedy the situation can sanctions be applied. Besides by a reconsideration of the lending policy of the European Investment Bank towards the member state concerned, the Council can require it "to make a

20 For a short overview over possible rules see e.g. BHF-Bank (1995).

non-interest-bearing deposit of an appropriate size with the Community until the excessive deficit has ... been corrected" (art. 104 c, para. 11). One has, however, to be afraid that these regulations will not effectively prevent a violation of budgetary discipline by single member states in the third stage since the most efficient sanction is then absent, namely the exclusion from participation in the EMU.

More severe rules would fix an upper limit to public debt and deficits combined with drastic sanctions taking effect *automatically* in case of violations. Since good economic reasons for such absolutely fixed rules can hardly be found more flexible rules are proposed. Here the upper limits are contingent upon the situation of the economy. An example for such a flexible rule is the requirement in the German financial constitution that the deficit should not exceed the level of investment expenditures. But it is even allowed to go just once beyond this limit for the purpose of fighting a disturbance of the macroeconomic equilibrium. Since the categories used are not clearly and properly defined a more specific and precise regulation would have to be found for the EMU. In my view the best solution would be to proceed on the basis of a relatively simple formula in which the permitted response of public deficits to certain economic situations and exogenous shocks is precisely fixed ex ante.

It is, however, important that in case of violations sanctions have to take effect automatically and not after discretionary decisions of the Council. One regulation in the case of excessive deficits could be that the member state concerned would automatically have to cut its public expenditure and to increase its taxes. If it will not obey this rule and will not even follow a last warning it has to be excluded from the EMU [21]. Another sanction as ultima ratio in the case of continued violations of budgetary discipline by a member state could be the temporary suspension of its right to vote in the Council. For the keeping up of its right to vote would give the member state some power to enforce a solidarity into instability [22].

21 See Gros (1995).
22 See Hasse (1995).

In a further proposal members of the EMU with excessive deficits would be obliged to make a non-interest-bearing stabilization deposit with the ECB of 0.3 per cent of the GDP which will be refunded after the Maastricht criteria of 3 percent deficit ratio and 60 per cent debt ratio are reached again [23]. In Waigel's stability pact refunding is only allowed for two years. If the criteria are not met again within this period the deposits remain with the ECB permanently and consequently become fines [24].

All the propoals mentioned before could only be realized by changing or amending the Maastricht treaty so that the whole ratification procedure would have to be repeated. Whether a binding stability pact outside the Maastricht treaty can effectively be concluded is a legal question which is to my knowledge not yet finally settled. It is, therefore, presently not sure at all that one of the proposals will politically be implemented. Even in case of a realization the problem of no bail out remains. In spite of an amendment or a stability pact a direct or indirect bail out could still take place. Therefore, it seems to me that one should not only rely on fiscal rules but even more on making the ECB accountable to the voters - as was described in the preceeding chapter - when looking for mechanismus which enforce a strict orientation of the European monetary policy towards price level stability.

5. Final Remarks

As was said before, a European stability culture would have to comprise a system of checks and balances by which incentives for the European central bankers to strive for price level stability and a broad public support for the pursuit of this goal and for the monetary policy required for it are created. It was impossible to discuss all relevant aspects of this problem here. An additional important question in this respect is whether the trade unions and the employer federations in the states participating in the EMU will realize when bargaining for wages that they will have a much higher responsibility for

23 See Lehment and Scheide (1995).

24 See Waigel (1995).

the level of employment than before. In the EMU setting wages which are too high will affect unemployment much more directly since their effects cannot be mitigated anymore by an expansionary national monetary and fiscal policy or a devaluation of the national currency. The bargaining process, however, only leads to a wage setting favourable to employment if the inflationary expectations of trade unions and employer federations adjust to the new course of monetary policy. If they do not deem it credible for bringing about a low inflation rate higher nominal wages will be agreed upon which will endanger price level stability and/or employment.

A further important question is the exchange rate arrangement of the EMU with the non-participating member states. If a system of fixed exchange rates similar to the EMS is introduced and unrealistic parities are fixed vis a vis the new European currency the ECB could be forced into interventions that make it impossible to control the money supply and, therefore, to defend price level stability. These additional two examples show that a European stability culture can only develop on the basis of a fundamental and lasting consensus in favour of price level stability. This cannot be simply prescribed politically. It will, however, emerge if the European monetary constitution is efficient, i.e. contains the right checks and balances. Some deficiencies in this respect were brought out in this paper. The Intergovernmental Conference in 1996 (Maastricht II) offers the chance to fill the gaps. This would be necessary if one is interested in making the EMU a sustainable and therefore long lasting solution. Only then will the EMU will contribute to successful and permanent European integration.

Annex
The fundamental regulations concerning price level stability - a comparison

Treaty on European Union	Bundesbank Act
1. The primary objective of the ESCB shall be to maintain price stability (article 105)	1. The Deutsche Bundesbank regulates the quantity of money in circulation and of credit supplied to the economy ... with the aim of safeguarding the currency ... (paragraph 3)
2. Without prejudice to the objective of price stability, the ESCB shall support the general economic policies in the Community ... (article 105)	2. Without prejudice to the performance of its functions, the Deutsche Bundesbank is required to support the general economic policy of the Federal Government (paragraph 12)
3. When exercising the powers and carrying out the tasks and duties conferred upon them by this Treaty and the Statute of ESCB, neither the ECB, nor a national central bank, nor any member of their decision-making bodies shall seek or take instructions from Community institutions or bodies, from any government of a Member State or from any other body. The Community institutions and bodies and the governments of the Member States undertake to respect this principle and not to seek to influence the members of the decision-making bodies of the ECB or of the national central banks in the performance of their taskes (article 107)	3. In exercising the powers conferred on it by this Act, it is independent of instructions from the Federal Government (paragraph 12)
4. Overdraft facilities or any other type of credit facility with the ECB or with the central banks of the Member States ... in favour of Community institutions or bodies, central governments, regional, local or other public authorities, other bodies governed by public law, or public undertakings of Member States shall be prohibited, as shall the puchase directly from them by the ECB or national central banks of debt instruments (article 104)	4. The Deutsche Bundesbank is authorised to ... grant the Federal Government, the Federal special funds ... and the Länder Governments short-term advances in the form of book credit and credit against Treasury bills (cash advances). The ceiling for cash advances, including the Treasury bills which the Deutsche Bundesbank has bought or undertaken to buy for its own account, is ... (paragraph 20)

Résumé

La culture de la stabilité comme prérequis d'une Union monétaire européenne (UME) durable

Cette contribution se propose de compléter le débat officiellement engagé sur la mise en oeuvre de l'UME.

Une première critique est adressée aux responsables politiques qui, dans l'ensemble, sousestiment le besoin de communication nécessaire pour susciter l'adhésion de l'opinion publique et des futurs utilisateurs de la monnaie unique au processus engagé. La signification du nouvel ordre monétaire européen est analysée ici sous l'angle de la politique de stabilité des prix, reconnue comme un objectif prioritaire pour les banques centrales. Mais la poursuite d'une politique monétaire allant dans ce sens suppose en fait une large acceptation du principe même de stabilité, concept présenté comme un élément "culturel" encore très hétérogène selon les pays de l'Union européenne. Cette "culture" de la stabilité ne saurait être simplement imposée par les gouvernements et parlements respectifs ; elle a besoin de l'appui, de la confiance de la base. La Conférence Intergouvernementale de 1996 encore appelé "Maastricht II", aura de ce point de vue aussi une mission importante car il s'agira de concrétiser ces exigences dans les textes, de finaliser les tenants et aboutissants de la politique financière programmée pour la troisième étape de l'UME (sous forme d'un "pacte de stabilité"). L'analyse de Wim Kösters éclaire utilement la problématique en jeu.

Zusammenfassung

Stabilitätskultur als Voraussetzung für die Dauerhaftigkeit der Europäischen Währungsunion (EWU)

In diesem Beitrag wird auf einige Defizite in der öffentlichen Debatte über die EWU hingewiesen. Vor allem wird kritisiert, daß insgesamt von den verantwortlichen Politikern zu wenig getan wird, um die Akzeptanz der zukünftigen europäischen Geldpolitik und der gemeinsamen Währung bei den Geldnachfragern sicherzustellen. Es wird die entscheidende Bedeutung der Ausgestaltung der Europäischen Geldordnung herausgestellt. Sie muß zum einen Anreize für die europäischen Zentralbanker enthalten, das Ziel Preisniveaustabilität auch tatsächlich anzustreben. Zum anderen muß eine breite öffentliche Unterstützung für die Verfolgung einer stabilitätsorientierten Geldpolitik entstehen. Es würde dann ein System von checks and balances für die europäische Geldpolitik existieren, das Stabilitätskultur genannt werden kann. Es ist notwendig, um eine dauerhafte Akzeptanz der EWU zu gewährleisten. Als Kernelement der Stabilitätskultur wird die accountability der Geldpolitik durch die Wähler (und nicht durch Regierungen und Parlamente) besonders hervorgehoben. Es fehlt jedoch bisher in der geplanten europäischen Geldverfassung. Beratungen auf der Regierungskonferenz 1996 (Maastricht II) darüber, wie dieses für die Dauerhaftigkeit der EWU sehr wichtige Element Berücksichtigung im Vertragswerk finden kann, werden für noch bedeutsamer gehalten als effizientere Regeln für die Finanzpolitik in der dritten Stufe der EWU (Stabilitätspakt), deren Problematik im Beitrag ausführlicher erörtert wird.

References

BERTHOLD, N. (1995): European Currency Union - Do We Need a Centralized Fiscal Stabilization Policy? in: Außenwirtschaft. Vol. 50. 399-422.
BHF-BANK (1995): Verschuldungsregeln als Sicherheitsgurt für die EWU. Wirtschaftsdienst Nr. 1795. September 2.
BUCHANAN, J.M. (1986): Can Policy Activism Succeed? A Public Choice Perspective. in: Hafer, R.W. (ed.). The Monetary versus Fiscal Policy Debate. Totowa N.J. 139-150.
CHANT, J.F./ACHESON, K. (1972): The Choice of Monetary Instruments and the Theory of Bureaucracy. Public Choice. Vol. 12. 13-33.
COMMERZBANK RESEARCH (1995): European Monetary Union. Prospects for European Monetary Union and Effects on the Bond Market. Frankfurt.
EUROPEAN COMMISSION (1995): Green Paper on the Practical Arrangements for the Introduction of the Single Currency. Brussels.
EUROPEAN MONETARY INSTITUTE (1995): Annual Report 1994. Frankfurt.
GROS, D. (1995): Zur Sicherung der Währungsunion vor exzessiven Defiziten. Ein Reformvorschlag zum "Verfahren bei einem übermäßigen Defizit". Geld und Währung Working Papers Nr. 43. Frankfurt.
HASSE, R.H. (1995): Europäische Währungsunion im Spannungsfeld zwischen politischem Wunsch und ökonomischer Realität. Discussion Papers in Economic Policy of the University of the Federal Armed Forces Nr. 51. Hamburg.
HEINEMANN, F. (1994): Verschuldungsanreize in der Wirtschafts- und Währungsunion. Discussion Paper No. 94-02 of the Zentrum für Europäische Wirtschaftsforschung. Mannheim.
KÖSTERS, W. (1991): Europäische Zentralbank und Preisniveaustabilität. Hamburger Jahrbuch für Wirtschafts- und Gesellschaftspolitik. Vol. 36. 155-167.
KÖSTERS, W. (1993): La conception de la stabilité dans le traité de Maastricht: interprétation et critique. in: Maillet, P. (ed.). Trois défis de Maastricht. Convergence, cohésion, subsidiarité. Paris.
KÖSTERS, W./BELKE, A./KRUTH, B.-J. (1992): Monetäre Integration in Europe - Grundlagen, Entwicklungen und Perspektiven nach den Maastrichter Beschlüssen. in: Wirtschaftliche Grundbildung. Der Verbraucher in der Sozialen Marktwirtschaft. Number 2. Münster.
LEHMENT, H./SCHEIDE J. (1995): Der Fahrplan für die Europäische Währungsunion: noch erheblicher Handlungs- und Klärungsbedarf. Kiel Discussion Papers No. 259. Kiel.
MADE IN GERMANY (1991): The Economist. November 2. p. 85.

MASERA, R. (1995): Haushalt und Verfassung. Revisionshypothesen im Lichte des Maastrichter Vertrages (Übersetzung aus dem Italienischen). in: Deutsche Bundesbank, Auszüge aus Presseartikeln Nr. 64. September 21. S. 1-5.

MISHKIN, F.S. (1993): The Economics of Money, Banking and Financial Markets. Boston and Toronto.

MUELLER, D.C. (1989): Public Choice II, rev. ed. Cambridge.

NEUMANN, M.J.M. (1991): Central Bank Independence as a Prerequisite of Price Stability. European Economy. special edition No. 1. 79-92.

OHR, R. (1995): Die Maastricht Kriterien sind zu weich. Die Sorgen um die Währungsunion bleiben berechtigt. Risiken der Währungsunion. in: Frankfurter Allgemeine Zeitung. Oktober 14. p. 14.

SCHMIDT, Ch./STRAUBHAAR, Th. (1995): Maastricht II: Are Real Convergence Criteria Needed? in: Intereconomics. Vol. 30. 211-220.

TOMA, E.F./TOMA, M. (ed.) (1986): Central Bankers, Bureaucratic Incentives and Monetary Policy. Dordrecht, Boston and Lancaster.

VAUBEL, R. (1990): Currency Competition and European Monetary Integration. The Economic Journal. Vol. 100. 936-946.

WAIGEL, T. (1995): Stabilitätspakt für Europa. in: Deutsche Bundesbank, Auszüge aus Presseartikeln Nr. 75. November.

Lewis D. Johnson

Financial Governance in the New Europe

1. Introduction

2. Financial system structure and performance

3. Theory of financial system organization

   A. Transactions economics
   B. Deal attributes and governance structure
   C. Agent capabilities and governance structure
   D. Schematic summary of the theory
   E. Financial system structure
   F. Policy implications

4. Implications for Europe

5. Whither Europe ?

6. Summary and policy conclusions

1. Introduction

The move to a unified European state has necessitated the harmonization and coordination of myriad activities and processes, including transporation, information systems, telecommunications and banking. An issue of vital importance to Europe's future economic health is the structure of its financial system. A financial system (which encompasses the entire process of amassing and allocating capital and is more than just banks) is charged with the task of ensuring the provision of adequate capital for optimal economic growth (the primary market) and the subsequent allocation of ownership and control of that capital (the secondary market), and the type of financial system which is appropriate for a country or a region depends on a variety of factors discussed below.

The purpose of this paper is to analyze the prospective financial system for the new Europe and to develop policy recommendations on its structure [1]. The paper is based on the seminal work of Oliver Williamson. It addresses the issue of the extent to which the existing heterogeneous financial system should continue to exist, and where there should be further harmonization of national financial systems. The answer will be seen to be dependent in part on the nature of transactions undertaken by different intermediaries, and in part on the prospective degree of harmonization of industrial structures and "white collar" infrastructures [2] in the new Europe.

The paper is organized as follows. The literature on differences between national financial systems is reviewed in Section 2, and a transactions economics theory of financial systems is introduced in Section 3. In Section 4, the current and prospective European financial systems are analyzed in light of the theory, while Section 5 extends this analysis to a discussion of the optimal

---

1 This paper builds on earlier joint work with Professors Edwin Neave and Bohumir Pazderka of the School of Business, Queen's University.

2 By "white collar" infrastructures I mean to describe the activities of the professional classes in areas such as the law, administration, accounting, and regulation.

financial structure for the new Europe. Section 6 concludes and provides policy recommendations.

2. Financial system structure and performance

There has been a considerable literature in recent years regarding the relationship between a country's financial system amd its economic growth. This literature was inspired in large part by attempts to explain the differential performance of the American and Japanese economies, but has broadened latterly to encompass a larger set of inter-country comparisons.

The Japan - U.S. comparison has highlighted the difference between bank-dominated and market-dominated financial systems [3]. In the bank-dominated economies (Japan and much of Continental Europe), Lester Thurow (1992) suggests that the ethos is one of "communitarian capitalism" (the state before the individual), in contrast to the "individualistic capitalism" of the market-dominated economies of North America and Britain. Thc U.S. in particular is often characterized as having a spirit of "cowboy capitalism". Michael Porter (1992) focusses on the issue of investment horizon, and concludes that the bank-dominated systems, with their "dedicated capital" (i.e., patient capital), take a longer-term strategic view than do the market-dominated systems, with their "fluid capital" (i.e., impatient capital) which, according to Porter, leads to myopic management and impaired lomg-term growth. Michel Albert (1993) further suggests that the "Alpine-Rhine" version of capitalism (bank-dominated) is superior to the "Anglo-American" version (market-dominated).

The core of the debate hinges on the differential "governance" capabilities of banks and markets. By governance is meant the ability to screen investment projects ("deals"), to monitor their progress, and to exercise control over their outcomes. Banks, with their closer relationships to lenders, are able to exercise closer governance of deals than can markets, with their more distant

3 Much of the debate to date has focussed on the two "polar" financial institutional types, banks and stock markets. Other elements of a financial system are examined later in the paper.

relationship. The main bank of the Japanese keiretsu and the German industrial and universal banks are generally perceived to have the ultimate degree of governance capability because of their close ties with their clients [4]. These ties mitigate many of the agency and other informational problems associated with market-style financing.

Johnson and Neave (1994) discuss many of the economic benefits derived from main banks in Japan (similar benefits would accrue to the industrial banks in Germany and other European countries). In essence, agency problems in Japan are lessened because banks hold equity as well as debt, and also take an active role in monitoring firms, to the extent of replacing incumbent management of ailing firms with bank employees (Prowse, 1990). Kester (1986) similarly notes the importance of banks being both lenders and owners, while Hoshi et al. (1990) argue that banks in Japan can bear more debt because of concentrated and dedicated ownership. Many analysts have observed (see, e.g., McCauley and Zimmer, 1989) that the apparently lower cost of capital enjoyed by Japan in recent years has derived in part from reduced agency costs (although other factors such as savings habits and tax laws play a part as well).

Higher-order governance does cost more, however, especially in terms of management time. As such, it is clearly not needed nor (because of cost) wanted for deals which do not require close supervision. As well, the nature of the optimal governance of a financial system depends on the level of a nation's economic development and on the degree of sophistication of its financial and regulatory infrastructure. In contrast to the "either/or" views of Albert and other commentators, Johnson and Neave (1994) show how the Japanese and American models should be and indeed are evolving toward a more sophisticated blend of the best features of each model. Further, Neave, Johnson and Pazderka (1994) argue that, for the transition economies of Eastern Europe, no one financial system is unambiguously preferrable, and that a country's

4 Urban and Vendemini (1992) discuss the role of Deutsche Bank as a universal bank and a center of German industrial networks.

financial system will evolve as the country passes through various stages of development. These results tend to moderate much of the current rhetoric in the literature, and to suggest that emerging European policy in this area should be neither static nor doctrinaire.

3. Theory of financial system organization

Most research to date on financial system organization has been anecdotal. The theories of market efficiency and of industrial organization have been widely applied to the banking industry, but not for the financial system as a whole. The theories of information economics (particularly agency theory and signalling theory) are rich with interpretation, but they are not amenable to convenient empirical verification. This paper draws on the theory of transactions economics (as developed by Oliver Williamson, 1985 and 1988) to provide structure for analysis. The application of the theory to financial system organization is based on Neave (1990, 1991).

A. Transactions economics

In transactions economics, an economic organization is not static but continually evolves so as to attain cost-effective governance of transactions. Williamson analyzes this process using the individual transaction (the "deal") as a basic unit of analysis. Cost-effective forms of governance are found through aligning the attributes of individual transactions with agents' governance capabilities. Different structures provide different capability to screen, monitor, and control deals through time. Closer governance, however, incurs higher costs, so organizations strive to attain the least-cost form of governance given deal attributes and agent capabilities.

Transactions economics has only recently been employed to analyze financial system organization. Williamson (1988) examines debt and equity as alternative governance mechanisms. Richter (1989) advances a theory of banking regulation based on what he calls the "New Institutional Economics", which builds on Williamson. Neave (1991) studies financial system organization, while Johnson and Neave analyze real estate investment management (1992) and international competitive advantage (1994). Neave, Johnson and Pazderka (1994) apply transactions economics to analyze the evolution into market economies of the former Communist states in Eastern Europe. The discussion that follows focusses on the "lending" side of intermediaries' activities; Johnson and Neave (1995) analyze in more detail the joint problem of managing both asset and liability portfolios.

B. Deal attributes and governance structure

Deals are characterized in terms of three attributes: their repetitiveness, their specificity, and their degree of risk or uncertainty. Repetitiveness of a transaction matters because transactions economics is a dynamic theory and agents learn through doing. Specificity matters because alternative uses for an asset reduce the need for closer governance. For financial deals, specificity can usefully be interpreted in liquidity terms; i.e., an asset with a high degree of specificity is "illiquid" [5]. Risk and uncertainty matter in the Knightian sense: deals under risk can be characterized by probability distributions while deals under uncertainty are less amenable to statistical projection, hence require more ongoing attention.

Individual deals differ in these attributes, and Williamson developed three classes of governance structure (markets, hybrids, and hierarchies) for governing these attributes. Market structures have the least governance capability, so they are most suitable for deals where complete contracting is possible; hence markets tend to have a short-term focus since complete contracting depends on availability of relevant information, which decreases the longer the time period [6]. For deals involving incomplete contracting,

5 One might better term this property "viscosity" in order to retain its monotonicity.

6 There are a number of other attributes of different governance structures which are not explicitly considered in this paper but which are nonetheless important. For example, markets provide useful objective information such as hurdle rates for capital investment, and they also provide a mechanism for diversification. Higher-level governance structures have diminished capabilities in these areas.

information is revealed through time, and the ongoing governance capabilities provided by hybrid or hierarchical governance are likely to prove more cost-effective than the shorter-term capabilities offered by market governance.

C. Agent capabilities and governance structure

Agents' capabilities are limited by bounded rationality and environmental uncertainty. Subject to these constraints, agents seek a cost-effective match between deal attributes (which evolve through time) and their governance capabilities (which also evolve through time, due to learning and technological change, among other factors). As well, the "white collar" infrastructure of regulation, accounting and legal standards, and related areas constrains both the agents' capabilities [7] and permissible actions [8].

D. Schematic summary of the theory

Figure 1 provides a schematic summary of the application of transactions economics to financial system structure. The first panel of Figure 1 shows that a financial system provides funds using the three governance mechanisms of markets, hybrids, and hierarchies. To emphasize the specialized context of financial system structure, the market, hybrid, and hierarchical forms of organizations are referred to as market, intermediary, and internal forms of financing.

7 For example, the amount and timing of disclosure of company information (as prescribed by regulators) have a profound effect on the ability of an agent to exercise looser forms of governance.

8 For example, the current state of banking regulation in the U.S. does not permit commercial banks to undertake investment banking activities (as is common in Japan and Germany).

Figure 1: Governance Capabilities, Deal Attributes and Alignment

Governance Structures

Markets		Hybrids (Intermediaries)		Hierarchies (Internal Financing)
Public Markets	Private Markets	Securities Firms		Holding Companies (Ownership Concentrations)
		Industrial Banks		Universal Banks
	Commercial Banks			
			Venture Capital Cos.	Financial Conglomerates
				Keiretsu

Governance Capabilities

---> Greater monitoring capabilities --------------------------------->
(particularly on a continuing basis)

Greater control capabilities
(auditing, replacement of key personnel)

Greater adjustment capabilities
(ability to alter contracts as circumstances change)

Governance Costs

---> Increasing --->

Deals' Attributes

---> Increasing information differences ----------------------------->

Perceived greater risk; uncertainty rather than risk

Increased asset specificity / decreased asset liquidity

Greater need for continued monitoring

Greater need for ex post adjustment

Increasing cost of default

Under each governance form are displayed various types of financial institutions, with governance capability increasing from left to right. For example, public markets are recorded to the left of private markets, because of greater investigative capability and greater freedom to negotiate terms of private markets. Similarly, commercial and industrial banks usually have less highly developed governance capabilities than do venture capital firms which tend to make greater use of discretionary arrangements. The highest degree of governance capability is offered by hierarchical organizations, examples of which include financial conglomerates and Japanese keiretsu. Industrial and universal banks such as found in Germany also offer capabilities close to the hierarchical form when they enter into long-term lending and share purchase arrangements with their clients.

The second panel of Figure 1 specifies agents' capabilities, and indicates that different governance mechanisms possess them in different degrees. For example, intermediaries and internal organizations have greater monitoring and control capabilities than do markets. The third panel shows that these greater capabilities incur higher costs.

The final panel of Figure 1 outlines the different deal attributes associated with different governance structures and governance capabilities. Deals characterized by greater informational differences between the two parties (the financiers typically having less information) are seen by financiers as involving higher degrees of risk, or as presenting uncertainty instead of risk, thereby posing a greater need for continuing governance. Similarly, less liquid assets require closer governance. Thus, market financing is more likely to be associated with symmetric information and liquid assets, with closer governance structures coming into play as the need to monitor and control deals increases (whenever it is cost-effective to do so).

Financiers have few monitoring and control capabilities if they hold debt or a minority share position, and greater capabilities if they are controlling shareholders. Thus, under uncertainty, greater relative use of equity can be expected, since greater capabilities for ex post adjustment are likely to prove cost-effective when it is not possible to write complete contracts (Williamson, 1988). There is also a temptation for more intensive government intervention and regulation in financial systems with a high degree of uncertainty.

E. Financial system structure

The aggregate financial structure of an economy will comprise a mixture of institutional types reflecting the attributes of the economy's deals, the capabilities of the economy's financiers, and the characteristics of its white collar infrastructure. Markets, intermediaries, and internal financing organizations each offer a unique combination of capabilities, at increasing cost. As such, each mechanism offers cost-effective governance of some deal types, but not of others. Financial system organization results from these governance structures being aligned with classes of deals on the basis of cost-effectiveness.

There is a natural evolution in any economy from the right to the left in Figure 1 (due in part to agent learning and information revelation) [9], but a continual infusion of new agents and new deals requires the maintenance of high capability governance structures even in highly developed economies. As well, some deals naturally require more governance than others. For example, Johnson and Neave (1992) show that managing real estate investment portfolios requires far more governance capability than than that required for managing a portfolio of personal loans. Similarly, financing established industries and technologies requires less governance than would financing new industries and new technologies.

9 A classic example is the process of "disintermediation" in which banks pool ("securitize") individual loans for sale in the secondary market. A further example is the market for swaps, which has evolved from illiquid, customized deals to liquid, standardized deals.

F. Policy implications

The preceding analysis explains why economies have complex financial structures (because of their mixture of deal attributes and agent capabilities), why the financial structure of an economy evolves over time (because of changes in the mix of deals and agents), and why some economies have different financial structures than others (because of different mixes of deals and attributes, different degrees of development, and different white collar infrastructures).

Many commentaters (e.g., Albert, 1993) fail to appreciate this complexity wherein different governance structures can be either complements or substitutes. To development economists in particular, different financial arrangements are only substitutes, and represent needless duplication. Hence development economists tend to develop policies aimed at reducing financial structures to a single type. In contrast, transaction economists see complementary governance structures as necessary to finance the many different forms of deals a developed economy can present: only some kinds of deals can cost-effectively be done by market financings, while others are more cost-effectively governed using intermediaries or internal financing organizations.

A flexible policy toward financial structure is especially important given that financial structure can affect both the rate and the type of economic growth. Financial structure determines which types of deals can be financed and governed cost-effectively, and the wrong structure can lead either to foregone investment activity or to the necessity of bringing in foreign financing and managerial assistance. This can have a profound effect on a country's or region's competitive position.

Other factors differ between countries, including the cost and availability of capital, and these factors also have important implications for economic development. In a global capital market, these constraints are not binding [10], but they offer potential loss of control over local resources and they have potential negative foreign exchange implications. The legal, administrative and regulatory infrastructure as well as the political climate can also affect the international flow of capital [11].

All of these factors highlight the importance to a country or region of a well-considered policy toward financial structure, a policy consistent with economic opportunities, managerial competence, and white collar infrastructure. The contribution of transactions economics to the debate is the suggestion that no single form of financing structure is appropriate for a country or region at a given point in time, nor does the optimal financing structure remain static over time.

4. Implications for Europe

Europe stands at a crossroads, with two policy issues to be addressed. The first issue is the form toward which individual European financial structures should evolve. The second issue is the extent to which a pan-European financial structure should be encouraged, to the possible detriment and disappearance of many national institutions.

There are few barriers at present to the development of pan-European financial services. Banking and insurance companies have increasingly gained reciprocal powers (formalized most recently in the Second Banking Directive) which permit the establishment of financial service institutions in any member country (the so-called "passport"). Stock markets have remained more insular

10 Indeed, there is evidence that real bond yields are converging as capital markets become more global. See "The Global Capital Market: Supply, Demand, Pricing and Allocation", a recent study by McKinsey Financial Institutions Group.

11 For example, limitations on repatriation of capital or the threat of expropriation will effectively dissuade foreign investment.

(to the extent that this is possible in a global economy) [12], but many of these restrictions will be lifted by the end of 1995 with the implementation of the Investment Services Directive. As well, plans were recently announced for a Europe-wide screen-based trading system aimed at smaller capitalised companies (the European Association of Securities Dealers Automated Quotation market, EASDAQ, modelled after NASDAQ in the U.S.) [13]. Paris and London have also announced plans for competing small-company exchanges [14]. The growth of Ecu-denominated financial markets in the last decade has also brought European financial institutions and instruments closer together (Leroux, 1995).

The remaining barriers are, principally, different national regulatory schemes and tax systems (e.g., Luxembourg's holding out on the imposition of withholding taxes), but pressures are increasing for further harmonization. These barriers can lead to a preferential advantage for institutions in certain countries, while at the same time possibly leading to an adverse selection problem, wherein institutions establish themselves in the least restrictive regulatory regime and use the "passport" to compete across borders.

The current structure of European finance is not homogeneous. Much is made of the difference between the Continent and the U.K., but Continental Europe itself has many inter-country differences in, for example, the structure and performance of individual banking systems and in the importance of stock markets to the domestic economy. These differences reflect different industrial structures, different experiences with government intervention (particularly in the case of banking), and a number of other economic, cultural and socio-economic factors. For example, people in the Mediterranean countries have until recently been underinsured relative to their northern European

12 Inter-market competition between counties has been so intense that most markets have until recently banned trading screens from other markets. Foreign companies wanting to join stock exchanges in Italy, France and Spain have to set up separate subsidiaries. Exchange membership requirements also vary across markets, with, for example, only banks allowed in Germany and no banks allowed in France. Source: "The Economist", November 5, 1994, p. 85.

13 The European, 28 October - 3 November 1994, p. 18.

14 The European, 20-26 January 1995, p. 20.

neighbours. Different countries have had different exposure to the emergence of market economies in Eastern Europe, with Germany obviously facing the most pressure. Standish (1995) discusses differences across countries in the evolution of the accounting and commercial law professions.

Molyneux, LLoyd-Williams, and Thornton (1994) show in their study of competitive conditions in European banking that banks have not yet responded to the new freedoms offered in a unified Europe, and that banks face different competitive conditions in different countries. For instance, banks in Germany, France, the U.K., and Spain behave as if they are under conditions of monopolistic competition, while results in Italy are consistent with a monopoly or short-run oligopoly.

Structurally, France and Italy have the most concentrated banking markets of the larger economies [15] (interestingly, they also have had the most government involvement in the past), while all of the smaller countries (with the exception of Luxembourg, which has many banks competing for tax-related business) had higher market concentrations than the larger economies. The threat of encroachment by large international institutions has led to further concentration in some countries. Lloyd-Williams, Molyneux, and Thornton (1994) report that Spanish public policy has been to encourage bank mergers while at the same time encouraging the sharing of branch networks with foreign banks. Zardkoohi and Kolari (1994) conclude that Finland is over-banked and should encourage further rationalization prior to joining the EC, in order to effectively compete against larger rivals. Italian banks are allegedly overstaffed and inefficient, unable to compete against larger European banks, and the government has begun to reduce restructions on branch networks and mergers; in response, steps have been taken to rationalize costs and, through mergers, to gain size [16]. Austria admits to being over-banked, and is also undergoing a restructuring of its banking system [17]. The Portugese banking

15 Concentration is measured as five- and ten-firm asset and deposit ratios.

16 "The Economist", November 5, 1994, p. 87.

17 International Herald Tribune, November 2, 1994, p. 11.

system is undergoing a drastic reorganization with current deals in the works resulting in the major banking groups controlling 70 percent of the domestic industry. Branch closures and further rationalization are expected to cut the cost structure dramatically [18].

Stock market capitalization is small in France and Germany versus the U.S. and U.K. (Dembinski and Schoenenberger, 1993, p. 51), but trends are shifting. France in particular has recently experienced a growing reliance on market financing, while even Germany and Japan have begun to move in that direction (ibid., pp. 24 - 25). In Germany, banks are divesting many of their industrial holdings and many industrial companies are "demerging", both of which activities have led to increasing use of (mostly foreign) investment banks and an increasing equity float [19]. As of 1994, about six percent of German households invested in stocks, compared with 16 percent in France and more than 20 percent in the U.S. and U.K. [20]

In other countries, however, such as Austria, investors have little experience with stock markets and have tended to invest in safer securities like government bonds. Italy also has not had a strong tradition of stock ownership, due in part to the large number of family-owned firms, and in part to a lack of transparency, a delayed settlement date, and no protection of minority shareholder rights. This situation is changing as more companies become privatized, more privately owned companies seek new capital, and major regulatory reforms come into effect [21].

Stock markets are often criticised for having a large-company bias (see, e.g., Albert, 1993 and Dembinski and Schoenenberger, 1993) and are seen as not being of much help when most new economic development is being created by small and medium enterprises. The announced establishment of EASDAQ and

18 The European, 13-19 January 1995, p. 16.
19 The Sunday Times, February 5, 1995, p. 2-7.
20 The European, 20-26 January 1995, p. 20.
21 The European, 27 January - 2 February 1995, p. 17.

its competitors in Paris and London should foster more meaningful market activity in the new Europe (although it is doubtful if all three exchanges are viable).

A further critique of stock markets is that small investors are disadvantaged because others (the "insiders") may have prior access to timely and meaningful information, hence the insiders can trade at the small investors' expense. Harmonization of financial disclosure requirements and coordination of insider trading prohibitions should alleviate many of these impediments to stock market growth. It is not necessary to standardize financial reporting guidelines, as is often touted by some critics, as long as the system is sufficiently transparent that investors can observe and interpret new information and act accordingly.

5. Whither Europe?

Europe is characterized by a variety of national economies, with differing mixes of new and old industry and service economies and varying white collar infrastructures. As such, and with respect to the first policy issue above (the form toward which individual European financial structures should evolve), the preceding analysis would suggest that a mixed financial structure comprising markets, intermediaries, and internal financing organizations is the appropriate model. Policies to encourage the simultaneous development of all elements of the system should be developed, and policymakers should be aware of the dynamic nature of financial systems and construct policies amenable to change. Flexible policies are particularly important for a unified Europe as future growth to the east and possibly the south is being considered [22].

22 See Neave, Johnson and Pazderka (1994) for a discussion of the importance of flexible policies to the economic well-being of the emerging markets in Eastern Europe.

With respect to the second policy issue (the extent to which a pan-European financial structure should be encouraged), there are benefits and disadvantages to a continental financial structure. The principal benefits are economies of scale and scope, the ability to amass the necessary critical mass of capital to compete globally, and the diversification offered by a continent-wide lending base. The principal disadvantage is the disappearance of many local and regional institutions, with consequent loss of national identity (which is happening anyway in the unified Europe) and (more significantly) possible loss of contact with local clients and their needs and special situations.

Previous experience in North American banking can help foreshadow the likely outcome of a continental system. In Canada, a branch banking system has allowed the major banks to prosper at home (in large part by being able to diversify across regions and industries) and to become large enough to compete globally. In contrast, the American state banking system to date has exposed individual banks disproportionately to regional econonic turmoil (as in oil and gas in Texas and and a rusting infrastructure in New England), with many regional American banks having gone bankrupt over the years as opposed to the handful in Canada. New regulation in the U.S. to allow inter-state banking and the development of "super banks" has inspired a burst of mergers by many banks (to attain competitive size) and a fear of dissolution by many others (because of their lack of competitive size). Similar activities are beginning in Europe (viz. Spain above) and will likely accelerate as further rationalization of the system occurs.

The issue of whether to encourage pan-European institutions is as political as it is economic. Transactions economics can provide some guidance on the matter, however. Higher-order governance by necessity requires more detailed access to information and a better capability to interpret the information and ability to act upon it. Markets, on the other hand, need only publicly available information and there is not the imminence of intervention by financiers that there is with intermediaries and internal financing organizations. In a similar vein, markets benefit from diversification (across regions and industries) while higher-order governance structures suffer from diversification (because of the dilution of managerial time and expertise and the lesser knowledge financiers have of the details and nuances of more remote deals).

This analysis suggests a natural spectrum of continental financial structures. Markets can only benefit from a continental structure (and the continent can only benefit from an increased supply of capital to small and medium enterprises, as proposed by EASDAQ). Capital markets require a critical mass to compete globally, and rationalization of smaller regional established markets will increase their ability to raise capital competitively.

This process has begun with the re-establishment of London as the pre-eminent regional financial centre (e.g., the move of Deutsche Banks's global investment banking activity to London) and with a move toward concentration of exchange listing by German companies on the Frankfurt Exchange (to provide adequate liquidity for active secondary trading). Currently, Frankfurt, Munich and Düsseldorf account for nearly 90 percent of German share trading (with Frankfurt alone accounting for 74 percent of the total) and the survival of smaller exchanges such as Berlin, Hanover, Bremen, Stuttgart and Hamburg is doubtful [23]. Frankfurt meanwhile has designs to challenge London as the central stock market, with its major strength being its access to and experience with the capital-hungry Eastern European countries. The process of rationalization will accelerate when the Investment Services Directive removes many of the existing barriers in 1995. Developments in electronic trading systems (and the relaxation of constraints on their cross-border use) will further centralize stock market activity.

Some intermediaries, such as commercial banks and insurance companies, could benefit from the diversication and larger markets of a continental structure without impairing unduly their governance capabilities. For banking, opportunities are likely to be concentrated in the commercial and industrial sector, since it is thought that retail customers will still prefer the comfort of

23 The European, 12-18 May 1995, p. 16.

dealing with their domestic institutions [24]; however, in the case of cross-border currency transactions (which are expensive and slow), a number of banks are setting up electronic on-line networks to permit instantaneous and inexpensive fund transfers (for both retail and commercial customers) [25]. Insurance companies have already begun to develop continental links with the establishment in 1992 of Eureko, a consortium of Dutch, British, Portugese, Danish and Swedish companies [26].

Other intermediaries, such as venture capital companies, should diversify with care, and internal financing organizations, such as universal banks, can only lose from a continental financial structure. The reason for this, as discussed above, is the higher governance capability needed for such intermediaries and the consequent excessive cost of extended operations and loss of local knowledge.

6. Summary and policy conclusions

The preceding analysis has applied the theory of transactions economics to the evolving European financial structure. The conclusions from the analysis are, first, that a mixed financial structure comprising markets, intermediaries, and internal financing organizations should be encouraged, and, second, that some types of intermediaries should pursue a pan-European structure and some should not.

European leaders, in planning for the optimal economic growth of the new Europe, should adopt the following principles in any new policy developments:

(1) The encouragement of a flexible financial structure.
(2) The elimination of remaining barriers to continental financial structures.

24 Thomson and Taylor, 1994.
25 International Herald Tribune, December 8, 1994, p. 11.
26 The European, 9-15 December 1994, p. 28.

(3) The harmonization of the white collar infrastructure, particularly with respect to disclosure standards, insider trading, and transparency guidelines.

Such a policy framework will facilitate European financial institutions in maximizing the potential of the new Europe.

Résumé

Le contrôle du système financier dans la nouvelle Europe

La réalisation de l'Union Européenne nécessite l'harmonisation ou la coordination d'innombrables activités et processus, incluant notamment les systèmes de communication, d'information et le système financier, ces derniers jouant un rôle particulièrement important. En effet le système financier (qui englobe la totalité du processus d'accumulation et l'allocation du capital, au-delà de la seule activité bancaire) a pour mission de dégager les ressources financières nécessaires à une croissance économique optimale (le marché primaire) et à en répartir la propriété et le contrôle (le marché secondaire). La détermination d'un système financier adéquat (pour un pays ou un ensemble de "régions" intégrées) dépend de nombreux facteurs, présentés et discutés par l'auteur.

Lewis D. Johnson passe d'abord en revue les différents types de systèmes nationaux en vigueur, distinguant ceux qui sont plutôt dominés par les institutions bancaires (Japon et la plupart des pays d'Europe Continentale), de ceux qui sont plutôt dominés par les marchés (Royaume-Uni et Amérique du Nord). Cette structure n'est pas neutre au regard de la dynamique à moyen-long terme de l'économie.

L'auteur se réfère à la théorie des transactions de O. Williamson pour étayer son argumentation et justifier une organisation, de complémentarité, diversifiée entre marchés et intermédiaires financiers. Cette problématique est appliquée au cas de l'Europe et à la restructuration en cours de son système financier, pour le moment hétérogène. Avantages et inconvénients réciproques sont présentés, aussi sous un angle prospectif (à la fois politique, financier et technologique).

Zusammenfassung

Steuerung und Kontrolle des Finanzsystems im neuen Europa

Die Verwirklichung der Europäischen Union erfordert die Harmonisierung oder Koordinierung unzähliger Geschäftstätigkeiten und -abläufe, insbesondere auch der Kommunikations-, der Informations- und Finanzsysteme, wobei den letzteren eine besondere Bedeutung zukommt. Das Finanzsystem (das neben den Bankgeschäften die gesamten Kapitalakkumulations- und Allokationsabläufe umfaßt) hat in der Tat die Aufgabe, die für ein optimales Wachstum notwendigen finanziellen Mittel bereitzustellen (Primärmarkt) sowie eine Verteilung von Eigentum und Kontrolle zu bewirken (Sekundärmarkt). Die Bestimmung eines (für ein Land oder eine Gesamtheit von integrierten "Regionen") adäquaten Finanzsystems ist abhängig von zahlreichen Faktoren, die vom Autor dargelegt und erörtert werden.

Lewis D. Johnson bietet zunächst einen Überblick über die verschiedenen nationalen Systeme. Hierbei unterscheidet er zwischen jenen Systemen, die eher durch die Geldinstitute dominiert werden (Japan und die meisten Länder Kontinentaleuropas) und denjenigen, welche eher von den Märkten dominiert werden (Vereinigtes Königreich und Nordamerika). Diese Struktur ist im Hinblick auf die mittel- und langfristige Wirtschaftsentwicklung nicht neutral.

Zur Untermauerung seiner Argumentation und um eine komplementäre, zwischen Märkten und Finanzinstituten unterscheidende Organisation zu rechtfertigen, verweist der Autor auf die Transaktionstheorie von O. Williamson. Diese Problematik wird dann auf Europa und sein zur Zeit noch in Gestaltung befindliches, heterogenes Finanzsystem angewendet. Die jeweiligen Vor- und Nachteile werden, mit einer gleichzeitig politischen, finanziellen und technologischen Vorausschau, dargelegt.

References

ALBERT, M. (1993): Capitalism vs. Capitalism. New York. Four Wall Eight Windows.

DEMBINSKI, P./SCHOENENBERGER, A. (1993): Financial Markets: Impossible Mission?. Paris. Fondation pour le progrès de l'homme.

HOSHI, T./KASHYAP, A. /SCHARFSTEIN, D. (1990): The role of banks in reducing the costs of distress in Japan. Journal of Financial Economics. September. pp. 67-88.

JOHNSON, L.D./NEAVE, E.H. (1992): Strategic Real Estate Management: The Case of Olympia & York. Canadian Investment Review 5. pp. 51-62.

JOHNSON, L.D./NEAVE, E.H. (1994): Governance and Comparative Advantage. Managerial Finance 20. pp. 54-68.

JOHNSON, L.D./NEAVE, E.H. (1995): Governance and Financial System Supervision, presented at the Conference on Corporate Decision-Making in Canada. Toronto. Ontario. March 20-21, 1995. Forthcoming in an Industry Canada publication of the Proceedings of the Conference on Corporate Decision-Making in Canada.

KESTER, W.C. (1986): Capital and Ownership Structure: A Comparison of United States and Japanese Manufacturing Corporations. Financial Management. Spring. pp. 5-16.

LEROUX, F. (1995): International Financial Markets in ECU: The Impact of a Difficult Consensus. in Sabine Urban (ed.). Europe in Progress: Model and Facts. Wiesbaden. Gabler Verlag.

LLOYD-WILLIAMS, D.M./MOLYNEUX, P./THORNTON, J. (1994): Market Structure and Performance in Spanish Banking. Journal of Banking and Finance. May. pp. 433-443.

McCAULEY, R./ZIMMER, S. (1989): Explaining International Differences in the Cost of Capital. Federal Reserve Bank of New York Quarterly Review. Summer. pp. 7-28.

MOLYNEUX, P./LLOYD-WILLIAMS, D.M./THORNTON, J. (1994): Competitive Conditions in European Banking. Journal of Banking and Finance. May. pp. 445-459.

NEAVE, E.H. (1990): How Financial Systems Evolve. Canadian Investment Review 3. pp. 11-26.

NEAVE, E.H. (1991): The Economic Organisation of a Financial System. London and New York. Routledge.

NEAVE, E.H./JOHNSON, L.D./PAZDERKA, B. (1994): Financial Governance in Transition Economies. Queen's University Working Paper # 94-13.

PORTER, M. (1992): Capital Choices: Changing the Way America Invests in Industry. Reported in The Economist. pp. 89-90.

PROWSE, S. (1990): Institutional investment patterns and corporate financial behavior in the United States and Japan. Journal of Financial Economics. September. pp. 43-66.
RICHTER, R. (1989/90): "Banking Regulation as Seen by the New Institutional Economics". in The Economics and Law of Banking Regulation. Occasional Papers Vol. 2. Winter 1989/90. Center for the Study of the New Institutional Economics. Universität des Saarlandes. pp. 135-160.
STANDISH, P. (1995): Public Accounting and Auditing in the European Union. in Sabine Urban (ed.). Europe in Progress: Model and Facts. Wiesbaden. Gabler Verlag.
THOMSON, G./TAYLOR, M. (1994): The Developing Single Market in Financial Services. Bank of England Quarterly Review. November, 99. pp. 341-346.
THUROW, L. (1992): Head to Head: The Coming Economic Battle Among Japan, Europe, and America. New York. William Morrow and Company.
URBAN, S./VENDEMINI, S. (1992): European Strategic Alliances: Co-operative Strategies in the New Europe. Oxford. Blackwell Publishers.
WILLIAMSON, O.E. (1985): The Economic Institutions of Capitalism. New York. Free Press.
WILLIAMSON, O.E. (1988): Corporate Finance and Corporate Governance. Journal of Finance 43. pp. 567-591.
ZARDKOOHI, A./KOLARI, J. (1994): Branch Office Economies of Scale and Scope: Evidence from Savings Banks in Finland. Journal of Banking and Finance. May. pp. 421-432.

Jim Stewart

Core-Periphery Interactions in European Stock Markets[1]

1. Introduction

2. Some differences between capital markets

   A. Why multiple listing?
   B. Institutional arrangements

3. The role of banks

4. The ownership of shares

5. Regulatory issues

6. Taxation

7. Correlation between capital markets

8. Differences in the financing of companies

9. Anglo-American markets versus the european model

1 The author would like to acknowledge helpful comments from Mairead Devine, David Jacobson and especially Bill Kingston.

1. Introduction

Free capital mobility is central to the further development of the European Union. The key idea is that capital including investment capital, should be free to flow to those sectors and countries that investors prefer. This objective has been supported by EU economic policy and directives. For example, directives have been introduced which harmonise corporate accounting standards and disclosure, taxation, and regulations for banks and other financial institutions.

However national institutional structures remain different, and this is particularly the case with institutional structures as they affect financial markets. These institutional structures may be classified into two broad types (1) the Anglo-American or Anglo-Saxon model and (2) the German banking model. The U.K. Ireland, and to some extent the Netherlands fit into the former category, while Germany and Austria are examples of the latter model. The financial systems of other countries in the union are evolving and have characteristics of both systems.

These financial systems also partly overlap with currency blocs, so that movements in German interest rates are regularly followed by changes in interest rates in Belgium, Holland and Austria. Switzerland, although outside the EU, also follows German interest rate movements. These countries' currencies have also moved together in recent periods of currency instability within the EMS (at the end of 1993 and Spring 1995). An important issue which arises from differences in institutional structures is the extent to which free capital mobility will result in uniform markets and, given economies of scale in share trading, the extent to which share trading becomes centralised. Two tier markets have already emerged in the capital markets of large countries. Free capital mobility is likely to further rationalise share trading so that peripheral capital markets will trade in purely domestic issues. Large companies from small countries will have shares traded on large country capital markets.

New issues in peripheral countries (unless of very small companies) will be marketed and traded in two or more centres. Apart from regulatory issues these developments raise other issues relating to the investment preferences of international investors versus the investment requirements of local economies.

This paper examines differences between the Anglo-American versus the German banking model, in the following sections and suggests some implications for peripheral capital markets.

2. Some differences between capital markets

It is not surprising that different countries have different sized capital markets, reflecting the different sizes of their GNP. These differences exist whether measured in terms of value of listed securities or turnover volumes, and have persisted over a long time period. The main exceptions are that for a brief period in the late 1980's Japanese stock market values and volumes were greater than those of the U.S. and for more recent years German stock market volumes have been greater than those for the U.K. although the value of quoted securities is higher on the London Stock Exchange. The number of quoted companies is also related to the aggregate value of shares. Table 1 shows the relative size of different stock markets within the EU for the year 1990.

It can also be deduced from Table 1 that German quoted companies are much larger in terms of stock market values than companies from other countries examined.

Table 1: Quoted Companies and Stock Market Capitalization for Various European Countries for the Year 1990

	Austria	Denmark	France	Germany	Holland	Ireland	U.K.
Number of companies(1)	n.a.	85917	699170	404195	257000	110418	1005300
Number of domestic quoted companies(2)	82	258	443	413	260	51	1946
Stock Market Capitalisation (ECU billions)(2)	18.1	28.5	223.7	7.6	259.9	91.7	601.4
Total Stock Market Value/GDP	14.6%	28.1%	24.5%	21.8%	42.1%	27.9%	79.0%

(1) Source: Ruding Report, Report of the Committee of Independent Experts on Company Taxation, Commission of the European Communities, 1992, p. 240. The data refers to 1989 for Denmark.
(2) Source: European Stock Exchange Statistics, 1991, Brussels: Federation of Stock Exchanges in the EC. The data refers to the end of year market value of domestic listed securities, excluding investment funds. Stock Market Values/GDP ratios were taken from Table XVI.

Table 2 shows the number of companies quoted on the main market in various EU countries. For some countries (Ireland, Denmark and the U.K.) there has been a steady decline in the number of quoted securities. There were 2356 domestic companies quoted on the London Stock Exchange in 1979 (Wilson Report, p. 496) compared with under 1800 in 1994. There were 677 listed companies in total in Germany in 1954 compared with 486 in 1989 (Edwards and Fisher, p. 77). In some instances trends are distorted because of reclassification of companies quoted on the main market, for example, the increase between 1993 and 1994 for Ireland, Denmark and the U.K. is partly explained by a reclassification of quoted companies between the main market and other markets. For other countries there has been some increase in the number of quoted companies. One common influence has been the role of privatizations in increasing the number of quoted companies and in particular the value of aggregate shares. New stock market quoted companies are far more common in Anglo-American financial markets compared with European markets. There were only 25 new companies quoted on German markets between 1959 and 1979, although the number of new companies quoted increased to 125 between 1983 to 1989. Whereas for most of the period 1965-79 there were more than 25 new quoted companies in each year on the London Stock Exchange [2]. During the period 1983-89 there were over 43 new quoted companies on average each year. Apart from privatisation new quoted companies are partly explained by the economic cycle. The number of new quoted companies is associated with periods of rising and high stock markets.

Table 2: Number of Domestic Quoted Companies for the Years 1988-1994(1)

	Austria	Denmark	France	Germany	Holland	Ireland	U.K.
1994	94	56	459	423	317	56	1747
1993	93	53	472	426	245	53	1646
1992	94	53	515	425	251	53	1816
1990	82	51	443	413	260	51	1946
1988		59	459	402	231	59	1804

(1) Refers to the main market.

Source: European Stock Exchange Statistics, Federation of European Stock Exchanges, Bruxelles, various years.

2 Source: Wilson Report, Committee to Review the Functioning of Financial Institutions, cmnd 7937, 1980, Table 3.64,; Davis and Yeoman, Table 1.1.

The discussion so far has centred on domestic companies but another feature of capital markets in different countries is the extent of multiple country listings. Table 3 shows that for more recent years the number of multiple country listings has tended to fall slightly or remain static. But relative to the size of their economies Holland and the U.K. have more foreign companies listed than other countries.

Table 3: Number of Foreign Quoted Companies for the Years 1988-1994(1)

	Austria	Denmark	France	Germany	Holland	Ireland	U.K.
1994	41	10	195	227	215	9	462
1993	43	11	205	229	224	9	479
1992	47	11	217	240	246	8	514
1990	44	10	226	234	238	8	613
1988		7	217	232	227	4	585

(1) Refers to the main market.

Source: European Stock Exchange Statistics, Federation of European Stock Exchanges, Bruxelles, various years.

A. Why multiple listing?

Multiple listings are a response to three main forces:

(1) International diversification by investors, in particular institutions such as pension funds. It is easier for a U.K. pension fund to trade in Swedish shares if they are quoted in London. For this reason large privatizations in the U.K. and elsewhere involved the sale and quotation of shares in a number of different stock markets;

(2) Related to this reason is the need for large companies to source finance in a number of different capital markets;

(3) A third reason is that given free capital mobility share trading will move to those capital markets with the most efficient (lowest cost) capital markets.

B. Institutional arrangements

Capital markets in different economies have many similarities but also important differences. For example non-voting or differential voting shares are rare in the U.K. and Ireland (as in other Anglo-Saxon financial markets) but are much more common in other European Stock Markets. One result of this is that hostile takeover bids are more difficult to execute and hence unusual in stock markets where shares are characterised by differential voting rights. The process of price setting is also different. Prices on the London Stock Exchange are determined by market makers who quote prices at which they both buy and sell shares, the difference between the buying and selling price being their profit margin. The Paris market is however organised as an auction market, although a continuous auction. The price setting process is organised by computer which balances supply and demand. Institutional arrangements in many markets have also been subject to a great deal of change in recent years. Pagano and Roell argue that the main agent of change has been competition between exchanges. The reason for this is that trading volume will flow to the lowest cost and most liquid markets. Some stock exchanges have been subject to greater competition than others. For example the 1994 Annual Report of the Danish Stock Exchange comments (p. 6) "Competition between the European stock exchanges has been intense during recent years", in particular from the London market. In 1993 over 30% of all trading in Dutch shares was undertaken on the London Stock Exchange. Recent reforms of the Dutch Stock Market were introduced with the intention of reducing this proportion (Financial Times, 16/6/94). Similar reforms on the French Bourse were also triggered by a loss of business to the London Exchange (Pagano and Roell). There are however some institutional differences which some argue are to the benefit of European economies compared with Anglo-Saxon economies. One of these differences relates to the role of banks in different economies.

3. The role of banks

There have been a number of attempts at classification of financial systems. For example Zysman (1983) classifies financial systems into (a) capital market based; (b) credit based financial systems with government administered prices, (sometimes described as an overdraft economy); (c) credit based financial systems dominated by financial institutions with considerable influence on industry. Zysman argues the U.S. and the U.K. are of the first type. France and Japan are of the second type and Germany is of the third type. Financial systems have changed substantially in recent years with a greater dominance of capital markets in all countries, but substantial differences remain. For example in France, State owned banks used to be the main providers of finance to the corporate sector. Credit was allocated by administrative mechanisms rather than capital markets, and interest rates were kept artificially low (Bruneel, p. 136) or subsidised (Zysman, p. 129). The French financial system has moved towards a greater reliance on capital markets in terms of equity issues and ownership of equity shares (Bruneel, p. 138-139). The net effect is that the intermediation ratio (the ratio of credit granted by financial institutions to total external financing) fell from almost 80% in 1981 to 40% in 1986 (Bruneel, p. 149). Similar trends have occurred in other countries (Bruneel, p. 150), although this ratio will also vary over the trade cycle. Despite these changes, Bruneel concludes that banks will continue to play a major role in the French financial system.

The distinctive nature of the provision of finance in Germany has been noted by many writers. Shonfield (writing in 1965) describes the close connections between banks and industrial firms in Germany to the mutual advantage to both and cites Marshall (writing in 1919) to the effect that these relationships have been long enduring.

Cable (1985) argues that "German companies make little use of their relatively undeveloped capital market, and depend heavily on the banking system for their external finance". Banks were also found to be the main source of external funds, two thirds of which were in the form of long term loans.

Edwards and Fisher (1994, p. 91) show that for the period 1965-71 for all productive enterprises while internal sources of funds are the largest component of net financing, bank borrowing accounted for just over 50% of external sources of finance compared with 7% for equity shares. Edwards and Fisher also report differences in firm financing depending on legal form, with quoted companies (AGs) relying to a greater extent on internal sources than other legal forms. Edwards and Fisher also argue that Bank loans are relatively more important as a source of finance for U.K. non-financial companies (NFC's) than for German NFC's but banks in Germany have a different relationship to NFC's than in the U.K. For example they are large shareholders and they have representatives on the boards of companies. It is often argued that because banks are both shareholders and providers of loan finance investment decision making is (a) more rational because of the reduction in information asymmetries, and (b) in particular there is far less emphasis on short term decision making. For example, Mayer (1987) concludes that the distinctive feature of successful financial systems is their close involvement in industry.

Capital markets in Anglo-American type financial systems have been criticised as emphasising the short term. Short termism has been defined as "the interaction of financial markets with managerial decision making [which] results in a sub-optimal level of long-term investment" (Miles, 1993). Miles estimates that for a sample of U.K. companies accounting for about one half of the market value of U.K. quoted companies, cash flows that occur more than five years in the future "are discounted at twice the rate the rate of shorter term cash flows" (p. 1394). Deducing short termism from returns is difficult because discount rates may reflect risk. Higher discounting may reflect higher risk rather than short termism (Satchell and Damant, 1995). Other authors have argued that short termism can be identified from comparisons of international spending on R & D and patents and trade statistics. Demirag, Tylecote and Morris argue from such an examination that much of UK industry suffers from short-term decision making.

Christopher Lorenz (Financial Times 12/3/93) has summarised the debate about short termism in the following way: "British manufacturing is crippled by short-termism. With rare exceptions such as once-glamorous Glaxo, companies cannot invest and innovate their way to greater international competitiveness because financial institutions and the stock market are interested only in the level of short-term profits and dividends". Best (1990) argues that the provision of long term finance is particularly striking in Japanese institutional structures. A public/private administrative interplay has a clear influence on long term industrial finance in Japan whereas "in the United States and the United Kingdom the stock market plays a leading role (p. 201)".

Best has also examined institutional arrrangements for the provision of finance to small firms in an industrial district in Northern Italy and notes the key role played by financial consortia of small firms in assessing projects and providing loan guarantees to banks which provide the funds. Effectively these financial consortia redress the imbalance of information asymmetries. In the U.K. and some other countries these are thought to result in too great an emphasis on collateral in providing loans. Best (p. 238) says "an individual firm cannot supply the requisite trust to a banker to obtain working capital, but a financial consortium can". Christensen (1992) argues that because there is no general clearing mechanism in the market for credit, credit is allocated by rationing. Hence mutual understanding, social and cultural coherence, and learning by financial institutions from diverse projects, as well as the behaviour of borrowers are all important in ensuring the financing of potentially successful projects. Similar ideas have been discussed in terms of asymmetries in information between borrowers and lenders and how a financial system can minimise the associated costs. In contrast Christensen argues that capital market based systems do not support the same degree of learning by financial institutions which in turn may impair their ability to select future projects.

Short termism in financial markets may also be associated with volatility and hence the focus of central banks may be on managing short term movements in interest and exchange rates. The president of the Bundesbank claims such a policy is in marked contrast to the policies pursued by this important institution:

> "We are following a steady policy with some fluctuations and this is probably different to the Anglo-Saxon world...the Anglo-Saxon markets are always looking for the need to an anti-cyclical policy which is based on the experience in the Anglo-Saxon world" (Source: The Guardian March 16 1995).

In the same interview the President of the Bundesbank also associated derivatives with volatility in financial markets.

The relative importance of bank borrowing in different financial systems may not vary with the financial system, but may vary with the nature of assets to be financed, the stage in the financial cycle and other factors. However all studies agree that a major difference between Anglo-Saxon Markets and Bank or credit dominated financial markets lies in the nature of shareholders.

4. The ownership of shares

The proportion of shares owned by individual shareholders has fallen in most economies during this century and the proportion of shares owned by financial and other institutions has increased correspondingly. Table 4 shows this data for the U.K.

Table 4: Share of U.K. Equities Held by Individuals %

	1957	1958	1963	1969	1979	1981	1984	1988	1992
Individuals (% of shares owned)	65,8	54		47,4		28		20	20
% of Population owning shares			7			4,5		7	21

Source: Central Statistics Office, London, Various issues.

It is interesting to note the increase in the percentage of the population owning shares. This is largely due to the privatisation programme. Privatisation is also associated with increases in the percentage of the population owning shares in other European countries.

The main difference between different economies relates to the nature of the institution which owns shares. Pension funds in the U.K. owned 31.1% of ordinary shares in 1991 and insurance companies 20.7%. This is likely to understate ownership as it does not adjust for nominee accounts [3]. One common way of assessing the relative importance of pension funds is to express their assets as a percentage of GNP. For 1992 this ratio was nearly 80% for the Netherlands, 66% for the U.K. and 35% for Ireland. This ratio was nearly 18% for Denmark and under 10% for all other EU countries [4]. Thus there is a clear distinction between the U.K. Holland and Ireland and other EU countries. Pension funds are also large as a per cent of GNP for the U.S. and Canada (Davis, 1990, Table A).

In contrast in Germany and other countries cross holdings of shares between non-financial firms are important. Edwards and Fisher (p. 180) estimate that non-financial enterprises owned 39% of the shares of German enterprises in 1988. Furthermore in a study of 301 of the largest quoted companies, in 1983, 88% had a single shareholder owning 25% or more of the equity shares (Edwards and Fisher, p. 183). The concentration of share holdings has also tended to increase through time. In addition banks owned 8.8 % of all shares in 1988, but controlled a higher percentage via proxy votes. A major difference between the Anglo-Saxon financial markets and the German model lies in the different ways that institutions as shareholders behave. The nature of the shareholder and the distribution of shares has considerable implications for stock market activity.

3 Source: Central Statistics Office, Economic Trends, no. 466, August 1992, H.M.S.O.

4 Source: European Federation for Retirement Provision, and European Economy Annual Economic Report for 1993, Table (5) p. 186, Directorate General for Economic and Social Affairs, 1993.

Pension funds have particular characteristics as investors. They are risk averse, and they seek to minimise risk by holding a diversified portfolio of assets. This portfolio may also be diversified across currencies. Hence U.S. and U.K. pension funds are large holders and traders in shares in a number of EU Stock Markets. One way of reducing risk is to invest in liquid assets, hence institutional investors have a positive preference for share holdings in larger companies whose shares are more liquid. Pension funds and Insurance companies can also be characterised as passive shareholders. They tend not to vote at Annual General Meetings, and they never seek board representation. Their most common way of expressing dissatisfaction is by selling shares. Hence one implication of large share holdings by pension funds and insurance companies is that stock market volumes are largely determined by institutional shareholders. The size of each trade is also larger, and this in turn has implications for the structures of share trading, which will become more capital intensive. So that in the U.K. Ireland and elsewhere stock broking firms are now often owned by financial institutions, in particular banks.

German banks are an important category of shareholder in German companies. They exercise voting rights on behalf of other shareholders. They appoint representatives to the main board. Their share holdings are held over long time periods. Cable and others have pointed out that banks control in excess of 50% of the number of votes (including proxy votes) in large German companies. Edwards and Fisher cite data from 1980 to the effect that 61 of the top 100 AGs had bank representatives on their boards. The three big banks in turn account for a majority of those appointed to supervisory boards by banks. Because big banks also control the new issue market it is likely that they can also influence the allocation of funds to particular firms. While Edwards and Fisher document the different shareholder firm relationship in the German banking model they question the widely accepted conclusion by Cable (1985) that "there is a significant positive relationship between the degree of bank involvement in leading industrial companies and their financial performance". Critics of the German banking model would also cite recent well publicised examples of the failure of corporate governance structures such as the cases of

Metallgesellschaft and Schneider. Krummel (1980) considers that "banks holding shares are rather more inclined to come to the aid of ailing companies in which participations are held". Hence it is probable that Anglo-Saxon financial relations would have resulted in the demise of Metallgesellschaft, rather than additional loans from its bankers and its ultimate survival.

There are other differences in shareholder patterns between Anglo-Saxon capital markets and EU country capital markets apart from differences in the nature of the financial institution owning shares. Cross holdings of shares are particularly important in some countries such as France. Privatisation of State owned companies further reinforced cross holdings of shares as large blocks of shares were sold to other companies. These holdings are regarded as long term investments. Perhaps as a result of such cross holdings and shared directors public criticism of French companies by shareholders is unusual despite some exceptions (for example the 1995 Annual Meeting of Elf Aquitaine as reported in Financial Times 28/6/95). Demsetz and Lehn (1985) argue that increasing the concentration of stockholders makes shareholders' monitoring more effective and lowers its cost. This proposition does however depend on shareholders exercising their control rights.

Current shareholdings and control patterns in a number of EU countries, for example, control by minority shareholders through differential voting rights and cross holdings, may not be compatible with the growth of cross border stock market flows and multiple listings [5].

5. Regulatory issues

Problems with corporate governance have emerged irrespective of the nature of the financial system. Large country capital markets have been particularly active in recent years to ensure that share trading systems protect investors. Insider trading on stock markets has been illegal for many years in the U.S.

---

5 Any Moves by the EU to remove differential voting rights would particularly affect the dominance of the Wallenberg family in the control of Swedish industry.

It has been illegal in the U.K. since 1980 and is now illegal in all EU capital markets. There have also been well publicised cases of insider trading on the Paris stock market (for example, Pechiney) as well as on the Frankfurt stock exchange. However to a certain extent there is a trade off between the effectiveness of regulation and the cost of regulation. To the extent that different centres are in competition for share trading the centre that has the lowest cost (least regulated) may attract the greatest share trading volume. This sort of competition is sometimes referred to as "the race to the bottom".

The economic case for regulation of non-bank financial firms is generally stated in terms of the nature of the services provided. They are credence goods, that is goods whose quality is difficult to establish or which may never be fully established such as investment advice. Problems of adverse selection and moral hazard may arise as follows. Because services provided are credence goods it is possible that pricing is based on an average rather than quality. Quality is difficult if not impossible to determine with credence goods. This may mean that firms providing higher quality cannot price their services accordingly, and firms providing lower than average quality may charge average prices. Hence below average quality firms will eventually replace above average quality firms. Financial firms also often combine the twin roles of principal and agent, which may also lead to conflict of interest problems.

There are broadly two models for the regulation of financial markets (1) self regulation and (2) State regulation. The U.K. financial markets are an example of self regulation and the U.S. State led regulation. In addition the EU has issued a number of directives which affect financial firms.

In the U.K. the Financial Services Act of 1986 established a statutory body known as the Securities Investment Board (S.I.B.) which in turn authorised self regulatory organisations (SRO's) to regulate financial firms and Recognised Investment Exchanges (R.I.E.s) which run financial markets. The S.I.B. is effectively a regulator of regulators, while the regulators are members of the industry being regulated.

The regulatory structure in London has been subject to a number of criticisms. For example the chairman of Prudential Corporation, the largest life insurance company in the U.K. has called for a move away from self regulation to a statutory basis under full government control. One reason for this viewpoint is the belief that the Prudential Corporation would be a major beneficiary of such an approach, indicating a 'free-rider' problem, that is the inability of potential customers to distinguish good from bad products, which adversely affects firms providing good products and the industry as a whole (Financial Times 4/11/92). The SIB has also been criticised by the retiring chairman in the Annual Review for 1991/92, as being too fragmented and consequent difficulties in investigating insider trading activities (Financial Times 4/6/92).

In contrast the Securities and Exchange Commission (SEC) in the U.S. regulates brokers/dealers in securities and mutual funds and screens security issues to ensure regulations are complied with. It employs a large specialised staff and may prosecute directly for fraud or insider trading rather than relying on other state agencies as in the case in the U.K. Insider trading in the U.S. is a civil offence rather than a criminal offence as it is in the U.K. A civil offence requires a less onerous level of proof making successful prosecutions easier.

Some critics of the SEC (Benston, p. 84) have argued "that the system in use in the UK is more effective, or at least as effective as the U.S. system but the costs are lower". Benston argues that corporations would disclose information voluntarily in the absence of SEC requirements. SEC requirements increase disclosure costs to firms and increase costs of issuing securities, because of the production of unneccessary information. Benston also argues that much of the mandatory disclosure requirements are misleading, for example the accounting treatment of goodwill. According to Benston "a program of government mandated disclosures may actually be unfair to shareholders".

While capital markets in the U.K. and other countries were deregulated in the sense of the removal of restrictive practices and the removal of restrictions on the formation of multiservice financial companies, the financial services industry remains subject to extensive regulation as the industry evolves.

In some European countries the main force for regulation of financial services is the EU. But within Europe the U.S. based SEC is also important in terms of influencing levels of disclosure and in the case of multiple listings providing information to markets with lower disclosure requirements [6]. One reason why the SEC is influential relates to the desire for large companies from different countries to obtain a stock market quotation in New York and hence the need to comply with SEC regulatory requirements. Because of the growth of cross border share trading and multiple listings on core country capital markets, increasingly core country regulatory requirements will determine small/periphery country regulations.

6. Taxation

Taxation is important in explaining differences in the operation of financial markets and in the financing of companies. A good example of tax driven market changes occurred in Sweden in 1984 when a new government introduced a tax of 1% on sales/purchases of securities. This was increased to 2% in 1986. Following these tax changes 60% of the trading volume of the 11 most actively traded Swedish stocks moved to London (Umlauf, 1991).

Taxation may also influence the form of financing of companies. While in all EU countries interest paid on debt is tax deductible, the taxation of dividend distributions varies, so that in effect the higher the payout ratio the higher the corporate tax rate, thus providing an incentive to finance by retentions. In some countries corporate tax rates are lower than in others. In Ireland companies classified as manufacturing pay corporate tax at a rate of 10%. Thus the tax deductibility of interest payments is much less important for these companies. Given free capital mobility in terms of investment and finance, there will be a tendency for risk adjusted rates of return on capital to become equal. Hence countries with high corporate tax rates may experience capital outflows.

---

6 The Guinness takeover of Distillers in the U.K. and the takeover by the French company Pechiney of Triangle are examples of information relating to insider dealing originating in the U.S. (Financial Times, 2/8/93).

Conversely countries with low corporate tax rates or low tax rates on investment income will experience capital inflows. The size of these inflows and outflows will in turn place constraints on possibilities for divergent tax strategies. In practice the larger capital exporting economies have considerable incentives to ensure that tax competition does not result in a reduction in tax revenues.

Apart from distortions in the allocation of investment, different rates of tax and tax systems result in incentives to avoid tax by using complex corporate structures and the use profit switching transfer pricing. Profit switching transfer pricing involves pricing intra-company transactions in such a way as to maximise profits in the lowest tax area. Apart from reductions in tax revenue, the pursuit of tax efficiency may also be at the expense of operational efficiency.

Harmonisation of corporate tax rates and tax rates on investment income within the EU is likely to prove difficult. The Ruding Report which investigated distortions within the EU due to different corporate tax regimes identified the absence of neutrality with respect to the location of investments as being an impediment to obtaining the benefits from a single market. The Ruding report identified two different types of neutrality (1) capital import neutrality which requires that the marginal effective tax rate on suppliers of capital in any country be the same. This principle would imply that income is taxed where it arises. (2) The second main principle is termed capital export neutrality which means that tax policy should not affect the location decisions of individuals or companies. This could be achieved if income were taxed on a residence basis. The Ruding Report made various recommendations which attempt to reduce tax distortion problems for example removing double taxation of dividends paid between subsidiaries and parent companies, implementation of rules to solve transfer pricing disputes, and introducing a minimum corporate tax rate.

The different ways that corporate taxes and individual income taxes interact can pose considerable distortions for example in the case of Advanced Corporation Tax in the U.K. This refers to the tax deducted from dividends on behalf of shareholders. The company was effectively collecting tax on behalf of the State.

This tax was then regarded as an advance payment of corporation tax. If a company paid no dividends no ACT was payable. Problems arise where there is a divergence between where profits are earned and where shareholders live. Where profits were earned abroad and taxed abroad, ACT could not be offset against foreign tax payments. This particular regime acted as a deterrent to foreign investment by U.K. companies and has resulted in a number of changes to the tax code.

In summary, fiscal systems in various European countries are not neutral with respect to the financing of companies and the taxation of corporate income, and returns to investors. Part of the observed differences in financing patterns may reflect these differences. Tax competition and the desire of capital exporting countries to protect their tax bases could result in greater harmonisation, but also a reduction in the ability of different countries to have different and perhaps more appropriate fiscal systems to their needs.

7. Correlation between capital markets

The international stock market crash of 1987 led to considerable research interest in the extent to which different stock markets are correlated. This research had two main motivations. The first of these was to discover whether some trading systems resulted in less volatility; the second objective was to discover the extent to which different stock markets were correlated which has implications for risk reduction via international portfolio diversification. This research is of considerable interest in examining dominant stock markets within the EU.

Roll (1988) examined monthly movements in stock market indicies in local currencies over the period June 1981-September 1987 for a number of countries. German stock market movements were found to be highly correlated with those of Switzerland, Holland and Austria. French and Belgian stock markets were also positively correlated. The U.S. Canadian and U.K. stock markets were also found to be positively correlated. Negative correlations were found between the Danish and Austrian Stock markets. An earlier study by Eun and Resnick examined monthly returns converted to $US from a sample of individual shares in different stock markets for the period 1973-82. Returns thus take into consideration currency movements and share price movements. Of the eight countries examined the stock market returns of Germany, the Netherlands and Switzerland had the highest correlation. In a later paper Eun and Resnick examined the effect of currency changes on stock market returns to a U.S. investor using weekly data for stock market indices for the period 1980-85. Of the countries examined exchange rate movements were more volatile than stock market movements for Switzerland and nearly as volatile for France and the U.K. Rather surprisingly these authors found a positive correlation between exchange rate movements and stock market movements for the countries examined (Canada, France, Germany, Japan, the U.K. and the U.S.).

Bertero and Mayer examined share price movements for 23 countries (including 13 European countries) both before and after the 1987 crash, using daily data relating to share indicies. Of the 23 markets examined they report four groups of countries whose stock market indicies were particularly closely correlated. These groups were: (1) Canada, the U.S. and the U.K. (2) Switzerland, the Netherlands and West Germany; (3) France, Belgium and Italy and (4) Singapore, Australia and Malayasia. Bertero and Meyer also conclude that all stock markets have become more correlated since the 1987 crash.

Roll (1992) examined intercountry correlation coefficients of stock market indicies for the period April 1988-March 1991. Similar results were found as for other studies. European stock markets in particular were found to have become more highly correlated. For example Roll reports correlation coefficients in terms of $US for the French Stock market with markets in Germany, the Netherlands and Switzerland of 0,68, 0,72 and 0,69 respectively. This increase in correlation in market movements in turn reflects closer integration with other European economies in terms of interest rates, currencies and the economic cycle. However Roll concludes that intercountry stock market correlations can be explained by similarities in their quoted industries. The more similar the quoted industrial structure the greater the intercountry correlation.

Roll also calculates a Herfindahl industry concentration index for 24 countries. In general smaller stock markets have higher concentration indicies with a large proportion of the value of the stock market accounted for by quoted companies in the financial sector in for example, Austria, Belgium and Ireland. Roll also reports that stock market returns when expressed in local currency are negatively correlated with currency changes.

8. Differences in the financing of companies

Although the capital markets of Anglo-Saxon countries are sometimes described as if they are homogeneous there are important differences between them. For example issues of bonds (in particular quoted bonds) are far larger than issues of equity shares in the U.S. (Masulis, Table 1.2). Quoted bonds are rarely issued in the U.K. It has been possible to repurchase ordinary shares in the U.S. for a number of years. This fact coupled with takeovers financed by debt resulted in a net reduction of issued ordinary shares in the U.S. over the period 1984-88 (Brealey and Myers, Fig. 14.1).

Despite the far greater size of capital markets in Anglo-Saxon financial systems compared with bank or credit dominated financial systems, internally generated funds are important in all economies and indeed are the single largest source of funds for firms in most years irrespective of the nature of the financial system. There are difficulties in making satisfactory inter-country comparisons because of different accounting conventions. For the same reason Balance Sheet analysis of debt/equity ratios is subject to considerable uncertainty.

Bank borrowing is also more important in the U.K. than the U.S. In a comparison of the financing of U.K. and German firms over the period 1970-89 Edwards and Fisher conclude most investment was financed with internally generated funds. Bank borrowing was the largest external source in both countries but was much less significant than internal sources. They conclude (p. 68) "There is no evidence to support the view that banks are a more important source of finance in Germany than the U.K.". Despite the importance of internally generated funds there are important differences between countries in the relative proportion of retained profits. Mayer and Alexander report that over the period 1982-88 U.K. firms had dividend payout ratios of 31% compared with 13% for German firms. These high payout ratios are in turn explained by some commentators as being due to (a) the relative importance of pension funds as shareholders and (b) an overemphasis on short term factors, the assumption being that high dividend payout ratios will result in higher share prices.

9. Anglo-American markets versus the european model

Removal of restrictions on capital flows and investment has resulted in greater capital mobility within the EU. This in turn has resulted in greater competition between capital markets both as a source of funds and as a location for secondary trading in shares. This competition has emphasised the differences that exist in the organisation of capital markets, the nature of shareholders, and the financing of companies. This chapter has considered some of these differences within the EU broadly characterised as: market based (Anglo-Saxon); and banking based (German model). Briefly, market based capital markets are characterised by a greater number of quoted companies, a higher ratio of stock market values to GNP; and by an active takeover market. In banking or credit based capital markets contested takeovers are rare. This may be explained by a number of factors, for example the existence of differential voting rights in non Anglo-American type stock markets. Some shares may have no votes or far more votes than other shares. Equity shares in Anglo-American markets are characterised by one share one vote (although there are rare exceptions). There are also differences in the nature of the shareholder and the extent of cross-holdings which result in differences in corporate governance, for example, in whether larger shareholders seek board representation. Finally, partly reflecting these different characteristics, there are differences in regulation. Regulatory structures themselves are responsive to competitive forces, with the more highly regulated markets, which have higher costs, experiencing a competitive disadvantage with less highly regulated markets.

One effect of this competition is to introduce changes in the organisation and operation of different capital markets. Change has also occurred as a result of various EU directives, for example in relation to the level of disclosure. One likely consequence of increased competition is the dominance of smaller country capital markets by larger country capital markets. This in turn will have implications for the sources of investment funds. For example, to the extent that the London exchange becomes dominant, larger companies within the EU will have shares quoted on London as well as on a domestic market. Markets are likely to become more alike in their price setting, with a wholesale/retail distinction in terms of the cost of trading. It is also likely that efficiency in terms of the cost of trading, uniform pricing and liquidity will result in regional markets within a country (such as the German exchanges) merging with the larger market within the country (Financial Times 9/5/95). Trading in small country capital markets may in turn consist largely of smaller domestic companies. Such distinctions are likely to further widen the costs of finance (and/or availability of finance) between peripheral capital markets and core capital markets.

A movement towards Anglo-American type financial markets may also increase the cost of equity capital (Mayer, 1994), because of the importance of dividends as a signaling device. While an active market for corporate control is seen as an essential element of Anglo-American capital markets its introduction into other markets could result in some disadvantages. Prevezer and Rickets (1994, p. 243) argue that well documented increases in returns to shareholders resulting from takeovers may not be derived from efficiency gains but from "redirected rents" or the returns to specific assets. Others have argued that takeover gains may be a result of the breaking of implicit contracts such as employee pension rights.

An emphasis on an active market for corporate control may also mean particular ownership structures may become difficult to achieve, for example cross-holdings and associated board representation. Mayer (1994, p. 191) argues this in turn could adversely affect activities requiring cooperation from different stakeholders (employees, supplying firms, banks), such as new markets and product development.

On balance it is likely that many differences in capital markets within the EU will persist. It is unlikely, for example, that pension funds will become as important in other EU countries as they are in the U.K. Differences in shareholders and in corporate governance are also likely to remain with the consequence that hostile takeovers will continue to remain less frequent in capital markets other than that of the U.K. For this and other reasons the London Stock Exchange is likely to remain the largest market in terms of secondary trading, but other regional centres (Frankfort and Paris) can be expected to become major centres for new capital issues for firms.

Résumé

Interactions entre les bourses européennes du centre et de la périphérie

L'espace financier européen devrait en principe devenir de plus en plus homogène en raison à la fois de la libre circulation des capitaux et des directives (ou politiques) inspirées par les organes communautaires. Pour le moment les systèmes institutionnels nationaux et la réalité de blocs monétaires distincts expliquent encore l'existence de nombreuses divergences qui s'expriment notamment par :

- l'importance relative des marchés financiers en termes de capitalisation boursière et de nombre de sociétés cotées,
- la part des sociétés domestiques et des sociétés internationales cotées sur les différentes places,
- les modes d'évaluation et d'échange des actions,
- le rôle des banques dans le financement des entreprises,
- la nature des actionnaires actifs sur les marchés (fonds de pension, sociétés d'assurance, banques, particuliers),
- des réglementations plus ou moins contraignantes,
- le coût des transactions,
- l'impact de la taxation des capitaux, évidemment loin d'être neutre.

L'auteur présente les études qui ont été faites sur les corrélations des mouvements boursiers (prix, rendements, échanges, cycles économiques...) calculées pour les principaux marchés européens et nord-américains. L'opposition entre un modèle anglo-américain et un modèle européen (continental) se trouve confirmée, mais ces différences vont-elles perdurer avec l'achèvement de l'Union européenne ? L'auteur donne une réponse positive et l'explicite, avec les conséquences que l'on peut en attendre notamment au niveau des marchés primaires (émission de capital) pour lesquels Francfort et Paris semblent bien placées et au niveau des marchés secondaires où Londres maintient sa domination.

Zusammenfassung

Interaktionen zwischen zentralen und peripհären europäischen Börsen

Der europäische Finanzraum müßte eigentlich als Folge des freien Kapitalverkehrs und der von den Organen der Europäischen Gemeinschaft erlassenen Richtlinien immer homogener werden. Die weiterhin bestehenden institutionellen Systeme der Mitgliedsstaaten und das Vorhandensein der verschiedenen Währungsblöcke erklären jedoch das Weiterbestehen zahlreicher Unterschiede. Diese sind im einzelnen:

- die relative Bedeutung der Finanzmärkte in bezug auf den Börsenwert und die Anzahl der an der Börse notierten Unternehmen,
- der Anteil der nationalen und der internationalen Unternehmen, die an den verschiedenen Plätzen gehandelt werden,
- die Modi der Aktienbewertung und des Aktienhandels,
- die Rolle der Banken bei der Finanzierung der Unternehmen,
- die Besonderheiten der am Markt tätigen Anteilseigner (Altersversorgungsfonds, Versicherungsgesellschaften, Banken, Privatpersonen),
- mehr oder weniger strenge gesetzliche Regelungen,
- die Transaktionskosten,
- die Wirkung der durchaus nicht neutralen Kapitalbesteuerung.

Der Autor legt die Ergebnisse der Untersuchungen vor, die über die Korrelationen der Börsenbewegungen (Preise, Erträge, Umsätze, Konjunkturzyklen...) an den bedeutendsten europäischen und nordamerikanischen Börsen durchgeführt wurden. Der Gegensatz zwischen dem angelsächsischen und dem kontinentaleuropäischen Modell wird dabei bestätigt. Werden diese Unterschiede nach der Vollendung der Europäischen Union weiterbestehen? Der Autor bejaht ausdrücklich diese Frage und verweist auf die Konsequenzen für den Primärmarkt (Kapitalemissionen), auf dem Frankfurt und Paris eine gute Ausgangsposition besitzen, und für den Sekundärmarkt, auf dem London seine Vorherrschaft beibehalten wird.

References

BENSTON, G.J. (1985): "Towards a Cost/Benefit Analysis of the SEC: Have the British a Better Way ?". Midland Corporate Finance Journal. vol. 3. no. 2. pp. 66-85.

BERTERO, E./MAYER C. (1989): "Structure and performance: Global Interdependence of Stock Markets Around the Crash of October 1987". London. Centre for Economic Policy Research. Discussion paper no. 307.

BEST, M.H. (1990): The New Competition; Institutions of Industrial Restructuring. Cambridge. Polity Press.

BREALEY R.A./MYERS S.C. (1991): Principles of Corporate Finance. 4th ed. New York. McGraw-Hill.

BRUNEEL, D. (1991): "The Reform of the French Financial System". in Cavanna H. Financial Innovation. London. Routledge.

CABLE, J. (1985): "Capital Market Information and Industrial Performance: The Role of West German Banks". Economic Journal. vol. 95. no. 377. pp. 118-132.

CHRISTENSEN, J.L. (1992): "The Role of Finance in National Systems of Innovation". in Bengt-Ake Lundvall (ed.). National Systems of Innovation: Towards a Theory of Innovation and Interactive Learning. London. Lintner.

DAVIS, E.P. (1990): "The Development of Pension Funds - An International Comparison". Bank of England Quarterly Report.

DAVIS, E.W./YEOMANS, K.A. (1974): Company Finance and the Capital Market. Cambridge. Cambridge University Press.

DEMSETZ/LEHN (1985): "The Structure of Corporate Ownership: Causes and Consequences. Journal of Political Economy. vol. 93. pp. 1155-77.

DEMIRAG, I./TYLECOTE, A./MORRIS, B. (1994): "Accounting for Financial and Managerial Causes of Short-Term Pressures in British Corporations". Journal of Business Finance and Accounting. vol. 21. no. 8. pp.1195-1213.

EDWARDS, J./FISHER K. Banks (1993): Finance and Investment in Germany. Cambridge. Cambridge University Press.

EITEMAN, D.K./STONEHILL , A.I./MOFFETT, M.H. (1992): Multinational Business Finance. 6th ed. New York. Addison-Wesley publishing Co.

EUN, C./RESNICK, B. (1984): "Estimating the Correlation Structure of International Share prices". Journal of Finance. December. pp. 1311-1344.

EUN, C./RESNICK, B. (1988): Exchange Rate Uncertainty, Forward Contract and International Portfolio Selection. Journal of Finance. March. pp. 197-215.

KRUMMEL, H.-J. (1980): "German Universal Banking Scrutinized". Journal of Banking and Finance. Vol. 4. pp. 33-55.

MASULIS, R.W. (1988): The Debt Equity Choice. New York. Ballinger Press..

MAYER, C./ALEXANDER, I. (1990): "Banks and Securities Markets: Corporate Financing in Germany and the United Kingdom". Journal of the Japanese and International Economies. vol. 4. pp. 450-475.

MAYER, C. (1994): "Stock Markets, Financial Institutions, and Corporate Performance". in N. Dimsdale and M. Prevezer. Capital Markets and Corporate Governance. Oxford. Clarendon Press.

MILES, D. (1993): "Testing for Short Termism in the UK Stock Market". Economic Journal. vol. 103. no. 421. pp.1379-1396.

PAGANO, M./ROELL, A. (1990): Trading Systems in European Stock Exchanges: Current Performance and Policy Options. London. Centre for Economic Policy Research.

PREVEZER, M./RICKETTS, M. (1994): "Corporate Governance: The UK Compared With Germany and Japan". in N. Dimsdale and M. Prevezer. Capital Markets and Corporate Governance. Oxford. Clarendon Press.

ROLL, R. (1988): "The International Crash of October 1987". Financial Analysts Journal. September-October. pp. 19-35.

ROLL, R. (1992): "Industrial Structure and the Comparative Behaviour of International Stock Market Indices". Journal of Finance. vol. XLVII. no. 1. pp. 3- 41.

RUDING REPORT (1992): Report of the Committee of Independent Experts on Company Taxation. Brussels. Commission of the European Communities.

SATCHELL, S.E./DAMANT, D.C. (1995): "Testing for Short Termism in the U.K. Stock Market: A Comment". Economic Journal. vol. 105. no. 432. pp. 1218-1223.

SHONFIELD, A. (1965): Modern Capitalism, The Changing Balance of Public and Private Power. London. Oxford University Press.

UMLAUF, S.R. (1991): "Transaction Taxes and Stock Market Behaviour: The Swedish Experience". Institute of Finance and Accounting London Business School. Working paper 150-91.

WILSON REPORT (1980): Committee to Review the Functioning of Financial Institutions. London. H.M.S.O. cmnd 7937.

ZYSMAN, J. (1983): Governments, Markets and Growth: Financial Systems and the Politics of Industrial Change. Oxford. Robertson.

William Kingston

What Kind of Patent System Does Europe Need?

1. Introduction

2. How well does the present patent system perform?

3. Why does the system work so badly?
   A. It protects invention, not innovation
   B. Much valuable information is not protected

4. The importance of "tacit" knowledge
   A. Technology and science

5. The "circles of meaning"
   A. Protectable "core" information
   B. "That something can be done"
   C. "There is a market for it"

6. Why patents work for chemical inventions

7. Alternative ways of protecting information
   A. Secrecy
   B. Capability, persuasive and specific market power
   C. Relative unimportance of patents

8. Excessive cost of patent litigation

9. International changes in protection means
   A. Loss of capability to the Pacific Rim
   B. U.S. retains dominance in persuasive market power
   C. Japan as a force in international patenting
   D. Europe's special need for effective patents

10. The funding crisis in basic research
    A. The "virtuous circle" of research funding
    B. Virtuous circle broken

11. How might the patent system be improved?

12. Reducing the cost of resolving disputes
    A. Compulsory arbitration with legal aid
    B. Sources of arbitrators and funds for legal aid

13. Direct protection of innovation

14. Compulsory licensing
    A. Capital payments as well as royalties?

15. Other possible improvements
    A. Giving weight to tacit knowledge
    B. The need for innovation offices
    C. Modification of "national treatment"
    D. Patents for scientific discoveries?

16. Conclusion

1. Introduction

The standard definition of a patent is that it is a bargain between an inventor and the State. In this, the inventor agrees not to keep what has been discovered secret, but to disclose it to the public through the formal mechanism of the system. In return for this disclosure, the State grants the inventor a monopoly of making, using and selling the invention for a prescribed period.

From this definition, it follows that patents are concerned with:

- Information, since this is what the inventor dedicates to the public; and
- Means of preventing others making use of the information disclosed, since this is what the State purports to give in exchange for the disclosure.

This Chapter will examine how well the performance of the existing patent system lives up to its promises, and will show that it does so very poorly. It will then show that this is largely due to failures to adapt the system to growth in our understanding of the nature of information and of the different means by which it it can be protected. It will be further shown that these failures have had a particularly adverse effect on innovation in Europe, and in the final section of the Chapter some suggestions will be offered for modifying the system in the interests of European economies.

2. How well does the present patent system perform?

There is now an irrefutable body of empirical evidence that the patent system fails to deliver the protection for information which it promises. Mansfield's research in the U.S. showed that effective duplication of a typical patented product is possible within 3 years, and, even worse, that it would not cost the imitator more than the innovator (Mansfield et al., 1981). The system works best for the chemical industry, but even for inventions of this type, patents raise imitation costs by no more than 40 percentage points. Poor as this is, it is far better than the 7 to 10 points for, e.g., electronics.

U.S. firms put Patent protection far behind marketing techniques as means for capturing the rewards of their investments in R&D (Levin et al., 1987). British engineering firms say that "very little" of their R&D depends upon the existence of the Patent system (Taylor and Silberston, 1973). Patents which were later held to be valid did not prevent the innovating firm from being driven out of the market for their CAT-Scanner invention - "the greatest advance in diagnostic technique since X-Rays".

3. Why does the system work so badly?

A. It protects invention, not innovation

The first reason for the poor performance of the modern patent system is that its objective is to protect invention, and not innovation. That is, its emphasis is on discoveries, rather than on the activity of turning discoveries into concrete reality. This is the opposite of what it did originally, as in the earliest grants to Alpine miners, in the Venetian Ordinance of 1474 and in the 1623 Statute of Monopolies in England. The modern Patent system has a quite different emphasis, because it is a creation of the nineteenth century. Because of its intellectual origins in the natural rights thinking which inspired both the French and American Revolutions, it protects inventors - "those who find new things" - in contrast to the earlier system, which protected innovators - "those who get new things *done*".

By protecting invention directly, it protects innovation only indirectly. What protection an innovation gets, therefore, depends upon how strong the link is between it and its related invention. This goes far to explain the differential performance of the patent system according to the subject matter of the invention. In chemicals this link is strong, so Patents work much better for them than they do for mechanical and electrical innovations, where the link is weak (for a more extensive treatment of these points, see Kingston, 1987).

B. Much valuable information is not protected

The patent system operates on the very simplistic assumption that information is a commodity. Beginning in 1713 in England, patent applications have included a written description of an invention which should enable someone else who is "skilled in the relevant art" to replicate it. For modern information theory, communication is a much more complex matter. As developed by writers such as Shannon and Weaver (1949) and McKay (1969) it distinguishes between "information", "knowledge" and "meaning". Information is measured in terms of "surprise", i.e., the probability that the recipient does not possess it already; knowledge is a loose structure made up of some of the items of information which have been received in the past; and meaning is the relationship between a particular knowledge structure and a new piece of information which reaches it.

Not all of the information which reaches a particular recipient becomes incorporated in the corresponding knowledge structure. Much information passes through the loose structure without having an impact upon it at all, some reinforces parts of the existing structure, and occasionally a message may have such an impact as to cause a radical rearrangement of the knowledge structure - i.e. it has a great deal of meaning. These relationships have been well summed up by Langlois:

> Information is not homogeneous, meaning is a matter of form, not of amount; and the value or significance of a message depends as much on the pre-existing form of the receiver as on the message itself...[I]nformation is stored in a system not as oil is stored in a tank, but by virtue of the change the information makes in the very organization of the system itself. In a fundamental sense, knowledge and organization are identical (1983, p. 593).

In terms of patents, the important point to note is that a message ("information") by itself is literally meaningless, since meaning implies a related mind. Because information only has meaning in relation to an existing knowledge structure, its meaning will be different for every recipient.

However, as it is operated at present, the patent system ignores this completely, assuming that precise, unambiguous meaning can be "poured" into a patent specification by the inventor, and that exactly the same meaning can be taken out by all other interested parties, from the Examiner in the Patent Office to a rival who wishes to "free-ride" on the inventor's labour and investment.

3. The importance of "tacit" knowledge

Another important dimension has been added to our modern understanding of information by the work of Michael Polanyi. It is to him above all that we owe the concept of "tacit" knowledge (which of course forms part of an individual's knowledge structure on which meaning depends, as noted above). Tacit knowledge only exists in actual use, and can only be articulated and communicated very partially. In Polanyi's famous phrase, "we always know more than we can tell". It can be contrasted with explicit or scientific knowledge, which is capable of being transmitted in symbolic form to anyone who learns the symbols. Because of this, a child today can come to have exactly the same understanding of the relationships of geometric shapes as Euclid had.

Obviously, the tacit part of our knowledge structure, in its relationship to messages which reach us, may have an important effect on the meaning which these messages have for us. In turn, this meaning changes our capacity to make decisions in respect of this information. Unfortunately, the source of this change is ignored by the patent system, which only recognises knowledge that is explicit. The patent system has no room - indeed, *can* have no room - for tacit knowledge.

It might be argued that to a very slight extent in its U.S. version it does recognise that a patent specification may not capture all the information there is in an invention because it allows "unexpected commercial success" as ground for overcoming a rejection by the examiner for lack of an inventive step. Such an argument is very weak because of the practical reality that commercial success may in fact be attributable to access to distribution, or to the scale of investment in advertising, much more than to any informational factors.

A. Technology and science

Tacit knowledge, therefore, is the type of knowledge which is related to technology, and is as old as the first tool-using animal. One learns a technique by practising it, just as one learns to play a game by playing it, not by reading books about how to do either. Scientific knowledge, as a part of explicit knowledge, had its origins as recently as the Classical period in Greece, and, moreover, only reached the Western world in medieval times, and then in a roundabout way through Islamic culture in North Africa and Spain.

In fact, the partial union between science and technology in the applied science and engineering which is typical today is much younger still, dating only from the middle of the last century, well after the industrial revolution got under way. The modern patent system, which in Europe can be dated from the 1877 German legislation, reflects an emphasis on science rather than technology in its simplistic approach to information. It completely ignores the importance - especially for decision-making - of tacit knowledge.

The relationship between science and technology is far from being fully explored, and how tacit knowledge interacts with explicit knowledge will certainly be an important part of the future study of this relationship. The effect of information that is significant to a recipient is to change that recipient's knowledge structure, and this change can apply to the tacit part of this structure as well as to the explicit (scientific) part. Since tacit knowledge only exists in use, and is only partly communicable, it is probably mainly used for the continuation of routines already learned (even though these routines may be extremely complex).

Nevertheless, tacit knowledge has a special part to play in innovation, which is the putting of new ideas into effect. This is because the explicit knowledge required for this is never complete, and doing anything new invariably means acting in the absence of some information which is theoretically desirable.

It is in fact a well-accepted characteristic of innovators and entrepreneurs, that they are able to take decisions and to act under these conditions. This suggests the possibility that it is their tacit knowledge which makes the difference to their power of decision-making - and patents, as has been seen, do not protect knowledge of this kind.

5. The "circles of meaning"

In terms of modern information theory, and especially in the light of knowledge having a tacit as well as an explicit component, the information which a particular invention generates can be illustrated in the following diagram of "Circles of Meaning".

A. Protectable "core" information

The innermost circle represents the invention itself, as it is supposed to be protected by the patent system. This consists of information that is of practical use, that is not already known anywhere in the world, and that involves an "inventive step", defined as "not obvious to one skilled in the relevant Art". All patent systems purport to protect technical equivalents of any of the elements of an invention, as well as its "preferred embodiment".

B. "That something can be done"

However, the invention also delivers the important and valuable information "that something can be done" (the second "circle of meaning") and this is not protected by the patent system. When this information reaches the knowledge structures of competitors, it brings about changes in both their tacit and explicit components. One of the most important aspects of the relationship between information about the invention and the tacit knowledge of a recipient, is the way it can stimulate advertence to other possible ways of achieving the same technical or commercial end.

'Circles of Meaning'

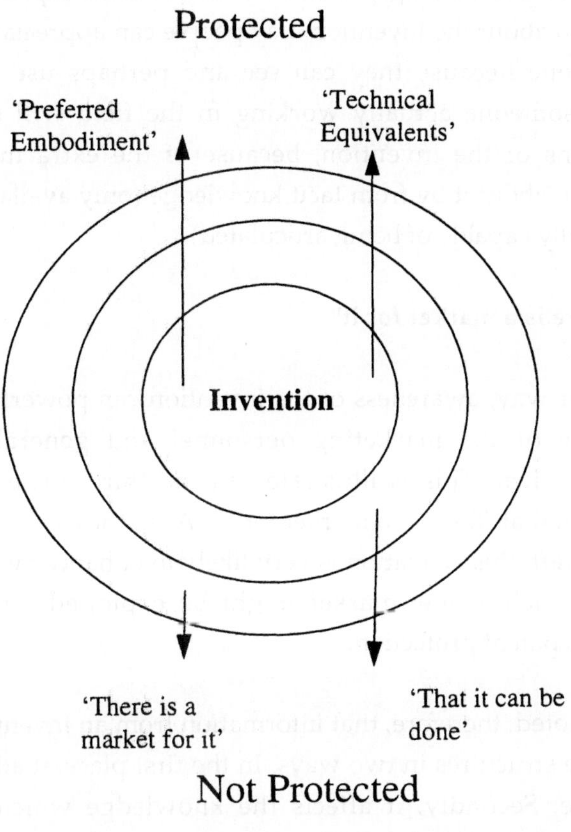

At least part of such ways will almost certainly have been present already in the recipient's tacit knowledge, but it may only become explicit in the context of the information about the invention. Lay people can appreciate that something can now be done because they can see and perhaps use the related product. But only someone actually working in the field will be alerted to all the implications of the invention, because of the extra meaning given to the information about it by from tacit knowledge (only available in actual use, and only partially capable of being articulated).

C. "There is a market for it"

In a similar way, awareness of the invention can powerfully activate the tacit knowledge of the marketing personnel and general management of a competitor firm. This is illustrated in the third circle, which contains the information that "there is a market for it". As in the case of the competitor firm's technical staff, this activation is very likely to enhance awareness of alternative ways in which a new market might be exploited without infringing the invention's patent protection.

It will be noted, therefore, that information from an invention modifies existing knowledge structures in two ways. In the first place, it adds to existing *explicit* knowledge. Secondly, it affects the knowledge which was *tacit* amongst recipients of the information, so as to make at least some of this explicit. These changes in the overall structure of knowledge (both tacit and explicit) of the technical, marketing and general management personnel of a firm in the same field as that of the firm which made the invention, or in a related field, gives information about the invention a quite special meaning for them. This meaning can have a powerful effect upon their capacity to make relevant decisions, notably, of course, decisions to compete with the originator of the invention to the latter's disadvantage. Yet none of the information which is literally "meaning-full" when it comes into relation with particular knowledge structures, is protected by a patent.

6. Why patents work for chemical inventions

Using the "circles of meaning" in relation to tacit and explicit knowledge also helps to explain why the patent system works so much better for chemical inventions than it does for other kinds. This is because in chemicals, the formula which has been arrived at in the laboratory, the formula which receives patent protection and the formula of the product which is eventually bought by the user, are all identical.

Further, competitors have no opportunity to produce a near-substitute by making small changes to the formula in the hope of producing a product which can obtain a share of the originator's market without infringing the patent monopoly. This is because the slightest change in a chemical formula may produce something which is radically different in performance from the original - in pharmaceuticals, a healing drug may even be turned into a harmful one.

Consequently, learning about a chemical invention brings about almost no stimulation of the tacit knowledge of chemists in competitive firms to envision alternative ways of achieving the same end without infringing the inventor's protection. Neither can information about the invention have an effect on the tacit knowledge of the competitor firm's marketing personnel, since they can have little possibility of being able to sell a minor variant of the invention. The information generated by a chemical patent is therefore virtually restricted to the core, explicit information about the invention, and this is protectable by the patent system. The information in the outer circles, "that it can be done" and "there is a market for it", has little "surprise" - and consequently little meaning - for the recipients of information about a chemical invention, whereas it is highly meaningful for recipients in non-chemical fields.

7. Alternative ways of protecting information

The patent system, then, does a very poor job of protecting investments in generating information, except for chemical inventions. This is partly because it only protects innovation indirectly, and partly because it fails to protect much information that is full of meaning for competitors of those who do innovate. Why is this failure important, and why, in particular, is it especially harmful to innovation and economic development in Europe? The first part of the answer lies in the fact that patents have never been the only way of protecting information.

A. Secrecy

Secrecy, if it can be maintained, protects tacit as well as explicit information perfectly. The Venetians were able to maintain a most valuable monopoly in respect of ornamental glass-blowing for several centuries in spite of the strong desire on the part of others throughout Europe to copy them. They achieved this through secrecy. Much of the information in this case must have been tacit, in the skills of the workers in the State glass factory, but the knowledge that if any of these went to work abroad in response to the tempting offers which were frequently made to them, the Venetian secret service would track them down and put out their eyes, seems to have been a most effective deterrent.

In the absence of such extreme sanctions, however, secrecy is very difficult to maintain over valuable information. This is probably the reason, indeed, why it was the Venetians themselves who established a very early patent system in 1474, as a means of attracting "ingenious men" to their city. This made grants of monopoly for as long as 80 years (Mandich, 1948). Patents are one alternative to secrecy, but there are others. In fact, a firm's activity of keeping "free-riders" away from its information can be seen as part of its wider activity of keeping competitors away from its markets. Clearly, if a competitor can use information which it has cost a particular firm money to develop, that competitor can share in the market for any resulting product or improvement to a product. A firm's ability to keep its information to itself, then, is an aspect of its ability to keep its markets to itself.

B. Capability, persuasive and specific market power

This ability is known as market power, which can be classified in three ways (for a detailed discussion of this classification, see Kingston, 1984). First of all, there is the market power of capability, obtained by investment in productive assets. These enable a firm to do something better than its competitors, or even do something which its competitors cannot do at all. Secondly, there is the market power of persuasion, obtained by investment in marketing resources, especially advertising. This enables the firm to add a "psychological ingredient" to its physical product. The combination is incorporated in a Brand, which has the great advantage of being a legal monopoly through Trade Mark registration law. Thirdly, there is Specific market power, which is any means of keeping competitors out of a market which results from Government action, through some edict or particular piece of legislation. Patents for invention, of course, are an important variant of Specific market power, as are most kinds of official license.

Every firm uses all three types of market power, although it uses them in different proportions. Also, all types of market power can deliver protection for investment in generating information. This has particularly important implications for European firms, which will be explored below.

C. Relative unimportance of patents

From the broad perspective of market power as protector of information, it is quite remarkable how small a part of economic activity is affected by the patent system today. A recent survey for the European Patent Office, for example, was carried out on the basis that only 3% of the 13 million firms in the EU (360,000 firms) are either actual or potential users of the system. These were 20% of firms in production industries. The survey found that only 56,000 firms had made a patent application at some stage, and estimated that a further 111,000 could be regarded as potential users of the patent system, since they did some research and development (Eposcript 3, 1994).

These last two figures are especially interesting, because what they show is that 2 out of every 3 firms which are specifically involved in generating information (because they do some R&D) must be using some other type of market power than the specific market power of the patent system, to prevent free-riders getting access to whatever valuable information they produce. It is a reasonable corollary that the remaining one-third of firms, which do use the patent system, also use the other types of market power to protect the results of their R&D.

The very narrow range of usage of the patent system is further confirmed by statistics which show that of the 120 classes of the International Patent Classification System, 48% of applications to the European Patent Office come from no more than 10. These classes relate mainly to the chemical and electrical/electronic industries (European Patent Office Report, 1994).

8. Excessive cost of patent litigation

Bouju's 1988 study of international patent litigation for the EU showed a clear need for drastic measures to reduce the cost of settling disputes. An official U.S. report recently concluded that:

> unless the problems of cost and delay in patent litigation are addressed now, the central purpose of the patent system to provide an effective incentive for development and commercialization of new technology will be seriously eroded. Such an erosion could well prove a threat to the very existence of the patent system..." (1992, p. 76).

Large firms have enormous opportunities at present for imposing burdens on their opponents in litigation in terms of delays and discovery actions. The result is to make the patent system virtually useless to all but the largest firms as a means of protecting investment in generating information. The same U.S. Commission observed that:

> the delays and complexity of modern patent litigation have provided overly aggressive lawyers with an ample assortment of opportunities to stall, delay and harass. The net of these factors is that patent litigation has become an increasingly inefficient, ineffective and undesirable means of resolving patent-related disputes (1992, p. 78).

Because of the scale of litigation costs, a series of alternative dispute resolution means has developed, mainly in the United States, Arbitration is the most promising of these procedures, but because this is voluntary, it is of no help in the many instances where the cost of litigation intimidates - and is indeed intended to intimidate - attempts to obtain justice in patent cases.

9. International changes in protection means

A problem which Europe shares with the United States is the modern strength of their rivals on the Pacific Rim. This has seriously undermined the ability of Western firms to protect the information which they generate, through their market power of capability. Up to World War II any failure of the patent system to protect the results of investment in R&D by Western firms could be compensated for by their market power of this type, since they possessed it to an unrivalled degree. This is well illustrated by a letter from Thomas Edison, whose firm (which became U.S. General Electric) was one of the most patent-conscious that has ever existed, but which decided to allow its electricity patents to be infringed. In this letter, Edison noted that they could safely do this, because "the business ascendancy we have acquired is of itself sufficient to give us a practical monopoly" (cf. Passer, 1953, p. 100). In other words, their market power of capability was able to substitute for the specific market power of the patent system.

As long as Western firms were dominant in terms of capability market power, any information which they generated which the patent system could not protect, was still barred to free-riders unless these possessed matching capability. Any Western firm which had the capability to invent, develop, manufacture and put on the market a new product or an old product with a new feature, before its competitors, could thereby gain a competitive advantage over them. It would not get the whole of any market, because its competitors would be able to gain access to the information generated by the originator and so catch up sooner or later. However, the originator's profits from the lead time gained would still be enough to justify the risk of investing to produce the information. The requirement of matching capability meant that any Pacific Rim firms of the time could not make commercial use of the information, even when they could obtain it, since either they could not produce the relevant product at all, or if they could produce it, they were unable to match product quality, nor to achieve the necessary economies of scale to compete in terms of price.

A. Loss of capability to the Pacific Rim

Today, this situation is completely changed. The balance of advantage in terms of capability market power has shifted definitively to the Pacific Rim countries. No Western firm can now rely only on its capability market power to protect an investment in generating information. All the information it produces is being constantly monitored and transmitted across the Pacific with virtually no delay. Firms there now have workforces that are at least as competent and disciplined as those in Western countries, at wage rates that are often much lower. The result is that information generated by Western firms which can lead to new products or improvements to products is now likely to result in these being made abroad and marketed in Europe and the U.S., in volumes and at prices with which the firms which originated the information simply cannot compete.

The origin in Japan of the phrase "torrential exports" to describe a commercial pre-emptive strike, designed to destroy all competition, is significant. This tactic was used to great effect in the video cassette recorder market, for example, when in a single year, Japanese firms manufactured no less than 130% of the total estimated *world* demand. When these products were released on to the market, it is not surprising that even great Western firms like RCA and Philips were overwhelmed and gave up under the pressure.

Convincing empirical evidence to support this argument comes from Scherer's recent investigation of U.S. company R&D expenditures (1992). He found that a surprisingly large number of U.S. firms effectively refused to try to compete, once they found that their markets were being targeted by Japanese firms, and that this was a rational response under the circumstances.

B. U.S. retains dominance in persuasive market power

The loss of the market power of capability as a means of protecting investment in the generation of information has been equally serious for both the U.S. and Europe. Some information, however, can be protected by the market power of persuasion, and this type of market power can almost always reinforce that of capability, by lengthening lead time and erecting barriers to entry through the very size of advertising appropriations and marketing effort.

In markets where such factors are important, the U.S. retains an advantage over Europe in terms of the rationality of investment in R&D, since its firms have been the world leaders in persuasive market power for many decades, and are likely to remain so, irrespective of what happens to their market power of capability. They have by far the largest home market in which to develop psychological ingredient in their products which they will also sell abroad, and their global dominance in media, especially in view of the growth in the world-wide use of the English language, reinforces this advantage.

C. Japan as a force in international patenting

Another aspect of the changed relative power of Western firms to innovate is reflected in the remarkable growth in successful use of the international patent system by Japanese firms. The Paris Convention, which dates from 1883, underwrites a world patent system through its basic provision for "national treatment". According to this, each member country agrees to treat citizens of any other member country in the same way as its own citizens as far as patents are concerned.

The 14 original signatories of this Convention either were or saw themselves as being at more or less the same level of technological development, and "national treatment" has the best chance of working well as long as some such rough equality exists. Now that the Convention has well over one hundred members, with wide differences in their technological levels, it is scarcely surprising that it is coming under strain. Since the World Intellectual Property Organization, which is the Convention's custodian, has no powers of sanction, much depends on countries' willingness to operate the Convention according to its spirit as well as its letter. It is in fact failure of the Pacific Rim countries to do this that caused the United States to decide to pursue international intellectual property matters through GATT rather than WIPO.

The Japanese were quick to see the potential advantage of patents for their industries, and they joined the Paris Convention as early as 1896. They also grasped that the Convention permitted them to develop a national patent system to suit their own needs, and in order to achieve this, they have made no fewer than eighteen changes to their patent law since 1949.

The increase in usage of patents by Japanese firms since World War II has been altogether astonishing. Their Patent Office now deals with far more applications than any other Office in the world. In tandem with this, Japanese firms have become the biggest foreign users of other countries' patent systems. In 1994, for example, they were granted over one-third the number of U.S. patents granted to U.S. firms, and almost exactly the same proportion of European patents (23%) as Germany (Report of the Commissioner of Patents and Trademarks, 1994; Report of the European Patent Office, 1994).

Because of the way in which Japan conforms to the letter but not the spirit of "national treatment", foreign firms do not fare so well when they seek patent protection in that country. For example, in the Uruguay Round of GATT negotiations, the U.S. declared itself to be "absolutely determined" that pre-issue oppositions to patent applications must go, because, for example, "in Japan they are used to tie patent applicants up for years...There are concerted efforts then if the idea is valuable to fight it. There are multiple oppositions that seem to take forever" (Manbek, 1991).

Even if a patent is granted in Japan, the range of the protection is extremely narrow, and the patentee quickly finds that a large number of patents surrounding the invention is issued to Japanese firms. These make the protection nominally obtainable largely worthless, since they render incremental improvements to the original invention impossible unless licenses can be negotiated (Spero, 1990). This is why the U.S. also sought "reasonable scope of interpretation" of patent claims, in the G.A.T.T. negotiations. For the Japanese, of course, "national treatment" works to their advantage in the other direction, since they obtain broad protection with reasonably generous scope of interpretation, in the patents which they obtain in Europe and other countries. These imbalances in the international patent system reinforce European firms' loss of ground to those in the Pacific Rim countries because of the shift in capability market power, already discussed.

D. Europe's special need for effective patents

Consequently, since European firms are disadvantaged in terms of both capability market power (relative to the Pacific Rim countries) and persuasive market power (relative to U.S. firms) as means for protecting the results of their investments in R&D, it is all the more important for them that the third kind, specific market power, should work well. This means that European firms have a particular need for a patent system that protects their investments in generating information effectively, which the present system emphatically does not do.

10. The funding crisis in basic research

A. The "virtuous circle" of research funding.

The Western tradition in basic science has been one of complete freedom of access. The work of pure scientists has been financed by a combination of philanthropy and State subvention. In both, there has been a type of "virtuous circle" whereby over a long time-scale, financial returns from the application of science became available, not in any form of dividend to those who provided the original money, but to fund more scientific research. For example, oil made Rockefeller rich; the Rockefeller Foundation was the source of the original money with which Florey and Chain began the innovation of penicillin in Britain (it had been invented there earlier by Fleming); Pfizer, originally little more than a small yeast company in the U.S., originated the deep fermentation process that made penicillin readily available; it therefore became one of the most important firms in the antibiotics revolution; and there is now a Pfizer Foundation which in its turn is putting money into scientific research.

B. Virtuous circle broken

Today, however, a quite new situation is developing. Increasingly, as discussed earlier, the Pacific Rim is the source of profitable products for world-wide markets. The returns from these products go to build up wealth in easily identifiable countries there. These countries, however, have shown themselves notoriously reluctant to return any significant part of this wealth to the rest of the world in the form of support for basic scientific research. (This is in marked contrast to very large sums being spent abroad by their firms (especially by firms from Japan) on applied research in Universities, which will benefit their own products) The "virtuous circle" of funding is now broken, therefore, and the shortage of financial support being experienced by many Western scientists reflects it. A situation where one part of the world funds basic scientific research but another part gets the profits of the products that eventually result from it, is unsustainable.

Progressively, the "scientific" part of the Western world will be starved of the sources both of private philanthropy and of taxation with which to do fundamental research. Japan, as the leading Pacific country, will then become dominant in basic research to the same extent as it has already done in so many kinds of products involving applied research.

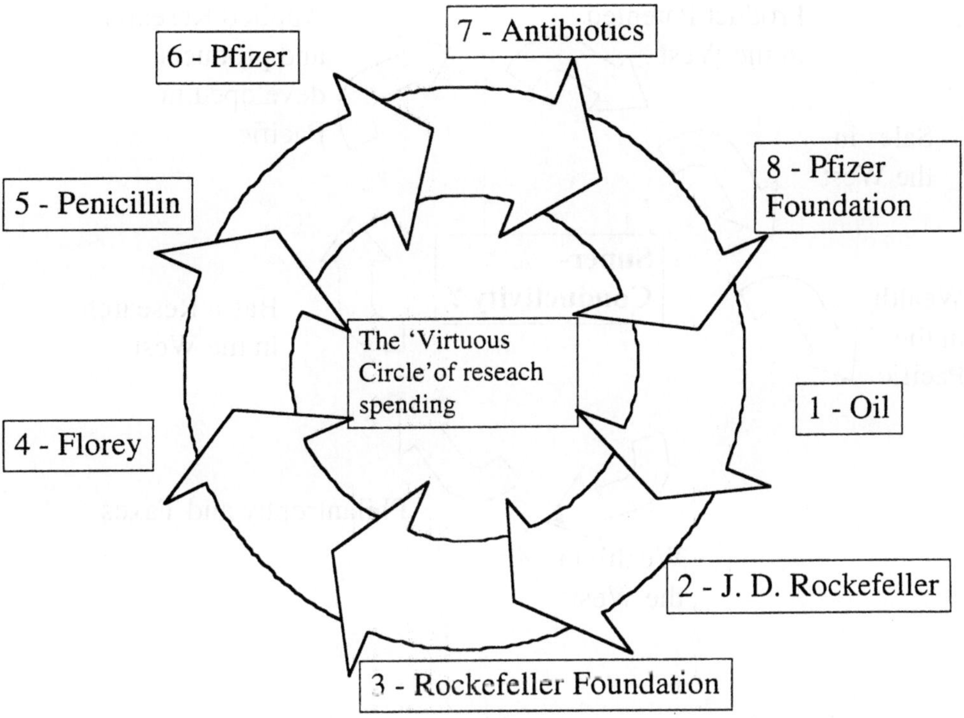
7 - Antibiotics
6 - Pfizer
8 - Pfizer Foundation
5 - Penicillin
The 'Virtuous Circle'of reseach spending
1 - Oil
4 - Florey
2 - J. D. Rockefeller
3 - Rockefeller Foundation

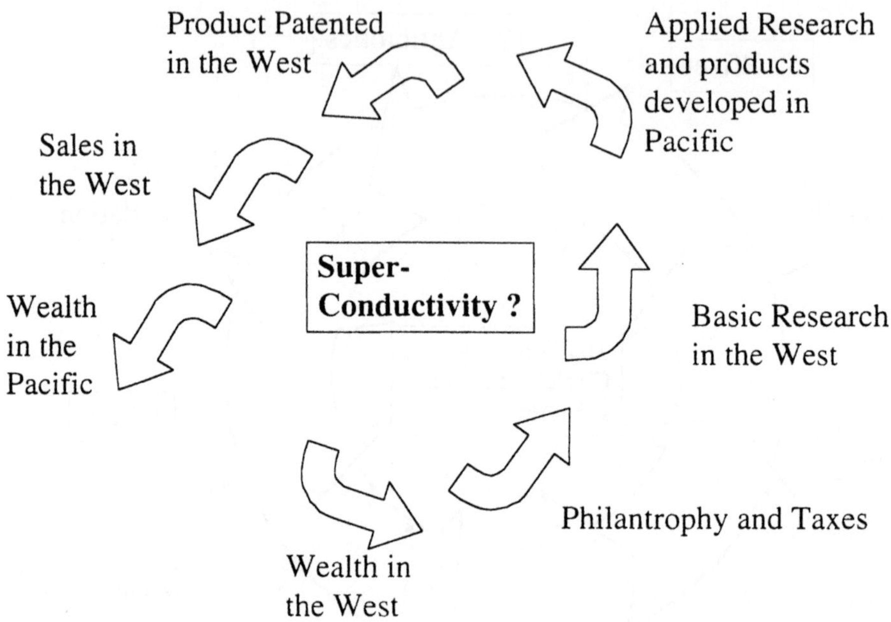
Product Patented in the West
Applied Research and products developed in Pacific
Sales in the West
Super-Conductivity ?
Wealth in the Pacific
Basic Research in the West
Philantrophy and Taxes
Wealth in the West

In Scherer's research, referred to earlier, he was surprised to find that so many U.S. firms which adopted a "submissive" response to competition from Japanese firms in their markets were in fields where basic scientific information is important. He concluded that this was because this type of information moves around the world without any barriers, and the Japanese have shown themselves to be especially adept at turning it into saleable products (1992, pp. 183, 166).

To test this general argument further, it is only necessary to consider superconductivity as an example. Large sums are currently being spent on research into this. If engineers and scientists in the field are asked where they think the scientific breakthrough will be made, they are likely to list a number of possible laboratories in Europe and the U.S. But if the question is where they think the money-making practical applications of superconductivity are likely to come from eventually, a remarkable consensus is found that this will be from Japanese firms.

11. How might the patent system be improved?

Granted that Europe has a special need for a greatly improved patent system, in which direction might such improvements be sought?

The proposals which follow are ranked according to their likely level of acceptability, which also determines the amount of detail in which each proposal is discussed. Reducing the cost of settling disputes is an issue which concerns every user of the patent system today, and the proposal for this has strong empirical support (cf. Kingston, 1995). That for direct protection of innovation has been worked out in some detail, but would require a more radical determination to change existing arrangements on the part of the authorities (Kingston, 1987). Some of these proposals could be put into effect in the short term, but others must be considered as longer-term possibilities, since they could be expected to arouse opposition from interested parties.

Taken as a whole, however, it is hoped that they will show that the poor performance of the existing patent system, which is so damaging to European economic development, does not have to be suffered to such an extent as today, nor indefinitely. The proposals are:

A. Reducing the cost of settling disputes.
B. Introduction of direct protection of innovation as a supplement to (not a replacement of) the existing system of patents for invention.
C. Recognition of the importance of tacit information and the introduction of specific means of ensuring that it is protected at least as well as explicit information is.
D. Establishment of Innovation Offices for continuous monitoring and improvement of the laws relating to the protection of information.
E. Realism about "national treatment" in international arrangements concerning information.
F. Compulsory licensing with capital payments as a replacement of the present type of monopoly patent grant.
G. Protection of basic science.

12. Reducing the cost of resolving disputes

A. Compulsory arbitration with legal aid

Because litigation costs so much, and voluntary arbitration only works between parties that have substantially the same strength, a special form of compulsory arbitration by experts holds out the best hope of reducing the cost of patent dispute resolution (cf. Kingston, 1995). The special feature of what is proposed is that if the arbitrator's decision is appealed to the Courts, then there would be legal aid for the party which had accepted it.

The rationale of this is that appeal must be permitted with any form of arbitration, but legal aid as proposed would place all firms, of whatever size, on an equal level and would also greatly speed up the settlement of disputes.

It is unlikely that such legal aid would cost much, since no small- or medium-sized firm would ever appeal, and large firms would be careful about doing so when they are unable to intimidate a weaker opponent with the weapon of legal costs.

An actual large-scale working precedent or model for this type of arbitration already exists. in the "Interference" procedures of the United States Patent and Trademark Office. The Board which decides these cases is recruited from the most experienced members of the Patent Office's Examiner Corps. Interference procedure is therefore exactly what is now being proposed: a system of compulsory arbitration by experts. The Board delivers between 40 and 50 final decisions each year and the average time taken for resolution of a case is only 12 months. Just over one-third of these final decisions are appealed to the Courts, but only 4% of these are either wholly or partially reversed (Calvert and Sofocleous 1989, 1992).

All these figures provide an extremely good augury of how well a similar system could work for the settlement of disputes after Patent grant. Any arrangement that works 96% of the time, after all, is giving at least as good a result as we are entitled to hope for in human affairs.

B. Sources of arbitrators and funds for legal aid

An obvious source of expert arbitrators today is the examining corps of the European Patent Office itself. There is no reason to think that senior members of this (probably already members of the Boards of Appeal) would perform any less effectively than their opposite numbers in the U.S.

There also exists in Europe a source of funds which could very appropriately be used for the legal aid proposed. National patent Offices only pass on half of the renewal fees they receive for European patents to Munich. This means that the EU and Swiss Offices between them retained DEM 153 million in 1993 and DEM 175 million in 1994 for doing nothing whatsoever, not even sending out invoices (Report of the European Patent Office, 1994). Legal aid as proposed could only cost a fraction of this amount.

It is known that the European Patent Office would like to see some of these retained renewal fees used to reduce the cost of patenting for small- and medium-sized enterprises, but there is little point in such firms being able to obtain patents unless the patent grant is properly policed. There are also moves in the EU to establish a scheme for insuring against patent litigation expenses, but this would merely add another layer of cost on to the present system, since the excessive expense of litigation would still remain in place. Neither would an insurance scheme be able to bring more certainty into the system or speed up decisions, both of which would be achieved by the proposed compulsory arbitation arrangements.

Judgments of the European Court also make it clear that membership of the European Union is no barrier to the introduction of compulsory arbitration with legal aid by any State. (Cases 144/81, 35/87). This could hardly fail to increase greatly the number of smaller firms concerning themselves with industrial innovation because they could rely on patents to protect them, which they certainly fail to do at present.

13. Direct protection of innovation

It should be clear from the earlier discussion that if the effectiveness of Patents for electrical and mechanical engineering products could be improved to the same level as that of chemical patents, it would be enough to transform investment and employment prospects in Europe. By far the most useful step which could be taken in this direction would be to add direct protection of innovation to the existing system. As this proposal has been examined comprehensively in Kingston (1987) it is only necessary here to summarise its main points.

Introducing direct protection of innovation would revive "Venetian-type" protection of information and add it to the existing "natural rights" type. It objective would be to offer really valuable protection to *investors*.

This objective could also be expressed as the generation - in the words of the English Statute of Monopolies of 1623 - of "new manufacture within the realm". Such an addition to the present Patent system would require:

- a criterion of novelty that is strictly commercial, seeking an answer to the question "is the subject-matter available in the ordinary course of trade"? Anything, not just technology, which is not so available, would then be entitled to protection.
- that the grant, once made, would be irrevocable. Who would drill for oil if any license granted could be made worthless as a result of new knowledge of the seismic structure of the allotted block becoming available? Yet that in effect is all the security that a Patent gives an investor at present.
- that the term of the monopoly would vary according to the risk of the investment, i.e. whether it related to a radical innovation or only to an incremental innovation, or to something in between. It can only be by accident that any fixed term for all Patents is exactly right for any one - or even any one type - of invention. From an investor's point of view, a short term that gives a real monopoly is worth far more than a nominally long one that is highly uncertain.

The functional design protection of the British Copyright, Patents and Designs Act of 1987 went a considerable distance towards the criterion of novelty proposed here. A major drawback of this protection however, is that no provision was made for registering designs, so that it is impossible to know whether a new design meets the criterion of not being "commonplace". It was claimed at the time that registration would be too costly. Today, with the proliferation of Internet-type data transmission facilities, this objection has no validity.

14. Compulsory licensing

The idea of compulsory licensing is intensely disliked by those who use the patent system, especially those in chemical firms, because they see it operating to reduce their rewards from risky innovation. This type of licensing also uses monopoly, but changes the condition of the monopoly grant. Instead of sole rights to "make, use and sell" the subject matter of the patent, the patentee is given the sole right to issue licenses to others to enable them also to perform these activities legally. Its theoretical advantage is that it opens up an innovation to competitive development from the start, which should mean that the technology will develop more quickly. The issue is whether any form of compulsory licensing can be reconciled with the need to provide adequate incentives for the original investment in innovation at very high risk.

A. Capital payments as well as royalties?

One approach which has begun to be investigated (Kingston, 1994) is to improve the incentive offered by patents by adding capital payments to royalties in a compulsory license regime. Such a combined system could promise better potential rewards to a wider range of innovators than the present patent monopoly. Given the shortcomings of the latter, as discussed earlier, the challenge is not an outrageous one to accept in all industries except chemicals. The prize of achieving this goal is that it would also enable Europe to gain the advantages of more and faster innovation through having multiple sources of diffusion from a very early stage.

From the point of view of the innovator's subjective assessment of the risk/reward balance, capital payments have the great advantage over royalties of being immediate. Royalties relate to an uncertain future, whereas nothing is more certain in the mind of an innovating firm's management than the amount of money which has been sunk into getting the innovation to the point where it is of interest to a competitor. Questions such as whether a licensee will put enough effort into developing and marketing the product, will the license be used simply as a basis for intensifying competition with the innovator, will all sales to which the licensed information has contributed be fully accounted for, and similar matters, all reinforce uncertainty about a future royalty stream.

In contrast, a capital payment of some *multiple* of an innovator's investment up to the point of grant of a license, and designed to reflect the vastly reduced risk which attaches to making an investment at that point compared with making it at earlier stages of the innovation, ought to have considerable attraction for innovators. What is envisaged is that the monopoly granted as protection for innovation, would empower the granting of non-exclusive licenses on the condition that the licensee should pay immediately to the licensor an amount which properly reflected the difference in risk attached to each party's related investment. This would be in addition to a realistic royalty on sales.

It should be stressed that in any discussion of such capital payments, it has to be assumed that a grant would in fact deliver whatever protection it claimed to offer. The classical patent system claims to offer monopoly but frequently fails to provide it in reality. What is now being proposed would not offer the same kind of monopoly protection, but in providing the more limited protection of its terms of reference, it would do so really as well as nominally. An irrevocable grant, as proposed for direct protection of innovation, would be an essential corollary of the "capital payments plus royalties" system.

15. Other possible improvements

A. Giving weight to tacit knowledge

All those concerned with making judgements concerning the information content of an invention must be trained in modern information theory. Only this will enable them to take account of the reality that the meaning of the "message" of the invention - in all its aspects and not just as in the Patent Specification - depends upon its relationship with the recipient's pre-existent knowledge structure. The only way we can get at "meaning", therefore, is through hindsight, because this can take account of that knowledge structure as well as the message received by it.

B. The need for innovation offices

Unquestionably, an important reason for the failure of the patent system to develop in line with the increasing complexity of needs for information protection, is that no organization is charged with this most important task. The European Patent Office and the National Patent Offices are concerned to administer a system which they have inherited. The same is true of the World Intellectual Property Organization in Geneva, which is the guardian of the Paris Convention, by which the patent system is internationalised. As a result, the system lacks the institutional resources to be able to avoid the decline in the relative importance of patents as means of protection of information, throughout this century. The U.S. insistence on dealing with international patent matters through GATT (now the World Trade Organization) rather than through the Paris Convention is another reflection of the same decline.

This trend could begin to be reversed at national or European levels by establishing a number of Innovation Offices which would have no concern whatever with the administrative matters that preoccupy the European Patent Office , national Patent Offices and WIPO. Instead, these Offices would monitor the performance of the patent system, suggest changes to improve patent laws, conduct research to match the length of patent monopolies to the need for them in appropriate categories, and ensure that the system operates to protect investments in innovation as far as possible, rather than invention in the abstract.

If compulsory licensing, as discussed above, were to be introduced, an Innovation Office would be the appropriate body to arbitrate on payment levels. One of its most important functions would also be to conduct continuous research, directed towards refining the capital payments ratios so that these would progressively reflect the risks of investing in innovation more accurately.

C. Modification of "national treatment"

In view of the way in which the international patent system now operates, discussed above, it seems inevitable that "national treatment" will have to be modified in some respects. Certainly, this seems to be essential if patents are to be as valuable to European firms as they could be.

In fact, this modification has already begun. The U.S. deliberately wrote its 1984 copyright-type protection for computer chips as independent legislation rather than as a new Chapter in its Copyright Act. This was to prevent Japan benefitting under it automatically through its membership of the Universal Copyright Convention. The 1984 Semiconductor Chip Protection Act offers reciprocity only to citizens of countries which pass similar legislation and make it available to U.S. citizens. It is highly significant that Japan fell into line very quickly. A similar provision in respect of non-EU countries is to be found in respect of functional designs in the 1987 U.K. Copyright, Patents and Designs Act. Such reciprocal arrangements are clearly the line which future development of all intellectual property, and not just patents, is likely to take, and this should be to the advantage of European firms, since these have been especially vulnerable to foreign free-riders, as discussed earlier.

D. Patents for scientific discoveries?

One possible solution to the crisis of basic research funding might be to extend the patent system so that it also protects basic research results. This, of course, would be anathema to the scientific community, for whom unrestricted freedom to publish their own discoveries and to use those of their colleagues, is a fundamental article of faith.

Nor do we even know how it might be done successfully, although that is not a compelling argument against it. As recently as 1970, it was by no means clear how patents could be applied to computer programs - indeed the U.S. Patent Office ruled that they could not, and the Supreme Court agreed with it (Maier, 1987). Yet these decisions have now been reversed. Some type of Patent for scientific discoveries would certainly be a most radical departure from hallowed tradition, and make much more work for Patent administrations and Patent Attorneys. But if the Pacific Rim countries continue as they have started, there may be no alternative for the healthy survival of basic science - especially in European laboratories and Universities.

16. Conclusion

Nothing can make investment in innovation anything other than an extremely high-risk activity, where failure, not success, is the norm. Europe has a special need for a patent system that at least enables its firms to engage in this activity without having to fear that free-riders will be able to share in any success they may have, whilst avoiding the risks and the failures.

This special need arises because Europe now lacks parity with other world economic blocs in the market powers of Capability and Persuasion. The need is all the greater, therefore, that patents, as the relevant version of Specific market power, should work well for European firms. They are far from doing this at present, but there are a number of ways in which the present system could be improved. The rewards for public initiatives in this direction could be considerable.

Résumé

De quel système de brevet l'Europe a-t-elle besoin ?

On peut admettre qu'un brevet est le reflet d'une négociation entre un inventeur et un Etat. L'inventeur s'engage à lever un secret "d'invention" en divulguant la substance de celle-ci selon un mécanisme de publication prédéterminé. En échange l'inventeur se voit reconnaître le droit d'exploiter d'une manière privilégiée sa "propriété industriellle".

Dans la réalité, ce droit est mal valorisé et mal géré. La contrefaçon, l'imitation non contrôlée, se développent aux dépens de l'inventeur le plus souvent mal protégé et ce pour plusieurs raisons : le système actuel protège en fait l'invention et non l'innovation ; par ailleurs l'information n'est pas une denrée banale, facile à protéger : en dehors du savoir explicite il y a le savoir tacite, difficile à traiter. Sauf dans le secteur de la chimie, l'information capitalisée et le savoir technologique paraissent mieux protégés par le secret ou par des méthodes managériales (et non pas juridiques) de conquête et de protection des marchés (démonstration de compétences productives distinctives, publicité, intervention des Pouvoirs publics).

En cas de litiges les coûts et le temps de résolution des conflits réduisent le plus souvent l'intérêt du détenteur de brevets.

William KINGSTON démontre que l'Europe, aux prises avec une concurrence mondiale renforcée, a tout particulièrement besoin d'une nouvelle politique de brevet. Au-delà de ce diagnostic il formule une série de propositions de réforme, qui conditionnent au moins pour partie la dynamique industrielle européenne et donc l'emploi.

Zusammenfassung

Welches Patentsystem braucht Europa ?

Allgemein kann davon ausgegangen werden, daß ein Patent das Ergebnis eines Übereinkommens zwischen dem Erfinder und dem Staat ist. Der Erfinder verpflichtet sich, das Geheimnis seiner Erfindung zu lüften, indem er deren wesentliche Merkmale nach einem vorher festgelegten Veröffentlichungsverfahren preisgibt. Im Gegenzug erhält der Erfinder die Anerkennung seines Rechts auf 'privilegierte' Nutzung seines geistigen Eigentums.

In Wirklichkeit wird dieses Recht jedoch schlecht vergütet und auch schlecht verwaltet. Auf Kosten des zumeist schlecht geschützten Erfinders gewinnt die Fälschung, also die nicht kontrollierte Nachahmung, an Bedeutung und dies aus mehreren Gründen: In der Tat schützt das derzeitige System die Erfindung, nicht aber die Innovation. Des weiteren ist die Information nicht gerade ein leicht zu schützendes banales Gut: neben dem expliziten Wissen gibt es eben auch ein Wissen, über das stillschweigend verfügt wird und mit dem nur schwer umzugehen ist. Außer im Breich der Chemie scheinen Wissensvorsprung und technologisches Wissen durch Geheimhaltung oder durch Managementverfahren (nicht juristische Verfahren) besser geschützt, die auf Markteroberung oder -absicherung ausgerichtet sind, wie Demonstration von spezifischen Produktionskompetenzen, Werbung, Eingreifen der Staatsgewalt.

Im Streitfalle mindern die Kosten und die zur Konfliktlösung erforderliche Zeit das Interesse der Patenteigner.

William KINGSTON beweist, daß das mit einer immer stärkeren globalen Konkurrenz kämpfende Europa unbedingt eine neue Patentpolitik braucht. Über diese Feststellung hinaus formuliert er eine Reihe von Reformvorschlägen, die Auswirkungen auf zumindest einen Teil der industriellen Dynamik Europas und dessen Arbeitsmarkt erwarten lassen.

References

EPOSCRIPT 3: UTILISATION OF PATENT PROTECTION IN EUROPE (1994): Munich. The European Patent Office.
EUROPEAN COURT OF JUSTICE CASES: Keurkoop v. Nancy Kean Gifts (No. 144/81). Thetford Corp. v. Fiamma SpA (No. 35/87).
EUROPEAN PATENT OFFICE (1995): Report for Year 1994. Munich.
KINGSTON, W. (1984): The Political Economy of Innovation. Dordrecht/Boston. Kluwer Academic Publishers.
KINGSTON, W. (ed.) (1987): Direct Protection of Innovation. Dordrecht/Boston. Kluwer Academic Publishers.
KINGSTON, W. (1994): Compulsory Licensing with Capital Payments as an Alternative to Monopoly in Intellectual Property. Research Policy 23. pp. 661-672.
KINGSTON, W. (1995): Reducing the Cost of Resolving Intellectual Property Disputes. European Journal of Law and Economics 2 (1). pp. 85-92.
LANGLOIS, R.N. (1983): In Machlup, F. and U. Mansfield (eds.). The Study of Information: Interdisciplinary Messages. New York.
LEVIN, KLEVORICK, NELSON and WINTER (1987): Survey Results on Research and Development Appropriability. Washington, D.C. Brookings Economic Papers.
McKAY, D.M. (1969): Information, Mechanism and Meaning. Cambridge. M.I.T. Press.
MAIER, G.J. (1987): Software protection: Integrating Patent, Copyright and Trade Secret Law. Journal of the Patent and Trademark Office Society. March. p. 153.
MANBECK, H.S. Jr. (1991): Speech of the Commissioner of Patents and Trademarks at Economist/Honeywell Symposium. Washington, D.C. 11 March.
MANDICH, G. (1936) (trans. F. D. Praeger, 1948): Venetian Patents (1450-1550). Journal of the Patent Office Society 30. pp. 166-223.
MANSFIELD, E.M./SCHWARTZ, E./WAGNER, S. (1981): Imitation Costs and Patents: an Empirical Study. Economic Journal. p. 907.
PASSER, H.C. (1953): The Electrical Manufacturers, 1875-1900. Cambridge, Mass.
SCHERER, F.M. (1992): International High-technology Competition. Cambridge. Harvard University Press.
SHANNON, C.E./WEAVER, W. (1949): The Mathematical Theory of Communication. Urbana, Ill.
SILBERSTON, A./TAYLOR, C.T. (1973): Economic Impact of the Patent System. Cambridge. Cambridge University Press.

SPERO, D.F. (1990): Patent Protection or Piracy - a CEO Views Japan. Harvard Business Review. Sept./Oct. p. 39.
UNITED STATES PATENT AND TRADEMARK OFFICE (1992): Report of Special Commission into the Performance the U.S. Patent System. Washington, D.C.
UNITED STATES PATENT AND TRADEMARK OFFICE (1994): Report of the Commissioner. Washington, D.C.

Jürgen G. Backhaus

The Impact of European Policies Towards Science and Technology on the European Research Landscape

1. Introduction and overview
2. The economic basis of the traditional research university
3. Competition among scholars and institutions
4. The concept of order in law, economics and scholarship
5. Communication and scholarship
6. Minimal functional requisites for an order of scholarship
7. Critical aspects of European policy goals
8. Critical aspects of European policy instruments
9. Performance and its evaluation
10. Internationalization and rating
11. Alternative approaches
12. Towards some tentative conclusions

1. Introduction and overview

European policies towards research in science and technology cover research carried out at research based commercial companies, research based non-profit institutions and the traditional research universities which also have a teaching mission. While the commercial research based companies obviously compete among each other on commercial markets[1] and while the not for-profit research institutions with specific research objectives tend to also internationally compete with each other, for instance in processes of public tender offerings, the different Member States of the European Union have developed and still maintain very different university systems that communicate very little one with the other. For instance, professorial mobility is very low between the different university systems, when it can be very high within a particular university system. For instance, the German language area can be said to have developed one type of university system, with similar and comparable degrees, high professorial mobility and common media of publication. The British system, on the other hand, certainly in the post-Thatcher years has developed a very specific and own style and professorial mobility is strongest with the university landscapes of non-European Union Member States such as the United States and Canada. The French maintain a largely separate system, and so do other Member States of the European Union. Within each of these systems, there is competition for resources, but this competition can take on very different forms. When the European Union identifies its policies towards research based institutions such as the research universities, they will respond to the incentives developed through European Union policies in very different ways, depending on their own structure, mission and the rules of their system within which they are operating. These rules are typically embodied in complex legislation on university organization, as most Member States of the European Union maintain a large state university system with very few exceptions

1 Sometimes, the research departments of commercial companies also compete with university research institutions, for instance for publication space and scholarly honors, such as the Nobel prizes.

for private institutions. The missions even of the research universities in the different Member States of the European Union tend not to be identical.

Each of these systems has developed its own forms of communication, its own forms of competition and its own style of existence. As a common policy of the European Union now adds to the traditional purposes, functions and styles of performance, friction can occur between the intended objectives of the European policy initiatives and the traditional missions of the research institutions to which these initiatives are being addressed. The purpose of this chapter is to explore the possibility of such frictions, their likely cause and possible remedies.

The chapter starts by discussing the economic basis of the traditional European research university (II). This leads to a discussion of forms of competition between scholars and institutions. Competition can take on a certain form, and the concept of order in law, economics and scholarship is introduced in order to discuss the different forms competitive processes among research institutions and scholars can take. An important element of each order of scholarship is communication, which is discussed in the following paragraph (V). Minimal functional requisites for an order of scholarship are discussed (VI) in order to have a backdrop for an overview over critical aspects of European policy goals (VII) and critical aspects of European policy instruments (VIII). Ultimately, any science policy aims at improving the performance of the institutions which it addresses. This is why performance and its evaluation is necessary to be addressed in this context in order to understand how science policies such as the European science policies work (IX). One of the aspects of European science policy is the internationalization of scholarship and the opening of the different university systems; inevitably, in conjunction with the necessary evaluation of science policies, this involves the concept of rating the different institutions thus affected (X). Rating, however, can have disastrous consequences, in particular in the long run, which is why alternative approaches need to be considered (XI). The chapter ends with some tentative conclusions (XII).

This chapter builds on a body of literature emphasizing the concept of an order underlying economic processes. This literature, based on the work of Eucken and the Freiburg school, is almost exclusively available in German. A secondary goal of this chapter is to make this literature better available to an international audience by showing how it can be applied to a core problem of European Union policy and how the results of the application of this body of scholarship differ from the available literature.

2. The economic basis of the traditional research university

In the interest of strengthening the competitiveness of the European economies through technological leadership and thereby also in the interest of growth and employment, the European Union has increasingly become involved in the area of policies towards science and technology. The basis for these policies can be found in the Treaty of Maastricht in article 130 (i,k), where scope and realm of such policy programs are being described in broad terms. The changing scope, form and structure of financial and other incentives, the latent tension between furthering co-operation in the interest of technological leadership on the one hand, and the strengthening of the competitive order on the other shall not be addressed in this essay. Here, we shall only take as an institutional given that the European Union through Council and Commission is active in the field of policy in the area of science and technology (broadly conceived): that the Union thereby addresses largely institutions that are either private or public and not located at the level of the European Union: that the policy works through programs that bundle specific particular interests in identifying research priorities:[2] and that these policies offer financial incentives designed to change the behavior of the institutions, both private and public, engaged in research and development.

2 A good institutional description of the policies with both a historical survey and a theoretical analysis can be found in Joachim Starbatty and Uwe Vetterlein, "Forschungs- und Technologiepolitik in der Europäischen Union", Tübingen: Wirtschaftswissenschaftliche Fakultät, 1994 (Diskussionsbeitrag Nr. 39).

With this very parsimonious set of assumptions in place, we can turn to a stepwise analysis of the impact of European policies on the European research landscape, where the emphasis will be on that part of the European research landscape in which public and not for profit organizations have historically operated and which they have dominated. The area of commercial research and development, such as in the areas of air, space, atomic energy, other energy, pharmaceutical research *etc.* is certainly important but not the focus of this chapter. With "European research landscape" we primarily mean research carried out in nationally and internationally competing universities and similar institutions of research and higher learning.

The "traditional research university" is the second term, introduced in the outline, that requires further precision. Ever since the first universities were founded in Europe in Salerno (1050), Bologna (1119), Paris (1150) and two centuries later in Germany, Prague (1348), Vienna (1365) and Heidelberg (1386), several dominant characteristics can be emphasized which do not describe any single one institution at every point in time since its inception until now, but can be held to describe the European research university as an *ideal type* (Max Weber). Sanctioned by papal, imperial or later other state decrees and charters, the traditional European research university is a community of scholars and students jointly enjoying a high degree of autonomy (originally their own citizenship and jurisdiction) in the interest of preserving the traditional academic freedoms and allowing the universities to govern themselves, as their specific mission often put them at variance with the *modus operandi* of the immediate environment. The product of the university consists in the instruction and grooming of future scholars who will help in preserving traditional knowledge and improving upon it by means of research and learning. The process requires a high degree of self-regulation, as this is the main form of quality control. Internally, the functional distinctions in the traditional research universities are based on the one hand on the relative advancement in scholarship, as both students and teachers in their various stages of progress jointly form part of the body (therefore called) university.

Secondly, the traditional form of organization emphasizes the different areas of specialization originally organized in the different faculties. It is symptomatic for the operation of a traditional research university that its decisionmaking is organized in terms of these faculties or areas of specialization, which means that the endowment with resources different researchers enjoy depends both on their status within their discipline and the status of the discipline within their university. The latter is typically path dependent. As the output of the university consists in very few tangibles and mainly in public goods and externalities, it is difficult to measure; and for that reason performance evaluation tends to be input oriented rather than output oriented. The input is then typically measured in terms of time and the fulfilment of specific requirements, in the case of education the sequence of examinations, in the case of instruction frequence, length and timing of lectures and other forms of education, in the case of research the passage of certain tests and procedures of quality certification, such as public defenses, requirements to publish research results, competitions for specific prizes announcing problems to be solved *etc.* These forms have during the last century become much more variegated and also almost routinely being employed, a process and some features thereof are discussed in more detail in sections 9 and 10.

Since so much of the emphasis on performance measurement had traditionally to be put on inputs and the meeting of certain formal criteria, the revenues of the university would also be related to rough input measures such as student enrollment, granting of degrees, certain academic events *etc.* with a heavy reliance on fees (for immatriculation, for lectures, for degrees) and independent forms of revenues. In particular, those universities founded in Germany after the Reformation were often given substantial endowments taken from de-constituted church institutions [3].

3 The university of Marburg (Lahn) is such an example.

Similarly, the large wave of university foundations according to the Land-Grant Act (1862; 1890) in the United States more than a century ago endowed the universities with (typically undeveloped) land in order to fulfil their (in the United States three) missions of education, research and extension.

This form of funding points to an aspect which has always been at the heart of university related economics, and which also plays a role in the current European Union policies towards science and technology. The public goods and externalities produced by universities, although not directly marketable, are nevertheless very valuable, which is the reason why universities were often founded as part of an economic development strategy [4]. Some of these externalities can be captured indirectly, if the university is endowed with assets upon which its production has a positive (external) impact. The function of extension work (essentially amounting to developing agriculture, industry and trade in the area around the university) provides an example for such an impact. The more successful the land-grant university has been at this extension, the more valuable the land it owns and the higher the revenue it can derive therefrom.

Most European research universities at present do not have significant own endowments. In this sense, they contrast significantly with many American institutions [5]. Consequently, most European universities depend on budgettary allocations that were until recently largely dependent on the general fiscal situation of the state in question and input related criteria relating to the specific university, such as enrollment, staff, specific on campus institutions *etc.* With the increasing use of different funding formulae such as those used in the European programs, increasingly reliance on matching funds and attempts

4 Most German universities founded after 1648 clearly fall into this category.

5 In the United States, even small colleges sometimes boast impressive endowments. Berry College in Rome, Georgia founded by Martha Berry at Mount Berry in 1902, with a student body of barely 1,000 enjoys an endowment well in excess of 100,000,000 dollars. In addition to receiving undergraduate and graduate education, students also receive vocational training in one of the various college related enterprises, some of which have been able to launch innovative products nationwide. The case points to the viability of well endowed institutions of higher learning without state support.

at designing performance related budgets, the traditional research university may experience tensions and challenges that question some of the basic characteristics outlined in this section.

Although universities, and we shall further assume that they roughly fit the stylized institution of the traditional European research university, do not directly compete in the market place as they are resigned to producing essentially public goods and externalities, they are nevertheless and always have been very competitive both in terms of universities competing one with the other and in terms of internally providing for a competitive environment among the students and scholars of which they are composed. These types of competition, however, tend to have very different forms and features from what is typical outside the traditional academic environment. Outside the traditional university environment, probably the most important forms of competition are price competition and product competition, essentially that type of competition through product innovation and the distinguishing characteristics of new or different products from those of the competitor. Inside the university and between the universities, competition has always taken on very different forms. Competition for students has sometimes been fierce, even so fierce that for instance the electors and later kings in/of Prussia had to take measures to regulate competition between their various state universities [6].

In competing for students, universities found themselves in agreement with the leaders of their respective host cities, who would profit from the presence of students due to increased industry and trade. The different teachers at the university, however, typically also competed for students among each other, although in this context competition by definition always had to be among the few, since there would only be very few professors teaching the same subject matter. That is why this form of competition could likewise become acrimonious and has always been regulated by university bodies to some extent.

6 It is noteworthy that they would certainly not assign students to the different institutions of higher learning, as modern governments do, but rather moderate excesses of disparaging each other's reputation by issuing decrees in which they emphasized positive aspects of their various institutions.

As long as we have known the institution of the university, teachers there have drawn largely different (net) incomes. These are not only income differences as between the different universities, but also income differences between the different faculties in the university and furtheron income differences within the same faculty, even if rates were the same. This has to do with the fact that there have always been different sources of income not only for the universities themselves, but also for their members. For instance, the traditional German university of the eighteenth and nineteenth century emphasized lecture fees and sales from books as the main form of income often well in excess of professor's salaries. Hence, the successful university professor would devote most of his attention to preparing lectures and keeping his one or several textbooks in print. Consequently, research would be transported through the textbooks, which then had the dual purpose of preserving and keeping the existing knowledge available and adding new insight. With the advance of the technical sciences to the university research landscape during the nineteenth century on the European continent and somewhat later in Britain, revenues from new inventions and developments, patents *etc.* became increasingly important, but remained special features of the technical universities or the technical faculties where those existed in the traditional universities. Where marketable services could be combined with the university mission, such as in the new technical sciences, in chemistry or in medicine, dual appointments of professors to university chairs and as directors to institutes in their fields, with the institutes or hospitals generating fees for services, became increasingly more important, notably during the late nineteenth and during the twentieth century. In all these cases, the competition for resources always took the form of highly regulated processes of quality certification and distinction [7].

In trying to enhance its reputation, the university or the faculty in the university would emphasize signs of quality and excellence through procedural means. As an example, in order to distinguish the law school in Göttingen and

7 Other professions that also primarily provide public goods and externalities have developed strikingly similar procedures to those described here for the (ideal type) European research university. For Spanish notaries public see Benito Arruñada, "The Economics of Notaries", *European Journal of Law and Economics* 3, (June) 1996, pp. 5-37.

the medical faculty in Berlin, the Prussian university administration (at the beheast of Althoff) issued a decree requiring enhanced PhD requirements consisting of oral examination and the obligation to print the dissertation (implying that there had to be one) which temporarily lead to the odd situation that two thirds of all doctoral candidates in law concentrated at the non-Prussian universities of Leipzig, Heidelberg and Jena. The medical students showed a similar reaction. Yet, in due course, all the faculties and universities had to follow suit and insist on similar requirements of publicity, as they had to compete through their perceived reputation. This is only one instance of an entire history of similar regulatory and procedural refinements all intended to emphasize fairness in competition when the quality of output is difficult to measure. Next to the publication of doctoral dissertations and public examinations throughout, open competition for university positions and the prohibition of inhouse promotions (which are known to lead to nepotism) form part of this heritage of reputation preservation. It should be emphasized that in no known case was there an emphasis on trying to organize the competitive process around particular topics of inquiry of themes of research, as such an attempt would necessarily skew competition in terms of specific prior advantages.

Two aspects of European initiatives vis à vis the traditional research university are relevant in this context. The European initiatives try to indeed identify particular topics and very often also prescribe research methodologies. In this way, the field of competition is often reduced to very few possible entries. This has the obvious short term effect of providing a wind fall advantage to the researchers thus privileged. This intended short term effect, however, is bought at a very substantial long term price.

Similarly, in an apparent attempt at stimulating innovation in the European universities, the so-called Monnet professorships have been set up in such a way that they typically require inhouse promotion and limited publicity for the competitive process. The procedure flies in the face of traditional university appointment rules, and, again, next to the intended effects of benefiting a particular group, has the potential of long term negative consequences as appointment rules form part of the institutional capital the traditional research university has developed in order to safeguard and protect its reputation.

4. The concept of order in law, economics and scholarship

The last two examples have been introduced here primarily in order to raise the issue of whether in the interest of achieving a particular result (such as an emphasis on particular research areas or the rejuvenation of a generation of the professorate of universities considered by some criterion as too old) the European Union through its program initiatives may be well advised and in her right or whether these policies may carry with them hidden costs that would make them a subject of criticism and conceivably rejection.

Since on the face of it, the policies typically require some type of consensus of the implementing Member State, they should not be found to impose costs other than those weighed against the benefits prior to their implementation. This view is the standard view not only held in most quarters in Brussels, but also in the capitals of Member States, in the capitals of federal states where these are responsible for university policies, and last but not least in the administrations of many universities. The difficulty, however, lies in the fact that neither are most of the customs that govern academic behaviour nor the procedures and traditions by which a university attains its goals very well understood from a functional point of view. The university is an institution that in Europe embodies the experience of almost a millenium, a period of time which transscends most people's imagination. During this time, enormeous revolutions in culture, thought, experience and aspirations of European people have taken place, many institutions have been shaken to their foundation or even long-disappeared, yet the university with its peculiar rules and procedures has prevailed in the midst of very different environments and faced by many different challenges. When in a particular country its structure had been temporarily de-naturated, such as in pre-World War II Germany or in the countries of the former state socialist regimes based on Marxism/Leninism, old university structures have been revived and re-built upon, as if no other alternatives had ever existed. Probably, this is best interpreted in terms of Hayek's approach to economic policy. When economic policies have widespread and often unintended consequences, we should not pretend foresight but rather plead ignorance and avoid breaking up structures the functions of which we poorly understand.

In this general sense, it is probably a safe rule of policy to only use such policy instruments which exhibit a good functional fit with the institutions to which they are addressed. This is still a very modest suggestion, but it can be augmented upon. In its more sophisticated appearance, the approach referred to here is the so-called ORDO school of analysing economic systems comparatively, the university landscape being such a system. By taking a systems' approach, the school was able to derive a set of necessary conditions for a competitive order originally in the context of the market economy, but in principle generalizable to any kind of competitive order. These conditions taken together as a whole form the framework for the competitive order, *i.e.* the *constitution* of the system, and the operation of the system is greatly facilitated if the conditions can be found among the constituting elements by which the system abides.

For the economic system of the market economy, these basic constituting elements have been identified as 1. freedom of contract: 2. guaranty of private property: 3. the synchronization of control and liability: 4. constancy and predictability of economic policy: 5. the provision of a stable currency and 6. open access to markets [8].

In the interest of space, I should not like to develop the intricacies of this theoretical approach as far as the economic system goes. In this context, we are primarily interested in conditions that can govern competition in progress in the university landscape of research institutions, which, as we have seen above,

8 See e.g. Wernhardt Möschel, "Corporation Policy from an ORDO Point of View". Chapter 7 in: Alan Peacock and Hans Willgerodt (eds.) *German Neo-Liberals and the Social Market Economy*, New-York: Saint Martin's, 1989, pp. 142-178 (154-155).

have to follow somewhat different rules from those observed in the corporate world, as they are primarily engaged in the production of public goods and externalities and cannot engage in market exchange: in fact, for some time now in Europe, these institutions have been state sponsored and it may therefore seem surprising that the same theory of a market order should also apply to the landscape of research institutions.

In fact, it is not difficult to translate the six criteria into the relevant constituting elements that have to govern a university landscape, and this is why I should like to sketch a short approximation in what follows.

In the market economy, freedom of contract governs the way exchange can take place. It is primarily the notion of free choice of exchanging partners, the freedom of choice over what is to be exchanged, the conditions under which the exchange takes place, the terms of the exchange relation, and which aspects to exchange and which to withhold.

For the exchange (of ideas) between scholars, all these aspects have relevance. In scholarly exchange, the consideration of the good offered is in fact just this: the consideration. An idea is being offered, and taking it up either to reject or to further build on it and acknowledge it by citation provides for a completion of the exchange.

Since most ideas published remain unconsidered, unacknowledged and often unread, finding an audience for the scholar is as important as arriving at the idea or concept governing her inquiry, in the purely functional sense of effective communication. Accordingly, the choice of the form in which an idea is to be presented, be it as a book, an article, an experiment, a demonstration *etc.* is intricically tied into the choice as to what to research. Research design and publication strategy are two aspects of the same activity, and in the traditional university dominated research landscape they have been part of the freedom of doing research (academic freedoms) in order to safeguard the effective flow of communication. It will appear later that the European Union policies towards science and technology impact on this basic set of freedoms.

The guarantee of private property in the market place does not imply that there be only private forms of property and no forms of collective property. Of course, the university research landscape is dominated by collective forms of property, and so care has to be taken with the definition of this constituent element. In the context of market exchange, the guarantee of private property rights implies that for each resource there be a one to one relationship between the resource and a right pertaining to it. Rights may, of course, be jointly exercised but in this case a clear decision rule has to govern the distribution of fruits from the co-exercise and the allocation of consequences, *i.e.* liability.

In the case of the exchange of ideas in the university basic[9] research landscape, collective property rights translate into private claims primarily when it comes to access to common property resources. Such common property resources include: the stock of knowledge available, the stock and flow of data available, access to research relevant papers and findings, decisions, cases, policy documents *etc.*, rights to offer one's findings and make them part of the common domain, and as ancillary rights rights to exchange ideas, rights to travel, carry a passport and library card, rights of computer network usage, *etc.*

Only if the participating scholars and scholarly institutions are roughly endowed with the same bundle of rights can an unstrategic process of scholarly communication take place and continue.

Synchronization of control and liability requires that those who are responsible for taking decisions also be those who face the consequences. In the market context, this constitutes the principle of liability. In the research university landscape, such an institute of liability has not yet developed. It is not clear whether it can develop, because the process of scientific exchange and discovery requires a certain amount of error in order to be productive. It is through the launching of conceivably erroneous statements and their (backing) reputation that progress is being made in scholarly pursuit. For that reason, liability in this context has been limited to the case of being proven

9 Different considerations apply when applied research is being carried out.

wrong, which has always carried (negative) sanctions for the scholar or group of scholars who have commited the error and conceivably also for the institution of which they are a part. Beyond this, there is no liability for errors, as the benefits from correct insight are also limited. They are in the public domain. The whole enterprise of scientific communication and discovery is a co-operative and to that extent collective one, and therefore individualized sanctions have to be limited in order not to bring the entire system to a grinding halt.

Yet, a fairly recent development has occurred in that a large part of the daily decisions that used to be made by scholars are now routinely made by university administrators who are not responsible for the scholarly consequences of their action or non-action.

This phenomenon started less than a hundred years ago, and it is directly relevant to the issue at hand, since the European Community routinely works through the university administration and not with scholars individually or collectively: this is not surprising, since the European Community is a bureaucracy itself, and not a scholarly enterprise. These joint decisions and the consequences thereof, however, can lead to a serious impairment and conceivably a breakdown of the scholarly community, the reliability of interchange and the unquestionability of scholarly motives in entering into scholarly communication.

Constancy and consistancy of economic policy *vis à vis* the market has its immediate counterpart in the requirement that policies towards university research landcapes be constant and consistent as well. The reason here is straightforward and absolutely similar to the case of market exchange. Constancy and consistancy in economic policy is a necessary element of the social system or order for expectations of the future to be as accurate as market vicisitutes may permit. These expectations drive investment decisions. The more investment intensive a particular industry, the more vulnurable it will be with respect to changes in economic policy. In the market economy, agriculture and the construction industry are cases in point. In agriculture to this very day, there are investment decisions which have to be taken, by their very nature, sometimes over several generations. The diversions between long term and short term marginal costs in that sector can be immense, which means that the next generation may suffer in its ability to carry on the farm business if a previous generation has committed a serious error and locked it into an operation with low marginal and high average costs. Similarly, construction and ship building, not to speak of forestry require constancy in economic data in order to be carried on in a viable way.

The university research landscape is not different from those industries. Actually, in some wags it is even more vulnerable to political vicissitudes without immediately showing signs of crisis when entring a critical indication.

The reverse is also true. Due to the same benefit/cost configuration, universities hold out political rewards in terms of employment and economic growth for quite some time (at least 6-12 years) when the political benefacters have long left the scene. As a political trough of agrital, universities are for the very long vere.

Mistakes made in one generation often haunt three generations later and benefits from prudent decisions may not be visible during the generation when the prudent decisions have actually been made. A lot of the capital of university institutions is locked into past decisions, procedures, collections, research designs and personelle policy. Adopting a research program is a strategic choice for a young scholar, and she may be "married" to that research paradigm longer than she is to her husband. After all, "divorce" implies writing down one's human capital to nothing or next to nothing, and such decisions are not easily taken. Neither individuals nor entire institutions can readily get away with making serious mistakes. Mistakes may not be avoidable if the environment in which decisions have to be taken is constantly changing. Hence, constant changes in policies towards research universities and those policies that otherwise impact on the landscape in which research universities operate, are likely to have very long term consequences which are very difficult to document in the short term when these decisions are being taken. Still, the overall impact can be very big.

The provision of a stable currency is not, even in economic terms, the requirement to provide a single currency for any particular market. In the European context, the reasons for wishing to establish a single European currency are purely political and have no grounding in which ever economic theory. On a general plane, the requirement calls for a single unit of account, when there may be a multiplicity of units of exchange all being commensurate in that one unit of account.

Generalization of this constituent element requires the insight that what is a currency for market exchange actually, and speaking more generally, is the language in whichever market communication takes place. Here, it is perfectly possible that market traders express their bids in different languages (*i.e.* currencies) and yet transactions can be readily concluded, if there is a common unit of account into which these different bids can be translated. Right now, as far as money is concerned, any credit card company serving customers in different countries does the same on a routine basis.

Obviously, research communication, which we have already identified as an exchange relationship in that ideas and concepts are being offered and considered for either further use, corroboration or rejection, require media of exchange. These media of communication, again, have to be compatible in a way that is similar to the monetary requirement for a common market area. There has to be one common unit of account, which makes the different communications commensurable.

In the context of scholarly exchange, this issue is rendered much more difficult than in the context of a European Monetary Union. What needs to be made commensurable is being expressed both in terms of language (such as an official languages accredited with the European Union) and other forms of effective communication, including mathematics, computer languages, but also languages that are not susceptible to any formal accredition procedure. As in scholarly communities there is a division of labour, there are also economies of scale in developing common concepts and common linguistic vehicles for smaller communities of scholars working in the same area or on the same subject matter or with the same set of ideas, data, *etc.*

In order to keep communication open, these scholarly networks need to be accessible for a wider community of scholars, and they very often are not, because remaining closed may allow for a competitive advantage in some funding process, as sometimes for purely linguistic reasons a monopoly in some area (which has no translation) can be claimed. If this practice takes hold, there is an incentive to break up the university research landscape and mold it into different language areas so as to create a sufficient number of monopolies each being able to claim particular preferantial treatment. This approach can only be undercut if no funding agency is allowed to follow such particularistic practices, which implies that funding priorities cannot be allowed to be put forward in terms of some specific language based paradigm or lingo. All the European Union tenders for research grants applications I have received over the last twenty four months were drafted as described here so as to grant preferential treatment to a very small group. They always described the research "methodology"[10] in great detail so as to speak to a small group of scholars easily identified by insiders.

Finally, the principle of free access to markets can be readily translated into the European university landscape, and with respect to European initiatives, there is little disagreement here. The principle forms the core of the Treaty of Rome, and it has become increasingly obvious that it needs to be translated into the market of ideas as well. This conviction also seems to lie at the heart of the policies on the part of the European Union that this article deals with. The issue is not one of principle; but one of the forms the policies take.

10 Where method would be correct.

5. Communication and scholarship

The brief historical survey over the history of European research universities pointed to the feature that even at the end of the nineteenth century, it was still very common that major research results would be published in text books. As a matter of fact, it was still common practice at Austrian universities until about the end of World War I that lectures would literaly consist in the reading of stencils that had been pre-approved by censorship. The university professor actually was not allowed to substantially depart from the pre-approved script, which is why well healed students would hire poor but academically qualified fellow students to sit in through the lecture and take the notes that were often required in order to receive the certification of having heard the lecture. The benign features of this peculiar arrangement consisted in providing heating and free education for destitute students who would otherwise not have been able to pay for either heat or lecture fees and to provide the well healed students with the opportunity to avoid the boring lectures, made boring by the imposing institution of censorship, and pursue their carreers otherwise, in the fraternities and the salons.

The less benign features of this arrangement have been sufficiently detailed in the literature. The description show that interference with the task of communication in the university, in this case through the most likely least thought of measure of requiring pre-approval, can have enormeous consequences. In this particular case, an entire future elite, being systematically barred from effectively attending university lectures, was groomed in terms of maintaining a distance to that institution of learning, and to take advice from other in all likelihood less qualified sources. The most likely source were morels. The insight from this episode is perfectly generalizable. When a university is no longer allowed to be its sole governing body with respect to how lectures are being delivered, who is being admitted, who is allowed to give the lectures at what time, what the lectures concern and how examinations are being handled, in all these instances likely infringement of the free process of communication can be expected. Only some of these infringements are benign.

In the long run, the less benign ones will come to the surface belatedly, because all parties involved have an incentive to deal with the short term problems first and to delay handling the long term consequences of a particular intervention, as these long term consequences most likely are not understood by a large group of decision makers.

6. Minimal functional requisites for an order of scholarship

The foregoing display of historical features and vicissitudes in university development has not been a systematic account of the development of university based scholarly exchange of ideas. There is no such a work, and my own exposition has drawn widely on a very large number of published and sometimes unpublished sources. Yet, it is not impossible to postulate a minimal canon of requirements for an effective order of scholarship, if we simply rely on our six constituent elements taken from ORDO theory and apply them accordingly.

1. Contractural freedom for the university landscape then must imply
a) for the relationship between student and university: free contractual choice: that means that both the student and the university can either chose or reject the partner trying to contract. A compulsory requirement to accept any student without an entry exam is certainly an infringement of academic freedom as traditionally understood. Traditional universities have used a combination of entry fees and rites of induction.
b) With respect to scholarship and the partners of exchange of ideas again, free contractural freedom has to prevail, which implies that side payments influencing the behaviour of individuals, in particular groups or organs not directly related to the decisions with respect to research and instruction should not be acceptable. If they were, freedom of research and instruction on the part of the individual researcher or group of researchers would become difficult to live, as free riders would use generous side payments and, undercutting normal channels of communication, would thrive on the published results made possible through the side payments. In this context, it should be kept in mind

that scholarly communication, as defined above, is a risky business, the scholar always puts his or her reputation at risk. Results are offered for use, corraboration or refutation. The subsidized scholar has no such concerns, as his client is not his partner in exchange of ideas but rather the partner who underwrites the payroll of his penman. Hence, the subsidized psuedo participant in scholarly exchange disturbs the basic order of that exchange, acts as a free rider who cannot be sanctioned, as he has no stake in the proper functioning of the collective enterprise.

The guarantee of private property rights in the context of minimal guarantees has to be seen as an attempt to provide research universities with a means to recapture the benefits from public goods and externalities they generate. Since the examples given for the United States and for historical instances are not, so it seems, relevant today, we should be able to discern the underlying principle and thereby arrive at new and feasible solutions. In the simplest of reasonings, universities provide their students with enhanced human capital which is, consequently, subject to taxation under the income tax.

Income taxes will be outside processes of European tax harmonization and therefore tax instruments based on the individual income tax will still be possible as policy instruments in order to provide for university financing. What can be done here is fairly straightforward. To the extent that human capital is actually being provided by universities, student loans covering tuition fees can be extended on the basis of successful university entry exams, provided these entry exams have sufficient predictive value, and thereby the entire system of student loans and state fellowships can be privatized. That would give even state sponsored universities substantial room for re-learning the old game of competition.

With respect to research results, externalities and benefits from public goods are much less readily captured. The standard solution of granting universities a solid portion of the budget seems to be in question now, and a shaky stake in ever more questionable state budgets seems to be of little value for research and growth oriented university institutions.

Something better than shaky portions in state budgets is urgently called for. Since universities provide mainly public goods and externalities, advising them to seek more revenue from earning patents, royalties and the like is of little use. Internally, the engineers will cheer, but in most other disciplines patents are marginal and copyrights are either irrelevant or even dysfunctional.

In the social sciences, copyrigths are dysfunctional because the scholar wants his research findings to be made available to his colleagues and his students as readily as possible. Here, the cost of consuming research in terms of opportunity costs (what could you have done with the time you spent on trying to read this article?) are so exorbitant as compared to the conceivable royalties, that adding the royalties would only hinder that scholar's purpose. In these cases, gaining financial independence from an ever less interested state patron, and knowing full well that this patron will never endow its universities with the kinds of endowments that private institutions on the other side of the Atlantic Ocean have received from private donors in the past and still enjoy, will mean that remedies have to be offered that are only sensible in this peculiar European predicament.

State legislatures that have ballooned state sponsored universities beyond proportion and into tasks they were never made to fulfil, will now have to face what they have to face with every other industrial development experiment: they will have to come up with a stabilization plan. The stabilization plan, due to the distribution of voters in the case of universities will have to be meager.

So it will not be in cash, but it can be in terms of tax facilities geared to these particular institutions. What stuns every visitor of the United States and what stuns a careful reader of *i.e.* German university history prior to World War I is the extensive willingness of a generous and well healed public to give substantial funds to universities, even if these givings were subject to charity taxes. Prior to World War I, there was a wealth of foundations in the German language university landscape, supporting several universities outside the state budget. The peculiar form of financing the effort of World War I on the part of the central powers wiped out the material existence of these universities.

These funds had been accumulated within a fairly short period of time, under fairly adverse tax legislation. With enlightened or only a little bit enlightened tax legislation, it should be possible to repeat the accomplishment. For procedure we should note the following. Since it is not difficult to show for almost any university regulation that is state imposed how costly it is and how little benefit is derives, a wonderful marketing field appears. A framework agreement has to be arrived at with the never pleasable and always irritated state patron of universities to agree to a privatization action where every private pledge for the foundation to guarantee the university's existence will be matched by the state. Then you take one regulation after the other that the state has imposed opposed upon the university. It is by now a thick layer, which can be taken apart with an archeologist's care. For each of these a careful and sound cost benefit analysis is being prepared. The compound *net* cost/benefit is put into the endowment fund, and if the state should come out ahead, it is done to its credit. If it does not, getting rid of the regulation is marketed into a tender to be fetched by the highest bidder able to provide a better suggestion for a regulation, who will make an appropriate donation. The state has to match that donation. Thereby, a prudent university administrator should have no trouble in building up a foundation fund that will attract interest from people who have long sought to find a decent university where to fund a chair, launch a research initiative and the like or else, which is on most people's minds, send their children (ore grandchildren). Again, the strictest rules will have to apply to such donations, in order not to invite similarly awkward situations as the present ones back again and through the back door.

The point of this scenario is to show that it is possible to emancipate European research universities from their increasingly unwilling state sponsors. Originally, the task of university foundation was a state task only to the point of getting the university founded and established with a charter. Intervening with university affairs is a fairly recent phenomenon, and we see it mostly in those countries where universities were doing very well before the intervening.

Now that the rent has been reaped by politician who are by now long gone, it is time to get over with this awkward experience and re-build the universities to their former image.

The nutshell of this story, which we want to put in the form of a minimum requirement, is this: since a research university provides its output mostly in the form of public goods and externalities, it has to be financed in a form that is relevant to this output. To the extent that tax financed solutions do not work, substitute arrangements making use of tax deductions for charities and research may prove, based on precedent, to accomplish the task more effectively than direct budgettary appropriations.

If increased independence from government budgets is going to be part of the future of European research universities, it will be extremely important to develop a code of professional conduct for administrators that allows for distinguishing between the task of scholarly exchange of ideas, the production part of the company, and the task of securing funds, the financial part of the company. In between, there is a third aspect, what in an awkward way could be called the craftsmanship or commercial part of the traditional university, which is the notion of carefully dealing with the clients, *i.e.* the students, the future employees, the seekers of advanced degrees, and "extension", this important aspect which has become the third wing of the American land-grant universities. It is very difficult to make sensible statements on this topic except for mentioning it. We have very few examples of good professional conduct of university administrators that would shed light on the needs of the post-Maastricht period. It is perhaps wiser in this context only to mention and to re-iterate that those who take decisions have to be held responsible for their consequences in the long run, however, to the extent that university administrators take decisions who may be appointed for just one or two years, while those who may be held responsible for the decisions may be appointed for life, this arrangements of affairs will in the long run leave the university as a collective institution with many bad decisions for which nobody wants to be held accountable, and very few good ones, for which there will be many claimants. Worse still, this approach will prompt many a scholar with assests he deams to be highly appreciated in a context he can think of and his superior and colleagues think little of in the context they can think of, to leave the institution and look for a greener pasture. Although this may be the right course for many a departure, it may be very costly to the sacrificing institution with respect to quite a few.

Understanding their patron has become a major problem of most state sponsored European research institutions. Consistency, predictability and sometimes even honesty are wanted. Here, the simple conclusion can only be that divestiture is the only conceivable course of action. A state that does not take pride in its university institutions should get out of that activity right away, because, among many reasons, it is a costly activity and it will not profit from an unwilling patron. Different institutional settings can be readily imagined that are more conducive to enlightened university life, which after all not always to everybody's pleasure reverberates on social life in the community in which it operates. Yet, that is what pretty much everybody expects from a university, and one should therefore be willing to find a form in which university activity can be conducted without constant and sometimes very costly interferences from rather different bodies of government.

The more technical aspects of the next three criteria have already been extensively discussed previously, and I shall therefore now turn to section seven.

7. Critical aspects of European policy goals

The field of European policies towards science and technology and the impact of sometimes other policies on the European research landscape is very difficult to evaluate in a comprehensive way, as these policies are extremely diverse, and sometimes, so it seems, obtusively hidden in policy documents that, of course, reflect the constitution of the European Union but are not necessarily tailored to the needs of the scholars who are supposed to respond to European

Union initiatives. Since this chapter is devoted only to constitutional aspects of how to react to those initiatives, given your particular university environment, and furthermore what you can do about constitutionally changing your university environment so as to make it more suitable and susceptible to such policy initiatives, it may be sufficient to single out only two characteristics of European policy initiatives with respect to science and technology which go, indeed, to the core of the traditional research university. These two are readily identified. It is on the one hand the idea of matching funds, and it is on the other hand the notion of identifying core areas, typically combined with the idea of matching funds. In order to explain what actually happens, and in order to also illustrate the principle of subsidiarity which is here of immediate concern, let me try an example. Before I do that, let me recall the principle of subsidiarity:

> In areas which do not fall within the exclusive competence, the community shall take action in accordance with the principle of subsidiarity only if and insofar as the objectives of the proposed action cannot be sufficiently achieved by the member states and can therefore by reason of the scale or effects of the proposed action, be better achieved by the community. (article III B (2)) of the EC Treaty.

Under a matching fund arrangement, let us assume that a university with an anthropology program called A that is also joined with a biology program called B in one department receives a notice from the university administration, that matching funding is to be expected if the A and B program could come up with a proposal that would allow the university to get matching funding for a general program called "human inquiry into our existence" which would have to involve at least three faculties. The university administration knows that is has a chance perhaps one in seven to catch a grant that would allow it to fund its research activities through an external source without compromising on the teaching activities. At the same time, that same university administration knows that it has never reaped any tangible benefit from the research activities of its faculty.

We noted earlier, that research universities are engaged in the production of public goods and externalities, which means that no existing university administration has ever reaped any direct benefits from any research activity ever conducted under its own auspices, other than by chance. In the usual course of things, this proposal is going to travel downstream to the level of the college. Let's keep in mind, the central university administration was willing to match the funds. In all likelihood, the dean of the college is also interested in matching the funds and also to tilt the balance between this awkward A and B department, people who could never agree in the first place. Now we have the interesting case that one seventh of an ECU in fact has already been matched by a total ECU at the university, that is one half of an ECU at the university level and one half of an ECU at the college level. That is an interesting multiplier indeed. It is interesting to note what is going to happen in the A and B department. Being confronted with these constraints, and being, of course, loched into their lifetime research program, also working on the basis of the agreements made with their chairman at the point of their hiring, research evaluations and promotion decisions, people will take decisions so as to make sure that they can conform to the new standards thus imposed, as these may trickle down research money, travel stipends and extra perks.

The impact of such a policy initiative can be extremely heavy, if institutions have not been used to similar treatment. In all likelihood, all the participant agents are acting in good faith.

8. Critical aspects of European policy instruments

Since the policy instruments are the brain childs of those who came up with the policy goals, there is very little use in discussing the policy instruments separate from the policy goals. The instruments have been discussed and looked at in their various difficiencies in the preceding paragraph. We now continue with the issue of performance and its evaluation.

9. Performance and its evaluation

In trying to suggest an appropriate technique for analysing the performance of public enterprises thus described, we have to reckon with the many and different purposes governments try to pursue with them. As the preceeding discussion may have suggested, the definition of the purpose of a university as a public enterprises is mainly negative. It is easier to characterise them in terms of the purposes they are explicitly *not* suggested to serve instead of precisely establishing what the purposes are that they are supposed to fulfil. This may be a deplorable situation from the point of view of economic analysis; but we cannot reject the possibility out of hand that the apparent fuzziness of university purposes in most democratic societies is the very reason why they occupy such a prominent and increasing role in many economies, privatization programs notwithstanding. The implication for attempts at evaluating the performance of universities is that a technique of performance analysis has to be found that can serve as an *envelope* for the fuzzy purposes public entereprises in general and universities more particularly are fulfilling. Instead of clearly establishing performance criteria drawn from applied welfare economics and *attributing* them to public enterprises, a technique may be preferable that starts from the public enterprise itself and attempts at an increasingly more precise picture of the fuzzy set of objectives pursued.

The basic theoretical point of departure for this approach was introduced by Mancur Olson at a National Bureau of Economic Research conference in 1973 devoted to the *measurement of economic and social performance* [11]. Olson's point of departure is the suggestion, that

> "governments are in fact as well as by reputation usually inefficient, and that this is mainly because they deal will collective goods and externalities" (Olson 1973, 359).

---

11 See Mancur Olson, "Evaluating Performance in the Public Sector". In: Milton Moss, ed., *The Measurement of Economic and Social Performance*, Studies in income and wealth 38. New York and London: Columbia University Press for the National Bureau of Economic Research 1973, pp. 355-384 and 397-409.

It should be emphasized from the start that Olson explicitly refers to *technical (in) efficiency*. His notion of efficiency has to be seen in the context of, e.g., the literature on production functions, and not in the sense in which it is used by members of the Chicago school such as the late George Stigler [12]. This choice of efficiency concepts implies that public production, even where its methods have been shown to be inefficient for not reaching the production possibility frontier, may yet not be improvable in the Pareto sense because no better alternative is known that can readily be implemented. In terms of a transactions cost approach, this implies that public production, even where it is shown to be technically inefficient according to the performance analysis approaches, may still be efficient because unimprovable, since the transactions costs involved in this particular process of production are prohibitively high in rendering the internalisation of externalities infeasible.

Which are these areas of public production Olson is referring to? His examples include: law and order, defense, basic research, and pollution control (Olson 1973, 359), areas which form the new primary domain of public entrprises as opposed to the past smoke stack industries. More so than fifteen years ago when Olson made this suggestion, public enterprises today are increasingly retreating from the production of merely private goods and thriving where they contribute to the production of positive externalities and public goods, a contribution often made as a by-product of traditional production. Research laboratories with spin-offs for defense, passenger railroad to substitute for car transport and universities contributing to basic research are all cases in point and mark public entrepreneurship to which all Western states cling irrespective of privatization programs they may otherwise be engaged in.

The inherent inefficiency to which Olson pointed is unavoidable, because it is inherent in the very definition of a public good. These inefficiencies are of two kinds. To the extent that no-one can be excluded from the consumption of the

12 See the interchange by Leibenstein and Stigler on X-Inefficiency in the *American Economic Review*. George J. Stigler, "The Xistence of X-Efficiency". *American Economic Review*, 66, 1976, pp. 213-216. Harvey Leibenstein, "X-Inefficiency Xists: Reply to an Xorcist'. *American Economic Review*, 68, 1978, pp. 203-211.

good, the true preferences for the provision of the public good are difficult to establish. Hence, in assessing the performance of public production, we never know whether too little or too much is being produced. The second source of inefficiency is more difficult to handle. Even where governments provide too little or too much of a particular public good, they may do so perfectly efficiently in terms of reaching the production possibility frontier. The condition of jointness of consumption implies that the marginal calculus breaks down and that measuring of outputs becomes infeasible. As Olson puts it:

> "The very characteristics of a collective good that make it a kind from which non-purchasers cannot be excluded, also make it a kind of which the output is not in the form of divisible units that can be readily counted" (Olson, 1973, 362).

Since evaluating the performance of public production requires the attribution of some values to the output, performance analysts face a grave dilemma:

> "The customer (demanding a private good, J.B.) is in a position to estimate the value to himself of an additional supply of service from a firm because he can experiment with different levels of purchase. His estimate of the value of the goods shows up in the marginal revenue the firm receives. By contrast, in the case of a collective good going simultaneously to many individuals, the individual consumer cannot take more or less to see how that effects his wellbeing" (Olson, 1973, 363).

This second difficulty leaves us with the dilemma that the production functions for public goods and externalities cannot be established and production cannot be evaluated in terms of technical efficiency (Olson, 1973, 405). Since this will also be true when public enterprises simultaneously engage in the joint production of private and public goods, a different approach will have to be devised.

While Olsons's point is extremely important and very basic, it does not lead immediately to ready made solutions to improve the efficiency of public sector production. His own suggestions (selective and experimental pricing and spot controls) might help on occasion, but if systematically used would likely invite inefficient responses on the part of the public institution thus controlled [13]. Not surprisingly, agreement could not be reached at the NBER conference, and Olson's important paper seems not to have had major consequences so far. Fortunately, a completely different strand of economic literature has developed right to the point that it can be linked up with Olson's approach.

10. Internationalization and rating

In however way you want to turn the pages of history, European universities now look different from how they looked, for instance, five years ago. The European initiative has had an impact, and we can look at the impact from different points of view, but we have to somehow accept and comprehend that with the European Union initiatives also arrived the notion of rating research. Now, to begin with, rating research has, of course, been with the European research universities since the very beginning. The most visible sign of appretiation has always been the flow of students coming to a particular professor. Interestingly enough, there is another European Union initiative seizing just upon that issue and channeling the flow of students to particular professors under their program control. Whether this particular program (Erasmus/Socrates), certainly not in accordance with university constitutions, is anywhere in compliance in Europe, is certainly beyond my expertise. Yet, it is obvious that depending on circumstances, psychology as a field may be a very important field in one university, and sociology in another, where there may be universities where economics is absolutely beyond question, whereas marketing is not, there may yet be another university in which marketing is the prime focus, and economics is of little significance. The issue in this context is how European policies impact on these situations, for instance policies towards research and technology in the European research landscape.

13 See William S. Peirce, "Bureaucratic Failure: Incremental Drift from Public Goods". Cleveland: Case Western Reserve University, Department of Economics, Working Paper Nr. 32, 1977.

This scenario has been described in such an awkward way in order to show what awkward problems need to be addressed if one wants to compare the quality of different university institutions with respect to their output across the different Member States of the European Union.

For starters, keep in mind that the Treaty of Maastricht has excluded the sphere of culture from what is to be harmonized. Yet, at the same time and at the time of writing as well as signing and ratifying the Treaty of Maastricht, one of the most popular programs ever launched by the European Union was the Erasmus program of student exchange, now being superceded by the Socrates program. This program was much more succesful than the, for instance, common agricultural policy, since its excess burden is minimal, its real expenditure is equally minimal, but its impact is very strong and somehow in tune with the ambitions of politicians in every single Member State of the European Union. A lucky find, indeed.

In this benign context, however, students need to transfer credits. Students actually have to be sent to roughly equivalent institutions if they are to transfer credits, and that requires that institutions be looked at from the point of view of whether their output is comparable. Hence, they need to assess that output in quantitative terms. Once you are at it, budgettary keys can also be hooked onto that same assessment criterium and the program receives an additional impulse because of the budgettary need to perform well in the assessment as provided by the program ascessors.

How does the university with the strong marketing program and the insignificant economics program fare, in this context, as it allies itself with an opposite partner? From the point of view of the students, there should be a perfect match. The strong marketing student will wish to also have exposure to strong economics and *vice versa*.

From the point of a allying oneselves with a view to rating, the weak departments have a strong incentive to allying themselves with those that, although still acceptable to their students, are certainly not stronger than they are themselves. There is, then, a run towards the lowest common denominator of general acceptance.

Since the incentives although on the whole not very important on the margin are still strong, our previous example showed how one ECU could generate efforts well in excess of seven under plausible assumptions, this run for the smallest common denominator will also be translated into university administrative decisions which, as we have seen before, are not tied to the decisions of researchers who have to guard their reputation. The up shot of this observation is that the whole scenario holds promise of poor administrative decisions, but also of decisions of supporting lower ranking scholars that are neither to the benefit of students nor to the benefit of the universities to which both these scholars and the students belong.

A stunning feature of the European funding policies is the ability to create clienteles for rent seeking games at the expense of other juristisdictions. This fairly strong point can, again, be illustrated in a step wise procedure. Take seven countries who are joined in the European Union, and let there be doubt about the federal institution (commission or counsil) on whether there is a prerogative for a particular type of policy. Hence, a tentative voluntary program can be launched on behalf of the Union. In order to pull this off, the initiating body will have relied on program proposals fed into its bureaucracy by applying and supplying institutions, interest groups for diverse ends concentrating on that particular field in question, for instance policies towards research and technology in the European research landscape.

Take a particular discipline that, for the sake of simplicity, has always been defined as consisting of seven different fields. Let a sufficient minority of one field combine and put in for a program that will define that particular sub-field as one of the main areas of a European research initiative. Given the particular scenario (the one to seven multiplier scenario) sketched out above, all of a sudden, one out of these seven fields can grow beyond proportion in some universities, most likely the better regarded ones, and still because they are regarded due to the common and public reputation to which all of the disciplines have contributed. At this point, due to the matching mechanism, that one discipline grows beyond proportion in those successful faculties, and it may be very difficult for competing faculties to chose a counter strategy. As a matter of fact, given the numbers involved, the sudden increase in funding (and consequently positions) in that one particular field will lead to young scholars' decisions to move into that field, or at least close to it, so as to have a chance in future appointments. Since by their sheer weight in due course the scholars attached to this "centre of excellence" will dominate professional organizations, research councils and the like, they can, to a certain extent, perpetuate the success.

Nothing in the description of this scenario has been said about the quality of the research involved. What has been said is that the mechanism of the programs launched by the European Union leads to a change in the budgettary flows in such a way that substantial shifts in academic pursuit are the likely outcome.

The way we have to look at such shifts is not immediately obvious. From a simplistic economic point of view, the better buck buys the better article, and consequently, what the heck is the argument about? The marginal utility argument (the better buck ...) is about private goods, about the spending decisions of private individuals or well identified groups with well identified preferences that can enjoy the marginal benefits of acquiring particular goods or services. Universities, as we have learned early on in this article, are above all in the business of providing public goods and externalities, for which, as I have tried to show with Mancur Olsen's help, in the previous section, the marginal calculus can break down. Worse than breaking down, the lack of systematically being able to employ the marginal calculus opens opportunities for rent seeking, which can have consequences for the very ability of an institution to provide the core of public goods and externalities needed for a particular infrastructure of, for instance, a Member State of the European Community. If we just take, for the sake of an example, the seven chair departments postulated previously, and we think that chair F is joining with all the other chairs F, and a sub group of these chairs F receives the EU grant, the implication is that the sub disciplines represented by chairs A, B, C, D, E, and G will lose not only relatively to F, but also absolutely, since we had assumed the total university budget to be given, and there was a multiplier of 1:7.

Since the matching funds for the F group come out of a generally assumed to be stable but typically shrinking general budget, it is necessary to show by some means of documentation why the other subject areas have to release funds to the privileged one. It will be necessary to show that the privileged area actually, by some measure, is deserving more funds than the others, and this excercise will somehow have to be carried out a) with a view to future initiatives to receive matching grants and b) with a view to the ability of the privileged department to perform according to the criteria to be found. Thirdly, European Union guidelines will have to be observed carefully in order to fullfil the goal pursued under a.

In this proposition of the task of the university administrator, the preservation of the field as it traditionally has been taught does not figure anywhere. This could be considered an advantage if the new way of conducting research in that particular subject area where somehow the response of a scholarly exchange as to the merits of those subject areas, which it is not among our assumptions of this scenario. In fact, this scenario leaves ample space for entire Member States of the European Union to leave out entire subject areas from their curricula and research activities, and certainly without at any point of decision consciously wishing to do so.

As a *preliminary conclusion*, we can note that the scenarios of European policies towards research in science and technology have the potential to skew the decisions of identifiable decision makers so as to obfuscate the opportunity costs of their decisions and to emphasize sometimes small marginal benefits.

The introduction of the so-called Monnet professorships is an interesting case in point. The guidelines for the selection of Monnet professors call for nominations, either by name or by subject area or by both through the head of the university with the consent of all the reporting organizational parts (college, faculty, department, supervising professor), and the apparant idea of the whole initiative is to create a breed of young European minded professors in the schools. This objective it may very well achieve, but the opportunity costs, again, may be very high.

Let us take a look at how such a procedure takes place in a typical Member State of the European Union. Consider a state monopoly system of the university landscape (most European Member States have such a system) with the consequent depressed salary levels and high regulatory burdens.

Dynamic administrators have little chance in retaining promising young staff, and they have an eye on keeping promising staff with an ability to network in European circles so as to attract grants money. (this would, again, follow the 7:1 matching system as explained above). Obviously, in a department composed of the seven sub-disciplines A through G, the choice of a suitable candidate will have to focus on a young person in set F, who has not yet shown credible signs of being an achieving scholar but who has shown signs of being able to network and create funding relationships. The first point is important. If sufficient qualities in research and teaching as well as conceivably extension exist, this person is a hot asset and cannot be home bidded from an international market, which the European Union provides, among others through the Treaty of Rome, the re-enforcement of that treaty through the Treaty of Maastricht and, last but certainly not least the Erasmus and Socrates programs. The successful candidate who has been selected in the way suggested will bypass many of his competitors in his age group who have chosen different carreer paths. This will not go unnoticed, and the departments A to D and G will be further weakened by not being able to attract hard working if conceivably rather less "European" minded future university professors. Since in most Member States of the European Union, administrators who take the Monnet decisions are sitting for only one or two years, they have a strong incentive to further the interests of their own - within reason of their colleagues - and look at the future consequences, notably with respect to the entire research landscape and to what students can now reasonably expect, with less intensity of purview.

The Monnet program then will have produced an interesting group of people who will interact with the traditionally appointed university professors, but the long term impact of the program on the progress in science and technology in the European Union will be very difficult to assess. It may be impossible to assess, although the damage of the program may be substantial. The main damage lies in breaking the traditional carreer patterns on which life orienting decisions had been based, which is important in the case of researchers who tie their human capital to their research outlook, and it is also important with respect to guaranteeing a reliable transfer of knowledge to the next generation. Several European Union members are no longer able to transfer the common European knowledge in my own discipline, economics, to the next generation, as they lack, to name just the simplest instance, a commonly accessible source for tapping the internationally common pool of (in my case: economic) knowledge.

11. Alternative approaches

This essay has been difficult to read because the author had to lead the reader to conclusions that are by no means obvious, and that have not at all been discussed in the popular or academic press. Actually, the findings here presented cannot readily be translated into research paradigms that could be conducted so as to survive, in their output, standard review procedures for research to be published.

However, I submit to the reader the question: what else can we do? The problems pointed at in this essay are by no means obvious, and they spring from a mind trained in thinking about orders of systems, when most economists are not even trained in terms of thinking about systems but rather in terms of processes within the systems they have learned to know since they were high school students. The bread and butter applications of my suggestions are more tangible than what could have been accomplished through a sociological approach, they are also more tangible and, I think more palatable than could have been accomplished through a post-modernist approach, and yet I remain unhappy about not being able to systemattically have this analysis be screened by an audience that actually knows the subject[14]. The sample for a critical inquiry about the merits of my study would have to be a group of economically trained university administrators. This group does exist, and I intend (with the consent of the editor) to conduct such a survey. If one takes a world wide view, a surprisingly large number of economists have actually ended up as university presidents. The survey would emphasize the issue of whether my rendition of the problems European research universities face vis à vis the current and upcoming European initiatives, is skowed, wrong headed or to the point.

Since most of the actual consequences of European Union initiatives described in this chapter are difficult to ascertain in clear quantitatives terms, and since there are certainly no data bases which can be readily accessed by ill-equiped students ready to finish a disseration project within their allotted time, where the allotted time again has no bearing on the importance of the subject, it is difficult to dispute my story. But this is deeply troubling to me, as I am one who should like to have his story disputed if it is not correct. In this case, it is difficult to dis-sociate the personality of the writer from the article that is being written. One way, so far the only way I know, there may be others, is the approach to influence studies, Peter Senn[15] has pioneered.

---

14 In my attempts to discuss these matters, I have been stunned by the lack of knowledge of well known university professors about the circumstances of their professional existence. In particular, I was stunned by the fact that more is always thought to be better than less, without due regard to whether more is coming, and why the less is being accepted.

15 Senn, P. R., "Where is Althoff? Looking for Friedrich Althoff in English Language Sources", in: Backhaus, J. (guest editor), *Journal of Economic Studies*, vol. 20, No. 4/5, 1993, pp.201-261.
Senn, P.R., "What has Happened to Gustav von Schmoller in English?" Paper read at the symposium, *Gustav von Schmoller und die Probleme von Heute*, 24-27 June in Heilbronn, Germany, 1988.
Senn, P.R., "What has Happened to Gustav von Schmoller in English?", *History of Economics Society Bulletin*, (forthcoming).

This is one approach addressed to the question raised. It is not the only possible approach, and it is not the last approach.

The main point of this study, that the European research university, given the shape of the current programs of the European Union, is being weakened by the European Union, will only be demonstrable after the readers of this essay have long passed their prime.

12. Towards some tentative conclusions

In this essay, I have tried to show that the European Union inititiatives towards science and technology, ostensibly in the interest of promoting employment and growth through technological advancement, have side effects that undermine the very purpose at which they aim. The funding formula and the way the programs are launched undermine the ability of leading research universities to be leading players in the international fields that is, of course, not dominated by European Union research priorities. The only way to make the program successful is, indeed, to make it universal, which is out of the question. More specifically, we have taken note of a number of points which are worth taking stock of at the end of this long essay.

They do not quite reveal the impact of the argument, but some preliminary statements may well be formulated on the basis thereof.

1. At the traditional European research university, next to the publication of doctoral disserations and public examinations throughout open competition for university positions and the prohibition of inhouse promotions (which are known to lead to nepotism) form part of the heritage of reputation preservation. In no known case was there an emphasis, during the era of the traditional European research university, on trying to organize the competitive process for resources around topics of inquiry of themes of research, as such attemps would necessarily skew competition in terms of the specific competitors aware of their prior advantage.

Secondly, with respect to scholarly communication we can note:

2. Only if the participating scholars and scholarly institutions are roughly endowed with the same bundle of rights can an unstrategic process of scholarly communication take place and continue with success.

3. Joint financing arrangements stemming from decisions involving the European Commission and the European Council, and the consequences thereof, can lead to serious impairment and conceivably a break down of the scholarly community, the reliability of interchange and the unquestionability of scholarly motives in entering into scholarly communication.

New forms of financing universities would give even former state sponsored universities substantial room for re-learning the old game of competition.

4. This scenario is credible. In one case, it can be demonstrated that substantial funds had been accumulated within a fairly short period of time, under fairly adverse tax legislation, and yet being sufficient to feed an entire university (the University of Frankfurt on the Main). With enlightened or only a little bit enlightened tax legislation, it should be possible to repeat the experience.

5. The mechanisms of the programs launched by the European Union lead to a change in the budgettary flows in such a way that substantial shifts in academic pursuit are the likely outcome.

6. The scenarios of European policies towards research in science and technology have the potential to skew the decisions of identifiable decision makers so as to obfuscate the opportunity costs of the decisions and to emphasize sometimes small marginal benefits.

7. The difficulty in forming an opinion about the relevance and significance of European research policies lies in the impossibility of economists taking a point of view. In this sense, Max Weber[16] has greatly helped in writing this article.

16 Max Weber, "Wissenschaft als Beruf". In: *Wissenschaft und Politik als Beruf.* Tübingen: Mohr, Siebeck 1919, 1983 (Max Weber Gesamtausgabe, vol. 15-2).

Résumé

L'impact des politiques européennes de la science et de la technologie sur l'orientation de la recherche en Europe

Quelle influence exerce la politique de l'Union Européenne en matière de technologie et de recherche scientifique ? L'étude est ici centrée sur le rôle des Universités idéalisé du moins dans l'espace germanophone par le "modèle de Humboldt" du nom du philologue, philosophe et diplomate allemand qui créa en 1810 l'université de Berlin.

Il s'avère en fait, sur la base d'une analyse économique, que les système universitaire n'est pas simple à évaluer : les rôles des acteurs, les procédures, les références scientifiques, la publication des travaux de recherche et leur utilisation ne répondent pas à des normes précises ou à des formes imposées.

Ce constat devient intrigant à partir du moment où on admet que les Universités constituent un bien commun, producteur d'externalités. Des mesures particulières telles que celles générées par la politique européenne sont-elles alors susceptibles d'engendrer des biais, des déviations dans les missions d'universalité de l'Université ? Des exemples concrets viennent étayer la problématique étudiée.

Zusammenfassung

Politik der Europäischen Union im Hinblick auf Technologie und Forschungsfragen

Dieses Kapitel gilt der Politik der Europäischen Union im Hinblick auf Technologie und Forschungsfragen. Die Fragestellung wird auf die traditionelle forschende europäische Universität eingegrenzt, die im deutschen Sprachraum mit dem Humboldtschen Ideal beschrieben wird.

Es wird aufgrund eines ökonomischen Modelles gezeigt, daß diese Universität als System zwar begreifbar, aber im Einzelnen schwer modellierbar ist. Ihre Effizienz ruht in der umsichtigen Beobachtung von erwarteten Rollen, Prozeduren, Akten mit ihren Vorgängen und einem bestimmten Comment wissenschaftlicher Arbeit, der die Publikation der Forschungsergebnisse gewiß verlangt, aber nicht die Formen vorschreibt, in denen diese Publikation erfolgt.

Unter der Annahme, daß Universitäten vor allem (volkswirtschaftlich gesehen) öffentliche Güter und Externalitäten produzieren, wird weiter der Frage nachgegangen, wie sich die Politik der Europäischen Gemeinschaft auf die universitäre Landschaft in Europa auswirkt. Idealtypisch wird an die traditionelle Humboldtsche Universität gedacht. In dem Aufsatz wird im einzelnen ausgeführt, welche erheblichen Verschiebungen und zum Teil auch Verwerfungen die europäische Politik bewerkstelligen kann, und es wird auch auf einige Beispiele eingegangen, bei denen dies wahrscheinlich jetzt schon abzusehen ist.

References

ARRUÑADA, B. (1996): The Economics of Notaries. *European Journal of Law and Economics* 3.1. (March). pp. 5-37.

LEIBENSTEIN/STIGLER: X-Inefficiency. in the *American Economic Review*.. Stigler, G.J. The Xistence of X-Efficiency. *American Economic Review*, 66. 1976 pp. 213-216. Harvey Leibenstein. X-Inefficiency Xists: Reply to an Xorcist. *American Economic Review*, 68. 1978. pp. 203-211.

MÖSCHEL, W. (1989): Corporation Policy from an ORDO Point of View. Chapter 7 in: Peacock, A. and Willgerodt, H. (eds.) *German Neo-Liberals and the Social Market Economy*. New York: Saint Martin's. pp. 142-178 (154-155).

OLSON, M. (1973): Evaluating Performance in the Public Sector. In: Moss, M. (ed.). *The Measurement of Economic and Social Performance*. Studies in Income and Wealth 38. New York and London: Columbia University Press for the National Bureau of Economic Research. pp. 355-384 and 397-409.

PEIRCE, W.S. (1977): Bureaucratic Failure: Incremental Drift from Public Goods. Cleveland: Case Western Reserve University, Department of Economics. Working Paper Nr. 32.

SENN, P. R. (1993): Where is Althoff? Looking for Friedrich Althoff in English Language Sources. in: Backhaus, J. (guest editor). The Economics of Science Policy. *Journal of Economic Studies*. vol. 20. No. 4/5. pp. 201-261.

SENN, P.R. (1988): What has Happened to Gustav von Schmoller in English? Paper read at the symposium. *Gustav von Schmoller und die Probleme von Heute*. 24-27 June in Heilbronn, Germany.

SENN, P.R.: What has Happened to Gustav von Schmoller in English? *History of Economics Society Bulletin*. (forthcoming).

STARBATTY, J./VETTERLEIN, U. (1994): Forschungs- und Technologiepolitik in der Europäischen Union. Tübingen: Wirtschaftswissenschaftliche Fakultät. (Diskussionsbeitrag Nr. 39).

Hanns A. Abele

The Technology of Communication and the Reshaping of the European Broadcasting Industry

1. Introduction

2. Development of the European broadcasting system

   A. The emergence of the dual system
   B. Theoretical issues
   C. Regulating a dual broadcasting sector

3. Technological change and its economic consequences in the broadcasting industry

   A. A review of the technological development and its economic impact
   B. Basic economic questions to be answered
   C. Some skeptical observations

4. Conclusions

1. Introduction

Technology can exert a very important influence on economic and social systems. Some people think that the breakdown of the communist system was a direct consequence of the technological race which became dominant in the global race for superiority. Since the liberalisation and globalisation of markets made a lot of traditional instruments of economic policy obsolete more and more activities concentrated to create the best environment for technical progress. The hope is that this will help the country or the continent to stay competitive and secure a standard of living better than somewhere else.

Information is necessary to reach decisions conforming to the objectives. In addition it may help to produce knowledge and thus further technical progress. Efficient communication paves the way for dissemination of information and contributes to the improvement of production in a very general sense besides enhancing the comfort of human beings by removing their individual isolation.

This chapter discusses some aspects of technological progress in the sector of electronic media. The move to a digital technology is well on its way and has attracted firms from other sectors to start or deliberate offering media products. These firms belong to the computer and telecommunication industries and are among the largest corporations worldwide. It is necessary to ponder their impact on the European broadcasters and discuss the implications of this change as well as the probability of a radical shift within a short time span. In addition this chapter will give some hints on the theoretical problems and proposed solutions.

2. Development of the European broadcasting system

A. The emergence of the dual system

For almost five decades broadcasting signals were delivered over-the-air. Households received the signals from terrestrial transmitters. Since technical reasons prohibited the use of one channel for more than one signal at any time in a particular area in order to avoid signal interference the availability of the radio spectrum was the scarce factor in the supply of broadcasting. International organizations and government authorities have allocated the scarce spectrum by different methods to the intended uses[1]. Thus there was almost no room for private television mainly for technical reasons and governments' preferences.

During the last two decades this situation changed dramatically. The constraint of the scarcity of available spectrum to provide broadcasting programmes was relaxed by technical developments. Broadband cable and satellite based systems increased the options for distribution of programmes[2]. Although at first cable was mainly used to serve those households who had difficulties in getting a useful signal for their receiver because of difficult transmission conditions the additional availability of programmes to choose from changed cable's competitive position. Similarly satellite technology focused on high powered signals but technological developments have allowed to shift to other systems and reduced costs drastically. Since both opportunities for enlarged programme consumption were increased and costs for this consumption have been decreased incessantly it is no big surprise that demand for additional broadcasting has increased in line with this development. One decisive argument for the restriction of private broadcasting, scarcity of spectrum, was no longer valid[3].

1 For the methods to allocate spectrum see OECD (1993b):

2 A discussion of the rise of the cable segment in broadcasting industry and its relative competitive position is given by Johnson (1994).

3 A general overview of the development may be found in OECD (1993a) and Noam (1985).

Consequently all over Europe the supply of private broadcasting increased but less marked in the radio segment of the electronic media. As a result a dual broadcasting sector became the dominant structure in European countries[4]. The European courts promoted in several decisions on human rights grounds the development of private broadcasting vis a vis reluctant regulatory authorities.

Table 1: Shares of Audience of Public, Private and Foreign TV Programmes in Western Europe (Yearly Average of Grown Ups in Households with TV, in %)

	Domestic Programmes						Foreign Programmes		
	public			private					
	1988	1990	1992	1988	1990	1992	1988	1990	1992
Germany	85,0	68,7	51,1	9,6	22,7	40,1	5,4	8,6	8,8
France	37,0	33,0	38,0	63,0	67,0	62,0	0,0	0,0	
Great Britain	49,0	48,0	44,0	51,0	52,0	56,0	0,0	0,0	0,0
Italy	49,8	52,2	47,5	50,2	47,8	52,5	0,0	0,0	0,0
Spain	100,0 1)	83,2 1)	62,0 1)	0,0	16,5	37,2	0,0	0,3	0,8
Austria	89,0	80,0	73,0	0,0	0,0	0,0	11,0	20,0	27,0
Switzerland	40,0	38,0	33,0	0,0	0,0	0,0	60,0	62,0	67,0
Belgium	43,6	27,1	24,7	15,9	35,6	37,1	40,5	37,3	38,2
Netherlands	80,0	59,7	46,8	0,0	20.5	30,1	20,0	19,8	23,1
Norway	85,0	81,0	63,0	10,0	14,0	30,0	5,0	5,0	7,0
Sweden	76,0	72,0	71,0	0,0	13,0	22,0	24,0	15,0	7,0
Finland	61,0	57,0	54,0	33,0	39,0	41,0	6,0	4,0	5,0
Ireland	68,0	67,0	63,0	0,0	0,0	0,0	32,0	33,0	37,0
Portugal	98,0	98,0	95,0	0,0	0,0	0,0	2,0	2,0	5,0

1) incl. regional public programmes
Source: EBU: Trends in European Public Service Broadcasting. 1993. Cited from Media Perspektiven 3/94, p. 150. (translation H.A.)

4 See Noam (1991).

Table 2: Shares of Listeners of Public Radio in Western Europe (Yearly Averages of Grown Ups in Housholds with Radio, in %)

		1988	1990	1992
Germany	ARD	84,6	78,8	69,8
France	Radio France	18,6	18,3	20,6
Great Britain	BBC	72,0	67,0	61,0
Italy	RAI	40,7	37,0	29,4
Spain	RTVE	19,0	17,6	16,4
Austria	ORF	92,0	92,0	91,0
Switzerland	SRG/DRS	66,0	60,0	56,0
	SRG/SR	57,0	58,0	52,0
	SRG/SI	81,0	77,0	74,0
Belgium	RTBF	67,0	75,0	50,0
	BRT	77,4	87,7	84,6
Netherlands	NOS	87,0	70,0	53,0
Denmark	DR	69,0	68,0	77,0
Norway	NRK	66,0	66,0	66,0
Sweden	SR	77,0	76,0	73,0
Finland	YLE	90,0	61,0	73,0
Ireland	RTE	72,0	68,0	57,0
Portugal	RDP	32,0	30,0	20,0

Source: EBU:Trends in European Public Service Broadcasting.1993. Cited from Media Perspektiven 3/94, p. 150. (Translation H.A.)

The general picture emerging from the data in table 1 and 2 is the loss of market share of public broadcasters in Europe as a consequence of the development of the so called dual system. In television this loss is much larger than in the radio sector (whereas only in rare situations a slight increase can be diagnosed, namely in France).

Only four countries had no private television in 1992 yet, Austria, Switzerland, Ireland, and Portugal. With respect to competition from abroad it is possible to distinguish three groups of countries: a low one comprises those countries with market shares of foreign programmes less than 20%, a middle group with a percentage between 20 and 50% and a high group of more than 50%. Overall it is clear that the market shares of private and foreign programmes indicate close substitutes in the preferences of the audience simply because they are often supplied by the same programme providers.

Given the cost structure of producing a television or radio programme it must be possible to generate much higher earnings from television than from radio. Thus it is natural from economic incentives to provide private television. However, any supply needs sufficient demand in order to be sustainable. One of the important distinctions between public and private television programmes is the different programme structure. Content and presentation vary substantially. An illustration of the main aggregate programme patterns is given in fig. 1 and more detailed data are provided in table 5.

Table 3: Costs of ARD TV Programmes (Average Costs per Minute in DM (1))

Programmes			1991	1992	1993
ARD					
	Own Production of Members				
		Policy and Society	4 530	4 992	5 264
		Culture and Science	4 633	4 958	4 371
		Religion	4 126	4 680	4 201
		TV-Shows	17 460	17 244	16 558
		Entertainment	10 700	10 760	10 380
		Music Programmes	5 329	4 828	6 149
		Family	3 497	4 231	4 316
		Education, Advice	-	-	-
		Promotion	1 101	1 386	1 295
		TOTAL	6 537	7 147	7 424
	Joint Productions				
		News	5 950	5 625	6 814
		Weather	1 745	1 763	2 502
		Sport Show	8 126	8 166	7 486
		Films (Degeto)	5 620	4 960	4 470
		Others	5 002	3 108	3 371
		TOTAL	6 285	5 851	5 605
Television Programme Total			6 437	6 578	6 593
Regional Programmes			1 638	1 706	1 436
ARD/ZDF Morning Programmes			496	972	999
Third Programmes			972	898	775

1) Costs of transmission not included
Source: ARD Yearbook

Table 4: Costs of ARD Radio Programmes (Average Costs per Minute in DM (1))

Programmes		1989	1990	1991	1992	1993
1) Music		69	72	70	69	62
	Classic	127	125	140	135	136
	Pop	43	48	43	43	36
2) Vocal		168	167	167	147	145
	Politics	165	168	153	143	127
	Culture	189	189	180	172	174
	Education	151	166	186	202	199
	Entertainment	250	243	275	141	167
	Drama	532	571	518	549	515
	Sport	204	190	222	201	198
	Family Programmes	199	208	218	124	207
	Features	112	108	124	119	112
	Other	137	91	46	63	118
1+2 TOTAL		104	106	105	103	95
3) Programmes for Foreigners		27	28	31	34	36
1+2+3 TOTAL		101	103	102	101	93
Overall Total		99	102	101	99	92

1) Costs of Transmission excluded
Source: ARD-Yearbooks.

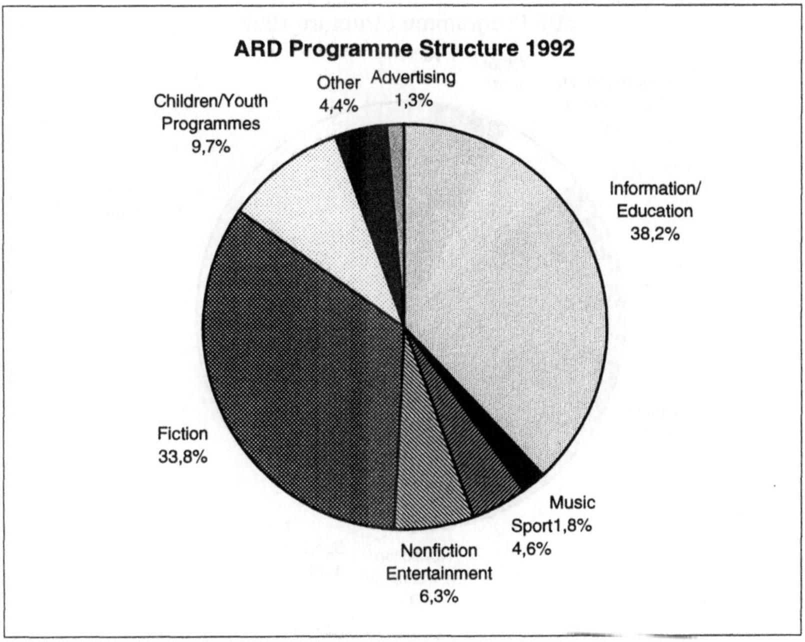
ARD Programme Structure 1992
Other 4,4%
Advertising 1,3%
Children/Youth Programmes 9,7%
Information/ Education 38,2%
Fiction 33,8%
Music
Sport1,8%
4,6%
Nonfiction Entertainment 6,3%

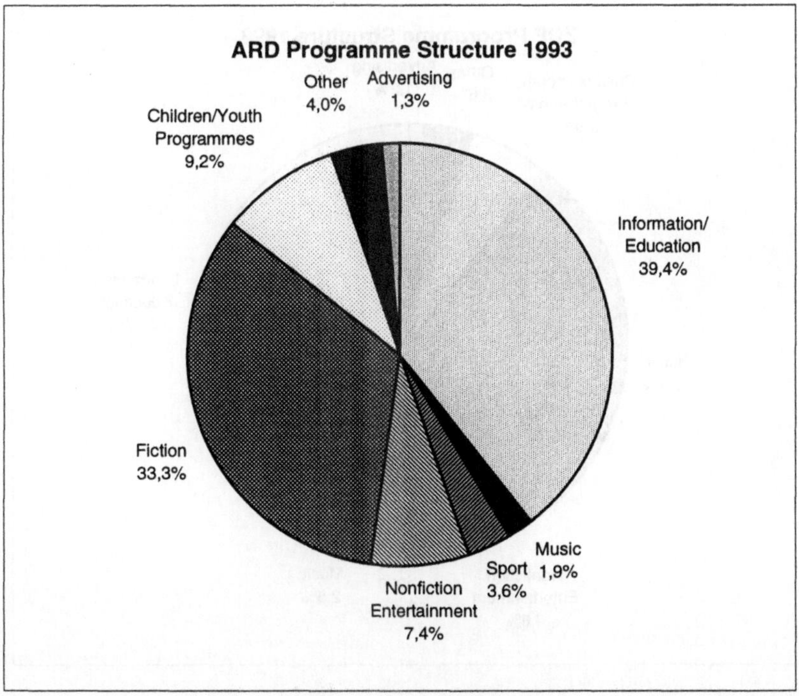
ARD Programme Structure 1993
Other 4,0%
Advertising 1,3%
Children/Youth Programmes 9,2%
Information/ Education 39,4%
Fiction 33,3%
Music 1,9%
Sport 3,6%
Nonfiction Entertainment 7,4%

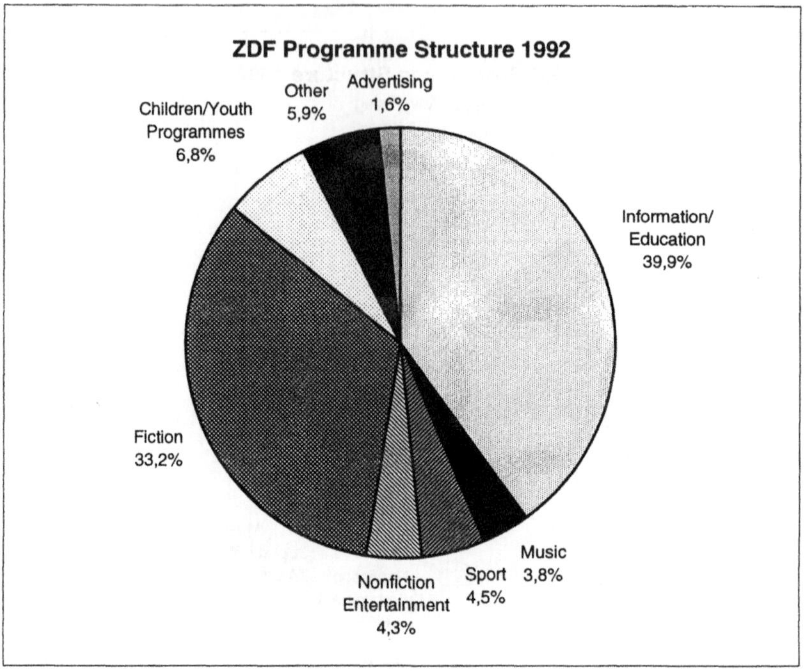
ZDF Programme Structure 1992
Other 5,9%
Advertising 1,6%
Children/Youth Programmes 6,8%
Information/ Education 39,9%
Fiction 33,2%
Music 3,8%
Sport 4,5%
Nonfiction Entertainment 4,3%

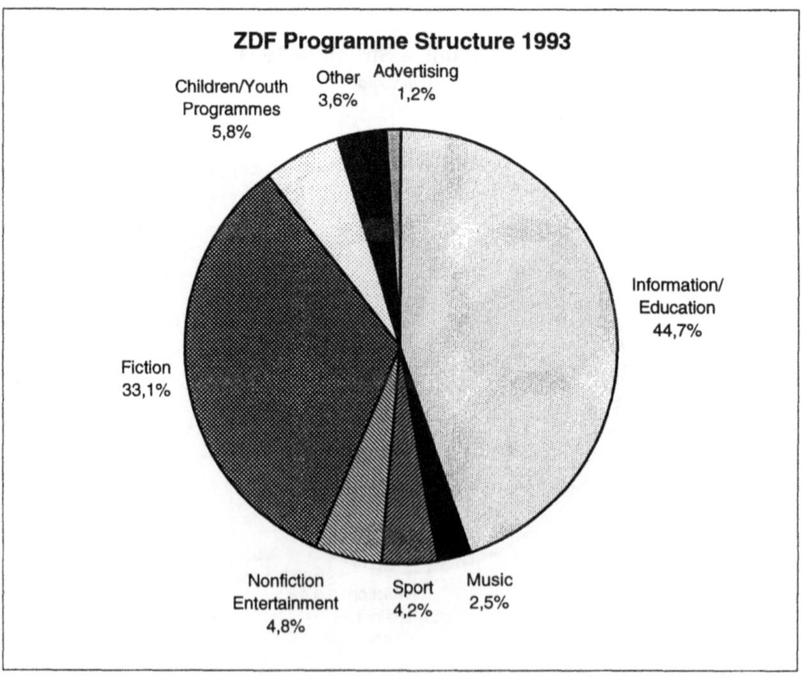
ZDF Programme Structure 1993
Other 3,6%
Advertising 1,2%
Children/Youth Programmes 5,8%
Information/ Education 44,7%
Fiction 33,1%
Nonfiction Entertainment 4,8%
Sport 4,2%
Music 2,5%

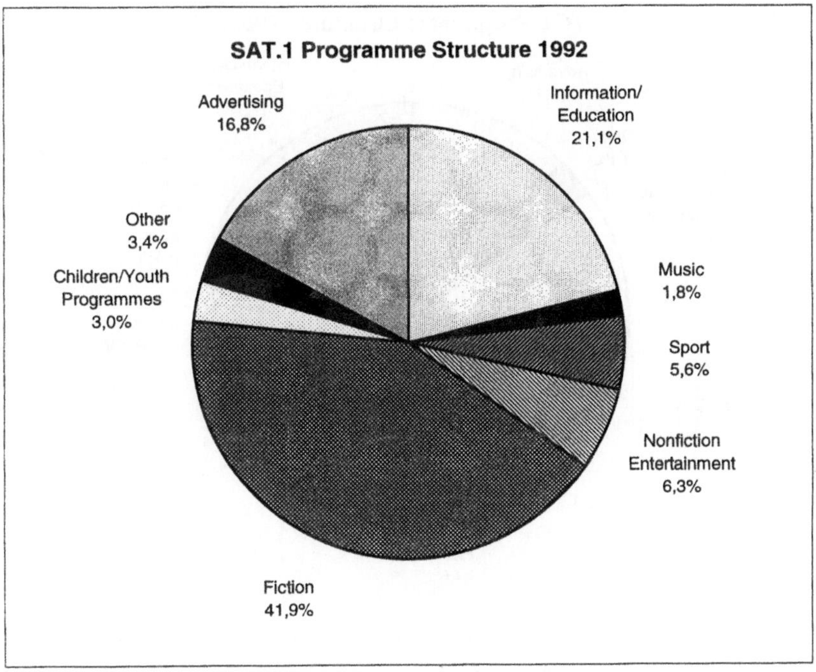
SAT.1 Programme Structure 1992
Advertising
16,8%
Information/
Education
21,1%
Other
3,4%
Children/Youth
Programmes
3,0%
Music
1,8%
Sport
5,6%
Nonfiction
Entertainment
6,3%
Fiction
41,9%

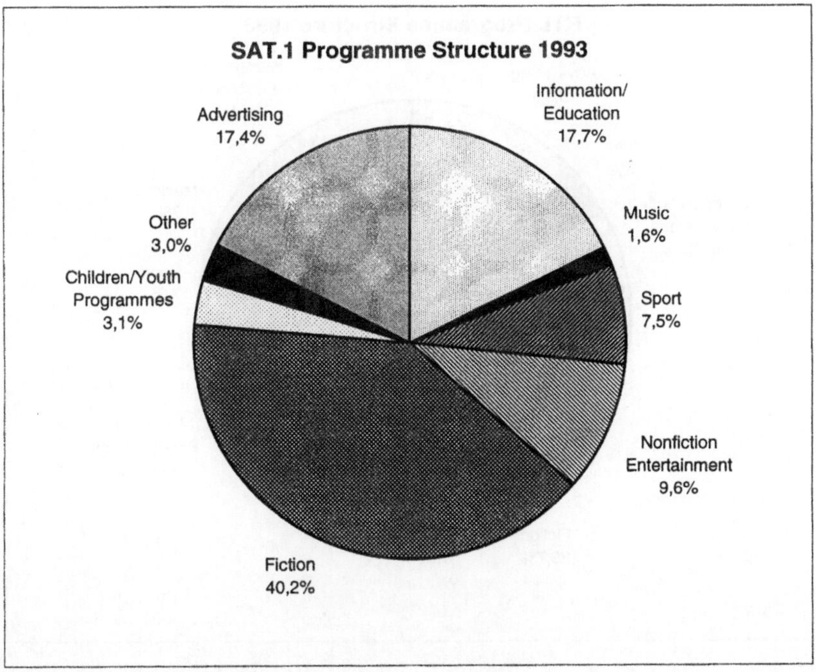
SAT.1 Programme Structure 1993
Advertising
17,4%
Information/
Education
17,7%
Other
3,0%
Children/Youth
Programmes
3,1%
Music
1,6%
Sport
7,5%
Nonfiction
Entertainment
9,6%
Fiction
40,2%

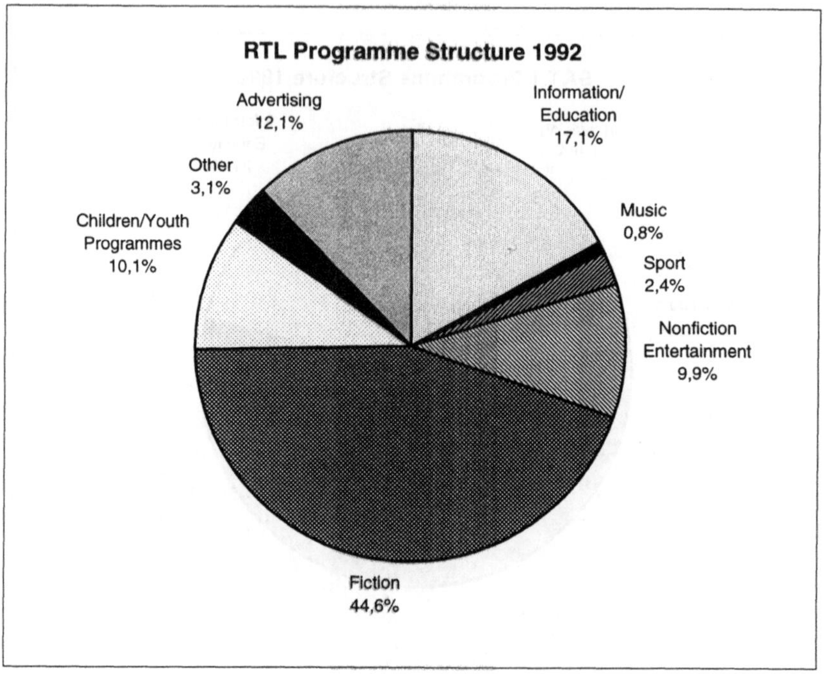
RTL Programme Structure 1992
Advertising
12,1%
Information/
Education
17,1%
Other
3,1%
Music
0,8%
Children/Youth
Programmes
10,1%
Sport
2,4%
Nonfiction
Entertainment
9,9%
Fiction
44,6%

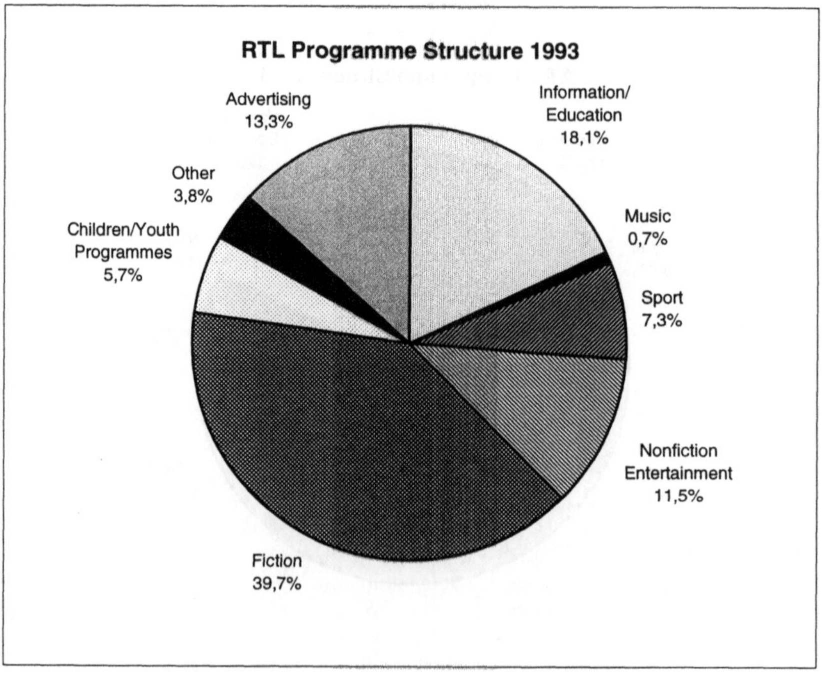
RTL Programme Structure 1993
Advertising
13,3%
Information/
Education
18,1%
Other
3,8%
Music
0,7%
Children/Youth
Programmes
5,7%
Sport
7,3%
Nonfiction
Entertainment
11,5%
Fiction
39,7%

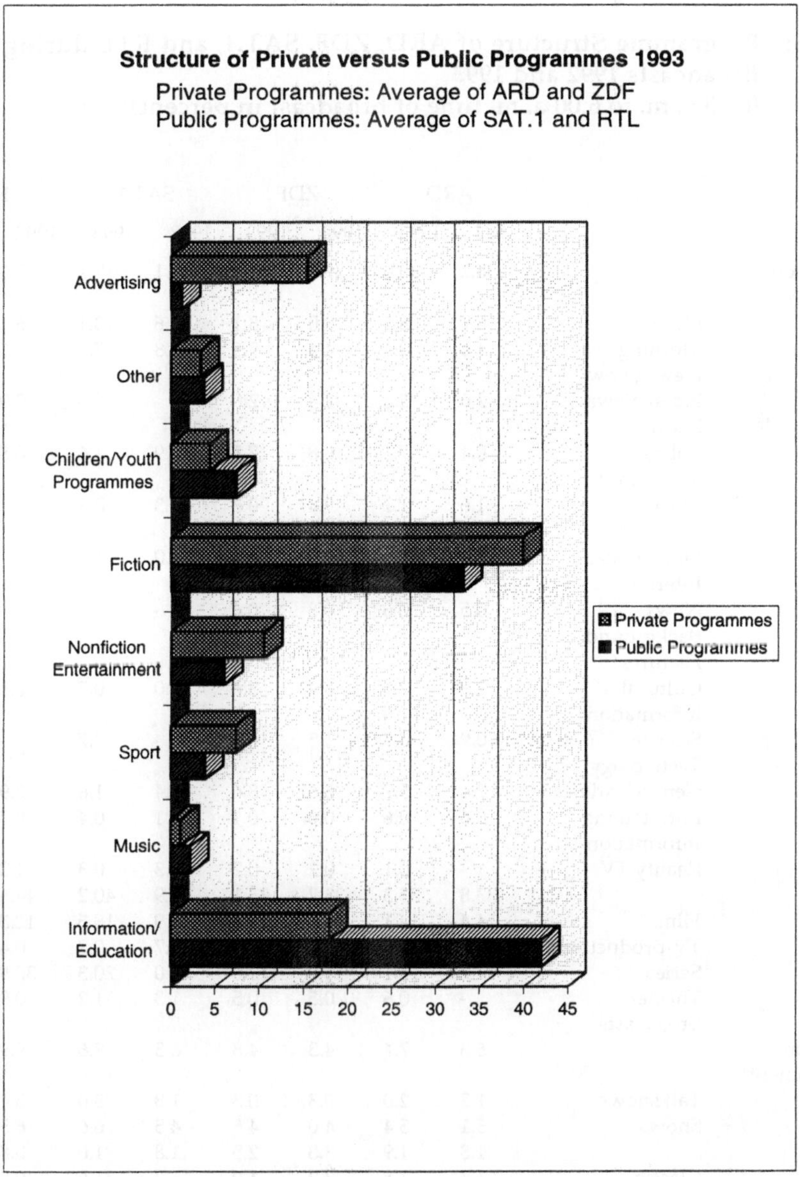
Structure of Private versus Public Programmes 1993
Private Programmes: Average of ARD and ZDF
Public Programmes: Average of SAT.1 and RTL
Advertising
Other
Children/Youth Programmes
Fiction
Nonfiction Entertainment
Sport
Music
Information/ Education
0
5
10
15
20
25
30
35
40
45
Private Programmes
Public Programmes

Table 5: Programme Structure of ARD, ZDF, SAT.1, and RTL during Total Broadcasts 1992 and 1993 (6.00 a. m. to 6.00 a. m. time of broadcast in percent)

		ARD		ZDF		SAT.1		RTL	
		1992	1993	1992	1993	1992	1993	1992	1993
Information/ Education		38.2	39.4	39.9	44.7	21.1	17.7	17.1	18.1
	News	8.7	8.3	8.0	8.1	5.6	3.1	5.1	4.5
	Morning News Show	4.6	9.4	4.4	9.5	4.8	7.4	5.0	6.2
	Noon News Show	2.6	2.3	2.4	2.0	-	-	0.9	1.0
	Policy Magazines	6.4	7.1	6.8	7.5	0.9	1.6	0.8	0.8
	Business Information	1.6	1.2	9.4	0.3	0.3	0.3	-	-
	Of Regional Interest	2.0	2.0	2.8	3.9	3.0	1.6	-	1.3
	News Background Features	0.5	0.6	0.8	0.4	-	-	-	0.1
	Cultural Information	2.9	2.1	3.4	3.6	1.0	0.7	0.6	0.6
	Science/ Technology	0.9	0.2	1.5	0.6	-	0.7	-	-
	General Advice	7.4	5.7	8.6	8.6	2.4	1.6	2.9	2.7
	Entertaining Information	0.6	0.6	0.6	0.1	0.1	0.4	0.7	0.2
	Reality TV	-	0.1	0.2	0.2	0.3	0.3	1.0	0.7
Fiction		33.8	33.3	33.2	33.1	41.9	40.2	44.6	39.7
	Films	14.4	14.1	14.5	11.4	15.9	18.5	12.3	7.1
	TV-productions	5.2	5.5	7.2	7.4	2.7	0.2	0.4	2.3
	Series	14.2	13.1	11.0	13.8	22.0	20.3	30.9	29.5
	Theater Broadcasts	-	0.6	0.5	0.5	1.3	1.2	0.9	0.6
Nonfiction Entertainment		6.3	7.4	4.3	4.8	6.3	9.6	9.9	11.5
	Talkshows	1.2	2.0	0.3	0.3	1.8	3.0	3.4	6.2
	Shows	5.1	5.4	4.0	4.5	4.5	6.6	6.5	5.3
Music		1.8	1.9	3.8	2.5	1.8	1.6	0.8	0.7
	Classic	1.4	1.8	3.2	1.9	1.8	1.6	0.8	0.7
	Pop	0.4	0.1	0.6	0.5	-	-	-	-
Sport		4.6	3.6	4.5	4.2	5.6	7.5	2.4	7.3
	Sport News	2.5	2.4	3.4	2.3	3.2	2.8	1.4	0.5
	Line Broadcasts	2.1	1.2	1.2	1.9	2.4	4.6	0.9	6.8

Children/Youth Programmes		9.7	9.2	6.8	5.8	3.0	3.1	10.1	5.7
	Children/Youth Non Fiction/ Fiction	5.2	5.6	2.1	2.0	0.9	0.7	4.6	0.6
	Children/ Youth/Fiction	4.5	3.5	4.7	3.7	2.2	2.3	5.5	5.1
Other		4.4	4.0	5.9	3.6	3.4	3.0	3.1	3.8
	Religious Broadcasts	0.1	0.9	0.8	0.8	0.0	0.1	-	-
	Other	2.2	1.2	1.4	1.1	0.8	0.5	0.3	0.3
	Station Identification, Programme Information	2.0	1.9	3.8	1.7	2.6	2.5	2.8	3.5
	Advertising	1.3	1.3	1.6	1.2	16.8	17.4	12.1	13.3
	Advertising Spots	1.2	1.3	1.6	1.2	9.6	11.6	9.8	12.2
	Teleshopping	-	-	-	-	0.3	0.1	0.3	0.0
	Other Advertising	0.1	0.1	0.0	0.1	6.9	5.6	1.9	1.1
Total		100	100	100	100	100	100	100	100
Broadcasted Time Min./Day		1085	1187	1125	1180	1285	1342	1440	1440

Source: KRÜGER, Udo Michael/ZAPF-SCHRAMM, Thomas, Programmanalyse 1993 von ARD, ZDF, SAT.1 und RTL. In: Media Perspektiven 3/1994. Adapted from Media Perspektiven. Basisdaten. Daten zur Mediensituation in Deutschland 1994.

With respect to time devoted to advertising there is a more than tenfold difference between the public broadcasters on the one hand and SAT.1 and RTL on the other hand. This difference leads to the second important distinction between private and public television suppliers: public broadcasters are predominantly financed by fees in Europe whereas private broadcasters rely on advertising revenue as their source of income.

Table 6: Sources of finance of public broadcasters in Europe (1) in %

	1988	1990	1992	1994 2)
fees	65,2	56,2	67,1	70,2
advertising	21,2	19,5	17,2	16,6
sponsoring	0,4	0,7	0,8	0,8
public subsidies	4,2	4,6	5,0	4,1
other	9,0	10,0	9,9	8,3
total	100,0	100,0	100,0	100,0

1) according to information by public broadcasters in 20 European countries.
2) estimates
Source: EBU: Trends in European Public Service Broadcasting. 1993.

B. Theoretical issues

From the theoretical viewpoint the dual broadcasting system generated two main areas for research, programme selection and welfare, as well as regulation. For quite some time economists elaborated a model proposed by Steiner[5]. Steiner used a framework which had been developed in a classic article by Hotelling and was able to mirror many institutional details of the broadcasting industry. In order to represent preferences of the audience he divided the audience in homogeneous subgroups with a preference ordering of the possible programmes. Two ownership structures of programme providers were studied. Steiner showed that the case of monopoly yielded greater programme diversity and thus higher consumer satisfaction. Competition resulted in programme duplication and forgone minority-taste programming. Despite the rather restrictive assumptions the results of Steiner's model were interesting. A number of modifications of the basic model were presented by different authors. Beebe (1971) presented the most elaborate model of this type which identified five factors determining the range of programmes being offered:

---

5 Cf. Steiner (1952).

(1) the number of channels for television
(2) the competitive or monopolistic control of the channels
(3) the cast of the programmes
(4) the financing of the programmes, advertising revenue and/or payments by viewers
(5) viewer's preference structure over programmes.

According to the richer structure of the model the results are more subtle and Steiner's conclusions may be reversed. Thus the judgement about the intensity of competition and its impact on the satisfaction of consumers can be found after studying all the determining factors of the model only. Spence and Owen (1977) provided significant progress in modeling demand for television programmes by using willingness-to-pay as a measure of preference intensity. They study four cases, namely advertiser supported TV or direct viewer payment (pay TV) both with either limited or unlimited number of channels, using as welfare criterion the gross dollar benefits minus the costs of the programmes being made possible by the decisions of agents. With some simplifying assumptions it is possible to summarize their model in a graph. Figure 10 illustrates possible equilibria in their model. The objective function being maximized depends on the case under study. Therefore there are three such functions:

(i) total surplus
$T(x,n) = nø\,(x) - Ax^2(n^2-n) - nF + nzx$ (1)

(ii) revenue function implicitly maximized by monopolistic competition
$R(x,n) = nxø' - Ax^2(n^2-n) - nF + nzx$ (2)

(iii) industry profits which is identical to the objective function of a monopolist
$((x,n) = nxø' - 2Ax^2(n^2-n) - nF + nzx.$ (3)

In this notation

n	number of programmes
x	audience size
z	price per viewer paid by advertiser

The function ø and the number A characterize demand and the substitutability of the programmes in the preference of viewers.

Figure 10

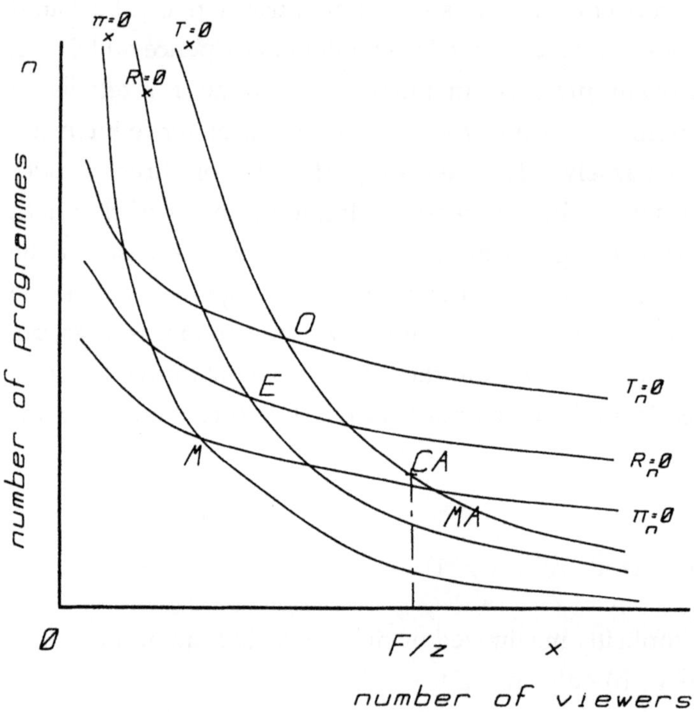

O	optimum
E	competitive pay TV equilibrium
M	monopoly pay TV
CA	competitve advertiser-support equilibrium (with unlimited channels)
MA	monopoly advertiser support

Source: adapted from Spence, Owen (1977)

Keeping in mind that the relative positions of the various maxima depend on the substitutability of the programmes it is easy to interpret the outcome by reading figure 10. The different competitive regimes may be ranked according to their desirability. For their example Spence and Owen conclude by using rather rough empirical estimates of costs and benefits that "advertizing prices fail by a wide margin to reflect viewers' valuations of programmes. This suggest that the competitive, advertiser-support equilibrium (CA...) is not in fact very close to the optimum in absolute terms, and increases the likelihood that E is superior to CA"[6]. This conclusion reinforces the result of a number of studies[7] that the way of financing the programmes may have a decisive impact on their contributions to the welfare and satisfaction of viewers. Dependence on advertisers' money makes a station less sensitive to the preferences of the viewers.

C. Regulating a dual broadcasting sector

As long as the availability of spectrum was the scarce resource the allocation of radio frequencies was of utmost importance[8]. The increased use of other distribution systems like cable and satellite generated a new situation for regulators. Among the issues to be considered in a dual broadcasting system were how to define the broadcasting market, how to analyze competition and concentration of media ownership, and what was the best policy response with respect to the approved goals[9].

By relying on the concept of elasticity regulators tried to define competition in the broadcasting industry and to compare diverse objects like networks and the cable industry. Although theoretically appealing it is very hard to get hold of necessary quantitative information to base decisions on good evaluation of factual circumstances.

---

6 Spence, Owen (1977), p. 119.

7 See Wildman, Owen (1985) and Owen, Wildman (1992) for extensive discussion and reference to the literature.

8 Some experiences with the allocation of commercial broadcasting are discussed in Dnes (1993).

9 See the discussion in OECD (1993a).

The rise of the private suppliers made the ability to secure sufficient funds of finance a thorny issue for regulators. Since public broadcasters have had fees as their basic finance they were restricted in their acquisition of advertising in order to allow the private programme providers to finance their activities almost exclusively by means of revenues from advertising. Since advertising has been not only an important source of finance for television but print media as well, another interest group entered the ring to fight for an additional share of profits. Crossownership among private television stations and publishing and media conglomerates brought the issue of concentration in the media market to the forefront. Public concern about the limits of tolerable concentration in the media sector is justified because democracy nowadays depends on a well developed media sector, especially the electronic media, for citizens' information and the political process itself.

The way regulators conduct their business changed as well. Theoretical developments, in particular in the realm of economics of information, led to a new understanding of the working of regulation. Rather naive mechanical conceptions were replaced by sophisticated strategic mechanism designs allowing regulation despite asymmetric informations and limited possibilities to collect additional information to pursue the goals which regulation wants to attain. One example, although from the telecom sector, is sufficient in this context. This is the ingenious auction of spectrum the Federal Communications Commission conducted at the end of 1994 and the beginning of 1995 using a specially designed format of an auction and the internet to kick off a new system of personal communication[10]. It is reasonable to borrow from these experiences in order to regulate the broadcasting sector.

10 The background and the deliberations leading to the choice of the specific auction format are reviewed by McMillan (1994).

3. Technological change and its economic consequences in the broadcasting industry

A. A review of the technological development and its economic impact

Digital signal processing has been a technology whose impact has steadily spread. The rise of the computer industry and the advent of the personal computer in particular demonstrated the superiority of digital technology for many applications. More and more people became aware of the potential of this technology for their purposes. Thus a rush to be ahead of others in exploiting the profit opportunities set in.

The computer industry regarded digital technology as its home turf, but the telecom sector moved to digital technology as well. There were early attempts to merge these two basic sectors when IBM bought ROLM and later AT&T bought NCR. These ventures failed, but the underlying economic factors urging such mergers were unchanged. Both the computer industry and the telecom firms have been facing saturated markets in their traditional acitivities and had to look for new fields to keep on expanding. The revival of the idea of MULTIMEDIA as an integration of text, image, and sound based on a unified technology, namely digital signals, was an attempt to create a catchy marketing concept to conquer new markets. As a consequence of the search for new markets and in line with pursuing the idea of MULTIMEDIA, computer firms and telecom firms set their eyes on entertainment and television. Especially television seemed to be a good candidate to provide a port of entry for the newcomers to expanded chances to sell new products to new costumers. Suddenly the broadcasting sector has been confronted with the possibility of serious competition from outside.

Add-ons and software make it possible to run videos on a PC or television programmes in a window of the PC. Because sound and vision are digitized they are easily manipulated. Similarly the transmission capabilities of increased bandwith allow for indiviualized consumption by pay per view or video on demand. On the other hand telephone services do not use a lot of bandwith and are therefore a possible addition to the products of the cable sector having normally high capacity networks. Telecom firms are forced to try to provide similar products on their networks in order to defend their position. Thus all the diverse sectors are feverishly working on invading each others markets and all together they are trying to establish themselves as suppliers of TV products and starting to compete with traditional broadcasters, networks or cable companies. In principle technology provides a framework for new dimensions of communication by paradoxically individualizing mass communication.

In addition to offering the ability for individual manipulation of the way to consume information and change this information digital technology holds another luring promise. For a long time mass communication was characterized by one way flows. The recipient had the choice to accept or to deny the message. However, the new technologies pave the way to increased interactivity. This means that two way communications can be realized technologically even with TV like products.

It is an interesting question to study the effects of technological developments on economic circumstances. Does technology drive the growth of markets? Are traditional broadcasters under pressure because their technology is superseded by another developed by different sectors and allowing two way communications? Principally the answer to these questions is related to Schumpeter's famous hypothesis of the role of entrepreneurship and technology in the dynamic evolution of an economy[11]. Although Schumpeter's ideas are now used even in colloquial discussions they resist strict theoretical investigation. It is easier to make the ideas plausible than to come up with adequate models empirical corroboration. The complexity of questions involved in the problem mentioned requests a variety of approaches to illustrate the different dimensions.

11 In contrast to Schumpeter's opinion the Nobel laureat Fogel (1964) showed that the contribution of railway construction to the growth of the growth of the US economy was rather small!

The technical consensus view about the implementation of the new possibilities consists of a network of some suitable topology and an interface to the consumer. Some think of huge servers sitting in the net holding all the software and providing the necessary information to the end user on demand. Not very surprising this is the view of firms being strong in databank software. Others conceive of an interface having high processing power, being able to decompress the material received, and handling all two way interaction. In any case the set-top box which is an implementation of the interface will control the admission to the services provided by the network. Therefore it is important for any content provider not to be excluded by the access capabilities for these boxes because otherwise demand for their products will be severely restricted.

Consequently there is a big fight to dominate the upcoming technology and market for set-top boxes. By now it is clear that control of an essential element of a technology is an important ingredient for economic success. This has been proven by the rise of Microsoft via control of the operating system for PCs. In addition it is very unlikely that households will be ready to buy several boxes to access different networks which enhances the importance to be accessible for all or the majority of households.

By analogy one may learn from similar but more isolated developments. A case in point is the attempt to improve the quality of television by introducing High-Definition Television (HDTV). The central question to study is the economics of standard setting[12]. On the one hand the failures of agreeing on a unique standard for videos, PCs and other areas and on the other hand the success of standards for audio cassettes and CDs sensitized managements of global firms and economic politicians for the impact of the decisions to be taken. Concerning HDTV Japan was the pioneer. Since the late 1960s Nippon Hoso Kyokai (NHK) has been proposing and developing HDTV and began experimental broadcasts in 1979. Europe lagged but was still far ahead of the USA. Thus concern spread that adoption of the Japanese system as a global standard would give enormous competitive advantages to Japanese industry. Hence the adoption was blocked.

12 Farrell, Shapiro (1992) are an excellent source to start with.

Meanwhile the United States tried to turn their disadvantage into a comparative advantage by moving from a system with analog technology to a fully digitalized system. This allowed to build on the strength of the computer industry in the USA. The move to a digital system by the FCC forced the competitors, Japan and Europe, to develop a similar system as well, consequently evaporating their advantages. Now even in Japan the only working system by NHK is almost completely digital.

Because of the increasing globalization of markets it is clear that a unified standard for set-top boxes is urgently needed and there will be considerable pressure from content providers to agree on such a standard. The recent negotiations to unite the competing formats for offering videos on CDs may illustrate the upcoming developments in the attempts to provide new television products and other forms of communication and entertainment.

The huge uncertainty accompanying technological shifts and the big amount of investment necessary to get a new system going induces big players to rely on a trial and error method. In the USA and in Europe there are a number of pilot experiments which help to collect experiences and try different technological layouts and various economic products. It is understandable that there are only few informations about these test sites available because they are set up to generate predominantly private information and nobody wants to pass on this information to the competitors[13]. However, it is astonishing how far most of these tests run behind initial expectations. E.g. Time Warner has recruited a handful only of interested households for the test in Orlando although it was initially offered as a free service. Somehow press reports seem to have, maybe deliberately, overstated the curiosity and interest of people for the new technological possibilities.

13 At least for Germany there is now available a summary report about the tests being conducted; cf. Felsenber, e.a.

In addition to the technological problems there are numerous legal questions open. The growth of the internet has made people sensitive for issues of security and privacy which are to be solved also for interactive services especially teleshoping. The software industry deplores huge losses because of piracy which for sure will not stop if video on demand will be broadly available. The economic question of how to price the new products is still very unclear as the households readiness and ability to pay for new services cannot be taken for granted.

B. Basic economic questions to be answered

Even if it is difficult to predict the outcome of the intensive activities to move to new technologies by merging telecom, computer, and broadcasting industries one aspect is very clear: there will be a vastly increased demand for inputs to be able to supply new and traditional products. This means that the upstream demand, e.g. for films, scripts, shows, news will increase dramatically. Sony learned from its lost battle about the format of videos, camcorders, and VCRs that even technical superiority will not make good for lack of software. Thus a big run to buy Hollywood studios, their creative talents, and their film archives set in. However, not all the investments in these entertainment producers turned out to be profitable, at least in the short run.

Vertical integration poses difficult strategic decisions for managers. Because of the rapidly changing market environment the competitive position of firms undergoes rather swift changes. In addition ties to upstream as well as downstream firms may be transformed similarly abrupt. Theoretical analysis relies on game theoretic methods to shed light on the options for firms in situations of vertically structured markets[14]. Foreclosure is a strategy which can increase profits in some situations. Oligopolistic markets are natural candidates for coalitions or exclusion. At least at the global level rather few players are active worldwide which enforces the necessity of a study of the strategic dimension.

14 One interesting example of this literature is Church, Gandal (1992).

The conclusions of the top players are different, sometimes almost contrary. Whereas AT&T decided to split up and form special units to cope with the changing markets after having tried to answer the challenge by buying other firms and merge with them, Disney moved to integrate upstream and downstream activities. Only future development will show which strategy will turn out to be better[15].

C. Some skeptical observations

The promotion of the vision of a new paradigm in the use of electronic media was at the beginning dominated by p.r. instruments conveying - on purpose - euphoric messages about the new possibilities. The Clinton/Gore Administration generated the idea of a national information (data) highway[16] which should be the vehicle for the glittering new world of MULTIMEDIA and use of information. Similarly the European Council tried to prevent another European fall back in an important industrial sector and set up a task force to develop ideas for the creation of a new information sector. The report of this group was presented at the Corfu conference of the EU[17].

Given the economic woes it is alluring to rely on some dynamic factor to revive economic growth. The big hope is that this will bring new jobs urgently needed in industrialized countries which have been plagued by stubborn unemployment. Unemployment in the OECD area has become a very disturbing factor since it has resisted traditional policy recipes and has been growing for decades[18]. A further advantage of the information highway is the

15 For background material see Egrine, Papathanassopoulos (1990). The Wall Street Journal Europe carried a supplement in June 1995 which was an illustration of the various forms of strategic alliances up to 25 May 1995 among the different camps with the title: Global Convergence ARCchart "Thinking Outside the Box". It looked like a spider web linking firms with a multimedia content, multimedia distribution, hardware/electronics, software, and telecommunications orientation.

16 See U.S. Department of Commerce (1993).

17 Cf. High Level Group on the Information Society (1994).

18 See OECD (1994) for an extensive discussion of theoretical, political, and factual aspects of the problem.

hope that the need for public funds seems to be limited. The main brunt of the financial burden is expected to fall on the private sector especially the newcomers to the multimedia business. This is essential because the general need to reduce public deficits - not only in Europe to fulfill the Maastricht criteria but also in the USA - severly limits the ability of governments to pump prime economic growth. During recent cyclical upswings the industrial countries experienced growth without increased employment, however, which casts serious doubts on the effectiveness of promoting the information sector as an instrument of employment policy.

Widely open is the demand side for the new technological opportunities as well. There are no reliable results on the willingness of households to pay for the new offers. In general, reduced employment perspectives mean diminished income and induce precautionary consumption. All outlays regarded as nonessential will be planned very carefully. New services and products face an uphill battle because they have to replace other budget items if they cannot be financed out of income growth. This makes it rather iinprobable to see explosive growth in the new fields which would be necessary to recover the big costs of inital investment.

But there are not only financial obstacles. Consumption of media products is time consuming. Although there are marked differences between age groups and media products the daily audiovisual consumption is between 5 an 6 hours as indicated in table 11 for Germany. Given the present institutional arrangements like working hours and education system it is difficult to expect a sizeable increase of the time devoted to audiovisual consumption. Thus there is the possibility of substitution only of older products by new products.

The development of this huge market is illustrated by the data in tables. Despite some crisis at the beginning of the 80s the sale of audio media is one of the most dynamic growth product in consumer goods markets. From 1985 to 1994 sales amost tripled.

Table 7: Global Sales of Audio Media

	Units (1 000 000)				Sales (1 000 000 US-Dollar) 2)
Year	Singles	LPs	Tapes 1)	CDs	
1981	550,0	1 140,0	510,0	-	12 300
1982	680,0	900,0	570,0	-	11 200
1983	800,0	850,0	660,0	5,5	12 000
1984	750,0	800,0	800,0	20,0	12 000
1985	650,0	730,0	950,0	61,0	12 250
1986	490,0	690,0	970,0	140,0	14 000
1987	390,0	590,0	1 150,0	260,0	17 000
1988	370,0	510,0	1 390,0	400,0	20 300
1989	357,0	450,0	1 540,0	600,0	21 600
1990	341,0	339,0	1 446,0	770,0	24 050
1991	330,0	157,0	1 428,2	977,8	26 203
1992	349,1	114,9	1 471,7	1 165,6	28 794
1993	405,6	80,5	1 348,7	1 392,8	30 492
1994	391,1	37,7	1 383,2	1 741,0	35 533

1) 8-track-cartridges and musicasettes
2) Sales at consumer prices
Source: International Federation of the Phonografic Industry (IFPI).

A decisive change in this market has been the shift towards CDs and digital technology. The latter opens up new ways for distribution and new opportunities to fight the high quantity of piracy. In general, one has to conclude that growth in the audio market was made possible by reduced prices, shifts to new products and only in part by an expansion of outlays for media products.

Table 8: Sales of Audio Media in USA, Japan, Great Britain, and France

	Units Sold (in 1 000 000)			
	Singles	LPs	Tapes 1)	CDs
USA				
1985	120,7	167,0	339,1	22,6
1986	93,9	125,2	344,5	53,0
1987	87,1	107,0	410,0	102,1
1988	89,7	72,4	450,1	149,7
1989	112,7	34,6	446,2	207,2
1990	116,1	11,7	442,2	286,5
1991	97,7	4,8	360,1	333,3
1992	111,7	2,3	355,4	407,5
1993	108,5	1,2	339,5	495,4
1994	102,1	1,9	345,4	662,1
Japan				
1985	53,2	46,4	59,6	16,5
1986	50,6	34,2	56,7	36,1
1987	38,4	20,8	59,9	52,0
1988	43,3	8,7	63,9	72,0
1989	44,0	1,7	59,2	114,7
1990	50,8	0,6	45,8	135,3
1991	89,6	0,7	19,4	171,8
1992	105,8	0,8	16,2	181,8
1993	145,3	0,6	14,0	191,8
1994	130,6	0,5	11,0	203,5
Great Britain				
1985	73,8	52,9	55,4	3,1
1986	67,4	52,3	69,6	8,4
1987	63,4	52,2	74,4	18,2
1988	60,1	50,2	80,9	29,2
1989	61,1	37,9	83,0	41,7
1990	58,9	24,7	75,1	50,9
1991	56,3	12,9	66,8	62,8
1992	52,9	6,7	56,4	70,5
1993	56,3	5,0	55,7	92,9
1994	63,0	4,5	56,0	116,4
France				
1985	64,0	33,9	22,3	2,4
1986	54,8	28,0	22,0	6,2
1987	49,4	20,4	22,1	12,5
1988	42,7	19,4	31,0	25,9
1989	36,3	16,2	40,1	40,3

1990	28,0	6,7	41,9	54,8
1991	21,7	1,4	41,6	72,6
1992	16,9	0,2	35,5	78,5
1993	20,8	0,1	31,2	86,6
1994	16,3	0,1	27,7	95,2

1) MusiCasetten in USA und Japan icluding 8-Track-Cartridges.
2) Sales in Consumerprices
Sources: Recording Industry Association of America (RIAA): International Federation of the Phonografic Industry (IFPI): British Phonografic Industry (BPI).

Similarly there seems to be a different pattern of uses of VCRs, telephone, and mailorder services as well as online services in Europe than in the USA.

Table 9: Videorecorder, Telefon, Mailorder: Uses in USA and Europa (% of households)

	USA	D	GB	F	I
Renting videos (households with VCRs) 1)	82	35	36	30	45
Using telefons for ...2)					
ordering meals/pizzas	45	21	14	1	11
homebanking	25	2	3	1	19
ordering tickets	23	12	15	1	9
information services	17	13	2	12	14
lotteries/betting	21	1	26	23	1
Mailorder 2)					
clothes, shoes	39	29	23	10	37
hardware, furniture	23	8	12	4	7
books, casettes, CDs	39	10	11	7	20
gifts, food, other	29	12	2	4	10

1) Share of households renting one or more videos during last month households with VCRs in %: USA=88, D=63, GB=74, F=60, I=57
2) regular uses
Source: Inteco/TV World.

Table 10: Subscribers of American online-services and Btx/Datex J 1990 - 1995 (in 1000)

	1990	1991	1992	1993	1994	1995
CompuServe	740	900	1 130	1 600	2 450	3 200
America Online	110	160	200	530	1 500	3 000
Prodigy	440	750	1 000	1 050	1 200	1 600
Delphi	70	75	80	85	100	140
Apple World	-	-	-	-	65	90
Genie	70	85	100	100	75	75
TOTAL+	1 600	2 200	2 700	3 750	6 300	8 600
Btx/Datex J	258	302	340	497	708	818

at yearend, 1995=June, rounded
+including others

Thus the consumers in Europe are more reluctant to use interactive services or the services are relatively more expensive in Europe than in the USA or both. In any case increased interactivity seems to be more attractive for sellers of services and their marketing campaigns than the consumers.

Even if consumers are going to look for the new trendy MULTIMEDIA products it is doubtful whether they will have enough time and money to buy and use these products. Given the use of time and the average income situation as demonstrated in tables 11 and 12 only substitution of present consumption can create room for a switch to new media products in the short run[19].

19 Like most of the other data used in this chapter German data are presented to secure within the given space limits comparable information.

Table 11: Time Used To Consume Audiovisual Media (min. per day, 5 a.m. to 12 p.m., Monday -Sunday)

		1992	1993	1994
Radio				
	Total	169	169	168
	Men	158	158	159
	Women	178	178	177
	14-19 y.	125	125	121
	20-29 y.	171	177	168
	30-39 y.	193	181	188
	40-49 y.	183	183	181
	50-59 y.	175	176	175
	60-69 y.	165	168	169
	70 y. +	137	140	142
TV				
	Total	177	177	178
	Men	176	176	176
	Women	178	179	181
	14-19 y.	137	133	142
	20-29 y.	141	138	141
	30-39 y.	166	166	159
	40-49 y.	165	166	169
	50-59 y.	189	189	190
	60-69 y.	226	223	224
	70 y. +	222	226	225
Video				
	Total	n.a.	4	4
	Men	n.a.	6	5
	Women	n.a.	3	3
	14-19 y.	n.a.	12	10
	20-29 y.	n.a.	8	8
	30-39 y.	n.a.	6	4
	40-49 y.	n.a.	4	3
	50-59 y.	n.a.	2	2
	60-69 y.	n.a.	1	1
	70 y. +	n.a.	0	1
Records, Casettes, CDs, Tapes				
	Total	13	13	13
	Men	14	15	15
	Women	11	11	11
	14-19 y.	42	44	36
	20-29 y.	25	24	26
	30-39 y.	13	13	14
	40-49 y.	9	9	9

	50-59 y.	5	5	6
	60-69 y.	3	3	4
	70 y. +	2	2	2
Audiovisuel Consumption				
	Total	357	361	361
	Men	347	352	352
	Women	365	369	369
	14-19 y.	300	309	305
	20-29 y.	335	345	340
	30-39 y.	369	363	364
	40-49 y.	355	359	361
	50-59 y.	367	370	370
	60-69 y.	392	394	396
	70 y. +	359	367	370

Source: Media Perspektiven, Basisdaten. Daten zur Mediensituation in Deutschland 1994. (translated and adapted H.A.)

Table 12: Monthly Outlays for Media Consumption: BRD (West) (in DM)

	4-Person medium income Household		
	1991	1992	1993
TV sets	11,34	10,10	11,68
Radio sets	10,68	12,62	9,58
Addous	5,15	6,52	3,89
Installation/Repair	2,74	3,88	1,91
Fees	21,87	26,68	28,62
Other hardware	3,52	3,45	3,35
VCRs	6,41	4,79	4,16
Records, Tapes, e.a.	12,59	14,65	16,23
Books	23,12	23,71	26,62
Newspapers	18,53	18,37	18,56
Magazines	13,73	13,59	14,85
Cinema	2,35	2,00	2,95
Theater	2,55	3,07	2,47
Concerts	1,41	1,39	1,69
TOTAL (+)	135,99	144,82	146,56
Average Income (-)	4 580,65	4 769,35	4 850,41
Share (+)/(-) in %	3,60	3,63	3,68

Source: Federal Statistical Office Media Perspektiven. Basisdaten. Daten zur Mediensituation in Deutschland 1994. (translated and adapted H.A.)

Economic reasons, reduced growth and increased unemployment risk, and social and behavioural factors cast some doubt on the readiness of consumers to embrace the new developments in the media industry. Even if this technology will be adopted in the long run which seems to be very likely given the economic power of those promoting this technology it seems to be very unlikely that this shift will take place in a rather short time.

4. Conclusions

In order to gain access to markets outside their traditional realm telecommunication and computer firms start to offer television like products and try to develop interactive multimedia services. They try to exploit their comparative advantages and aim at developing digital technology in a way to supplement their existing installations. Broadcasters are normally not well positioned to provide interactivity except when they distribute their programmes via cable.

Interactivity may be one strength of the position of telecom firms, however, their networks are very often still lacking capacity for bandwith to transmit moving images satisfactorily. The best position in relation to the enlarged and intensified competition seem to have the cable industry. A way out of this dilemma for the disadvantaged is to develop hybrid systems relying in part on existing installations and complementing them with new links and/or new technology.

The new technical opportunities create for traditional broadcasters enhanced competition not only in their programming and transmitting activities but at the upstream level as well. Vastly increased numbers of channels need to be filled with content. Therefore there will be fierce competition for talent, films, series and the rights to cover events like the olympic games or other well known sport contests. A clear indication of this development is the dramatic increase of the prices to cover olympic games or soccer world championship or the national soccer champions league.

On the other hand the value of production capacity and archives will increase. A multiplicity of channels makes sense only if each is able to attract consumers and therefore interesting material has to be presented. Otherwise the new technological options are void of content and are sure to be extinct within a short time.

One of the features embedded in the new technological opportunities is intensified interactivity. Most implementations rely on high capacity networks and efficient compression techniques. The importance of the distribution channels increases for broadcasters because access to a suitable system is decisive for the possibility to reach recipients. If traditional broadcasters are excluded from access to these transmission systems they will vanish in the long run. Consequently they will have to fight hard that set-top boxes are not used as an instrument to exclude them from distributing their products.

The present discussion of upcoming changes in television seems to suggest that the competitive position of private programme providers will be deteriorating more than their public counterpart's. One of their strength, providing interesting and recent films, may be substituted by video on demand allowing a viewer to fine tune the time structure of his consumption according to his preferences. In the same direction work the changes with respect to advertising.

Digital technology allows more manipulation of the programme by the enduser. This ability might be used to avoid advertising inserts. Reduced visibility of their messages leads advertisers to look for alternative ways to reach their target groups undermining the main source of finance for private programme providers. New pricing schemes like pay per view may compensate for lost advertising revenues. Increased use of fees by private broadcasters blurs an important distinction between private and public suppliers. Because the way of financing programmes has an important influence on the contents and the structure of programmes this change reduces further the difference between private and public broadcasters and their antithesis in the dual system.

Both globalisation of media markets and a multitude of technological options make it of utmost importance to look for potent partners. Broadcasters have to enter strategic alliances to respond to their new business environment. This represents a big unusual challenge for them because it implies a repositioning in a changing market.

Last but not least it is important to point to the need for new concepts of policy responses as well. Evolutionary changes of economic activities need an appropriate institutional framework. The conduct of policy has to be revised accordingly. Otherwise policy is in danger to become irrelevant at best or detrimental at worst. In addition it should be remembered that previous technological shifts were engineered using public broadcasters as a vehicle for innovation. Because of the huge sums required to finance any system of interactive television industry is reluctant to invest. For political reasons and competitive pressure the increases of fees for public broadcasters are under tight control and do no longer allow accumulation of substantial reserves. Thus it may be the case that the public broadcasting sector no longer can be a leader in the transition to new technologies. Since politicians expect the developments under the slogan of information highway as a long needed help for the European employment problem this development may pose a dilemma endangering fundamental goals of economic policy. In any case technological developments hold the potential for fascinating reconfigurations of the sector of electronic media which can have far reaching impacts for the economies and societies in Europe.

Résumé

Les technologies de communication et la réorganisation des secteurs de la radio et de la télévision européens

Les nouvelles technologies du cable et de la transmission par satellites ont élargi d'une manière considérable les possibilités de diffusion de l'information et de l'image. C'est aussi par la suite un système dual de médias électroniques qui s'est développé, marqué par la rivalité des émetteurs publics et privés avec des incidences réglementaires et politiques.

L'évolution vers un système entièrement digital entraîne des modifications considérables aux plans de la production et de l'utilisation des biens et services en question. Des questions stratégiques se trouvent posées au niveau socio-économique. La dynamique globale impulsée par "les autoroutes de l'information" et en particulier leur impact sur l'emploi, tant espéré par les hommes politiques, reste cependant problématique.

L'évolution du système dual actuellement en vigueur en Europe est en marche et de nouvelles configurations vont voir le jour.

Zusammenfassung

Technologie der Kommunikation und die Neugestaltung des Europäischen TV- und Radiosektors

Durch die technischen Neuerungen der Kabel- und Satellitentransmission wurde die Knappheit des Wellenspektrums überwunden, und es konnte sich in Europa ein duales System im Bereich der elektronischen Medien entwickeln. Dies hat eine Reihe von spezifischen Problemen aus der Rivalität von öffentlich-rechtlichen und privaten kommerziellen Rundfunkveranstaltern gebracht, die ihren Niederschlag in theoretischen und politischen Fragen, insbesondere der Regulierung fanden.

Der Übergang zu voll digitalen Systemen bringt im Bereich der elektronischen Medien zusätzlich zum Technologieschub auch eine dramatische Veränderung der wirtschaftlichen Rahmenbedingungen, da die Unternehmen der Computerindustrie und des Telekommunikationssektors in den Bereich der elektronischen Medien eindringen und versuchen, neue stärker interaktiv ausgerichtete Produkte anzubieten. Aus diesem Grund stellt sich für die Beteiligten eine Reihe strategischer Fragen, die für den weiteren wirtschaftlichen Erfolg, möglicherweise sogar für das künftige Weiterbestehen, entscheidend sein werden.

Die wirtschaftspolitische Hoffnung, von der Dynamik der Informationsgesellschaft vermehrte Beschäftigungseffekte zu erhalten, scheint möglicherweise voreilig zu sein, da die Akzeptanz angesichts der gegebenen Umstände - geringere Einkommensdynamik, weitreichende Sättigung im Konsum audio-visueller Medienprodukte - zweifelhaft erscheint.

Zu den künftigen Entwicklungen gehört mit hoher Wahrscheinlichkeit, daß das duale System in Europa an Bedeutung verliert und eine neue Konzeption für die institutionelle Gestaltung des Bereiches der elektronischen Medien entwickelt werden muß.

References

ALEXANDER, P. J. (1994): Entry Barriers, Release Behavior, and Multi-Product Firms in the Music Recording Industry. Review of Industrial Organization. 9. 85-98.

BEEBE, J.H. (1977): Institutional Structure and Program Choices in Television Markets. Quaterly Journal of Economics. 41 (1). 15-37.

CHURCH, J./GANDAL, N. (1992): Integration, Complementarity Products, and Variety. Journal of Economics and Management Strategy. 1(4). 651-675.

DNES, A.W. (1993): Bidding for Commercial Broadcasting: an Analysis of UK Experience. Scottish Journal of Political Economy. 40 (1). 104-115.

EGRINE, R./PAPATHANASSOPOULOS, S. (1990): The Internationalisation of Television. London. New York.

FARRELL, J./SHAPIRO, C. (1992): Standard Setting in High-Definition Televison. Brookings Papers on Economic Activity: Microeconomics. 1-77.

FELSENBERG, A./KIND, T./SCHANZE, H./TABELING, P. (1995): Statusbericht zur Situation der deutschen Pilotprojekte zum "Interaktiven Fernsehen". Siegen. (Report about the German pilot projects in Interactive Television; preliminary working paper).

FOGEL, R.W. (1964): Railroads and American Economic Growth: Essays in Econometric History. Baltimore.

HIGH-LEVEL GROUP ON THE INFORMATION SOCIETY, EUROPE AND THE GLOBAL INFORMATION SOCIETY (1994): Recommendations to the European Council. Brussels (often referred to as Bangemann-Report).

JOHNSON, L.L. (1994): Toward Competition in Cable Television. Cambridge, Mass. London.

MCMILLAN, J. (1994): Selling Spectrum Rights. Journal of Economic Perspectives. 8(3). 145-162.

NOAM, E. (1991): Television in Europe. New York. Oxford.

NOAM, E. (ed) (1985): Video Media Competition. Regulation, Economics, and Technology. New York.

OECD (1993): Competition Policy and a Changing Broadcasting Industry. Paris. (OECD 1993a)

OECD (1993): The Economics of Radio Frequency Allocation. Paris. (OECD 1993b)

OECD (1994): The OECD Jos Study. Paris.

OWEN, B.M./WILDMAN, S.S. (1992): Video Economics. Cambridge, Mass. London.

SPENCE, M./OWEN, B. (1977): Television Programming, Monopolistic Competition, and Welfare. Quarterly Journal of Economics. 41(1). 103-216.

STEINER, P.O. (1952): Program Patterns and Preferences, and the Workability of Competition in Radio Broadcasting. Quarterly Journal of Economics. 66(1). 194-223.

DEPARTMENT OF COMMERCE, INFORMATION INFRASTRUCTURE TASK FORCE (1993): The National Information Infrastructure - Agenda for Action. Washington, D.C.

WILDMAN, S.S./OWEN, B.M. (1985): Program Competition, Diversity, and Multichannel Bundling in the New Video Industry. In: NOAM, E.M.(ed.). Video Media Competition - Regulation, Economics and Technology. New York. pp.244-273.

WILDMAN, S.S./SIWEK, S. (eds.) (1988): International Trade in Films and Television Programs. Cambridge, Mass.

Youri Roubinski

The European Union and Russia

1. Between Europe and Asia

2. Between past and future

3. The first steps

The radical transformation of the European landscape since the end of the Eighties - the fall of the Berlin wall, German reunification, the collapse of Communist regimes and finally the disintegration of the USSR - has created an historic opportunity to redraw the map of Europe which was divided after World Wars I and II into two opposing economic, political and social camps. In the euphoria of the immediate post-Communist era, it may have seemed that General de Gaulle's dream of "a Europe from the Atlantic to the Urals" built upon common values of pluralistic democracy, human rights and market economy, was soon to become true. It was not long, however, before the question of Russia's place within Europe led to a bitter debate which even now is far from being resolved.

1. Between Europe and Asia

The interesting feature of this debate is that the dividing line between the advocates and opponents of Russia's "Europeanisation" is not between East and West but through them.

A number of western analysts believe that by definition Russia - Communist or not - cannot and must not be considered as a fully European state, and therefore rule out any involvement of Russia in EU activities, both now and in the future. "We must recognise once and for all that Europe stretches at least from Brest to Brest-Litovsk and that it is our duty to consodidate the democracies reconquered from the former Soviet empire", observes the French essayist Alain Minc (1). He goes on to express with a hint of cynicism his satisfaction at the rising influence of nationalist and neo-Communist forces in Russia, which, in his view, will deal a mortal blow to the illusions formed by the West towards the end of the Soviet regime. And because of this "salutary ogre" the USA will avoid the isolationist trap, NATO consolidated and extended to the East, and a united Germany remain formally linked to the western structures without yielding to the temptation of reverting to its pivotal role in the old balancing act between East and West.

This sentiment portrays obvious nostalgia for the Cold War when the act of European construction was stimulated to a large extent by western fears of the Soviet threat. Thus Stalin could be considered the "godfather" of a united Western Europe, though obviously not in the same way as Robert Schuman or Jean Monnet. Alain Minc is also influenced by old anti-Russian intellectual arguments going back to the Marquis of Custine or even to the Duke of Sully. The latter described Russia as "a barbaric country on a par with Turkey, even though it has been a Christian power for 500 years. The Tsar of Muscovy must therefore be deprived of his European possessions and relegated to Asia".

According to modern proponents of Sully's "Grand Design", Russia's whole 1,000 year history has been marked, due to the absence of natural frontiers, by expansion of its empire towards the warm seas under the pretext first of promoting Orthodox Christianity ("Moscow, the third Rome") to overcome Catholicism or Islam, then of defending the Slav peoples (pan-slavism) and finally of spreading the messianic revolution of Marxist Leninism.

According to this view, with its imperial vocation stemming from a tradition of strong centralised power (from the Tsarist autocracy to Communist totalitarianism), has been capable on its own of exercising control over an ethnically and religiously heterogenuous population inhabiting the vast territory from Smolensk to Vladivostok. Each time its power was undermined, the ensuing anarchy threatened to spread chaos to its neighbouring countries. It follows that the political cultures of Russia and Europe, based since the Age of Enlightenment on the Supremacy of the State, are fundamentally incompatible.

Another argument against rapprochement between a united Europe and Moscow is Russia's precarious strategic position and its neo-imperialist designs as evidenced by the bloody conflicts currently raging in Transnistria, Transcaucasia and Central Asia. Those who espouse this view maintain that the West should eliminate Russian influence not only in the ex-satellite countries of Central and Eastern Europe, but also in the countries in the

European part of the former USSR. The French historian Alain Besançon writes: "It is obviously in Europe's interests to close off the vast Soviet arena in order to prevent potential shock waves from spreading unchecked from Brest-Litovsk to the Pacific. It would be desirable, if Utopean, to create a Third Europe from the Ukraine to the Baltic which would join our Europe once the Second Europe had also done so"(2).

Finally, the opponents of EU overtures towards Moscow point to the slow pace of Russia's economic and democratic reforms, to its fragile institutional and legal infrastructure and to its economic and socio-political instability. Given that Russia still has enormous military and above all nuclear capabilities, they believe mutual confidence to be a long way off and East-West dialogue to be too risky.

It is paradoxical that these arguments coincide with the views of the ultra-nationalist Russian conservatives who could not be more anti the West. Inspired by Slavophile ideas of the mid 19th century and by the "Eurasian" current of though espoused by White Russian émigrés in the inter-war period (Prince Trubetskoi, P. Savitski et al), they too stress the fundamental incompatibility between European civilisation, with its individualistic, mercenary and permissive characteristics and Russia with its own traditional values. In their view, Russia is destined to follow its own path, which is based more on spirituality, collectivism ("sobornost") and social justice than on liberal democracy and free market economy. They prefer to guard jealously all that is Russian, with Slav, Turkish, Greek, Byzantine and Islamic elements all mixed in, rather than the proclaim the achievements of Peter the Great who opened "a window into Europe" modelled on the West, in the name of the modernisation.

These rather abstract and vague notions lead to very precise political conclusions: Russia, currently weakened by political and economic crisis, cannot establish relations with the European Union on the same footing.

The West, Russia's eternal enemy, will not fail to take advantage of the present situation and exploit the natural riches of Russia, corrupt its soul with American mass culture, undermine its morale and tranform it into a kind of semi-colony comparable to China at the beginning of the century.

Thus we hear calls for the radical revision of Russian foreign policy priorities, firstly to move towards full integration of the former Soviet Republics within the framework of the Commonwealth of Independent States (CIS), and secondly to turn to the Asian powers (China, India, Iran, and parts of the Arab world). It is only by doing so that Russia can reestablish its former links with its traditional allies and partners which were severed after the collapse of the USSR; only in this way can it reexploit their markets, notably the arms market, and restore its status as a greater power. Russia must make the best possible use of its geographical position linking Europe and Asia, the North and the South, and the prosperous West and the Third World.

Those in favour of such a programme clearly want the Russian State to maintain quasi-monopolistic control over its natural resources, production apparatus and market by means of rigid protectionism. They would like to see the State returning to its dominant role in the economy, supporting state subsidies for the military-industrial complex, collectivist agriculture, and a political shift towards authoritarianism.

This is the platform of the "national-patriots", be they Monarchist or neo-Fascist, who together with the neo-Communists are nostalgic for the USSR and represent the main hard-line opposition to the Yeltsin administration, in power since 1992. They are all hoping to gain from the fact that the Russian population is completely demoralised, having been traumatised by the high social price that had to be paid for transition towards a free market economy. They are also taking advantage of the national humiliation suffered by the Russian people, whose pride has been sorely wounded.

Russia gained historic victory in the Second World War at the price of tremendous sacrifice, and has now suffered defeat in the Cold War without putting up much of a fight. It is not surprising that the Russian man in the street feels tremendous bitterness at his country's loss of prestige abroad and at the need to ask its former enemies for help.

Naturally the West is their scape-goat and Russian liberals seen as docile instruments in the hands of foreign secret services and possibly even as part of the global "judeo-masonic conspiracy" against Russia. They are held responsible for the country's misfortunes - inflation, poverty, corruption, crime and the often tragic fate of the 25 million Russians living in exile in the "near abroad", i.e. in the independent states that were once part of the USSR, where they suffer all kinds of discrimination.

Like the opponents of rapprochement between the European Union and Russia or between Russia and a united Europe, its advocates can also be heard on both sides of the former iron curtain.

Western advocates of extending the EU to Russia reject the caricature of Western Europe which portrays it as a minuscule and vulnerable "peninsula of the Eurasian continent", threatened by the Russian colossus and obliged to seek support from beyond the Atlantic. The dissolution of the Warsaw Pact and of the Soviet Union has radically changed the balance of power. Russia has lost more than its "external empire", i.e. its former satellites in Central and Eastern Europe conquered in 1945. In recognising the sovereignty of the 14 Republics of the former USSR, Moscow has also destroyed its "internal empire" which it inherited from the tsars over three centuries. Its territory has now shrunk by a quarter (17 million km^2), its population decreased by 40% (149 million inhabitants from 289 million), and in the process it has lost a lot of its natural resources and of its industrial and agricultural potential.

Meanwhile the European Union has grown from six to nine member states, then to ten and twelve, and now to fifteen. Its population of 450 million and its GDP is greater not only than that of Russia, but also than that of the United States. And this trend is set to continue.

So, the balance of power in Europe has changed dramatically. The geater part of the USSR's military infrastructure, including its nuclear capacity and its defense industry, used to be based in the Ukraine, Belorussia and the Baltic States, in direct opposition to NATO deployments in the West. Under these conditions the United States felt able to reduce its military presence in Europe by two-thirds while still maintaining its nuclear umbrella, and the member states of the EU sought to form a "second pillar" of NATO comprising French and British nuclear deterrents.

In answer to those who accuse Moscow of neo-imperialist ambitions in the post-Soviet era, the historian Hélène Carrère d'Encausse of the Académie Française reminds us that it was Russia who chose to relinquish her empire. "The very fact that the world is focussing on Russia's progress is in itself the safest bulwark against imperialist temptation"(3).

Her colleague, the late Annie Kriegel, stressed that western fears of a resurgence of Moscovite imperialism are inconsistent with European interests. She sees Russia as able to spare Europe from Yugoslav-type destabilisation on its south-eastern flank. "The time had to come for wounds to heal. But the United States and the West failed to understand for many years that a sick, dismembered geo-political zone had to be supported if it was to be patched up. Resurrection of the former Soviet Union was out of the question. Instead the CIS emerged as the framework for a new relationship between the Republics of the former Soviet Union. The experience of the British Commonwealth and the special relationship between France and Africa following the process of decolonisation are cited as examples of similar international groupings" (4).

Furthermore, Russia's cultural and spiritual identity is not completely alien to western civilisation: it has made a major contribution to it and has indeed been an integral part of it. In the USSR, ethnic Russians made up just about half of the total population; in the Russian Federation they represent 80%. Christianity and liberal and socialist ideas came to Russia from Europe, undergoing significant changes in the process. Just as Russia has ties with Asia, Great Britain has similar ones with North America, and Spain and Portugal with South America, due to their Anglo-Saxon and Iberian cultures respectively. "Russia is an integral part of Europe", wrote the Austrian Foreign Affairs Minister Aloïs Mock. "Who could seriously wish to exclude the country of Tchaikovsky, Pushkin, Turgenev, Dostoevsky, Gogol and Tolstoy from a common Europe while seeking to belong to it oneself?"

Russian advocates of cooperation with the EU think along the same lines. They represent not only liberal intellecuals and traditional westernisers who fear revenge from those who are nostalgic for the totalitarian state and see in Europe a guarantee of irreversible democratic reforms. This stance has also been adopted by those who have already embraced the market and in whose interests it is, for the sake of trade, to advocate rapprochement between Russia and the outside world. They realise that any attempt to isolate Russia from Europe and to turn it once again into the enemy of the West, could only result in severing their country from the most vibrant centres of scientific and technical progress and from the foreign capital and high-tech equipment Russia urgently needs in order to weather the current crisis and to lay the foundations for a truly great Russia of tomorrow.

It is doubtful whether the debate on Russia's place in Europe will culminate in a clear victory for one side. Arguments on both sides are reflections of a complex and multi-faceted reality. The likely scenario is a pragmatic compromise between the two, based on a common denominator. What this will be will depend above all on Russia's economic development, which for the moment remains uncertain.

2. Between past and future

The balance-sheet of the first four years of reforms in Russia has been interpreted in so many different ways that we are reminded of the well-known metaphor of the bottle which can be perceived either as half-full or as half-empty. There is the same ambiguity about projections for the future. The OECD's report on the state of the Russian economy published in October 1995 concludes that if macro-economic stabilisation succeeds, Russia could, in 1996, embark upon a period of rapid growth of up to 10% of GDP per annum. But if high inflation persists and macro-economic policy is unable to improve the conditions for trade or encourage more productive use of resources, output would be likely to fall once again (5).

The current state of crisis is an inevitable consequence of Russia's transition from ultra-centralised state planning to a supply and demand based market, from total state ownership of property to a mixed economy boasting a large private sector, and from semi-autarcy to openness in its relationship with the outside world. Changes such as these have proved more profound, painful and prolonged in Russia than in the countries of Central and Eastern Europe or even in China, where the old political system based on total domination by the Communist Party is still intact.

Official statistics show that since the beginning of radical economic reform in 1992, Russia's GDP has fallen drastically. Since 1990 it has decreased by half, even though in 1993-94 it fell by only a quarter. During these last two years, industrial output has fallen by almost a third. Production of electricity has fallen by 13%, of non-ferrous metals and fuels by 21-22%, of steel by 21-31%, of chemicals and petro-chemicals by 40-48%, and of light industrial goods by 59% (6).

Above all the crisis has affected the manufacturing and processing sector, from the defense industry (in 1994, arms production fell to 45.1% of the 1992 level) to consumer goods. The main reason for this is a reduction in purchasing power combined with a dirth of state orders.

In agriculture, gross output has declined by 13%. The wheat harvest shrank from 106.9 million tons in 1992 to 87.3 million tons in 1994, with forecasts for 1995 a worrying 65-66 million tons. The sugar beet harvest fell from 25.5 million tons to 13.9 million tons. Numbers of livestock decreased dramatically (cattle by 8%, pigs, sheep and goats by 21-30%). Consequently, meat production fell from 12.9 million tons to 10.8 million tons.

Rapid bursts of inflation were both a cause and a consequence of the free-fall in output. From the brutal liberalisation of prices at the beginning of 1992 until the end of 1995, retail prices rose astronomically, increasing five to ten thousand fold, while average wages rose only three to five thousand fold.

Meanwhile inflation has been fired by the huge budget deficit (10% of GDP) which was financed for a while by the increasing volume of money in circulation and credits issued by the Central Bank. Numerous attempts to curb it have been cancelled out by enormous increases in public debt, regional authority debt and, above all, company debt. Bad debts within the production chain have been preventing deliveries and leading to delays in wage payments. Furthermore, high cost prices in production are serving to fuel the inflationary process: machinery is old or obsolete (capital investment fell by 13% in 1993 and 26% in 1994), there is heavy taxation (even though only two thirds of taxes are collected), raw materials and fuel are expensive, interest rates high, and we must not forget the quasi-monopolistic position of a number of big companies.

The fact that wage rises are lagging behind price increases has resulted in lower purchasing power for the average Russian, and worsening standards of living are being aggravated still further by delays in wage payments. Even taking into account the social welfare benefits which since the Soviet era have constituted 12 to 25% of income, total remunerations packages fell by 26% in 1993-94. In the first half of 1995, 44.5 million people - at least 30% of the population - saw their income fall below the official subsistence level of 277.4 thousand roubles, a worsening trend of about 25% on the previous year. By mid-1995 the average family was spending 54% of its income on food.

The situation is particularly difficult for social groups living on incomes fixed by the state: especially pensioners and students, but also junior civil servants, teachers, doctors, researchers, actors and artists, etc. Of these, 70% are living below subsistence level. It is therefore hardly surprising that the once impressive stock of Russian scientists, who were the beneficiaries of hand-outs from the military-industrial complex, has shrunk considerably. In 1994 alone, the number of researchers in specialised institutes fell by 20.5%.

Meanwhile, the disparities in wealth are growing larger between the small number of very rich in society, the so-called "new Russians", most of whom are engaged in some form of international trade or banking, and society's most vulnerable. The top 10% share 28% of total incomes, while the bottom 10% share only 2.8%.

Russia's ecological and demographic situations have been causing alarm for some time. Air pollution in the big industrial cities is ten to fifteen times too high to comply with international norms, while a quarter of drinking water does not comply either. Leakages from oil pipelines have become a daily occurance with consequent irremediable damage to the environment.

The birth rate has fallen by a third. Since 1992 the total population has decreased by 462,000. Without the influx of 796,000 Russians from the "near abroad", the decrease would have been much more substantial. At the beginning of 1995, life expectancy for men was 58.2 years and for women 71.6. The vast increases in alcohol intake and drug-taking are partly responsible. Serious infectious diseases such as cholera, tuberculosis, dissentry and smallpox are becoming more and more common.

All these negative phenomena can be easily explained. The Soviet regime lasted for 73 years in Russia, which was its birthplace, as opposed to 45 years in other former Communist countries. It therefore had time to destroy the foundations of a free market economy in Russia in a much more radical manner, not only physically (in terms of private property, legislation, and financial and commercial infrastructure) but also, and above all, psychologically. Three generations of Russians were brought up in the spirit of egalitarianism and state provision. Having long since lost faith in the bright future promised by the founders of the regime, people expected the omnipotent state to give them a job that was reasonably paid, secure and not too taxing, allowing them to indulge in other more or less tolerated activities.

In order to be accepted into the privileged ranks of the nomenklatura and to be spared from such hassles of daily life as shortages, queues, and arbitrary bureaucracy, it was better to avoid taking any initiative or assuming responsibility.

Bad habits do not disappear overnight. The disintegration of the totalitarian Soviet state, hastened by the stagnation of the Brezhnev era and pompted by Gorbachev's perestroika, happened in the absence of an independent, politically stable and economically progressive civil society based on a dominant middle class. Instead of strenghening the middle class, the sheer brutality of the liberal reforms all but destroyed it.

As the Communist Party lost its stronghold on power and the political police was weakened, a source of fear was removed from the lives of the ordinary people. This led in some cases to anarchy bordering on total chaos. The breakdown of authority and the rise of civil disobedience were exaccerbated by a shaky legal framework. One of the most disturbing features of the current situation in Russia is widespread organised crime. Mafia-like criminal networks are growing fast, and gaining momentum in both government circles and the police force as corruption spreads.

In the first half of 1995 the number of reported crimes and serious offences was 924,000, compared to 899,000 in the first six months of the previous year. 59% of the crimes involved property.

These socio-psychological phenomena were aggravated by the heavy burden placed on society by an economic structure which was more distorted in Russia than anywhere else in the Communist world. The dogma proclaiming the supremacy of heavy industry, or the means of production ("group A"), over the consumer goods industry ("group B"), which lay at the heart of Stalin's industrial model, had catastrophic results. Having been successful during the War and in the immediate pre-war and post-war periods, this model turned out to be disastrous in the long run. The country's economy became literally buried under the weight of the gigantic industrial machine whose primary purpose was to serve the bloated military-industrial complex. As most modern equipment and research were devoted to this sector, the rest of the economy was condemned to lag behing technologically, suffering from a severe lack of resources for investment and even depreciation, from high cost prices and from low or even negative profitability.

Under the old system of centralised planning and state control over prices, wages, buyers, suppliers and investment, these structural faults remained largely concealed. They showed up only in the general shortage of goods and in relatively high but non-satisfied purchasing power which was artificially inflated by forced savings. But with the sudden liberalisation of prices, they were laid bare by galoping inflation.

It must be added that company managing directors feared the explosive social consequences of too rapid a reform process and of massive unemployment, especially in the "closed towns" where nearly everyone worked in one or two armament factories. These factories had once provided all the local social infrastructure - housing, nurseries, hospitals, schools and public transport. In the first half of 1995 at least 30% of Russian firms were unprofitable but were not closed down. They artificially avoided bankruptcy by leaving bills and wages unpaid and by sending workers on "administrative leave". In 1995, thanks to these devices, unemployment did not exceed 8% of the working population.

The disintegration of the Soviet Union has also meant an end to regional specialisation and division of labour, which in places had been in existence for several centuries. Traditional economic links between firms and regions were broken, a fact which explains at least a third of the fall in output.

Given these handicaps, it is hardly surprising that attempts to curb spiralling inflation by traditional means were only moderately successful, resulting in a sheer fall in production. Under these conditions, "shock therapy", chosen by Egor Gaidar's team at the beginning of 1992 under the influence of ultra-liberal American economists of the "Chicago school" (J. Sachs), was unable to achive the results obtained by L. Balzerovich in Poland. Having failed in its mission, Gaidar's team was replaced at the end of 1992 by a government led by Viktor Chernomyrdin who adopted a more pragmatic approach.

It would be wrong, however, to present an entirely apocalyptic picture of Russia today. The reforms over the last four years have not been in vain: they have changed the country almost beyond all recognition, are starting to bear fruit and to prepare the ground for close cooperation with the EU.

In this respect, Russia has a lot in its favour. Even after the disintegration of the USSR, Russia, covering one seventh of the earth's surface, remains the biggest country in the world. Its share of world coal production is 8-9%, electricity 9-10%, oil 16-17%, and natural gas 30%. Russia also produces 10-12% of fertilizers, 15-17% of timber, 10-12% of steel, 6-8% of cement, 13-15% of woollen textiles, 5-6% of wheat, 8-10% of sugar beet and 10-12% of potatoes. Price liberalisation restored the balance between supply and demand in the market and ended decades of chronic shortages and bureaucratic distribution mechanisms. Despite on-going price rises the Russian economy has managed to avoid the supreme danger of Brazilian- style hyper-inflation and the collapse of the rouble. While in 1992 prices rose 26 times in real terms, they increased only 9-10 fold in 1993 and 3.2-3.3 fold in 1994. In 1995, the average monthly increase in prices was no higher than 6-7% and the government is expecting a figure of 1-2% for the end of the year.

In order to reach this ambitious goal the government is counting on the reduction of the budget deficit from 10% to 5% of GDP, on restricting the amount of money in circulation and Central Bank loans to companies, on the rise of interest rates, on issues of treasury bonds and on government loans with interest payable every quarter in order to guard against inflation.

The spectacular bankruptcies of some big private companies like MMM and Tchara and of dozens of commercial banks specialising in dubious operations have dealt a blow to many small shareholders, but have also served to stabilise the burgeoning financial market. The negative effects of the internal convertibility of the rouble and especially of speculation against the national currency, for example in October 1994 when the rouble lost a quarter of its value during one session, have been contained by the introduction in mid-1995 of fluctuation limits in the Dollar-Rouble exchange rate, the so-called "corridor". This has reduced the likelihood of a "dollarisation" of the Russian economy, in which there are currently about 20 billion Dollars in circulation.

The first encouraging signs of an upward swing are in production. Many analysts think that if official Soviet statistics used to exaggerate growth rates for propaganda reasons, their Russian successors are tending to do the opposite. This is easy to explain: in the old days, Soviet managers fiddled their balance sheets to give the impression that they had fulfilled the Plan in order to get their bonus. Today managers understate their results in order to reduce their tax burden. Were this not the case, how could one explain the fact that GDP fell by half in 1990-94 while energy consumption fell only by 20%?

Since the end of 1994, some sectors have stabilised. This is especially noticeable in the car industry and in the chemical and petrochemical industries, while the construction and public works sectors have experienced net growth. IMF experts predict that Russia will see a 2% growth in 1996. Michel Moussa, the chief economist at the IMF, justifies this view by highlighting the positive effects that the current structural reforms will have on the Russian economy, above all on inflation (7).

Structural changes are well underway. The reduction in the number of state orders has meant a lesser role for the military-industrial complex. The number of unprofitable coal mines is diminishing and modern production methods are being introduced into the steel industry. A better balance between heavy industry, especially the defense sector, and the consumer goods industry, to the latter's advantage, goes hand in hand with the rapid development of the tertiary sector, which played an insignificant role under the old regime. The Russian economy today prides itself on modern commercial and financial enterprises, private banking and services. The volume of private bank loans to industry and agriculture is growing, and healthy companies are increasingly able to have adequate current assets by self-financing.

Real incomes are now beginning to rise after experiencing a sharp decline. In 1993 they grew by 10% and in 1994 by 16%. This phenomenon is not so much due to increases in wages or social security benefits as to indirect gains through small businesses, black market activities, and private allotments which contribute significantly to family food supplies. In 1995, these sources of revenue accounted for 30% of the total income of modest households. Furthermore, families are beginning to save again, though this time of their own volition.

One of the most tangible results of the Russian reforms is the privatisation of the state sector, which once had absolute control over the national economy. By mid-1995, 120,000 firms had been affected in one way or another by privatisation. In 1994 the private and semi-independent sectors made up 62% of GDP. Fully privatised companies were responsible for 25% of the total, while state enterprises accounted for only 15% of retail trade.

These far-reaching changes were bound to cause some problems. A large number of shares in the old state-owned companies were exchanged for privatisation vouchers. These were distributed free to the public or to workers' collectives, a policy which enabled company directors and senior managers to gain control of their firms for a pittance. However, many of the companies to be privatised were grossly undervalued, causing state revenues to be much lower than expected.

Privatisation is progressing at a much slower pace in the countryside where it is being met by solid resistance by collective and state farm bosses who have found a mutual home in the Agrarian Party. The crucial question of private land owvership has not yet been resolved and might become the subject of a referendum. In 1995, 246,000 private farms accounted for only 2% of total livestock.

On the other hand, radical changes have taken place in the most important area for future relations between the European Union and Russia: foreign trade. The end of the state monopoly over foreign trade has meant that thousands of firms, both big and small, as well as private businessmen, the so-called "shuttles", have emerged into the import-export market. As a result, the portion of foreign trade in Russia's GDP has grown, and Russia has become more and more integrated into the world economy. In 1995, half of Russia's consumer retail goods were imported.

The alleged drop by 50% in Russia's foreign trade between 1991 and 1992, according to Russian official statistics, is even less credible than official figures relating to output and revenues. The reason is tax evasion. In 1993 there was a net increase in foreign trade, reaching $99 billion in 1995. This growth was due to new trading partners as well as to changes in the nature of the goods traded.

The list of Russia's major trading partners has altered dramatically. Trade with the former Soviet Republics, considered to be domestic trade until 1992, is in constant decline. In 1992-94, its volume dropped threefold. In 1991 it accounted for 65.8% of exports and 70% of imports, while three years later it accounted for 22.5% and 25.8% respectively. In 1990, the Socialist countries which were members of the Council for Mutual Economic Assistance (CMEA) accounted for 43% of Russia's exports and 44% of its imports. In 1994, they accounted for 12.7% and 9% respectively. Finally, trade with developing countries fell in 1993-94 by 11.3%, and with China, North Korea, Laos and the former Yugoslavia by 13.2%.

On the other hand, trade with OECD members has grown considerably. In 1990-94 exports here increased from 35% to 67% and imports from 44% to 69%.

Bearing in mind that the Republics of the former USSR, the countries of the former CMEA and developing countries were the largest importers of finished goods, including machine tools, Russian exports in this field have fallen from 9% to 5% of total exports. Meanwhile, exports of raw materials, already occupying a dominant share, have continued to grow: oil and gas account for 46% and metals for 27%. In 1994, Russia exported 89 million tons of oil, 39 million tons of oil products, 109 billion cubic metres of gas, 12.8 million tons of wood, 3.4 million tons of wrought iron, 5.8 million tons of nitrate fertilizers and 2.2 million tons of aluminium.

Of Russia's total imports in 1994, machine tools account for 34%, or $9.5 billion, food and food-production equipment for 31% and chemical products for 11%. Imports of textiles and shoes fell from 12% to 7%.

Generally speaking, this changing import-export pattern is detrimental to Russia as it negatively affects its terms of trade. The fall in world oil prices is forcing Russia to export more in terms of volume for the same revenue (or less). Nevertheless, Russia's trade balance has been positive over the last few years, showing a considerable surplus of $12-15 billion. This means that the Russian market, still small in relation to the enormous size of the country, holds great potential as it forges a place among the "emerging markets".

3. The first steps

The European Union has clearly established its position as the leading trading partner of the Russian Federation: its share of Russian foreign trade was over 37% in 1995 and continues to rise.

The foreign trade of the EU with Russia (in thousand ECUs)

	1993	1994
Imports	15 543 035	17 918 251
Exports	11 541 160	11 971 781
Total volume	27 084 195	29 890 032
Trade balance	- 4 002 875	- 5 946 370

Source: Eurostat Brussels.

These figures are no coincidence. Russia's huge natural resources, skilled workforce, engineers of international standing, and industrial, scientific and technical potential, are solid grounds for linking its economy, even in its present state of transition, to that of the EU.

The extension of the EU to the North and to the East will no doubt contribute to this process. The former GDR, now part of one united Germany, was for nearly half a century the leading trading partner of the USSR, at the same time enjoying a special relationship with West Germany through "inter-German trade" and thus earning itself the title of "13th member of the Common Market". The membership of Finland and Austria, two neutral countries which greatly benefited from their role as intermediaries between East and West during the Cold War, will also be a strong factor in rapprochement between Brussels and Moscow.

The process of integrating the countries of Central and Eastern Europe into the EU will likewise play an important role. It will be a long and difficult process which, according to the European commissioner Sir Leon Brittan, will take at least until the beginning of the twenty-first century to complete. In the meantime these countries, which were closely linked to the USSR for 45 years within the framework of the CMEA, have an objective interest in clinging onto the attractive markets of Russia and the other Republics in the CIS.

It is clear that economic interdependence between the EU and Russia will not always be based on a relationship whereby Russia is the poor relation and provider of raw materials and cheap labour for Western Europe. Such a relationsahip would not only be unacceptable for the Russians, but also counter-productive economically. Experience throughout the world, and notably in Europe, has shown that the most highly industrialised countries make the best partners for one another, both as customers and suppliers. International division of labour and regional specialisation tend to cut across industrial sectors rather than between them. Cooperation between the EU and Russia must therefore evolve naturally, taking account of the Russian economy's current transitory status, and look to a future in which Russia will firmly establish itself as a free market economy.

The starting point for creating a legal framework for cooperation was the Agreement between the USSR and the European Community signed on 18 December 1989. In concluding this agreement, Moscow recognised the failure of her attempt to impose the CMEA on Western Europe as its economic counterweight by trying implicitly to gain Western recognition of Russia's domination on the economies of its then satellites.

However, the Agreement of 1989 was still based upon the principle of peaceful co-existence of the capitalist and socialist systems in Europe. Mikhail Gorbachev was trying in vain to adapt the latter in line with the new political climate, without changing its essence. The negotiations leading up to the Agreement took place when the Soviet Union still had control over Eastern Europe, but the signature took place after the fall of the Berlin Wall when the Communist regimes started to fall one after the other. Very soon, not only the CMEA and the Warsaw Pact, but the USSR itself ceased to exist. At the end of 1991, the Russian Federation and the 14 other Republics of the former USSR proclained their independence and announced that they had broken with their Communist past.

In this new climate the EU's approach towards Russia inevitably changed. The *modus vivendi* of two fundamentally different systems evolved into one of mutual cooperation based on the common values of the rule of law, human rights and equal opportunities, multi-party politics with democratic elections and, finally, free market economy.

The first country to draw logical conclusions from this new situation was the united Germany. In 1992 it took the initiative of proposing to its European partners a new contractual framework for dealings with Russia with the longer-term objective of creating a free trade zone. At the beginning of 1993 the European Commission granted Russia some of the tariff facilities available under the General System of Preferences (GSP), conceived originally for developing countries, while excluding some of the more "vulnerable" goods.

The next step was the signing of bilateral Agreements for Partnership and Cooperation (APC) between the EU and each of the independent states of the European part of the former USSR, i.e. the three Baltic states (Lithuania, Latvia and Estonia) and the three countries which had been the founding members of the CIS: Russia, Belorussia and the Ukraine. All six countries have signed the agreements and await their ratification.

The difference between these two groups of countries is that the Baltic states want eventually to obtain full membership of the EU on the same footing as the countries of Central and Eastern Europe, formerly members of the CMEA. As a preliminary step the EU may sign special additional agreements with them to open the way for a free trade zone before doing so with the three Slav Republics.

The Agreement on Partnership and Cooperation (APC) between the EU and Russia was signed at the meeting of the European Council on the island of Corfu in Greece on 24 June 1994 by the President of the Russian Federation, Boris Yeltsin, and the heads of state and of government of the twelve countries which then formed the Community (Germany, France, Great Britain, Italy, Belgium, the Netherlands, Luxemburg, Spain, Portugal, Greece, Ireland and Denmark).

The signing ceremony was predeeded by long and difficult negotiations. The biggest obstacles were the different legislative and fiscal systems of the two sides and the need to settle the delicate question of allowing a number of Russian goods into the EU. After considerable efforts by both parties, the talks were concluded successfully.

On both sides there was the political will to come to an agreement. However, it must be said that Russia is a much less significant competitor for the EU than are the countries of Central and Eastern Europe (CCEE). Their foreign exports are mainly finished industrial and agricultural consumer goods, creating a clash of interests between themselves and the Mediterranean member states of the EU of which France is the most vociferous. Other problems may arise with CCEE participation in the EU's common agricultural policy and the effect this would have on the Community budget. CCEE membership of the EU, which has been agreed upon in principle, turns out to be a very delicate issue and has been postponed until the end of the century at the earliest. In any case it will not go ahead without a long transitory period. Even Great Britain, a strong advocate of free trade, believes that it would be foolish to proceed more quickly.

However, clashes of interest between the EU and Russia are potentially few. They concern fissile matter, ferrous and non-ferrous metals (aluminium), some chemical products, fertilizers, and to a lesser degree textiles - on which Brussels imposes restrictions due to its anti-dumping rules. As far as other markets are concerned, some EU members compete with Russia in arms exports and the building of nuclear power stations. Most controversial issues could not only be overcome but even transformed into areas for cooperation, such as aeronautics, space programmes and nuclear energy.

The Agreement on Partnership and Cooperation with Russia is a voluminous document made up of 112 articles, 10 annexes and 2 protocols. Its stated objective is to create a framework for political dialogue in order to promote trade and investment, to help consolidate democracy in Russia and to ensure the development of a free market. Pointing to the fact that Russia is no longer a country with state-controlled trade and that its economy is in transition, the documeny emphasises the progress that Russia has made towards a free market economy, a trend that can only be accelerated with cooperation between the signatories to the agreement.

The APC lists nine specific fields of mutual interest: political dialogue; tariffs and trade; companies and investment; payment and capital; competition and protection of intellectual property; legislative cooperation; economic and social cooperation; transport, telecommunications, finance and tourism; cultural cooperation and the fight against organised crime (illegal immigration, corruption and drugs).

With the objective of creating a free trade zone based on the most favoured nation principle, the APC does not abolish all tariffs and quotas on imports from Russia. They are maintained, at least for the time-being, for fissile materials (on the insistance of the French), certain textiles, furs, metals and fertilizers. Meanwhile Russia has the right to impose tariffs on imported goods which are most likely to penalise Russian firms in their home market and create difficulties for start-up firms in Russia. These conditions are similar to those accorded by the EU to Mediterranean countries.

The APC also sets up a mechanism for regular political dialogue in the form of two annual meetings between the President of the Russian Federation and the President of the European Commission or of the EU Council. It stipulates that a Council for cooperation be set up at ministerial level, likewise a Committee for cooperation at senior civil servant level and a Committee for cooperation between parliaments. The Agreement is due to last for ten years with the possiblity of automatic extension. The first review of progress is planned for 1998. It will assess to what extent Russia's economic reforms justify a Treaty on free trade.

Given the fact that the ratification process and the necessary vote of endorsement by the European Parliament stipulated in the text will take rather a long time, the European Commission in Brussels proposed to the EU Council of Ministers in June 1994 that it should sign a provisional trade agreement with Russia. The main objective of this initiative was to speed up the procedure allowing Moscow to benefit from the most-favoured-nation clause which the APC would be putting off for 3-5 years depending on the time it would take for Russia to become a full member of GATT, now the WTO.

The Provisional Agreement is supposed to reduce this period to a bare minimum, as it is not subject to ratification by national or European parliaments. Preferential tariffs accorded by the parties to members of customs unions and free trade zones and to neighbouring countries for cross-border trade and to developing countries are excluded from this agreement. Import quotas are lifted, but the right to impose anti-dumping measures is kept. Also, the text provides for the free transit of goods and payment in fully convertible currencies.

Although the provisional arrangement was worked out rather rapidly, its signature was delayed by at least six months because of the war in Chechnya which provoked a negative reaction by EU member states. It was only after the cessation of heavy fighting in this small Caucasian republic which wanted independence from the Russian Federation, and after the opening of negotiations under the auspices of the OSCE, that the situation changed.

On 17 June 1995, EU representatives and the Russian Foreign Minister, Andrei Kozyrev, signed the Provisional Agreement on Trade and Related Matters. This agreement came into effect on 1 February 1996. It consists of 36 articles, 4 annexes and 2 protocols and a Final Act with 2 protocols and 16 mutual declarations. Four declarations were made unilaterally.

The APC and the Provisional Agreement pave the way for gradual rapprochement between the European Union and Russia, provided that Moscow's transition to a free market economy continues and that the necessary fundamental changes to the structures inherited from the Soviet past take place.

The role of catalist in this transition falls to the EU's Programme of Technical Assistance for the CIS and Mongolia, called TACIS, which was created in 1991, just before the disintegration of the USSR. During its four years of existence, 1,700 million ECUs have been spent, of which 60% (1,020 million ECUs) have gone to Russia. After the initial phase which was mainly intended for humanitarian aid, TACIS has concentrated on short term objectives in certain sectors and regions. The priority sectors are agriculture, help for small and medium businesses, privatisation, reconversion of the arms industry, transport (notably the port of St. Petersburg and air-traffic control), the safety of nuclear installations, telecommunications and management training.

The inter-state projects which concern all member countries of the CIS relate to banking, energy, the setting-up of customs and fiscal services, etc.

On a regional level, TACIS' priorities are the North-West of Russia, Karelia, Murmansk, the Kola peninsula and the region of Lake Baikal in Eastern Siberia, where ecological damage is threatening to destroy the unique flora and fauna. The regional projects of TACIS account for one third of the total sum available to it.

In spite of non-negligeable results, the TACIS programme has some shortcomings. The selection procedure for projects takes a long time: 3-4 weeks for presentations in Brussels, then another 6-8 months for examination due to the fact that each case has to be translated into all the languages of the EU. Therefore, it has been decided to adopt an accelerated programme called "Bistro", with 4 million ECUs for smaller projects which can be examined within 5 days.

The total amount of aid provided by TACIS is small when one considers the size of Russia: it provides less than half of the amount that the EU programme for technical assistance (PHARE) provides for Poland and Hungary. Russia has received from the EU the same amount as Hungary, whose population is 18 times smaller.

Even if one considers all the other western aid programmes and the sizeable credits granted by the IMF, the World Bank and the EBRD, and on a bilateral level technical assistance from the EU, it is obvious that even combined they cannot ensure Russia's economic recovery: Russia's own efforts will be decisive. Of all the foreign aid programmes, the most important are the rescheduling of Russia's foreign debt and private foreign investment. In both cases, Europe is at the forefront.

Russia's foreign debt is generally estimated at $115 billion, of which $90 billion was inherited from the former USSR. The payment of interest on this debt and of the principal would amount to a quarter of Russia's total annual exports. The Russian Federation has accepted responsibility for paying back the foreign debt of all the former Soviet Republics, and in exchange these Republics have given up their claims to foreign assets of the former USSR, with the exception of the Ukraine, where the issue is still open. Recognising that Russia had to carry the main burden of expenditure at the end of the Cold War - for the destruction of weaponry, above all of nuclear and chemical weapons, reconversion of the arms industry, the repatriation of soldiers stationed abroad, etc. - the Club of Paris (governments) and the Club of London (private banks) have agreed to reschedule payments to the tune of about $30 billion.

It must also be noted that Russia itself has in the past given big loans to Third World countries, the total amount of which surpasses the accumulated Russian debt. Although these former clients of the ex-USSR are incapable of paying back their debt in full, Russia is unwilling to cancel them and has formally requested membership of the Club of Paris as a creditor nation.

The volume of private foreign investment in Russia still leaves a lot to be desired, and the same is true of investment from EU member states, the leading investors in the East. Since 1992, foreign capital has been flowing in at an average of $1-1.2 billion a year, six times less than the amount of private Russian capital flowing the other way, totalling over $4 billion, or only half the capital going into Hungary. This may be explained predominantly by imperfections in the Russian legal system, the fragile and onerous fiscal system and the risks caused by widespread corruption and crime.

Foreign investors are nevertheless becoming more and more interested in Russia. By the beginning of 1995, there were already about 10,000 joint ventures and foreign companies in operation on Russian soil, four times the number two years previously. In 1994 they exported goods and services to a value of $4.6 billion, 9.8% of all Russian exports to the "far abroad", i.e. outside the CIS. 24.6% of foreign investment has been in the energy sector, 17.2% in machine-building and mechanics, 13.3% in trade. Most foreign investment has gone to Moscow (25%), Northern Russia, the Volga region, Siberia, and St. Petersburg.

The EU's relationship with Russia is now at a turning point similar to that reached in the Fifties by Europe and United States. Now, as then, trade is taking the place of aid programmes: "trade not aid". Today Russia does not want to beg for humanitarian aid or to obtain new loans which would only add to its already high debt burden, but wants instead to import capital investment in order to be able to export more and better goods. In both cases the role of leading partner can only be played by the European Union.

There is a fundamental difference in the nature of the economic relationship between the USA and the EU on the one hand and between the EU and Russia on the other. The economic interests of the USA, an important political and military ally of Western Europe within NATO, are slowly gravitating towards the North and South American continents as well as the Asia Pacific region. However, the USA and the EU are also competitors both in industry (telecommunications, aeronautics, nuclear power and arms) and in services, and above all in agriculture.

Meanwhile, since the collapse of the USSR, Russia's economic axis has moved towards Europe, where three quarters of its population and industrial potential is concentrated in one third of its territory. It is clear that Russia cannot possibly conceive of full membership of the EU in the foreseeable future. In any case, Russia does not aspire to this: "The difference between Western and Eastern Europe is an objective one and should be maintained. A "single market" does not exist. The East European market, utterly deformed during the Eighties, will sooner or later regain its former character, having shed its ideological mantle", observes the economist and Russian Member of Parliament Pavel Bounitch, a liberal reformer. He does not believe that most favoured nation status or a free trade zone can be instated overnight. For a number of goods Russia is unprepared to open its borders, as is the EU (9).

However, the process is now in motion and nothing will stop it. The most likely scenario for European economic union in the 21st century is an amalgamation of a number of continental sub-blocks: on the one hand the European Union (with or without a common currency) with Germany, at its hub, sustaining a special reltionship with France, and with Great Britain and Scandinavia to the North, the CCEE to the East and the Mediterranean countries to the South; on the other hand, the CIS, in which Russia will continue to carry the most weight. Only a Europe which is both united and multi-faceted can ensure an equilibrium between America and Asia Pacific in this multipolar world.

It was in this spirit that representatives of a number of European countries came together in Vienna on 28 May 1993. Amongst their number were Jacques Chirac, the Mayor of Paris and future President of France, Count Otto von Lambsdorf, former German Minister for the Economy and President of the Liberal Internationale, Aloïs Mok, the Austrian Foreign Affairs Minister and President of the Democratic Internationale, Anatoli Chubais, then Russian First Deputy Prime Minister responsible for privatisation, Anatoli Sobchak, the Mayor of St Petersburg, and others. The "Greater Europe" Commission they created sounded a word of warning: no great Europe without Russia, no great Russia without Europe (10). The events which have taken place since prove that there can be no alternative.

Résumé

L'Union européenne et la Russie

Les changements spectaculaires dans le paysage européen depuis la fin des années 80 ont provoqué un débat passionné sur la place de la Russie dans l'Europe de demain. La ligne de partage entre ceux qui préconisent pour elle un destin particulier aux confins de l'Asie et les partisans de son intégration organique dans l'ensemble européen passe moins entre l'Est et l'Ouest qu'à travers les deux.

L'issue de ce débat dont les origines remontent loin dans l'histoire dépend essentiellement du progrès de la transition de la Russie vers les valeurs communes européennes - l'économie de marché et la démocratie politique d'autant plus que la crise qui accompagne la rupture de Moscou avec le passé communiste est plus profonde d'ailleurs. Les résultats atteints au milieu des années 90 sont assez mitigés, mais la tendance générale est plutôt encourageante.

L'Union européenne peut contribuer dans une mesure non négligeable à l'évolution de la situation en Russie dans le bon sens ce qui correspond à ces propres intérêts économiques et géopolitiques fondamentaux. En dépit d'obstacles non négligeables on peut enregistrer les premiers pas sur la voie de rapprochement entre Bruxelles et Moscou. L'UE est devenu le premier partenaire commercial de la Russie (37% du volume total des échanges extérieurs russes). L'Accord sur le partenariat et la coopération (APC) signé le 24 juin 1994 à Corfou et l'Accord provisoire sur le commerce signé le 17 juillet 1995 à Bruxelles ont créé le cadre juridique de coopération dont les objectifs déclarés sont l'octroi réciproque de la clause de la nation la plus favorisée et la mise en place de la zone de libre échange. Ainsi commence à se profiler les contours de la "Grande Europe" dont deux piliers seront l'UE et la CEI.

Zusammenfassung

Die Europäische Union und Rußland

Die spektakulären, am Ende der achtziger Jahre in Europa erfolgten Veränderungen haben eine leidenschaftliche Debatte über den Platz Rußlands im zukünftigen Europa ausgelöst. Die Trennungslinie zwischen denjenigen, die Rußland vor allem am Rande Asiens sehen und jenen, die seine Integration in das europäische System anstreben, verläuft weniger zwischen Ost und West als innerhalb beider Räume.

Der Ausgang dieser Diskussion, deren Ursprünge weit in die Geschichte zurückreichen, hängt hauptsächlich vom Übergang Rußlands zu gemeinsamen europäischen Werten ab, nämlich zu Marktwirtschaft und Demokratie. Dies gilt um so mehr als die durch den Bruch Moskaus mit der Vergangenheit verursachte Krise tiefer geht als anderswo. Die in der Mitte der 90er Jahre erreichten Ergebnisse sind eher bescheiden, die allgemeine Tendenz ist jedoch ermutigend.

Die Europäische Union kann in erheblichem Maße zu einer positiven Entwicklung in Rußland beitragen, was auch in ihrem eigenen wirtschaftlichen und geopolitischen Interesse liegt. Trotz nicht unerheblicher Hindernisse lassen sich erste Schritte einer Annäherung zwischen Brüssel und Moskau feststellen. Die Europäische Union ist inzwischen der erste Handelspartner Rußlands geworden (mit einem Anteil von 37% am russischen Außenhandel). Das am 24. Juni 1994 in Korfu unterzeichnete Abkommen über eine partnerschaftliche Zusammenarbeit und das am 17. Juli 1995 in Brüssel unterzeichnete vorläufige Handelsabkommen schufen für die Zusammenarbeit einen rechtlichen Rahmen, dessen erklärte Ziele die Meistbegünstigung und die Bildung einer Freihandelszone sind. So zeichnen sich die Umrisse eines "Großen Europas" ab, dessen Säulen die E.U. und die G.U.S. sind.

References

1) MINC, A. (1993): Un salutaire épouvantail. in Le Monde. 23 déc.
2) BESANCON, A. (1993): Russie, L'enjeu impérial. in Le Monde. 08 oct.
3) CARRERE D'ENCAUSSE, H. (1994): Faut-il avoir peur de la Grande Russie? in Le Figaro. 01 fév.
4) KRIEGEL, A. (1994): Russie: vers la renaissance. in Le Figaro. 22 fév.
5) OECD ECONOMIC SURVEYS (1995): The Russian Federation. Paris. p. 22-23.
6) All statistics are taken from official sources:
GOSKOMSTAT (1995): Sotsialno-economicheskoe polozhenie Rossii 1993-94. Moscow; Goskomstat Rossii, Rossiiskii statisticheskii ezhegodnik. Moscow. 1995.
7) INTERNATIONAL MONETARY FUND (1993): Perspectives économiques mondiales. in Le Monde. 06 janv.
8) Source : Eurostat Brussels.
9) ITAR-TASS, 26.09.1995.
10) REPORT OF THE COMMISSION FOR THE GREAT EUROPE (1994): No Great Europe without Russia -No Great Russia without Europe. Finland.

Waldfried Schliesser

Consolidation and Expansion of the European Single Insurance Market

1. Introduction

2. The present situation of the European single insurance market

3. Consolidation or expansion ?

4. The single market maturity of Central/East European insurance markets

   A. Central/East Europe
   B. South-East Europe
   C. The Baltic countries
   D. Russia, White Russia and the Ukraine

5. Final remarks

1. Introduction

It may appear to be premature to ponder over consolidation and expansion so shortly after the European Single Insurance Market had basically been brought life on July 1, 1994, because it has had some shortcomings from its very birth which would have to be cured first. Quite obviously cuts were made on the original objectives in the course of its genesis. Would it not be better to focus attention on some finishing touches before talking about consolidation and expansion ?

Both approaches are necessary. Therefore, first of all, there will be an investigation on the basis of the original objectives of the EC Commission, to find out what has been achieved and what has not. Then some deliberations will be made as a basis for discussing whether consolidation and expansion of the European Single Insurance Market are really necessary and how they could be put into practice. Special emphasis is laid on the expansion to East Europe because the Central/East European countries represent the biggest European market potential which is not yet included in the single market.

2. The present situation of the European single insurance market

In order to be able to assess the significance the European single insurance market in its present state one should start from the basic ideas and objectives of the European Community. Its objective was to promote balanced and lasting economic and social progress, in particular by creating the single market (an area without any national boundaries), by promoting economic and social cohesion and by establishing an economic and monetary union [1].

The single market and the further development of the EEC to become an economic and monetary union are the pillars of the progressing economic integration of Europe. And the economic integration has proved to be the foundation for steps towards political and social union.

1 Cf. Art. B (Objectives of the Union and their realization) in the Agreement on the European Union of 7th February, 1992.

The single market in terms of the Treaty on the Foundation of the European Community "... comprises an area without national boundaries in which the free movement of goods, persons, services and capital is possible according to the regulations of this contract" [2]. The whole activity of the community in the economic and monetary union is "...committed to the principle of an *open market with free competition*" [3].

The insurance market is an indispensable part of the single market. According to the tasks and the political and economic maxim of economic integration, the insurance market had the following objectives:

1. Freedom of settlement for all insurance companies
2. EC-wide insurance possibilities offered of each insurance company and access to them for each customer
3. Equal terms of competition for each insurance company
4. The same basic insurance supervision terms and control of marketing methods and insurance products
5. EC-wide field of activity for insurance mediators under equal terms of competition
6. Registration of comparable financial data for all insurance companies
7. Equal treatment of all policy-holders in case an insurance company is subjected to compulsory winding-up
8. Choice of insurance legislation
9. Approximation between insurance tax rates and the taxation of insurance companies
10. Free movement of the capital of insurance companies, of policy-holders and insurance mediators.

2 Art. 7a of the Agreement on the Foundation of the European Union, (AFE), of February 7, 1992.
3 Art. 3a, para 1 of the AFE; passages emphasized by author.

The establishment of the freedoms of settlement and services, i.e. opening up more or less closed national insurance markets and safeguarding a single-market-wide competition has been at the centre of efforts.

That this would become a very complicated and lengthy process may have been underestimated at the beginning, but it is not really surprising in the face of the different starting points (in the development of the insurance industries, in the economic and social framework, in the legal and supervision systems and in the cultural traditions and consumer habits) and the resulting conflicts of interest (e.g. free competition versus consumer protection). All the more significant is the result of more than 30 years' efforts which, through the purposeful work of the EC Commission, the willingness to compromise of the representatives of the member states and the authority of the European High Court, finally led to success [4].

Since the translation of the 3rd generation of EC insurance guidelines into national law, it has been possible for the insurance companies and insurance mediators registered in one country to market insurance products single-market-wide and to establish settlements; the consumer has access to single-market-wide insurance possibilities offered.

The size and attractiveness of the European single insurance market have been further increased by the conclusion of the European Economic Area (EEA) Agreement which includes the EFTA countries (except Switzerland) [5].

On the basis of a theoretical model and after setting a legal framework, a common insurance market has emerged as part of the European Single Market, which is now one of the 3 biggest insurance markets in the world, in 1993 accounting for a world share of 27.67%, after the US (31.31%)

---

4 See Kammerer, Martina: The origin of EU market rules for the insurance industry. Vienna, 1994, p. 37 ff.

5 As Austria, Sweden and Finland have been EU members since 1995, the EEA expansion concerns Norway, Iceland and Liechtenstein.

and Japan (30.36%). Europe as a whole had a premium growth of 7.5% compared with the previous year, which was higher than that of the US (5.0%) and Japan (5.2%) [6].

The European single insurance market is characterized by:
. freedom of settlement and services for insurance companies and insurance mediators;
. a single registration, single-market-wide, for business based on concurrent criteria (single licence);
. financial and misuse supervision of insurance companies neutral to competitors, through the supervision board of the home country, on the basis of similar standards which follow mutually agreed principles (home country control);
. a European cartel law applied by the EC Commission as cartel board;
. steps towards a harmonization of national insurance law.

These market rules facilitate the single-market-wide competition of insurance companies, which is able to release innovative forces. Now that the national supervision board is solely competent for insurance companies having their main office in their country, the higher supervisory standards lead to a competitive disadvantage for local insurance companies (native discrimination) and which not expected continue to exist in the long run.

The emergence of one common insurance market from more than a dozen quite different national markets has no historical parallel [7], and can be considered a great success that may give an impetus to further integration.

6 World market share in premiums in US-dollars, calculated on the basis of data from: sigma, Wirtschaftsstudien Nr. 5/95, Assekuranz Global 1993, statistics appendix, pp. 2-3.

7 In the US, insurance supervision differs from state to state. Therefore one insurance company requires more than 50 concessions from the various states to be able to operate in all US states.

On the other hand, open problems and unfulfilled expectations should not be overrated but made the subject of continued constructive shaping of the single insurance market. This concerns, above all, these areas:

- In practice, the chances for concluding insurance contracts across borders in the free service business are made little use of [8].
- Equality of chances for insurance companies in competition across borders has not been achieved to the desired degree because there are considerable differences between the various countries in the taxation of insurance contracts and of insurance companies.
- The single-market-wide equal treatment of policy-holders in case of the compulsory winding up of an insurance company has not been secured.
- There is no arrangement yet for the supervision of groups of insurance companies and finance agglomerates (global financial companies) who operate across borders.
- Currency fluctuations can distort competition as long as exchange rates are not even fixed between the currencies of the member states.

On the basis of previous experience and progress made so far, the problems addressed and the open issues in shaping the single insurance market appear to be solvable. This can be considered as a logical continuation, as consolidation work, since the legal framework for the single insurance market has basically been completed. Consolidation, however, includes some more tasks:

- translation of the recommendation on insurance mediators [9] which in Germany and Austria, for instance, has not found its way into national legislation;
- building and consolidating European company law for insurance companies;

---

8 Inquiries showed that even in the Elsaß/Baden-Würtemberg border region, characterized by intensive business activity and passenger services, insurance contracts across borders are the exception. Even in industrial business, insurance protection from the home country dominates.

9 Recommendation No. 92/48 of EC Commission, EC.

- deepening the cooperation between national insurance control boards, and in due course checking the necessity to centralize control authority;
- Further harmonization of insurance legislation.

One task for the consolidation of the single insurance market is becoming more and more important for the work of the EC Commission: a continuous check on the effectiveness of existing regulations, and, if necessary, reacting on changed conditions with new regulations. It is doubtful whether there will be re-regulation as long as the principle of an "open market with free competition" is valid. In addition, sufficient experience with the existing market rules would have to be collected in order to accept as necessary a change of direction, which would be equivalent to a change of paradigms.

The progress made by the Community towards a monetary union should be of great importance for the consolidation of the single insurance market. The insurance industry, in particular, can draw advantages from the introduction of a stable Euro-currency because it meets the requirements of long-term risk coverage and associated capital investment in the single-market-wide business better than a variety of national currencies of varying strength.

3. Consolidation or expansion?

At present for the single insurance market, too, the strategic question arises whether consolidation should take preference over expansion, or whether consolidation and expansion should be pursued more or less simultaneously.

Before going into this question in more detail three remarks should be made.

First: The single insurance market is a part of the single EC market and partly determined by its underlying principles; nevertheless, the peculiarities of the insurance market should not be neglected. They result from the peculiarities of the insurance product. Stremitzer and Ennsfeller emphasize the immaterial nature of the insurance product, the difficulty an inquirer has in assessing product use, the need to explain the insurance product, the irradiation phenomenon when people try to visualize the insurance product, and the inclusion of the policy-holder in providing insurance benefits [10]. The policy-holder is a "prosumer". These product peculiarities caused the insurance market to emerge and develop as a specialized market, standing out and distinct from other markets. The special legislation for insurance companies and for the insurance contract, and a government supervision of the insurance industry have further strengthened separation.

The characteristics of the insurance market are not in conflict with the important role the insurance industry plays as a risk bearer and stabilizer of national economic circulation systems and as a collecting tank for capital, i.e. with its use for the national economy and the single company.

The independence and autonomous laws governing the insurance market facilitate partial and temporary deviations from the general internationalization trend of economic life. For instance, insurance companies can enter new markets before these have been opened up for commerce and industrial cooperation, if only the legal framework of these markets permits. The issue of consolidation and/or expansion of the single insurance market does not passively depend on the decision on the consolidation or expansion of the EU as a whole but can be answered independently.

Second: Eurosceptics may not consider consolidation and expansion to be a current issue, especially if they mainly strive for disintegration. Therefore, the possibility of a retrograde development or even a dissolution of the single market must be taken into account. However, such a development is improbable. On the one hand it is much more difficult to remove a given reality than to create a new one. No wish works as strongly as the practical requirement of insurance coverage for business activities across borders,

10 Stremitzer, Heinrich and Ennsfellner, Karl: thoughts on the customer-oriented quality of insurance services. In: Risiko Versicherung Markt. Festschrift for Walter Karten, edited by Hesberg, Nell, Schott: Karlsruhe, 1994, p. 385 ff.

and the advantages one has experienced in the single insurance market. On the other hand, one cannot rule out the possibility that further steps in integration might not be agreed upon at the present time. But this does not mean abandoning the level of integration already achieved.

Third: If expansion of the single insurance market is talked about, this relates essentially to expansion in the East. Central and East European insurance markets represent the big expansion potential. In Western Europe only a few countries are outside the single insurance market. Apart from Switzerland as the most important insurance country not integrated, these are miniature states: the British Channel Islands, the Isle of Man and Gibralter. Turkey has not been included, either.

Basically, the expansion of the single market is one of the fundamental intentions of the European Union. In the Agreement on the European Union of 7th February, 1992 the preamble expressly emphasizes "the historical importance of overcoming the division of the European Continent", and the necessity "to create firm bases for shaping the future Europe". So far the question is not really whether the single market should be expanded or not, but rather under which prerequisites this is possible.

As far as the European Community is concerned, there are basic obstacles. As in the EEA Agreement, membership of the single insurance market could be agreed upon with countries willing and able to join. This could be done without any changes to existing market rules and regulations. The relative independence of the single insurance market permits it to be expanded even before the countries concerned have become EU members. This means that the complicated problems of reforming EU institutions and the EU mechanism, which would have to be solved before the Union is further expanded, do not stand in the way of an integration of Central and East European insurance markets.

Most of the countries concerned have already signalled their intention to join and their readiness to follow the principles and regulations of the single insurance market.

The main issue in expanding the single insurance market is rather to create the necessary prerequisites in the countries that want to join, i.e. compatible insurance markets and rules and the economic and legal field associated with it. The so-called reform countries are undergoing a difficult transformation process, from the Soviet-type planned economy to a market economy system like the single market. How big these difficulties are becomes clear when you consider the starting positions. The planned economy type of insurance industry was characterized by the following features:

1. Undeveloped or limited functioning of the insurance industry as a category of the money economy. An insurance industry providing risk precaution presupposes a developed, functioning money economy. If an economic system is dominated by ideas and regulations based on payment in kind, if the function of money as a general medium of exchange is undeveloped or restricted, the insurance industry cannot develop its immanent possibilities as risk bearer and capital tank. How useful is an insurance benefit for a policy-holder if it is paid in worthless money, and if he cannot buy the goods he requires in the case of a loss?
2. The insurance industry was a state monopoly. Non-government or even foreign insurance companies were refused a concession. So there was no competition. Product variety and innovation were insufficient. Standardized legislation governing insurance protection was in the way of individual shaping that matched demand.
3. Fiscal deformation of the insurance industry. If the government insurance company is subordinate to the minister of finance, the latter's decisions on shaping insurance conditions and business practices may be overlaid by considerations and requirements of financial policy. This was regularly the case. Remitting profits and government recourse to insurance provisions and reserves obstructed actuarial business practices.

4. Dominance of the backward Soviet insurance model in the dependent countries even in cases where before 1945 the insurance industry had been highly developed, as in the east of Germany and the Czech Republic. That way, existing actuarial know-how went to pieces or could not develop when contact with modern developments in the outside world was lost due to self-isolation.

In addition, insurance for government institutions and facilities lost all sense because these were not really independent. For them, in the last analysis, the government budget acted as bearer of financial risks of all kinds. That way the insurance yield in business management and the national economy as a whole was restricted. The insurance industry led a Cinderella existence. In view of this starting position, the transformation of the insurance industry has the character of a complex new layout. How far the road to an insurance industry in a market economy may be will become clear if you compare the starting position described with the indispensable features of modern insurance markets. These are:

First: Private insurance companies.
As private property forms the basis of a modern market economy private insurance companies in the legal form authorized for the insurance business are typical. The existence of public law insurance companies does not alter this in so far, as in the single market they have only been authorized as competitive enterprises. Insurance monopolies as they existed in some German lands for instance for compulsory fire insurance on buildings had to be abolished.

Second : Free competition.
Competition is the most important characteristic of the market, of modern insurance markets, as well. This implies that market and competition rules secure the functioning of the market, preventing excesses and misuse without impairing competition.

Third : Free price fixing and product shaping.
Private insurance companies should be allowed to fix their prices and shape their products in free competition, to meet market conditions. In keeping with this is government insurance supervision relating not to products but to companies, which is, therefore, neutral in competition.

Fourth : Free movement of services.
It is granted in the European single insurance market by the freedoms of settlement, of services and of capital movement. For the reform countries in Central and East Europe the starting point was and the goal of the tranformation process is essentially the same, but the transformation strategy and policy, which have to take into account the concrete national conditions, are not. But in every instance there were basic tasks in creating the legal and economic prerequisites for a functioning insurance market. The immediate basic tasks of transformation include:

. Abolishing the government insurance monopoly;
. setting up market rules by shaping and carrying through the legal framework (insurance supervision and contract law);
. authorizing private insurance companies;
. training and further education of capable insurance experts
  equipped with the know-how of the insurance business in a market economy;
. opening up of national insurance markets.

A functioning insurance market requires a national economic framework which includes privatization of the industry, a roughly stabilized currency and positively developing economic, income and social conditions.

The reform countries' advance on the road towards transformation differs. But on the whole, in all these countries the insurance industry is still largely underdeveloped. Insurance penetration (premiums in per cent of the gross home product) in 1993 accounted for between 0.3% in Romania and 3.4% in Slovenia, while it attained an average of 6.9 per cent in the EC.

Differences in insurance density in 1993 were even bigger (premiums per capita). In the EC it averaged US $ 1234.00. In Slovenia the insurance density was US $ 213.60, while in the other countries it is even further behind, between US $ 2.90 in Romania and US $ 78.10 in Hungary. It is noticeable that insurance density is especially low in life assurance, namely US $ 0.30 in Romania and up to US $ 22.60 in Slovenia, the EC average being US $ 623.00 [11].

The progress made in transformation differs widely. The Central/East European countries (Poland, Slovakia, Slovenia, the Czech Republic and Hungary) are ahead of the Southeast-European countries (Albania, Bulgaria and Romania), of the Baltic countries (Estonia, Latvia and Lithuania) and of Russia, White Russia and the Ukraine. The present situation in the ex-Yugoslavian countries (Slovenia excepted) does not make a reliable statement possible at the moment.

In all these countries new legal insurance frameworks have been created, many of which are orientated to EU insurance guidelines. But the complexity, stability, the realization and the effectiveness of legal rules are still insufficient, least satisfactory in South-East Europe, and especially in the former Soviet Union.

The privatization of the insurance industry has also made varied progress. Most of the insurance companies emerged from former government insurance institutions still have a dominating market position, even if they have lost some market shares to newly founded insurance companies. Foreign insurers who might speed up the transformation process with their market economy know-how and financial power have gained influence in Hungary and the Czech Republic. In contrast, Poland and Slovenia have so far pursued a restrictive policy towards licensing foreign insurers, obviously with the intention of not exposing their national insurance companies to the tough competitive pressure of foreign competitors. In the economically less stable countries of the former Soviet Union and of South-East Europe foreign direct insurance companies are still keeping back their engagement, anyhow.

11 See sigma 4/95, p. 10.

1. The reform countries in Central/East and South-East Europe and in the Baltic, as well as some forces in Russia, White Russia and the Ukraine are endeavouring to create prerequisites for their membership of the single European market. They have made varied progress so far.
2. The economic framework continues to be difficult and hinders faster progress on the insurance markets. In Central/East Europe there has been a certain economic stabilization, but since the reform started prosperity has sunk by 10 to 35%, and except in Central/East Europe production is further decreasing, there being a high inflation rate [12].
3. The increasing engagement of foreign insurers, in as far as they have access to the insurance markets, facilitates the transformation process.
4. At present no reform country has achieved the prerequisites for membership in the European single insurance market. This will probably take a few more years.
5. The reform countries will not get to the single insurance market at the same time. Slovenia, the Czech Republic, Poland, Hungary and Slovakia as well as the Baltic countries will have the best chances.
6. In all reform countries one can feel that the European single insurance market is a model and that it is attractive.

Full membership of the reform countries in the European single insurance market may be preceded by steps towards the internationalization of the insurance business. This concerns, above all, further steps towards liberalizing and opening up the insurance markets in the reform countries by granting freedom of settlement, and via intergovernmental agreements on facilitating insurance business across borders.

Insurance companies, insurance associations, universities and other educational establishments from single market countries support the transformation process in the reform countries with numerous training and further training facilities for insurance experts. The TACIS programme of the EC Commission for Russia may serve as an example here. It is carried through by the European

12 See sigma 4/95, p. 3.

Insurance Association VCEA, and the insurance associations of Great Britain, Italy, France, Germany and scientific institutions from these countries [13].

4. The single market maturity of Central/East European insurance markets

A. Central/East Europe

This region includes Poland, Slovakia, Slovenia, the Czech Republic and Hungary. In **Poland** the first signs of a transformation of the insurance market appeared as early as 1984. The insurance law of 1984 permitted the authorization of new insurance companies. But it was only in 1988 that 7 private insurance companies emerged, among them WESTA [14], POLSIA and VARSOVIA, who had great difficulty entering the market. The established government insurance firms PZU and WARTA dominated the market with the help of their dense network of branch offices and agents, as well as the monopoly for compulsory insurance, which was a bigger insurance field.

The unsatisfactory effects of the 1984 insurance law, including its 1989 amendment, caused a new insurance bill to be prepared which was agreed upon on 27 July 1990. The British model served as an example, and advice given by the EC Commission was helpful. The 1990 insurance law basically met the requirements of the EC insurance guidelines then in existence. It restricted the range of compulsory insurance. The ruling on the opening up of the Polish insurance market is quite interesting. It was accepted as a basic goal, but not put into practice immediately. It rather provided a transition period which was obviously meant to give Polish insurance companies the chance to become competitive. This period has meanwhile been extended to 1 January 1999 [15]. During this transition period foreigners are not permitted to open any settlement or agency in Poland. Foreign capital stakes in Polish

13 See CEA Annual Report 1993-1994, pp. 27-28.

14 WESTA went bankrupt in 1992/93.

15 See S. Wlodyka: Basic Problems of Polish Insurance Law. In: Zeitschrift für das Versicherungswesen, issue 18-1993, pp. 446-451.

joint-stock insurance companies and the foundation of subsidiaries are possible, though. The insurance law of 1990 forms the legal framework for the emergence of the present Polish insurance market [16]. In 1993 thirty-six insurance companies were active, 10 in the field of life assurance and 26 in non-life insurance. The former government companies PZU and WARTA are still domineering. Their market share was 79.6% in 1994 [17].

In 1993 the total premium volume amounted to 30,955,816 million old zlotys, which was the equivalent of US $ 1.706 million [18]. The insurance density (premiums per capita in US-Dollars) was $ 44, in life assurance $ 12.70 and in non-life insurance $ 31.70. Insurance penetration (premiums in % of the gross domestic product) ran to 2.0 in 1993. In both cases Poland is behind the other Central/East European countries. Obviously there is considerable growth potential in the Polish insurance market.

With regard to the market structure one must realize that the motor (motor vehicle) insurance and the fire/non-life insurances dominate with market shares of 57% and 23%, whereas the private health and accident insurances, and especially the third party liability insurance, are underdeveloped.

An assessment of the inland market maturity of the Polish insurance market shows that the legal framework and real growth of the gross domestic product observed since 1993 are positive features. The principal disadvantage should be the high inflation rate which amounted to 43% in 1992, and was higher than 30% even in 1994.

16 The draft of an amendment shows the intention to strengthen protection of policy-holders and to establish an independent supervisory board.

17 See D. Fedczyn: Biuletyn Informacyjny; in: Pomorskiego Towarzystwa Obezpieczeniowego GRYF S.A., Luty 1995, Bydgoszcz, p. 3.

18 Statistical data based on sigma 5-1995, unless noted otherwise.

In the *Czech Republic* the transformation process in the insurance industry started after the political changes. The abolition of the government insurance monopoly and the passing of privatization laws facilitated the setting up of private insurance companies. The most important new legal basis for the activity of insurance companies and their government supervision is the law of the Czech National Council on the insurance industry of 27 April, 1991. It resembles the former strict regulations in Germany and Austria, formerly in the frame of so-called material government supervision, which may have served as a model. Later regulations like the tendering of account regulations of 1994 take account of the corresponding EU insurance guidelines. The licensing of an insurance company is decided upon by the ministry of finance functioning as the government control board. At the beginning of 1995, 28 domestic and foreign insurance companies were licensed. Czech citizens have to conclude insurance contracts with these companies.

Premium income in 1993 amounted to a total of 22,775 million CZK, the equivalent of US $ 781 million. Life assurance accounts for 5,826 million CZK, non-life insurance 16.949 CZK. With an insurance penetration of 2.5% the Czech Republic holds the third place among the reform countries. The insurance density of US $ 75.61 per capita also places the Czech Republic in the front ranks.

The market leader is the Ceska Poistovna a.s. with a market share of 68.9%, followed by the Ceska Kooperativa druzst.poj. a.s. with 4.82%. All the other newly licensed insurance companies remained below the 1% limit. As in Poland, the former government insurance company is dominant.

Unlike Poland, however, numerous foreign insurance companies are on the market with their subsidiaries, for instance the Allianz, the Gothaer and the Nürnberger insurance groups and the Gerling concern from Germany. The Erste Allgemeine, the Austria-Collegialität and the Bundesländer Versicherung from Austria, the Winterthur and the Zürich from Switzerland, the Nationale Nederlanden and some companies from Great Britain and the US.

They see growth chances on the Czech insurance market, which, as in other reform countries, are presently still restricted by the low incomes of the population, weak private insurance precautions and an unfinished privatization of the economy. The foreign engagement can be explained by the hitherto relatively low inflation rate.

In non-life insurance, fire/property insurance holds the first place with a premium share of 45%, followed by motor insurance with 29% and agricultural with 10%. Private health, accident and third party liability insurances are behind, similar to those in Poland and other reform countries. In **Slovakia** the framework of the insurance market does not differ widely from the Czech framework, even after their government separated from the Czech Republic in 1993. However, separate insurance laws existed before that, for instance the law of the Slovak National Council of 18 December 1990 on the insurance industry, which incorporates company law and supervision regulations. Insurance contract law is a subject of the civil code and the special economic code.

Premium income in 1993 amounted to 8,075 SKK, that is US $ 262 million. Life assurance accounted for 1,971 million SKK, non-life insurance for 6,104 million crowns. Insurance penetration is 2.37% and only a little below the Czech value, but there is a considerable difference in insurance density (US $ 49.20 per capita), which points to the lower level of economic development.

Twelve insurance companies work on the Slovak market (1993), the former government insurance company Slovenska poistovna a.s. dominating the market even more than in the Czech Republic. In 1993, 99.8% of the life assurance premium income came from the 3 biggest companies, as well as the Slovenska, the Kooperativa Druz stevna Poistovna a.s. and the Poistovna Otcina a.s., and 98.7% from the Slovenska alone. In non-life insurance the market share of the three was 98.1%, that of the Slovenska 84.7%. Until 1993 the market shares of the three foreign insurance companies were rather insignificant, but it should be noted that the Wiener Städtische has a share in the Kooperativa and the Östereichische Bundesländer has a capital share of 25%

in the Otcina. It can be noted, then, that in the face of a nearly monopolist market structure, competition is not sufficiently developed. Competition, however, is an important indicator of market maturity.

As to insurance fields, on the Slovak insurance market (non-life) in 1993 motor insurance (35.5%), fire/property insurance (35%) and agricultural insurance (18.0%) were in the foreground. As in the Czech Republic, private health, accident and third party liability insurances are underdeveloped. This factor and the low share in life assurance shows that the urgent demand for financial precaution is restricted by the low income of the population. That means: growing future incomes should provide for a more than proportional growth of these insurance fields.

In **Hungary** the transformation process has so far taken a different course. Thinking in terms of the market economy began even before the political changes at the end of the eighties, and influenced policy more strongly than in other reform countries. In 1986 a duopoly emerged from the government insurance monopoly, when the Hungaria took its place beside the Allami Biztosito. In order to speed up the privatization and modernization of the insurance industry Hungary, unlike other reform countries, put a stake on foreign capital. West European insurance companies used this chance of access immediately, acquired capital shares, even majority shares, and founded subsidiaries. Today the Hungarian insurance market is mainly owned by insurance companies from Germany, Austria, the Netherlands, Italy, France, Belgium and the US. Their market in Life assurance is 99.5 %, in non-life insurance 94.0%. There is only one insurance company wholly in Hungarian hands, the OTP-Garancia, a company of the savings banks. A total of 14 insurance companies are on the market (1933). The total premium received was 73,958 HUF in 1993, that is US $ 614 million. Insurance penetration (2.23%) and density (US $ 78.09 per capita) are on a similar level to the Czech Republic. Hungary amazingly left itself a lot of time for passing insurance laws. As late as 1994 a new insurance bill was handed in to parliament. Until that time the insurance market was regulated by government decrees, and quite strictly, following the principles of material government supervision.

Market leader in life assurance is the Ab-Aegon Altalanos Biztosito which emerged from the government insurance board, and is is today 100% owned by the Dutch Aegon. Their market share was 35% in 1993. The Hungaria also emerged from the government insurance board. Today it is 90% owned by the German Allianz. Its market share is 38.3%. It is the market leader in motor insurance. As the third biggest company the Nationale Nederlanden should be mentioned,which only works in the field of life assurance, but is the second biggest supplier after the AB-Aegon. Further, the Providencia should be mentioned, where the EA-Generali holds 78% of the ordinary capital. Their market share in non-life insurance was 8.6% in 1993.

In the various fields of the Hungarian insurance market, the motor insurance (39.5%) and the fire/property insurance (35.0%) are dominant. In Hungary, too, the private health, accident and third party liability insurances, but also the agricultural insurance are less developed. Problems are obviously created by a rising rate of inflation and decreasing real incomes of the population, which restrict the growth of the business.

In **Slovenia** the Soviet insurance model existed only until 1961. A market-oriented policy in Yugoslavia paved the way for the Slovenian insurance market after the country had achieved its political independence. Judged by insurance penetration (3.5%) and density (US $ 245.60 per head of population), it takes the first place among all the other reform countries, with a big lead over the majority of these countries. The premium income was 48.141 million SIT (equal to US $ 425 million), 5,097 million SIT from life assurance and 43,044 million SIT from non-life insurance.

In the various fields of the Slovenian insurance market in 1993, 39.5% were accounted for by the motor insurance, 35% by the fire/property insurance, and, after all, 10.5% by the private health and accident insurance. On the relatively developed but small Slovenian market there work 12 insurance companies; three have a dominating position with 85.9% of premium income in life assurance and 88.1% in non-life insurance. They are the Triglv, Ljubljana (life 28.6%, non-life 61%), the Maribor (life 28.6%, non-life 15.8%), and the Adriatic, Koper (life 5.5% and non-life 11.3%). There are three companies with foreign capital shares: Adriatic - Lloyd Adriatico Triest; Merkur - Merkur Graz; Prima - Grazer Wechselseitige. On the whole, however, foreign insurance companies are almost totally refused access to the Slovenian market, quite unlike conditions in Hungary. It is obviously the aim of Slovenian insurance policy to establish an independent market with competitive domestic insurance companies. The insurance law of November 1994, too, does not permit any foreigners to set up insurance companies in Slovenia.

An examination of the Central/East European group of countries shows that their insurance markets, with little differences, have made the biggest progress on the road to a market economy. However, they have not yet achieved market maturity by the standards of the European single insurance market.

A high degree of concentration has not permitted a sufficient development of competition. The application of legal regulations has to be further stabilized. Capital investments by insurance companies are difficult to make because the capital markets are not fully functioning yet. The efforts of the EC Commission and the European Insurance Association CEA to promote insurance know-how in these countries have yet to take their full effect. The preparation of reliable loss statistics for premium calculation is still under way. Therefore it may be justified to expect that it will take some more years to achieve single market maturity.

B. South-East Europe

This group of countries comprises Romania, Bulgaria and Albania whose insurance markets are usually given little attention. A certain self-isolation of Romania and especially Albania contributed to this.

In **Romania** the insurance market is little developed, judged by insurance penetration (0.27%) and density (US $ 2.93 per capita) in 1993. The premium income amounted to 50,6625 ROL, that is US $ 67 million, US $ 6 million accounting for life and US $ 61 million for non-life insurance. In the field of non-life insurance the motor (42%) and transport insurance (33%) had a dominating position.

After the government insurance monopoly had been abolished in 1990, the government insurance board split into three joint stock companies, and the licensing of new insurance companies had been made possible, at present about 30 insurance companies work on the market, some with foreign capital shares. Market leaders are two companies that emerged from the government insurance board, the ASIROM S.A. and the Astra S.A. In the field of life assurance, ASIROM held a market share of 98% in 1992; in non-life insurance 73% and Astra 24%.

As the political, economic and legal framework is little consolidated, the Romanian insurance market is expected to require a lot of time before it reaches market maturity. This is even more true of **Albania**. Insurance penetration reached 1.07% in 1994, insurance density was US $ 3.47 per capita. The premium income was only 1.204 ALL, that is US $ 12 million. Life assurance plays practically no role at all. 70% of the premiums came from the motor vehicle liability insurance introduced in November 1992. In 1993 there existed only one insurance company, the INSIG, a government company, based on the insurance law of July 31 1991. You can say, therefore, that the Albanian insurance market is not undergoing a process of transformation but is in the early stages of its formation.

Quite a different development in **Bulgaria**, where in 1993 insurance penetration at 2.28% and insurance density at US $ 29.13 per head of population were much higher. The premium income was 6.800 million BGL, that is US $ 246 million, and 29% came from life assurance, after all. The structure of insurance is more balanced, but the private health and accident and the third party liability insurances are weakly developed.

About 30 companies work on the Bulgarian insurance market. The two former government insurance companies DZI and Bulstrad, now joint-stock companies, are the market leaders with 40% and 10% in non-life and the DZI with 71% in life insurance. Newly set up insurance companies have placed themselves on the market, the MIC car insurance company founded in 1990 already holding a considerable market share in non-life insurance.

The more favourable position of the Bulgarian insurance market as compared with the two other South European countries, how ever, is impaired by legal uncertainty, a decreasing gross domestic product and high inflation. There is no new insurance law yet [19]. There is no legal basis for licensing foreign insurers. Therefore much has to be done to achieve market maturity.

C. The Baltic countries

The Baltic countries of Estonia, Latvia and Lithuania achieved their political independence in 1991. In a short period of time they have done a lot to build up their insurance markets with West European support. But they have not been able yet to overcome their enormous backwardness.

In **Estonia** in 1993 the premium income was 191 million EEK, that is US $ 14 million. Insurance penetration reached 0.82%, density US $ 9.03 per head of population. This approximately corresponds to the Russian insurance

19 The draft of new insurance law on the Polish model, prepared with the help of foreign consultants, has been in existence since 1992. The bill is to be passed in 1995.

market. The Estonian insurance law, which came into force on December 10 1992, is among the most up-to-date laws in Central/East Europe, and basically meets the requirements of the then EU insurance guidelines.

On this basis an interesting supplier structure emerged, interesting because foreign engagement is promoted and, after all, 16 non-life and 5 life insurance companies are active. The first foreign insurer in Estonia, the Swedish Trygg-Hansa, had merged as early as 1990 with the Eesti Kindlutus, the former Swedish subsidiary of the Soviet government insurance board, and the Bank Tartu to form the Hansa Kindlutus. The Seesam Ltd. was set up in 1991 with Finnish and US American shares. Swiss and German insurers became active, too. In non-life insurance foreign companies held a market share of 23%. While in non-life insurance the Eesti Kindlutus is leading with a market share of 30% without dominating it, it holds 91.3% in life assurance.

All in all: Estonia had a good start, but it is still a long way from a developed insurance market, mature enough for the single market. This is also true for **Latvia**, where in 1993 insurance penetration at 1.09% and insurance density at US $ 9.88 are somewhat above the value for Esthonia. The premium volume was 16 million LVL, that is US $ 27 million, US $ 8 million accounting for life and US $ 18 million for non-life insurance.

Latvian insurance laws are oriented on the EU insurance guidelines in order to create prerequisites for the later entry on the single market. The insurance law of 1991 was amended in 1995. At the beginning of 1995 a law on the government supervisory board was passed. Now there is an up-to-date legal framework, but in practice it is obviously not easy to get used to new legal regulations.

The Latvian insurance market experienced a foundation boom for new insurance companies in 1993/4. At the beginning of 1995 43 companies existed, but not all of them were able to maintain their hold on the market.

The concentration on the Latvian insurance market is lower than in other Central/East European countries. The market leader is the Balta Versicherungs-AG founded in 1992, a Danish-Latvian joint venture which took over the non-life portfolio of the former government Latva in 1994. Her non-life market share was 31% in 1994.

Among the bigger insurance companies there are also VIRA-A, Balva and Estora. Foreign insurers have capital shares, among them the German Alte Leipziger which holds 79% of RIGAS Fenikss, and the Finnish Phojola and American AIG, who jointly hold 100% of the capital of Famlat (First International Insurance Company of Latvia).

In life insurance, Ezerzem and Estoria are the market leaders. The Latvian insurance market, similar to the Estonian, showed a promising start, but it will have to take a longer road to market maturity.

Lithuania has the weakest insurance market of the Baltic countries. The 1993 premium income of 56 million LTL (US $ 14 million) signify an insurance penetration of 0.5% and an insurance density of US $ 3.82 per head of population. The insurance density is low; it is lower only in White Russia and Albania.

With the insurance law of 1990 and its amendment of 1995 satisfactory legal bases were created, but the insurance market is still little consolidated. This is shown on the one hand by the dominating role which the government insurance company Valstybine Draudimo Istaiga (market share of 77.3%), which has not been privatized yet, plays, and on the other hand by numerous new company establishments, almost 50 per cent of which had to leave the market in the meantime. Apart from the government-based Valstybine, the Drauda (set up in 1991 by the German Alten Leipziger and the Valstybine), the Preventa and the Vicura (a Swiss firm) are of importance.

D. Russia, White Russia and the Ukraine

This group of countries is of considerable importance because of its size. Their insurance markets are characterized by the most difficult problems found in all groups of countries. The question arises whether in these countries a development oriented on the European single market is being strived for at all. There are voices in favour. But there are also voices in favour of a Russian-dominated economic zone as a counterweight to the European single market.

In considering the insurance market of **Russia** one has to start from the fact that there is no market-based insurance tradition, even if temporarily disrupted, as it exists in the Czech Republic, in Poland or Hungary, which could be taken up. This and, above all, the continuing economic decline of the country, the weak political and legal situation and last not but least, the high crime rate impair the building of the insurance market. The premium income reached 1,257 billion RUR in 1993, that is US $ 1,348 million, US $ 436 million coming from life, US $ 912 million coming from non-life insurance. Insurance penetration was 0.77%, density came to US $ 9.09 per capita.

Until the beginning of 1994 a host of insurance companies were set up in an unregulated way. Out of about 2900 companies 1000 did not have a licence. It was the insurance law that came into force on January 12 1993, that brought the indispensable legal framework. The activity of a large number of untrustworthy companies impaired the development of the customers' trust so essential for the insurance business.

The Russian insurance market is characterized by the dominating position of the continuing government insurance companies. The Gostrach (not Rogostrach) held a market share of 90% in 1992. Ingostrach, the former insurer abroad, now works on the domestic market, too, focussing on transport insurance. The third government insurer is the Podmoskovje, a subsidiary of Rogostrach focussing on the area around Moscow. Foreign insurance companies are approaching Russia on a passive basis. They are going in slowly and waiting to see what occurs. "My advice to insurance companies: don't extend yourself too far, too fast" [20]. This advice is followed to the greatest possible extent. A contributing factor is that foreigners are granted only a minority share in Russian companies, anyhow. This chance was used by the Kölnische Rück (now owned by the American Re) which is holding 10% of the capital of ASKO, the biggest private insurance company. The second biggest, Rossia, cooperates with the Cologne company Colonia. It is worth mentioning that the 3 Russian government insurance companies work also in White Russia and the Ukraine.

In **White Russia** the Russian insurance market may even appear to be advanced. Factors with a negative influence carry more weight here. One must add that in the centralist Soviet Union the former insurance centre (and the currency reserves) were in Moscow. The consequences in White Russia today are widespread incompetence and a currency shortage. The premium income in 1993 of 70,900 million BYB (US $ 10 million) and the insurance penetration of US $ 0.98 per head represent the lowest values of all the countries under consideration.

The supplier structure resembles that of Russia. The White Russian subsidiaries of the former Soviet government insurance companies are now the White Russian government companies Belgostrach and Belingostrach. They account for approximately half the premium income. It is remarkable for the structure of insurance that credit insurance is most widespread. As the companies have hardly any securities for bank credits, the banks regularly demand the taking out of a credit insurance.

The situation on the insurance market is only slightly better in **the Ukraine**. A premium income in 1993 of 883.430 million UAK [21], that is US $ 202 million, signifies an insurance penetration of 0.58% and a density of US $ 3.87 per head.

20 J.M. Covalevski: After the Bloodshed, Russia Holds Promise; In: Best's Review, December 1993, p. 27.

21 A Ukrainian analysis of the insurance market notes a premium income of 937,493 million UAK for 1993 and of 14,4218,038 million UAK for 1994.

Basically the statements made for Russia and White Russia are valid here, too. The negative effect of the highest inflation rate of countries under consideration is particularly strong. The insurance law that came into force in 1995, is meant to clean up and stabilize the insurance market.

5. Final remarks

An examination of the Central/East European insurance markets under the aspect of an expansion of the European single market yields quite a varied picture for the four groups of countries. In all countries of central/east Europe a continued economic growth has started. The inflation rates are dropping, and it is to be hoped that the setbacks in Hungary and Slovakia will only be temporary. Privatization has made headway. The legal frameworks are EU-oriented, the political conditions somewhat stable and there is a firm intention of getting nearer to the European single market and to become a member. In all 5 countries a growth of premium income can be observed since 1991 (Hungary since 1992), a powerful growth in the Czech Republic and Slovenia. Opening up the markets is handled differently. While Hungary was quick in opening its market to foreign insurance companies, the Czech Republic and Slovakia were more cautious and Poland and Slovenia are more restrictive in order to give domestic insurance companies a chance to become competitive. All five countries are open for market economy know-how and training support. The efficiency of the insurance markets is strengthened by reinsurance with foreign insurers.

The transformation process is making successful progress so that single market maturity can be expected in the foreseeable future. The South-East European countries are following the same road, but the development and transformation of their insurance markets has not made such big progress, the biggest advance having been made by Bulgaria. The political, economic and legal frameworks are less powerful. Therefore more time is needed here to achieve market maturity. On the basis of the dynamic development observed last, the Baltic countries might succeed here somewhat earlier.

The insurance markets of Russia, White Russia and the Ukraine are furthest behind. The development and transformation of their insurance markets is still in the beginning, and is largely impaired by further economic decline and political instability. It has not yet been decided whether an approach to the European single insurance market should be striven for.

In summary one can conclude that an eastern expansion of the single insurance market to include the insurance markets of Poland, the Czech Republic, Slovakia, Hungary and Slovenia will be feasible and can be expected in the next few years. The Baltic insurance markets and, though not at the same time, those of Bulgaria, Romania and Albania could follow after a longer period. An expansion to include Russia, White Russia and the Ukraine cannot be foreseen. But in the long run these European countries, too, will not be able to ignore the attraction of the single insurance market.

Résumé

Le marché unique européen de l'assurance : consolidation ou expansion ?

Le marché de l'assurance s'est "unifié" à partir du 1er juillet 1994 dans le respect de la doctrine définie par la Communauté européenne. L'ouverture du marché de l'assurance s'avère inéluctable en raison de l'importance sociale et du poids économique de ce secteur. L'auteur en illustre les caractéristiques, en les comparant aux marchés nord-américain et japonais, tout en présentant les problèmes spécifiques posés par ce secteur des services aux fondements historiques marqués par de grandes différences nationales.

Les stratégies de développement de sociétés européennes d'assurance doivent aujourd'hui, et finalement d'une manière assez brutale, tenir compte à la fois des contraintes d'une nécessaire harmonisation dans les pays actuels de l'Union et des opportunités d'expansion considérables à l'Est où les systèmes d'assurance socialisée sont à la dérive. Waldfried SCHLIESSER décrit d'une manière détaillée, par pays, les données de la période de transition et les perspectives d'évolution. Le champ d'action est immense en raison du sous-développement actuel de système de marché.

Zusammenfassung

Der europäische Versicherungsbinnenmarkt: Vertiefung und Erweiterung

Nach dem Entstehen des europäischen Versicherungsbinnenmarktes sind Vertiefung und Erweiterung seine bestimmenden Entwicklungsprozesse geworden. Vertiefung bedeutet vor allem, die Chancengleichheit der Wettbewerber und die Gleichbehandlung der Versicherungsnehmer vollends durchzusetzen sowie die praktische Umsetzung der Binnenmarktordnung ständig zu überprüfen und diese rechtzeitig neuen Entwicklungen anzupassen.

Erweiterung bedeutet vor allem Osterweiterung durch schrittweise Einbeziehung der Reformländer in den Versicherungsbinnenmarkt.

Dies dürfte am ehesten in den Ländern Ostmitteleuropas (Polen, Tschechien, Slowakei, Ungarn und Slowenien) möglich sein, die die größten Fortschritte beim Transformationsprozeß zur marktwirtschaftlichen Versicherungswirtschaft erreicht haben und deren Marktordnungen bereits vielfach binnenmarktorientiert sind. Mit einem zeitlichen Abstand könnten die baltischen Länder (Estland, Lettland und Litauen) und die südosteuropäischen Länder (Rumanien, Bulgarien und Albanien) folgen. Über die Länder des ehemaligen Jugoslawien (mit Ausnahme Sloweniens) können wegen der zur Zeit gegebenen Lage keine verläßlichen Aussagen getroffen werden.

Ob Rußland, Weißrußland und die Ukraine in den Versicherungsbinnenmarkt einbezogen werden wollen und können, ist derzeit nicht absehbar, doch werden sie sich seiner Anziehungskraft auf Dauer nicht entziehen können.

References

EAST EUROPE: INSURANCE INDUSTRY MARKED BY ECONOMIC TRANSFORMATION (1994): Wirtschaftsstudien No 1. Schweizerische Rückversicherungsgesellschaft. Zürich.

INSURANCE INDUSTRY IN EAST EUROPE: RECOVERY HAS STARTED (1995): Wirtschaftsstudien No 4. Schweizerische Rückversicherungsgesellschaft. Zürich.

VERSICHERUNGSWIRTSCHAFT 1/93, 8/93, 13/93, 1/94, 2/94: Verlag Versicherungswirtschaft. Karlsruhe.

THE EUROPEAN INSURANCE INDUSTRY IN FIGURES 1993 (1994): Comite European des Assurances. Paris.

Adamantios Diamantopoulos
and Heidi Winklhofer

Differences in the Export Profiles Among Users of Export Marketing Research: Evidence from Two European Countries

1. Introduction

2. Background and literature

3. Methodology

   A. Data collection
   B. Variables

4. Results; analysis

   A. Firm demographics
   B. Objective indicators of the firm's export involvement
   C. Subjective assessments of the firm's export situation
   D. Managerial perceptions about the strategic role of exporting in their firm

5. Discussion and conclusions

1. Introduction

Some years ago, in their classic article on company internationalisation, Johanson and Vahlne (1977, p. 26) argued that "the lack of knowledge due to differences between countries... is an important obstacle to decision making connected with the development of international operations". However, the available empirical evidence indicates that information gathering in export markets is rather underresourced and the process itself less than systematic (e.g. Sood, 1981; Cavusgil, 1984a, 1985). This is both surprising and disconcerting, given the importance of information as a source of competitive advantage (Parsons, 1983; Porter and Millar, 1985; Turner, 1991; Glazer, 1991) and a pillar of market orientation (Kohli and Jaworski, 1990; Dalgic, 1994; Cadogan and Diamantopoulos, 1995).

While the export literature is full of examples of costly mistakes and lost opportunities as a result of inadequate information (e.g. Ricks, 1983) and while "failures continue to occur because firms either do not believe that international market research is worthwhile or face manpower and resource bottlenecks that impede research" (Czinkota and Ronkainen, 1990, p. 322), relatively few empirical studies have been conducted on the use of export marketing research (EMR) in practice. Even fewer studies focus on EMR as conducted by European firms as most research in this area comes from other countries (e.g. Walters, 1983; Cavusgil, 1984a, 1984b, 1985; Bodur and Cavusgil, 1985; Wood and Goolsby, 1987; Koh, 1991; Koh et al., 1993). Given the implications of the Single European Market for the development of marketing strategies (e.g. Kaynak and Ghauri, 1994; Leeflang and de Mortanges, 1994, Catalantone et al., 1991; Guido, 1991; Varaldo and Piccaluga, 1994), the role of marketing research becomes increasingly important for a firm's successful export operations. Consequently, investigation of the characteristics of European exporters using such research as input to their decision making is an important area for investigation.

The present investigation builds upon previous research seeking to provide insights into the use of marketing research by exporting firms. Past studies have either concentrated on *within*-country comparisons of users versus non-users of EMR in terms of firm characteristics and export profiles (e.g. Schlegelmilch et al., 1993) or on *between*-country comparisons of the actual implementation of EMR by user firms (e.g. Diamantopoulos et al., 1991); single-country descriptive studies of profiles of EMR users are also available (e.g. Hart et al., 1994). Interestingly, to the authors' best knowledge, no cross-country comparison of the export profiles of European EMR users has yet been undertaken despite the fact that there is evidence indicating that the allocation of resources to international research activities varies considerably across countries (e.g. Gofton, 1994). The current study attempts to redress this research gap by contrasting exporters located in different European Union countries (notably the UK and Finland) but who all use EMR in terms of their export characteristics. Taken in conjunction with the findings of previous research, the results of the present investigation should facilitate the development of a comprehensive framework specifying the conditions under which EMR is likely to be used by European firms. Knowing the latter would be beneficial to both marketing research agencies seeking to identify clients and to public bodies providing export promotion/assistance services, since EMR is only *one* possible information gathering mechanism available to the firm - the others being export intelligence (e.g. Denis and Depelteau, 1985) and export assistance (e.g. Diamantopoulos et al., 1993). It would also benefit export managers wishing to obtain an understanding of the circumstances under which European firms find it useful to employ EMR in their export operations.

2. Background and literature

Compared to the well established body of literature on domestic marketing research, (see Schlegelmilch and Therivel, 1988 for a review) substantially less has been written about EMR. The majority of contributions examine methodological problems (e.g. Mayer, 1978; Davis et al., 1981; Douglas and Shoemaker, 1981; Douglas and Craig, 1983; Parameswaran and Yaprak, 1987), describe techniques useful for EMR (e.g. Munson and McIntyre, 1979; Douglas et al., 1982; Stout and Dalvi, 1989), or give normative advice on how to go about researching export markets (e.g. Gasman, 1982; Gordon, 1984; Business America, 1987).

Empirical investigations focusing on the use of EMR by exporting firms originate in three different areas: First, in the general exporting literature, where EMR is treated as one of many variables investigated (see Gemünden, 1991 for a review of such studies); here use of EMR is typically treated as a background variable to the main issues of interest (e.g. internationalisation or export performance). Second, in the export promotion or export assistance literature (see Seringhaus, 1985 and Diamantopoulos et al., 1993 for reviews), as help with subsidising EMR costs is often one form of assistance provided by governmental bodies (e.g. The Export Market Research Scheme offered by the Overseas Trade Services section of the Department of Trade and Industry in the UK). Third, in the (limited) EMR literature itself which focuses on such issues as the information needs of exporters (e.g. Wood and Goolsby, 1987), the sources consulted (e.g. Walters, 1983), the type of research studies undertaken (e.g. Bodur and Cavusgil, 1985), and the application of EMR information on export decision making (e.g. Diamantopoulos and Horncastle, 1994).

From these latter studies, the use and sophistication of EMR has been found to be dependent on the following factors: company size (Walters, 1983; Reid, 1984; Cavusgil, 1984a, 1985; Diamantopoulos et al., 1990; Koh, 1991; Schlegelmilch et al., 1993; McAuley, 1993; Hart et al., 1994), type of industry and nature of product (Cavusgil, 1984a; Wood and Goolsby, 1987; Garrett and Hart, 1993), location of export markets (Bodur and Cavusgil, 1985), number of export markets served (Diamantopoulos et al., 1990; Hart et al., 1994; Schlegelmilch et al., 1993), export involvement/dependence (Walters, 1983; Cavusgil, 1984a, 1985; Seringhaus, 1988; Koh, 1991; Schlegelmilch et al., 1993; Koh et al., 1993, McAuley, 1993) and internationalisation stage (Cavusgil, 1984b; Reid, 1984; Yaprak, 1985; Seringhaus, 1987). In a cross-country comparison of EMR users, Diamantopoulos et al. (1991) found little support that the implementation of export marketing research is country-specific but various aspects of EMR implementation (e.g. number of research personnel and frequency of use of EMR information at different planning levels) were affected by both company-specific and environment-specific variables. The latter finding seems to suggest that it is the characteristics of the firm and the nature of its export operations that dictates how EMR is likely to be used rather than idiosyncratic factors related to the country of origin of the exporter. However, Diamantopoulos et al. (1991) did not formally investigate whether the *export profiles* of their EMR users were in fact similar.

The present paper reports on potential cross-country differences between UK and Finnish EMR users (both operating in the same industry sector) with respect to their export characteristics. It is important to note, in this context, that the UK has been found to lag behind other European Union countries in terms of commitment to international marketing research; a recent *EuroNet* survey of 550 marketing research buyers in 11 countries found that UK exporters ranked significantly below Finland, Denmark, Sweden and France on international marketing research resource allocation.

The two groups are contrasted in terms of four sets of variables drawn largely from previous research, namely (a) firm demographics, (b) "objective" indicators of the firm's export involvement, (c) "subjective" assessments of the firm's export situation and (d) managerial perceptions about the strategic role of exporting in their firm. The next section outlines the methodological framework of the study, highlighting the sampling procedure and the variables considered. This is followed by the presentation of the results under each of the four headings mentioned above. The paper is concluded by examining the implications of the findings and drawing an agenda for future research.

3. Methodology

A. Data collection

Data for the present investigation were gathered by means of a mail questionnaire sent to a sample of 80 Finnish and 245 UK exporters operating in the "design" sector (comprising furniture, clothing, leather & fur, jewellery, and glass & ceramics). The sampling frames utilised were the *Register of Finnish Exporters* and *Kompass UK* directory respectively; the cover letter was addressed to the Managing Director or the Export Director if the latter was identifiable. The small size of the Finnish sample reflects the limited number of firms in the relevant population; it represents virtually a census within the industry sector considered. Altogether 80 usable replies were received from the UK sample and a further 33 usable questionnaires were returned from the Finnish sample, resulting in effective response rates of 33% and 41% respectively; these are comparable to the response rates achieved in previous mail surveys of EMR practices (e.g. Hart el al., 1994). The higher response rate for the Finnish sample may partly reflect the fact that the questionnaire originated in another country and, thus, respondents felt they were participating in an "international" survey (Jobber and Saunders, 1988); it may also reflect the Finnish respondents' appreciation for receiving the questionnaire in their own language. The questionnaire was professionally translated into Finnish prior to dispatch; backtranslation procedures as recommended by Douglas and Craig (1983) were also employed to ensure comparability of the Finnish and UK versions.

The focus on a single industry sector reflects an attempt to control for industry-specific factors while undertaking cross-country comparisons; otherwise significant differences may reflect the confounding influence of industry practices, habits and norms. The chosen sector is characterised by high levels of export activity in both countries concerned and, in particular, Finnish design products enjoy worldwide reputation for their quality; thus the design sector provides a good empirical setting for a comparative study of export behaviour, at least for the countries concerned.

B. Variables

Following Cavusgil (1984a, p. 262), EMR was defined as "the research activities of firms, carried out either in the home market or in foreign markets, for the purpose of reducing uncertainty surrounding international marketing decisions". Companies who undertook such activities either internally (i.e. via an in-house marketing research unit) and/or externally (i.e. by commissioning research to specialised agencies) are classified as EMR users. Table 1 shows the breakdown of the two country samples into users and non-users.

Table 1: Sample breakdown according to the use or non-use of export marketing research

	Use of Export Marketing Research		*Total*
	Yes	*No*	
Finnish Companies	*16*	*17*	*33*
UK Companies	*42*	*38*	*80*

[Table entries are number of firms]

Altogether just over 50% of the respondent firms undertake some form of EMR, the proportions of users being rather similar across the two samples (48.5% versus. 52.5% for the Finnish and UK exporters respectively). The rather low proportion of EMR users in the overall sample may be partly attributed to the added complexities and resource demands associated with researching international markets which act as barriers to employing formal EMR (for a review see, Douglas and Craig, 1983). It may also reflect reliance on other (non-research) information-gathering mechanisms such as trade shows (e.g. Kleinschmidt and Ross, 1984) overseas distributors (e.g. Cook and Shipley, 1988), or foreign visits (e.g. Denis and Depelteau, 1985).

For purposes of the subsequent analysis, four sets of variables were employed to contrast the two EMR *user* groups. *Firm demographics* include indicators of company size, age and product range diversity. *"Objective" indicators* of the firms' export involvement include variables such as the organisation of exports, the number and geographical spread of export destinations and the firm's export intensity ratio. *"Subjective" indicators* of export involvement are captured by respondents' self-reports of export obstacles, the nature of competition and their comparative position versus competitors on elements of the export marketing mix. Lastly, managerial perceptions of the *strategic role of exporting* relate to the firm's position on the export life-cycle (i.e. its internationalisation stage) and the relative profitability of its export operations. Wherever feasible interval- or ratio-level scales were used to measure the above variables. However, the small sample size of the Finnish EMR user group dictated that non-parametric procedures had still to be used for significance-testing purposes. Thus two-sample chi-square tests for independence were applied to nominally-scaled variables and Mann-Whitney-U tests on all other scale types.

4. Results; analysis

A. Firm demographics

As Table 2 shows, UK EMR users are significantly older than their Finnish counterparts. However both samples contain, on average, a lot of "mature" firms; for example the oldest British company in this sample was founded 233 years ago, whereas the oldest Finnish one was "only" 115 years old. No significant differences could be found regarding the number of employees and total number of different product groups produced. Sixty-nine per cent of the UK respondents produce fewer than ten product groups and this applies also to all Finnish firms in the sample. The number of employees in the UK sample ranges from 14 to 24,000 as compared to between 5 and 700 people in the Finnish sample. Although these figures are rather different, these are non-significant; this can be largely attributed to the very wide variation in employment levels within the UK sample (in the latter, the standard deviation comes to 3,977 i.e. about three times its mean).

Table 2: Differences in terms of firm demographics

Firm Demographics	*Mean Values*		*M-W-U** 2-tailed Probability
	UK	*Finnish*	
Company age (years)	*96.12*	*44.25*	*0.001*
Number of product groups	*27.64*	*4.06*	*0.356*
Number of (full-time) employees	*1,343.48*	*307.25*	*0.531*

[Mann-Whitney-U]*

B. Objective indicators of the firm's export involvement

Seventy-one per cent of the UK EMR users and 88% of the Finnish sample claim to have an export department; however the application of a chi-square to the relevant frequencies did not produce a significant result. In terms of export staff, all Finnish firms employ a maximum of eight people and this applies also to 86% of the UK companies. Comparing the companies' years of export experience, UK firms have been significantly longer in the export business than the Finnish exporters. This is not entirely surprising, given that the UK companies are, on average, older than the Finnish (see Table 2 earlier); it may also reflect the long history of the UK as an export nation. As Table 3 shows, there are similarities between the two EMR user groups with respect to both the number and the percentage of product groups exported (the latter being defined as the number of groups exported as a proportion of all product groups produced). Also no difference can be detected in terms of export intensity levels (i.e. the proportion of total sales derived from export operations). However, UK products can be bought in more countries and a larger number of regions than Finnish products, reflecting a greater market-spreading tendency among the UK sample.

Table 3: Differences in terms of export involvement

Export Involvement	*Mean Values*		*M-W-U* 2-tailed Probability*
	UK	*Finnish*	
Number of export staff	8.69	3.81	0.604
Years of export experience	58.69	30.38	0.053
Number of product groups exported	7.62	3.13	0.664
Percentage of product groups exported	80.35	80.10	0.764
Export intensity (% export sales)	31.91	36.50	0.380
Number of export destinations	27.24	17.13	0.043
Number of regions	5.17	3.31	0.003

*[*Mann-Whitney-U]*

Examining the kind of regions respondents serve as export markets, reveals the following results: UK EMR users are involved more in Non-EU European countries, Oceania, Far East and other Asian countries (Table 4); the reason for this could well reflect traditional UK trading patterns which reach back to the time of the Commonwealth. No differences were obtained in terms of serving the EU, North America and the Ex-Comecon region. Thus, despite differences in the length of EU-membership between the UK and Finland both groups of exporters are involved in exports to the EU markets in similar proportions; note that Table 4 does not reveal *how much* of the total exports of each sample is destined for the EU and it may well be the case that these are dissimilar.

Table 4: Sample breakdown according to export regions served

Regions Served	*% of Companies*		*Chi-Square Probability*
	UK	*Finnish*	
EU	*93*	*100*	*0.272*
NON-EU	*86*	*44*	*0.001*
Oceania	*50*	*25*	*0.086*
Far-East	*76*	*19*	*0.001*
North America	*81*	*94*	*0.229*
Ex-Comecon	*19*	*31*	*0.319*
Other Asian Countries	*45*	*19*	*0.063*

C. Subjective assessments of the firm's export situation

Focusing initially on export obstacles, locating and working with distributors in export markets are regarded by both country samples as considerable obstacles to exporting, while economic differences and language difficulties seem to be less important (Table 5). UK EMR users see more difficulties with exchange rate fluctuations and political instabilities of foreign markets while the Finnish firms put more emphasis on cultural difficulties. These differences may well reflect the different geographic spread of exports between the UK and Finnish firms identified in the previous section (see Table 4).

Table 5: Differences in the perception of export obstacles

Export Obstacles	*Mean Values (1= unimportant 5= very important)*		*M-W-U* 2-tailed Probability*
	UK	*Finnish*	
Language difficulties	2.57	2.94	0.506
Cultural difficulties	2.43	3.00	0.099
Economic differences	2.90	2.38	0.141
Exchange rate fluctuation	3.55	2.75	0.018
Locating suitable distributors	3.64	3.94	0.571
Working with existing distributors	3.10	2.75	0.331
Political instability	2.40	1.69	0.039

[Mann Whitney-U]*

In both samples, product quality and style are perceived to be the strongest element of the export marketing-mix, while promotion and distribution activities are regarded as rather similar to those of competitors in export markets (Table 6). Cross-country differences exist only with regard to product price; specifically, Finnish exporters indicate that their price is higher compared to that of their competitors compared with the UK firms. This result is consistent with their attitude to the competitive situation because, for the Finnish sample, price competition is perceived to be *less* important than for the UK sample; moreover the Finnish firms put significantly more emphasis on non-price competition than UK firms. This suggests that the manner in which the two groups of exporter position themselves in the market is very different.

Table 6: Differences in the comparative export marketing mix and the intensity of competition in export markets

Comparative Export Marketing Mix	*Mean Values (1=inferior 5=superior)*		*M-W-U* 2-tailed Probability*
	UK	*Finnish*	
Product quality	*4.17*	*4.06*	*0.751*
Product style	*3.88*	*3.88*	*0.963*
Product promotion	*3.33*	*2.88*	*0.167*
*Product price***	*3.52*	*4.00*	*0.031*
Product distribution	*3.26*	*3.31*	*0.632*
Intensity of Competition in Export Markets	*Mean Values (1 = unimportant, 5 = important)*		
Price competition	*3.98*	*3.38*	*0.048*
Non-price-competition	*3.29*	*4.69*	*0.000*

*[*Mann-Whitney-U; ** 5=higher, 1=lower]*

D. Managerial perceptions about the strategic role of exporting in their firm

In terms of the firm's position in the export life-cycle, 43% of the UK EMR users indicate that they examine potential markets on a global basis as part of their international marketing strategy, whereas all but one of the Finnish respondents position themselves in the "experienced exporter" category. While this may reflect the greater export experience of the UK sample (see Table 3 earlier), it may also be partly due to the few very large UK firms responding to the survey; the latter are likely to operate more than one mode of foreign market entry (e.g. licences and joint ventures *in addition* to exporting) and thus view exports as only part of their global strategy. On the whole, and over both samples, the respondent firms appear to be quite advanced in internationalisation terms.

Table 7: Differences in managerial perceptions about the strategic role of exporting

	% of Firms		*Chi-Square Probability*
	UK	*Finnish*	
Company internationalisation:			*0.010*
a) Unsolicited orders only	*2.38*	*0.00*	
b) Examining export possibilities	*9.52*	*0.00*	
c) Export experimentally	*0.00*	*0.00*	
d) Experienced in exporting	*45.24*	*93.75*	
e) Exporting is part of global strategy	*42.86*	*6.25*	

Finally, respondents were asked to assess the profitability of their firm's export sales in relation to their sales in their domestic market. The answers, as shown in Table 8, indicate that both country groups regard export sales as equally profitable to home market sales.

Table 8: Differences in relative export profitability

	Mean Values (1 = much less profitable 5 = much more profitable)		*M-W-U* 2-tailed Probability*
	UK	*Finnish*	
Export profitability relative to home markets	*3.05*	*3.19*	*0.644*

*[*Mann-Whitney-U]*

5. Discussion and conclusions

The objective of the present investigation was to identify whether there is a common export profile of EMR users based in different countries. According to the findings, a single profile does seem to exist but *only* if one concentrates on "objective", more or less easily observable characteristics such as size, export intensity and export experience. Thus both groups of exporters are mature firms of medium- or large size, which have been exporting for a good many years and which obtain about a third of their total sales from overseas markets; they also manage to export about 80% of their total product range (as already mentioned, the fact that the UK firms are somewhat older and have been exporting longer than the Finnish ones is of little substantive importance given the numbers involved). In addition, most firms in both samples have formalised their export operations as indicated in the existence of a separate export department and the allocation of dedicated personnel to exporting. However, once attention is directed towards more *strategic* variables, substantial differences seem to characterise the two groups of EMR users. Such differences are manifested both in their export coverage strategies (i.e. market concentration vs market spreading) and their export positioning strategies (i.e. price vs non-price emphasis). Specifically, the UK EMR users prefer a market spreading strategy coupled with emphasis on price as a means for obtaining competitive advantage. Their choices are reflected in the large number of export destinations served and the geographical diversity of export locations as well as in their concern with exchange rate fluctuations and the intensity of price competition. In contrast, the Finnish EMR users follow a market concentration strategy and compete along non-price dimensions; they direct their exports towards a much smaller number of countries located in a smaller number of regions and are particularly concerned with the impact of cultural differences on their export operations. Whether the observed differences in strategic postures have implications for export performance is, unfortunately, hard to determine from the data. While no differences were observed in terms of export intensity (see Table 3) or relative export profitability (see Table 8), there are several other dimensions of export performance such as growth, rate of new market entry and export market share, none of which were considered in the present study. Given the complex and multidimensional nature of the export performance construct (for relevant reviews, see Madsen, 1987; Shoham, 1991; Matthyssens and Pauwels, 1995; Al-Khalifa and Morgan, 1995), one must reserve judgement as to the relative effectiveness of the different strategies pursued by the UK and Finnish firms investigated in this study.

Taking the above similarities and differences in conjunction, the country-specific patterns observed suggest that the needs of EMR users based in different countries are likely to differ substantially. The kind of research requirements associated with serving a large number of geographically dispersed markets while using price as a competitive weapon are unlikely to be the same (both in terms of information sources and data collection methods) with the requirements of a smaller number of clustered countries in which non-price considerations are perceived to predominate. While the specific nature of differences in research requirements is outside the scope of the present paper and left as an avenue for further research, it would appear that the kind of research services needed/utilised by UK and Finnish exporters are likely to vary, despite the fact that both groups operate in the same industry. What this implies is that a "standardised" package of EMR services tailored to a given industry may not be sufficient to meet the needs of all exporters (particularly if the latter are based in different countries), because of differences in the strategies of the latter. They may all be large, they may all be experienced, they may all export a substantial proportion of their output and they may all have an export department. In fact they may all look alike from the outside; but they may still need very different things indeed.

Placing the findings of the present study in the context of previous research is rather problematic as no other cross-country comparison of EMR *users* (not exporters in general) in terms of export profiles was uncovered during the literature review. However, some of the variables that differentiated between the two EMR user groups were also identified in previous studies as differentiating between users and *non-users* of EMR; for example, users are more likely to export to a larger number of markets than non-users (e.g. Diamantopoulos et al, 1990). On the other hand, variables such as size and export dependence which have been found to discriminate between EMR users and non-users (e.g. Cavusgil, 1984a) did not display significant cross-country differences among user groups according to the findings of the present study. Lastly, there are variables on which cross-country differences were noted (e.g. perceptions of export obstacles) but have not been shown to impinge upon whether a firm is *likely* to use EMR or not (e.g. Schlegelmilch et al, 1993). What these patterns suggest is that what differentiates between users and non-users of EMR in a *single-country* setting may or may not differentiate among user groups (e.g. EMR users based in different countries). In this context, an *ideal* discriminating variable enabling universal generalisations to take place, should (a) show *significant* differences between users and non-users of EMR in all *within-country* comparisons, (b) produce *non-significant* results in *between-country* comparisons. If it fails to do either, then it is not possible to generalise as to the differences between users and non-users in a multi-country setting *simultaneously*. Firm size is an example of a variable that fulfils these criteria in the present investigation, while the number of export destinations is not.

With regard to future research directions, three areas appear to hold a lot of promise. First, comparative investigations of the actual research activities of exporters would be useful to relate export profiles in general and export strategies in particular to EMR utilisation. Second, the way in which non-research information-gathering mechanisms (e.g. distributor intelligence and trade fair participation) is combined with formal EMR is in need of further investigation to paint a more comprehensive picture of the use of export information in the firm. Third, the linkage between the research orientation of the firm in general (as reflected, for example, in its domestic market research activities) and the sophistication of its EMR deserves attention. The combined insights from such investigations would enable the identification of the proper role of EMR, the factors facilitating its adoption as well as the limitations of its contribution to the firm's export success.

Résumé

Caractéristiques distinctives d'entreprises exportatrices utilisatrices de recherches en marketing. Illustration de deux pays européens.

Il est généralement admis que l'information est une source d'avantage compétitif ; à l'échelle internationale ce facteur semble particulièrement pertinent mais il présente de sérieuses difficultés d'élaboration et de diffusion. L'étude présentée par A. Diamantopoulos innove en ce sens qu'elle porte sur l'utilisation qui est faite en pratique de ces informations en marketing par les entreprises exportatrices au Royaume-Uni et en Finlande ; elle permet dès lors de mieux cibler ces informations en fonction des besoins réels des utilisateurs. Les entreprises étudiées (113 au total) dans les deux pays ont été sélectionnées dans le même secteur industriel afin d'éviter un éventuel biais méthodologique résultant de la diversité d'activité. Les deux groupes d'entreprises sont analysés sous le même angle de diverses variables, et révèlent finalement des situations et des comportements différents. La réalité de gestion à l'exportation reste multiple.

Zusammenfassung

Unterscheidungsmerkmale für Exportfirmen, die Marketingforschung betreiben. Darstellung am Beispiel zweier europäischer Staaten

Allgemein wird davon ausgegangen, daß Information Wettbewerbsvorteile verschafft. Gerade im internationalen Rahmen ist dieser Faktor ausschlaggebend; bei seiner Schaffung und Verwertung stößt er jedoch auf größere Schwierigkeiten. Die von A. DIAMANTOPOULOS vorgelegte Studie bringt insofern eine Neuerung, als sie sich mit der praktischen Verwendung von Marketinginformationen durch Exportunternehmen in Großbritannien und Finnland auseinandersetzt. Damit wird es möglich, die Informationen besser auf die wirklichen Bedürfnisse der Verwender auszurichten. Um eventuelle methodologische, durch verschiedenen Geschäftstätigkeiten bedingte Abweichungen zu vermeiden, wurden die insgesamt 113 Firmen aus beiden Ländern innerhalb derselben Industriebranche ausgewählt. Die beiden Gruppen werden dann in gleicher Weise hinsichtlich verschiedener Variablen analysiert, womit unterschiedliche Situationen und Verhaltensmuster aufgezeigt werden. Diese ergeben ein vielfältiges Bild des Exportmanagements.

References

AL-KHALIFA, A./MORGAN, N.A., (1995): Export Performance Measurement: a Review and Suggested Directions. in AMA - Marketing Theory and Applications. Vol. 6. Winter. pp. 313-318.

BUSINESS AMERICA (1987): A Step-By-Step Approach to Market Research. Vol. 10. No. 6. March. pp. 10-11.

BODUR, M./CAVUSGIL, S.T. (1985): Export Market Research Orientations of Turkish Firms. European Journal of Marketing. Vol. 19. No. 2. pp. 5-16.

CADOGAN, J.W./DIAMANTOPOULOS, A. (1995): Narver and Slater, Kohli and Jaworski and the Market Orientation Construct: Integration and Internationalization. Journal of Strategic Marketing. Vol. 3. pp. 41-60.

CALANTONE, R.J./di BENEDETTO, C.A./HARVEY, C.E. (1991): A Model for Defensive Marketing Strategy with Examples from the Europe 1992 Context. Journal of Euromarketing. Vol. 1. No. 1/2. pp. 9-38.

CAVUSGIL, S. T. (1984a): International Marketing Research: Insights into Company Practices. Research in Marketing. Vol. 7. pp. 261-288.

CAVUSGIL, S. T. (1984b): Differences Among Exporting Firms Based on their Degree of Internationalisation. Journal of Business Research. Vol. 12. pp. 195-208.

CAVUSGIL, S. T. (1985): Guidelines for EMR. Business Horizons. November - December. pp. 27-33.

COOK, D./SHIPLEY, D. (1988): The Search for and Evaluation of Overseas Distributors: An Exploratory Study. in Blois, K. and Parkison, S. T. (Eds.). Innovative Marketing: A European Perspective. Proceedings of the 17th Annual Conference of the European Marketing Academy. Bradford. England. pp. 115-137.

CZINKOTA, M.R./RONKAINEN, I.A. (1990): International Marketing. 2nd Edition. New York: Dryden. 1990.

DALGIC, T., (1994): International Marketing and Marketing Orientation: An Early Conceptual Attempt. Advances in International Marketing. Vol. 6. pp. 69-82.

DAVIS, H. L./DOUGLAS, S. P./SILK, A. J. (1981): Measure Unreliability: A Hidden Threat to Cross-National Marketing Research? Journal of Marketing. Vol. 45. Spring. pp. 98-109.

DENIS, J.E./DEPELTEAU, D. (1985): Market Knowledge, Diversification and Export Expansion. Journal of International Business Studies. Vol. 15. Fall. pp. 77-89.

DIAMANTOPOULOS, A./SCHLEGELMILCH, B.B./ALLPRESS, C. (1990): Export Marketing Research in Practice: A Comparison of Users and Non-Users. Journal of Marketing Management. Special Issue on International Marketing. Vol. 6. No. 3. pp. 257-273.

DIAMANTOPOULOS, A./SCHLEGELMILCH, B.B./TSE, K./ALLPRESS, C. (1991): Export Marketing Research: A Comparative Analysis of Finnish and British Firms. in King, R.L. (Ed.). Developments in Marketing Science. Vol. 14. Proceedings of the 15th Annual Conference of the Academy of Marketing Science. Ford Lauderdale. Florida. pp. 112-118.

DIAMANTOPOULOS, A./SCHLEGELMILCH, B.B./TSE, K. (1993): Understanding the Role of Export Marketing Assistance: Empirical Evidence and Research Needs. European Journal of Marketing. Vol. 27. No. 4. pp. 5-18.

DIAMANTOPOULOS, A./HORNCASTLE, S., (1994): Use of Export Marketing Research by Industrial Firms: An Application of Deshpande and Zaltman's Model. in Biemans, W.G. and Ghauri, P.N. (Eds). Meeting the Challenges of New Frontiers. Vol. 1. Proceedings of the 10th IMP Annual Conference. Groningen. The Netherlands. pp. 313-336.

DOUGLAS, S.P./SHOEMAKER, R. (1981): Item Non-Response in Cross-National Attitude Surveys. European Research. Vol. 9. pp. 124-132.

DOUGLAS, S.P./CRAIG, C.S./KEEGAN, W.J. (1982): Approaches to Assessing International Marketing Opportunities for Small and Medium-Sized Companies. Columbia Journal of World Business. Fall. pp. 26-32.

DOUGLAS, S.P./CRAIG, C.S. (1983): International Marketing Research. Englewood Cliffs. Prentice-Hall, Inc.

GARRETT, K./HART, S. (1993): An Investigation of Market Research Activities of Multinational SBUs. in Chiar, J. and Sureda, J. (Eds.). Marketing for the New Europe: Dealing With Complexity. Proceedings of the 22nd Annual Conference of the European Marketing Academy. Vol. 1. pp. 519-542.

GASMAN, L.D. (1982): Seven Rules for International Research. Marketing News-USA. September. p. 17.

GEMÜNDEN, H.G. (1991): Success Factors of Export Marketing - A Meta-Analytic Critique of the Empirical Studies. Paliwoda, S. J. (Ed.). New Perspectives on International Marketing. Routledge. London. pp. 33-62.

GLAZER, R. (1991): Marketing in and Information-Intensive Environment: Strategic Implications of Knowledge to an Asset. Journal of Marketing. Vol. 55. October. pp. 1-19.

GOFTON, K. (1994): Moving in on More Markets. Marketing. March, 10. pp. 26-27.

GORDON, I. (1984): How to Research your Export Markets. Sales and Marketing Management in Canada. November. pp. 10-11.

GUIDO, G. (1991): Marketing Mix Strategies in the Europe of 1992. Journal of Euromarketing. Vol. 1. No. 1/2. pp. 129-150.

HART, S.J./WEBB, J.R. /JONES, M.V. (1994): Export Marketing Research and the Effect of Export Experience in Industrial SMEs. International Marketing Review. Vol. 11. No.6. pp. 4-22.

JOBBER, D./SAUNDERS, J. (1988): An Experimental Investigation into Cross-National Mail Survey Response Rates. Journal of Marketing. Vol. 44. Fall. pp. 38-43.

JOHANSON, J./VAHLNE, J.E., (1977): The Internationalisation Process of the Firm - A Model of Knowledge Development and Increasing Foreign Market Commitments. Journal of International Business Studies. Spring/Summer. pp. 23-32.

KAYNAK, E./GHAURI, P.N. (1994): Consumer Behavior and Marketing Issues in the Europe of Post-1992. in Kaunak, E. and Ghauri, P.N. (Eds). Euromarketing Effective Strategies for International Trade and Export. New York. International Business Press. pp. 57-84.

KLEINSCHMIDT, E.J./ROSS, R.E. (1984): Export Performance and Foreign Market Information: Relationships for Small High-Technology Firms. Canadian Journal of Small Business and Entrepreneurship. Vol. 2. No. 4. pp. 8-23.

KOH, A. C. (1991): An Evaluation of International Marketing Research Planning in United States Export Firms. Journal of Global Marketing. Vol. 4. No. 3. pp. 7-25.

KOH, A.C./CHOW, J./SMITTIVATE, S. (1993): The Practice of International Marketing Research by Thai Exporters. Journal of Global Marketing. Vol. 7. No. 2. pp. 7-26.

KOHLI, A.J./JAWORSKI, B.J. (1990): Market Orientation: the Construct, Research Propositions, and Managerial Implications. Journal of Marketing. Vol. 43. pp. 1-18.

LEEFLANG, P.S.H./de MORTANGES, C.P. (1994): Marketing Planning and 1992: Observations and Expectations. in Kaunak, E. and Ghauri, P.N. (Eds). Euromarketing Effective Strategies for International Trade and Export. New York. International Business Press. pp. 85- 106.

MADSEN, T.K. (1987): Empirical Export Performance Studies: A Review of Conceptualizations and Findings. Advances in International Marketing. Vol. 2. pp. 177-198.

MATTHYSSENS, P./PAUWELS, P. (1995): Measuring Success in Export Marketing Strategy - A Critical Review. CIMaR Conference. pp. 1-20.

MAYER, C.S. (1978): Multinational Marketing Research: The Magnifying Glass of Methodological Problems. European Research. March. pp. 77-84.

McAULEY, A. (1993): The Perceived Usefulness of Export Information Sources. European Journal of Marketing. Vol. 27. No. 10. pp. 52-64.

MUNSON, J. M./McINTYRE, S. H. (1979): Developing Practical Procedures for the Measurement of Personal Values in Cross-Cultural Marketing. Journal of Marketing Research. Vol. 16. February. pp. 48-52.

PARAMESWARAN, R./YAPRAK, A. (1987): A Cross-National Comparison of Consumer Research Measures. Journal of International Business Studies. Vol. 18. Spring. pp. 35-49.

PARSONS, G. (1983): Information Technology: A New Competitive Weapon. Sloan Management Review. Vol. 25. No.1. pp. 3-14.
PORTER, M./MILLAR, V. (1985): How Information Gives You Competitive Advantage. Harvard Business Review. July/August. pp. 149-160.
REID, S. (1984): Information Acquisition and Export Entry Decisions in Small Firms. Journal of Business Research. Vol. 12. pp. 141-157.
RICKS, D.A. (1983): Big Business Blunders. Homewood. IL: Irwin.
SCHLEGELMILCH, B.B./THERIVEL, S. (1988): The Use of Marketing Research in Engineering Companies: Empirical Evidence from the U.S. and the UK. in Woodside, A.G. (Ed.). Advances in Business Marketing. Greenwich. CT, Jai Press. Vol. 3. pp. 249-291.
SCHLEGELMILCH, B.B./DIAMANTOPOULOS, A./TSE, K. (1993): Determinants of Export Marketing Research Usage: Testing Some Hypotheses on UK Exporters. in Baker, M. J. (Ed.). Perspectives on Marketing Management. John Wiley & Sons Ltd. Vol. 3. pp. 119-139.
SERINGHAUS, R.F.H. (1985): Private/Public Sector Interaction: How Effective is Export Marketing Assistance by Government: A Review of the Issues and Current Research. Proceedings of the Annual Conference of the European Marketing Academy. Bielefeld. Germany.
SERINGHAUS, R.F.H. (1987): Export Promotion: The Role and Impact of Government Services. Irish Marketing Review. Vol. 2. 1987. pp. 106-116.
SERINGHAUS, R.F.H. (1988): Export Knowledge, Strategy and Performance. Developments in Marketing Science. Vol. 10. pp. 97-101.
SHOHAM, A. (1991): Performance in Exporting: State-of-the-Art Literature Review and Synthesis and Directions for Future Research. Academy of International Business Annual Meeting. Miami. Florida.
SOOD, J. H. (1981): The International Market Information Model of Export Behaviour: An Empirical Investigation Based on the Size of the Exporting Firm. Proceedings of the European Academy of Advanced Research in Marketing. Kopenhagen. March.
STOUT, R. G./DALVI, N. (1989): Improving the Effectiveness of Multi-Country Consumer Tracking. Journal of the Market Research Society. Vol. 31. No. 4. pp. 545-550.
TURNER, P. (1991): Using Information to Enhance Competitive Advantage - The Marketing Options. European Journal of Marketing. Vol. 25. No. 6. pp. 55-64.
VARALDO, R./PICCALUGA, A. (1994): Marketing in Europe Beyond 1992: The Challenge of a Mix Between Global and Local Marketing Strategies. in Kaunak, E. and Ghauri, P.N. (Eds). Euromarketing Effective Strategies for International Trade and Export. New York. International Business Press. pp. 163-181.

WALTERS, P.G., (1983): Export Information Sources - A Study of their Usage and Utility. International Marketing Review. Vol. 1. Winter. pp. 34-43.

WOOD, R./GOOLSBY, J.R. (1987): Foreign Market Information Preferences of Established U.S. Exporters. International Marketing Review. Vol. 4. Winter. pp. 43-52.

YAPRAK, A. (1985): An Empirical Study of the Differences Between Small Exporting and Non-Exporting U.S. Firms. International Marketing Review. Summer. pp. 72-83.

Peter Standish

Accounting Codification: Experience and Prospects in the European Context

1. Introduction

2. Nature and scope of a national accounting code

3. The French national accounting code: origins and development

4. French experience with a national accounting code

   A. Application and adaptation of the code
   B. Structure and process for accounting standardisation

5. Applying French experience to the present European context

   A. Securities markets and international accounting standards
   B. Significance of changes in Eastern Europe

6. Conclusion

1. Introduction

This Chapter concerns the role played by standardised national accounting codes in the current European context and its relevance to changing ideas and influences on organisation of financial accounting and reporting for the needs of a market economy. Its starting point is the particular experience of France, the first European nation to adopt a national accounting code after the Second World War as the basis for organising enterprise accounting systems and presentation of annual accounts. The French model has influenced other European nations to adopt broadly similar codes of accounts, as well as Francophone nations outside Europe. Adopted in 1947, the French code, the *Plan comptable général* (PCG), was revised and reissued in 1957, 1982 and 1986 (Conseil National de la Comptabilité, 1986), and is undergoing current revision.

The purpose of the Chapter is to explain the role and nature of national accounting codes in contrast with the dominant approach toward accounting standardisation in the English-speaking world and at international level. This will be followed by assessment of the particular strengths and weaknesses revealed by French experience and their relevance to development of the Single Market and economic transformation of the nations of Eastern Europe.

2. Nature and scope of a national accounting code

The concept of a national accounting code is of a nationally observed set of requirements or guidelines for the systematic organisation of the financial accounts of entities engaged in economic activity. Entities for this purpose may be conducted for profit or non-profit objectives by individual persons, partnerships, associations, incorporated entities, or government operating through public administrative bodies or commercial undertakings. The defining financial characteristics of entities engaged in economic activity are that they operate with an acquired set of scarce resources or assets, finance their activities by some mix of contributions from owners and creditors, generate revenue from operating income or grants substituting for income, and incur charges against revenues. A comprehensive national code comprises the following elements:

1) A standardised chart of accounts

An entity chart of accounts comprises the set of separate accounts sufficient to meet the information needs of its users for a comprehensive and classified record of transactions having financial consequences, with the following attributes:

- Each account within the chart, as its basic building block, is established to represent, collect and aggregate dated monetary inflows and outflows, as well as residual monetary balances, of a specified well-defined category of financial transaction effects.
- The chart has a hierarchical structure, comprising account classes at the highest level of aggregation, one or more sub-classes, and individual accounts, providing for increasingly detailed representation of financial effects at each successive level.
- Account classes represent the fundamental components of financial position and performance, namely the financing of entity activity, the investment of resources provided by its financing, its revenue and charges against revenue.
- Coding of the chart comprises descriptive titles for classes, sub-classes and individual accounts, together with code signifiers for each component of the chart, such as all-numeric references.
- The structure and functioning of the chart provides for reclassification and transfer of financial effects between its components.

A national accounting code will include a model standardised chart of accounts containing a specified minimum set of account classes, sub-classes and individual accounts with the foregoing attributes, to be universally applied by entities as their accounting system, either in its nationally stated form or as adapted by a nationally specified process.

2) Instructions and guidelines for application of the chart of accounts

The code will provide instructions and guidelines, including explanation of its basic accounting principles, as reasonably needed for effective application of the model chart of accounts in documenting, recording, classifying and aggregating entity financial transactions, and for users of financial accounts to understand and interpret the attributes of information processed on this basis.

3) Requirements for annual accounts and notes on the accounts

The documentation of the code will also set out model formats for annual financial accounts to be presented to owners or bodies responsible for the entity, together with instructions and guidelines for such notes on the accounts as may reasonably be needed by informed users of accounts having a recognised interest and expectations regarding the financial position and performance of the entity.

Historically, systematic keeping of accounts was importantly driven by the need for an enterprise to maintain effective records of transactions for value with third parties. The state also had an interest in encouraging enterprises to maintain proper records in the event of dispute between parties requiring recourse to tribunals created or authorised by the state for resolution of commercial disputes[1]. Together with accounting for relations between parties at arms-length came concepts for the measurement of owner equity and distributable surplus on commercial transactions. These were required so that proprietors and equity partners might periodically determine the accumulated capital of an enterprise and the return on that capital as a reward to the risk of investing financial and other resources having alternative opportunities[2].

1 This interest of the state finds expression in the first French law for the keeping of accounts by merchants and traders, the *Ordonnance de Colbert*, 1673.

2 On the historical context for the emergence of financial accounting and the forms this took in various European countries, see Bérard and Lemarchand, 1994.

With the advent of industrialisation and technologically driven opportunities in mining, manufacturing, transport and other fields to construct large-scale enterprises and achieve economies of scale, the accounting task became more complex. Concepts had to be developed to deal with the need to account for usage of fixed assets over extended periods and periodic depreciation of those resources[3], for multiple classification of cost information for purposes of product costing and responsibility accounting[4], and for the emergence of a widening set of economic interests in entity financial performance consequent on the development of securities markets and complex instruments of financing[5].

In an unregulated environment, each enterprise would have the opportunity and necessity to devise the accounting code best suited to its needs. Experience shows that the expression of those needs leads to divergent outcomes in terms of the sophistication of individual enterprise accounting codes, their transparency to managers, let alone external parties, and their effectiveness in terms of information reliability and timeliness. The enterprise addressing these issues faces the choice between costly construction of its individual accounting code or foregoing individuality by recourse to commercially available information system products with elements of standardised accounting code design and implementation. Developments in computer-based software are shifting the cost advantage in this latter direction.

Prior to these developments, there was no realistic possibility of widespread voluntary adoption of standardised accounting codes. Reverting to the start of this century rather than contemplating its end is to enter a time with little or no income tax on enterprise profit, of securities markets with few listed companies, and of undemanding or effectively non-existent financial reporting requirements. There was little need for the enterprise to address wider issues of information reliability and financial communication to the general public.

3 Lemarchand, 1993, presents a detailed history of the development of depreciation concepts and accounting in France.

4 On the development of cost accounting for management control, see Johnson and Kaplan, 1987.

5 Dealt with in various milestone US and UK statements, notably, American Institute of Certified Public Accountants, 1973; (UK) Accounting Standards Steering Committee, 1975.

Nevertheless, the enterprise faced costly accounting system design and implementation. In this context, numerous proposals were advanced for accounting codes intended for particular industries, offering a way to reduce costs to enterprises in those industries and a basis for inter-firm comparisons of financial performance[6]. In due course, ideas for accounting codes emerged that presented more universal structures of accounting classification and relationships to concepts of capital, surplus and operating cycles. Of particular importance, both in terms of its theoretical weight and for its subsequent history was the contribution during the 1920s by the German accounting professor, Schmalenbach (Forrester, 1977).

By now, there were within Europe various fleshed out proposals for standardised accounting codes capable of application at a national level. These mostly emerged within Continental Europe, possibly reflecting less extensive development of the accounting profession and the role of securities markets throughout Continental Europe than in the UK or USA. Whilst construction of all manner of national arrangements for standardisation is forever a utopian dream, the possibility of a national accounting code arising from the voluntary agreement of innumerable competing individual enterprises and their professional accounting advisers is not realistic. If a national accounting code were ever to be implemented, it would have to be imposed by government fiat. The spark that achieved this was the widespread awareness of Schmalenbachís ideas in Germany and their attraction for the Nazi government as it set about moving the economy onto a war footing. The attraction was that by converting these ideas into a national accounting code, the government would achieve an instrument for cost control and prices regulation. In 1937, the German government proclaimed by decree the first such code, known as the Goering Plan, to be adopted within a short time throughout German industry and commerce (Singer, 1943). Similar ideas also took root in the Soviet Union,

6 The diversity of classification concepts in accounting is studied in Hain, 1980. For an extensive history of industry accounting codes, see Mommen, 1957.

initially as part of the process for specification and monitoring of national economic plans, but after the German onslaught in 1941 as a further tool in the massive redeployment of the economy for war needs.

3. The French national accounting code: origins and development[7]

In France, the German Occupation from 1940 onward was marked by rapid moves on the part of the French Vichy administration to undertake development of a national accounting code. Though there is evidence of German pressure for development of a code, there was no direct instruction to the French authorities to proceed. The commission charged in 1941 with the task produced its proposed code, the *Plan comptable général,* in 1942. Of particular influence in this speedy outcome was a group of influential industrialists and bureaucrats who accepted the superior merits of German economic organisation and sought to draw on its example for the reform of French economic life. They saw that France was seriously deficient in accounting skills, national economic statistics and organisation of its liberal professions. All three issues became of the highest priority and the subject for sweeping reforms. The proposed accounting code was, not surprisingly, closely similar to the Goering Plan, though with some elements of French accounting ideas[8]. Before measures could be taken to promulgate the code and apply it throughout industry, however, the authority of the Vichy government crumbled and conditions no longer existed for effective introduction of major social change.

With the post-war restoration of national government, attention turned to urgent tasks of economic and social reconstruction. The difficulties to be faced were familiar everywhere at that time in war-torn countries: rampant inflation,

7 See Standish, 1990, on the origins of the *Plan comptable général*. Its later development is dealt with in Standish, 1996 (forthcoming).

8 For comparison of the Goering Plan with the 1942 and 1947 PCG, see Richard, 1995.

chronic shortages and a poorly maintained or badly damaged economic infrastructure. The mood was for political change. Possibilities of national economic direction and planning beckoned as seemingly better alternatives to previous experience of largely unregulated capitalism and economic fluctuation. Wartime experience in France of national vulnerability created a determination that the state should have a greater say in the operation of the economy and performance of key sectors. Part of the path followed to achieve this was a programme of nationalisation of utilities, financial institutions and industrial enterprises which greatly expanded the task of managing the public sector and associated needs for improved accounting.

In these conditions, the concept of a national accounting code and accumulated experience with the 1942 PCG provided the impetus for its redevelopment and validation free from association with war-time conditions. This was expressed in the establishment in 1946 of a commission for accounting standardisation which in turn produced a code, revised from the 1942 proposals and embodying all the elements of a national accounting code specified above. Officially adopted in 1947, the *Plan comptable général* was to be applied in the first instance to state-owned enterprises of an industrial or commercial nature and private sector enterprises receiving state financial guarantees above a defined amount. At the same time as its adoption, the government established under the direction of the Finance Ministry the agency, the Conseil Supérieur de la Comptabilité, charged with responsibility for future development and application of the PCG. The clearest initial expression of benefits sought from the code is found in the report of the 1946 commission, summarised as follows:

- Transparency in accounting would provide users with information for proper evaluation that is denied when accounting operates inconsistently, and for more effective control by public authorities.
- Better financial performance information from enterprises would provide the basis for a more equitable tax system by contributing to an understanding of the sources and distribution of national income.
- Standardised enterprise financial accounting would contribute to the construction of national income statistics.

In performing their task, the reformers were effectively having to address the following issues of policy choice:

(1) Should development of a code have been the task of government or instead handed to the accounting profession or the private sector?
(2) Was there a need for a national accounting code or could financial accounting standardisation have been left to normal market forces?
(3) Should accounting standardisation have been primarily concerned with the information needs of investors in traded securities and to a lesser extent with other policy issues regarding financial reporting?

The answers to these choices need to be understood within the context of the early post-war period. As regards the first choice and compared with the UK, France had available a very low number of professionally qualified accountants and an immature structure of organisation of the accounting profession dating only from the wartime reforms. Handing the task of accounting standardisation to the profession was therefore not a practical possibility. As regards the second choice, the government of the day and influential civil servants saw their role as leading social reconstruction, rather than responding to market forces. Moreover, there was a considerable degree of political hostility toward the alleged past sins and failures of the private sector during the depression years before the war and the war itself. Finally, the role of financial accounting information in securities investment decisions was not a pressing issue given the relative insignificance of the French stock market.

Crucial to effective implementation of a national accounting code was the attitude of the private sector upon which the burden of application would largely fall. In that regard, reactions were mixed. The private sector was struggling to find a confident voice to deal with government and had to live with an administration fortified by experience with war-time regulation and control. As the 1947 PCG was not mandatory for private sector enterprises other than those receiving significant state financial guarantees, the possibility of extended application may have seemed distant. Moreover, the process for development of the 1947 PCG had provided a useful degree of input from recognised industry bodies and leaders of the accounting profession. Separation within the PCG of financial from cost accounting had been a significant concession to quell private sector fears of state surveillance, with organisation of cost accounting and associated private information about product cost margins left to the discretion of enterprises. As well, for some enterprise managers, the PCG may have offered a useful path to simplification of the accounting task through its standardisation. Finally, any private sector concern that application of the PCG might become part of procedures for compliance with income tax requirements was allayed by silence on that aspect.

In the years following adoption of the 1947 PCG, it became clear that it was having an increasing impact on French financial accounting practice as the core reference source for education and training of accountants. The PCG may be said to have established a national accounting language. Its revision in 1957 was followed by two public policy measures that made it a central element in the national organisation of financial accounting.

1) Adaptation of the PCG to the needs of industry sectors

Both with the proposed 1942 PCG and 1947 PCG, it had been accepted that the overall national accounting code would require adaptation to the information needs of particular industry activity sectors. The types of adaptations envisaged would be the substitution where appropriate of more industry-specific descriptive titles for accounts and extension of the code to insert sub-classes and individual accounts to reflect specific industry accounting practices (for example, regarding categories of fixed assets, stocks, turnover). Commencing in 1959, a procedure for progressive application of the PCG was enacted. Within a five year period, industry committees were to be established with the task of proposing such adaptations as they deemed desirable, with their work being coordinated by the reconstituted agency now responsible for the PCG, the Conseil National de la Comptabilité (CNC, or National Accounting Council), and ultimately requiring its approval. This produced results, if over a longer interval than originally envisaged. In the period 1968-1979, the CNC approved 55 industry sector adaptations of the financial accounting requirements of the PCG. There were also procedures for adaptation of the PCG to the needs of public agencies and nationalised enterprises, with 63 adaptations approved in the period 1958-1973.

2) Harmonising tax requirements with the PCG

Experience with the PCG and reactions of enterprises in the private sector showed the need to address its relationship with law and administrative requirements for determining enterprise income tax liability. There were many respects in which enterprises adopted accounting methods for tax purposes with unsatisfactory effects on the balance sheet and profit and loss account. Promoting what it saw as the cause of proper accounting, the CNC advocated the position that tax requirements should not affect accounting terminology or PCG rules for keeping of accounts. Prior to 1965, tax law definitions of taxable income and its components applied independently of the PCG. Similarly, procedural requirements for compiling accounting statements for tax return purposes were unrelated to the PCG. As from 1965, a tax decree specified the formats and descriptions to be adopted by enterprises for the annual declaration of profits and losses for tax purposes and the valuation rules directly affecting calculation of taxable income. The effect of the decree was to require conformity of enterprise accounting records and annual accounts with the PCG to the extent compatible with rules for tax assessment, a linkage retained to the present.

During the 1970s, it became clear that the PCG was increasingly in need of reform to take account of changing needs and circumstances. A particular limitation was that it had nothing to say on the subject of consolidated accounts, required if investors are to be presented with a composite view of the group financial performance and position of a holding company, its subsidiaries and significant but non-controlling equity investments outside the group. At that time, few French company groups prepared consolidated accounts, at least for public consumption, or were listed on stock exchanges outside France. Nevertheless, it was becoming important for French multinational companies to be more aware of international accounting standards and practices. The European Community (as then styled) was developing company law directives for the European harmonisation of financial accounting and reporting by enterprises, intended to reduce differences between rules and practices of the constituent Member States. Following accession of the UK to the EC and its participation in those developments, other Member States were brought directly into contact with British perspectives and practices from a context more heavily influenced by market considerations.

The ensuing EC Fourth Directive on requirements for the annual accounts of individual companies and Seventh Directive on requirements for group accounts were adopted by France in 1982 and 1985 respectively. In doing so, France chose to extend the requirements of the Fourth Directive to all enterprises, incorporated or otherwise and, in applying the Seventh Directive, to permit a number of optional accounting treatments for groups not available for the accounts of the individual enterprise. The legal position of the PCG was clarified at the same time, with application to all enterprises registered under the commercial code, as well as public sector enterprises of a commercial character. With major revisions in 1982 and in 1986 to incorporate requirements for consolidated accounts, the PCG arrived at its current form and contents.

4. French experience with a national accounting code

French experience with a national accounting code is significant both in terms of its national setting and the process adopted for its development and application. The national context over the life of the PCG has evolved from a high degree of state control and intervention in economic affairs to one where increasing attention has to be paid to international influences, directly as regards accounting standards and generally to the impact of international securities and currency markets.

A. Application and adaptation of the code

Since 1947, the French national accounting code has been progressively applied to a widening range of commercial and other activities. Procedures for its adaptation to the needs of particular industries or activities have been extensively employed, though perhaps not in the ways earlier anticipated. Adaptations occur in response to the following circumstances:

- As proposed by the trade association for a particular industry sector;
- Government ministry requests that the CNC consider a proposed adaptation or that the CNC itself develop an adaptation for an industry or trade sector, or a public agency or agency category;
- Initiation of a CNC project for adaptation to a particular sector.

Since adoption of the 1982 PCG, there have been 63 approvals of industry sector proposals by trade associations, with 48 containing modifications to the PCG. Where there has been no proposed adaptation on behalf of a sector, the PCG applies as it stands to enterprises in that sector. Whether or not an adaptation has been approved for its sector, an individual enterprise may adapt the PCG to its needs by further extension of the PCG chart of accounts but must respect the usage of account classes, sub-classes and individual accounts designated in the PCG as obligatory. Nearly all sector adaptations of the 1982 PCG were approved shortly after its adoption, suggesting that for other sectors the PCG is sufficiently flexible without the need for taking a similar step. In addition to adaptations for trade associations, the CNC has recommended adaptations for a number of important sectors of economic activity. These include legal entities in the agriculture sector (for example, cooperatives), managed securities and real estate investment funds, chambers of commerce, health and social welfare establishments, and non-profit associations.

In regard to the public sector, the PCG has been individually adapted for major state utilities such as the railways and electricity, and for many categories of public establishments, both of a commercial and an administrative character.

Some categories comprise thousands of individual establishments. Extension of the PCG to administrative establishments was brought about by a 1962 decree specifying requirements for financial accounting, management accounting and special accounting for physical items, valuables and securities, with a basic distinction to be drawn between accounting for transactions of the state itself and public national establishments. Key requirements applicable to financial accounting for the transactions of these two categories are as follows:

1) The state

Accounting for transactions funded from the general state budget and special treasury accounts, as well as from related budgets and special commercial accounts, is to be in accordance with an adapted code based on the PCG.

2) Public national establishments

Establishments of an administrative character are to apply specific accounting codes conforming to a model code based on the PCG and approved by the Finance Minister. Establishments of an industrial and commercial character are to apply a specific code based on the PCG and approved by the CNC.

B. Structure and process for accounting standardisation

The UK and US national accounting standard setting bodies, the Accounting Standards Board and Financial Accounting Standards Board respectively, operate as follows:

- Financed largely or wholly by the private sector;
- Boards each with fewer than a dozen members, mostly senior public accountants or auditors, enterprise finance directors, financial analysts or accounting professors, serving on a full- or part-time basis;
- Direction and staffing largely or wholly drawn from public accounting practice or private enterprise;
- A consultative process for establishing standards through stages of issuing proposals for public comment, revision and final adoption.

By contrast, the French government agency, the CNC, is wholly funded and staffed by government. It is a consultative body without regulatory powers which issues stated opinions for interpretation of the PCG and recommendations for its adaptation. Proposed opinions or recommendations are not issued for public comment prior to adoption. Its full council has over 100 members nominated from a wide range of public and private sector bodies and interests, all serving part-time other than its secretary-general. In practice, proposals for opinions and recommendations are dealt with by its other deliberative organs, namely the Bureau comprising the CNC president, its five vice-presidents and secretary-general, or sections respectively dealing with accounting for non-commercial activity (principally government accounting), enterprises, and accounting principles. Supporting the deliberative organs are four standing commissions of members and external experts for management accounting, consolidated accounts, accounting for financial instruments and small and medium enterprises. Groundwork on proposed opinions and recommendations is carried out by the commissions prior to transmission to the Bureau or relevant section for final decision.

The broad formalised constituency of the CNC effectively gives a place in its process to all groups with an interest in the PCG. For 1992, the latest year of available data, Table 1 shows its membership composition by public and private sector affiliation, and by category within those sectors, with the former comprising 28 and the latter 75 of the total 103 members at that time. The potential of membership constituencies for influencing the CNC process, considered below, is not simply a function of their size but also of their cohesion or commitment to the process.

1.1. Accounting profession and other accounting experts

Given its mission, an apparently obvious issue is whether accounting expertise dominates the CNC process and outcomes. Though not directly shown in Table 1, accounting experts numbered 53 of the 75 private sector members, made up of public accountants, auditors, enterprise chief accountants, accounting professors (some as trade union representatives), as well as certain representatives of other professional bodies and persons of recognised standing. In all, representatives of the accounting profession were the largest single constituency. Its ability to exert a coordinated influence is affected by its institutional structure organised on functional lines, with separate bodies for practising public accountants and statutory auditors[9]. As these are two distinctly different sets of responsibilities, it is not to be expected that the two bodies need or are in a position to maintain a common viewpoint in regard to CNC process or the PCG.

Given that membership of the French accounting profession is restricted to persons in public practice, the possible influence on the CNC process of its representatives needs to be considered in light of the demands of their professional institutions, individual accounting firms and clients. For these members, the economic structure of public accounting and auditing firms, in which chargeable hours drive income, imposes a direct opportunity cost on participation in CNC technical activity, which is on a non-fee basis. This factor is adverse to significant participation in CNC technical activities and to arriving at sustainable common ground on issues of CNC process and its outcomes. Analysis of published 1992 data shows that participation in commissions by the accounting profession representatives and eminent members of the profession was the lowest of any major constituent group.

In contrast, enterprise chief accountants are not directly subject to opportunity costs pressures. Habitually drawn from major French company groups, all members of this constituency participated in CNC commissions, particularly in relation to consolidated accounts and accounting for financial instruments, both key subjects for major groups. Accounting experts representing professional bodies for the advancement of their discipline and accounting professors had a high level of participation but, given their diverse constituencies, it is unlikely that they would find much sustainable common ground on accounting issues before the CNC.

9 Ordre des Experts Comptables et des Comptables agréés and Compagnie Nationale des Commissaires aux Comptes, each separately constituted and regulated under the Finance and Justice Ministries respectively.

Table 1: CNC 1992 membership by public or private sector, by membership category within those sectors

Public sector		
CNC President, Vice-Presidents and Secretary-General		4
Government ministries, councils, agencies:		
Audit	2	
Finance	2	
Industry/commerce/financial statement analysis agencies	4	
Justice	1	
National economic statistics	1	
Securities Commission	1	
Tax administration	3	
Other	10	24
Total public sector		28
Private sector		
Vice-Presidents		3
Institutions of the accounting profession:		
Practising public accountants	8	
Statutory auditors	9	17
Other professional bodies for the advancement of:		
Accounting	6	
Education	1	
Financial analysis, investment, fund management	4	
Management	6	17
Economic interest groups:		
Enterprise chief accountants	6	
Employer organisations	2	
Chambers and tribunals of commerce and trades	5	
Trade unions	5	
Other	5	23
Nominated by CNC President		5
Persons of recognised standing in accounting or related fields		10
Total private sector		75
Total CNC membership		103

Source: Conseil National de la Comptabilité, Rapport d'Activité 1992.

The conclusion from the foregoing is that CNC members with accounting expertise, though a majority of the private sector members, do not exert a coordinated influence commensurate with their numbers. This is partly because there is no common economic interest to unite them on issues of accounting doctrine. With representatives of the accounting profession, the demands and opportunity cost of public practice are a further factor, acting as an effective brake on their participation in CNC technical activity. It is notable that the French accounting profession as such has not at any stage strongly sought control over accounting standardisation, as might have been expected by comparison with the UK or USA.

1.2. Business enterprise sector and securities markets

The business enterprise sector is collectively represented on CNC through the national employer council, commerce and trades chambers, and the national conference of commerce tribunals. Their representatives had a high level of participation in CNC commissions, especially on consolidated accounts and accounting for financial instruments. Commerce chamber representatives participated in the CNC commission on accounting responsibilities of small and medium enterprises.

Business sector bodies represented on the CNC have broad constituencies. It is accordingly unlikely that they advance narrow interests in that forum, especially given availability of the procedure for industry sector associations to seek approval for adaptations of the PCG. Instead, these broadly-based business sector bodies can be expected to concentrate on items of general interest to their members. An obvious example of concern both to large or small enterprises is the relationship between rules for accounting profit and those for taxable income. It is likely that the business sector bodies maintain a close interest in this aspect of the PCG and its linkages with tax law and administration (see discussion of this issue from the state viewpoint in 3.2.3 below).

The interests of securities markets in the PCG are catered for through representation on the CNC of several professional bodies and economic interest groups, such as financial analysts and stock market agents. As a small group of members affiliated to individual bodies, they do not form a naturally cohesive group. Although reference occurs in early documentation on the PCG to the shareholder needs for improved financial information, addressing those needs has not historically been a driving priority in development of the PCG or CNC technical activity. This reflects important elements of the organisation of the French economy and related public policy, at the time of instituting the PCG and subsequently. Compared with the UK or USA, the stock market has to the present time played a relatively modest role in France in terms of numbers of listed companies, risk capital raised through securities issues, and total capitalisation of listed securities. In turn, its restricted role denotes the relative absence of an equity securities investment culture.

1.3. Interests of the state

The broad CNC public sector membership category comprises civil servants representing a wide range of government agencies. Their likely motivation is to maximise outcomes consistent with the policies and priorities of their particular agencies. In doing so, their roles are generally supported by legislation and regulation which they are bound to uphold. The agencies of most evident importance for identifying the various interests of the state and their influence on the PCG and CNC process are as follows:

1) Commission des Opérations de Bourse (COB, the securities commission)

With establishment of the COB in 1967, a regulatory voice to speak for securities markets and investor needs was accorded a place in the CNC. Through the 1970s, growth in the number of French listed companies meant that attention to investor needs was accepted by degrees as an important aspect of the PCG and CNC process. Nationalisation of companies following the change to a socialist government in 1981 again diminished the role of the stock market through significant reduction in the number of major listed companies and their aggregate market capitalisation. With privatisation since 1986 partly reversing previous nationalisation, attention has again been directed to financial accounting issues of consolidated accounts, recognition and valuation of fixed assets including intangible and financial assets, and adequacy of provisions for liabilities and charges. COB representation on the CNC therefore has an important role to play, with participation in the commission for consolidated accounts. There appears at times to have been competition between the CNC and COB over which body might best address issues of financial reporting by listed companies. Possibly to deal with this, there is now a COB-CNC commission to address matters of common interest.

2) Direction générale des impôts (DGI, the tax administration)

The early interest of the DGI in the potential of a national accounting code for improved determination of enterprise taxable surplus is clear from the work of the commission to develop the 1942 PCG. Notwithstanding this, there was no linkage between the 1947 PCG and definition of taxable income or tax declaration procedures, perhaps as a concession to sensitivities of the private sector over possible state surveillance of enterprise affairs through the PCG. Nevertheless, the interest of the DGI in the PCG was reasserted by the 1965 tax decree previously indicated, with the establishment of precise links between accounting and tax rules, and of subsequent procedures for basing the tax declaration schedules on information making up the annual accounts. The importance from a tax administration viewpoint of maintaining these links gives the DGI a significant continuing role in the CNC process as defender of its interests. In 1992 individual DGI representatives were the only CNC members to participate in all four CNC commissions. The DGI has a particular interest in requirements for financial information from enterprises subject to income tax and procedures to be followed for this purpose. Of recent years, this interest has concentrated on automated data exchange.

3) Lawmaking

The place of the PCG in commercial, company, tax and public administrative law gives the Justice Ministry a significant interest in the CNC process, signified by the participation in 1992 of its representative in all CNC commissions other than that for management accounting (an optional part of the PCG).

4) Institut National de la Statistique et des Etudes Economiques (INSEE, the national statistical office)

An early priority for the PCG was as a source of more reliable and standardised financial performance data from private sector enterprises on which to develop improved national economic statistics. This has had enduring effects on the PCG, which in some ways retains a conceptual framework appropriate to the production-driven economy characteristic of its early post-war origin. An example is seen in the requirement in all successive versions of the PCG that charges against income be classified in the annual accounts on the basis of their nature or type, rather than by purpose or destination as preferred generally for management purposes. A further example is seen in the importance given to measurement of value added, a key concept in statistics on financial enterprise performance by industry sector and nationally. This is reflected in the 1982 PCG with its set of management performance measures recommended to be prepared and disclosed by enterprises showing value added by their operations. Meanwhile, contemporary market conditions have become increasingly consumer-dominated, with enterprise financial management needing to pay increasing attention to investor priorities and the criterion of adding to shareholder value. In this context, profitability and cash flows are of paramount importance, with an associated need for improved financial accounting measures and values reflective of changing conditions, including circumstances pointing to drastic provisioning against asset values. This economic reality points to the difficulty of making distinctions between current operating profit or loss and extraordinary profit or loss, which in turn affect the validity of value added measures as defined in the PCG as a basis for consistent classification of charges, income, assets and liabilities across enterprises and industry sectors.

In reviewing the influence of interest groups on the structure and process for accounting standardisation in France, allowance must be made for changing conditions. EU Directives have been external factors to strengthen the influence of constituencies speaking for the role of accounting information in a securities market context. This is because the Directives themselves were only intended to apply to companies, their development was influenced by British perspectives and experience drawing on the importance of securities markets to financial risk assessment and pricing, and the Seventh Directive brought consolidation of accounts by groups to the forefront of attention. A further and more recent factor of change has been the emergence of the International Accounting Standards Committee as the pre-eminent body to develop international accounting standards and the consequent need for the CNC to address issues of compatibility of the PCG with IASC standards.

The importance of acceptability of financial reporting by major French groups to international financial markets and the particular issue of compatibility of the PCG requirements with IASC standards affect a wide band of interest groups represented on the CNC. They include public accountants, statutory auditors, the COB, enterprise chief accountants, and private sector bodies representing the business sector and securities markets. In the face of this coalition of interests, the state made a significant concession to private sector priorities by allowing important optional alternatives for consolidated accounts to the requirements for individual enterprise accounts, namely:

- Inclusion of interest charges in cost of fixed or current assets, without necessary regard to the length of the operating cycle;
- Balance sheet capitalisation of the effects of leasing transactions;
- Taking year-end foreign currency translation gains or losses on receivables and payables to the profit and loss account;

- Optional revaluation of fixed tangible and financial assets;
- Basing annual accounts on end-of-period monetary purchasing power;
- Valuation of depreciable fixed assets and stocks at replacement value;
- Use of last in, first out (LIFO) for cost of sales and stocks, whether for the group as a whole or for particular segments or regions of activity.

The state nevertheless shows every sign of retaining its long-standing interest in coherence between the PCG and its legal framework, particularly as regards tax law. Experience suggests that foreign influences in relation to accounting principles and their application are unlikely to affect the PCG without support from relevant state agencies represented on the CNC. Nor is there any sign of their causing a reconsideration of whether France is now best served by a process for accounting standardisation so firmly under the control of the state.

5. Applying French experience to the present European context

In considering French experience with a national accounting code in the present European context, two aspects of internationalisation and reform in the former Eastern European command economies warrant attention. In important ways, they are distinct issues but in others they overlap.

A. Securities markets and international accounting standards

The major contribution of the PCG has been in standardising the chart of accounts underlying the entity accounting system and the annual account formats constructed within the rules for that system. In its development there has been relatively little attention to construction of a conceptual framework for financial accounting and reporting. By this is meant the enunciation of a structure of broad interrelated concepts concerned with:

- Objectives for financial reporting, in terms of user needs;
- Criteria for recognition of the asset, external liability and owner equity components of financial position and changes in position;

- Criteria for bringing income and charges to account, and for distinguishing between their ordinary and extraordinary components;
- Presentation of periodic financial statements and associated information.

Intellectual leadership in this task was initially demonstrated in the USA through successive experiences with evolving a process for accounting standard setting, culminating thus far in the FASB *Statements of Financial Accounting Concepts* and various studies at conceptual level of particular financial accounting issues[10]. In recent years, the work of the UK Accounting Standards Board and the International Accounting Standards Committee have established them as important partners in the task. By contrast, the pace of development of the PCG and its outcomes have been more limited in scope and effect. In particular, in dealing with financial reporting to securities investors, France has been a follower rather than a contributor at an international level. The considerable advantages created over a long period from standardisation in annual accounts are being vitiated by the divergent response of French groups to the choices created from uncoupling requirements for consolidated accounts from those for individual entity accounts. For want of more specific direction, some French groups follow IASC standards, some follow US FASB standards, and others pick and choose. Within France, the most widely used enterprise financial performance databases continue to concentrate on individual entity data, as though consolidated accounts were yet to be invented. Moreover, in relation to consolidated accounts, the mechanism for supervising company practices and enforcing compliance with best standards does not have the robustness of the US Securities and Exchange Commission.

These uncoordinated developments reflect the structure for accounting standardisation. Relaxation by the state of the PCG requirements to be applied to consolidated accounts was a response to a coalition of the COB and private sector interests but the coalition has not been sustained as a basis for addressing problems emerging from responses to that relaxation. For the structure to regain effective authority, it needs more decisive involvement from the private

10 For example, the FASB, 1991.

sector and attainment of a faster tempo of activity. There may be interests of the state that would find it unpalatable to cede authority in this matter to the private sector. American experience in particular shows, however, that the diversity of private sector interests in accounting standard setting is too wide for a conspiracy against the public interest. Companies, their auditors, financial analysts and investment fund managers experience constantly shifting alliances of convenience, but they know that their many constituencies are closely watching what they do.

B. Significance of changes in Eastern Europe

The PCG was born out of convulsive experiences of change. Dominant interests of the state interpreted those circumstances as requiring firmer state direction of the economy, a position modified over time by fluctuating recognition and acceptance of the significance of market forces. In Eastern Europe, the convulsive change brought about by the collapse of communist control was initially hailed as the prerequisite for a rapid embrace of market capitalism. Subsequent events in that direction have been marked in much of the region by massive privatisation with markedly varying degrees of transparency applied to determination of transfer prices and selection of new equity owners. This has occurred in a context of unfamiliarity with international accounting standards, advanced financial accounting concepts and Western models for accounting standard setting.

In much of Central and Eastern Europe, national accounting codes have long been familiar, initially imposed by the state, in some cases still retained in the legal framework and in others adhered to through familiarity and absence of evident alternatives[11]. In those conditions, the concept of a code and its social and informational advantages are generally understood, at least for public policy purposes of production of statistics and tax administration.

11 For extensive discussion of developments in other European countries with experience of national accounting codes, see Bechtel, 1994, on Germany; Richard, 1995, on Russia and Romania, and the entire issue of *European Accounting Review*, 4/4, 1995, "Accounting in Central and Eastern Europe".

For the countries in question, there are no obvious advantages from abandoning this approach to accounting standardisation provided that it does not impede privatisation and development of properly regulated securities markets. Indeed, the matter can be put the other way round. Mitigation of divisive political and social consequences from privatisation and securities market development are contingent on social acceptance of these changes and the resulting distribution of economic gains and losses. There are similar risks related to the construction and operation of a system of enterprise profit taxation. In these uncertain circumstances, promotion of economic welfare requires close state attention to creating and sustaining conditions for application of effective accounting standards by enterprises (Bailey, 1995). Whereas Eastern Europe experience with national accounting codes was in the context of central command economies, without significant private equity ownership and associated securities markets and taxation systems, French experience under diverse conditions provides a relevant model.

6. Conclusion

In summary, the concept of a national accounting code is compatible with producing financial information flows for securities markets and accommodating pressures for more uniform international accounting standards. There is no reason to abandon its underlying basis in a standardised chart of accounts and associated terminology, which offer economies of scale in training accountants and users of accounting information, accounting system design and analytic approaches to financial statement interpretation. For the concept to retain authority, French experience suggests that it is important to loosen state control over development of the code as the market economy develops and to allow more play for the very market forces that the code is in important measure intended to serve. The state can reasonably retain a role of oversight in the process and will still be required to maintain and apply an appropriate regulatory framework.

Résumé

La codification comptable : expérience et projets dans le contexte européen

Partant de l'expérience du Plan comptable français adopté en 1947 et révisé à quatre reprises depuis, celui-ci ayant influencé d'autres pays européens et francophones en dehors de l'Europe, l'étude présentée dans ce chapitre se propose d'expliquer le rôle et la nature d'un plan comptable en comparaison du principe plus souple de standardisation comptable appliqué dans les pays anglo-saxons et dans la plupart des pays au monde. L'auteur porte un jugement très argumenté sur le système français en dégageant ses forces et ses faiblesses et en posant la question de sa pertinence pour l'Union européenne et les pays en transition de l'Europe de l'Est. Le débat porte sur l'information des acteurs, sur le contrôle des pouvoirs publics, et sur l'harmonisation des évaluations comptables dans une économie mondialisée. Les enjeux sont importants.

Zusammenfassung

Der Grundregeln der Buchführung : Erfahrung und Vorhaben im europäischen Kontext

Die vorliegende Untersuchung soll Sinn und Zweck des französischen Kontenplans darstellen und mit den weniger standardisierten Buchungsregeln vergleichen, die in den angelsächsischen Ländern und in den meisten anderen Staaten der Welt gelten. Sie baut dabei auf den Erfahrungen auf, die mit den 1947 verabschiedeten und seither viermal modifizierten Grundregeln der Buchführung gemacht wurden und großen Einfluß auf die anderen europäischen und außereuropäischen frankophonen Staaten ausübten.

Der Autor begründet eingehend seine Analyse der Stärken und Schwächen des französischen Systems und beurteilt dessen Einschlägigkeit für die Europäische Union und für die sich im Umbruch befindlichen osteuropäischen Staaten. Dabei geht es ihm um die Information der für die Buchhaltung Verantwortlichen, um die Kontrolle durch die öffentliche Hand und um eine Harmonisierung der Bewertungsgrundsätze im Rechnungswesen in einer sich weltweit organisierenden Wirtschaft. Beträchtliches steht dabei auf dem Spiel!

References

AMERICAN INSTITUTE OF CERTIFIED PUBLIC ACCOUNTANTS (1973): Objectives of Financial Statements. New York. AICPA.

ACCOUNTING STANDARDS STEERING COMMITTEE (1975): The Corporate Report. London. ASSC. 1-103.

BAILEY, D. (ed.) (1995): Accounting in transition in the transitional economy. The European Accounting Review, 4/4. 595-623.

BECHTEL, W. (1995): Charts of accounts in Germany. The European Accounting Review, 4/2. 283-304.

BERARD, V./LEMARCHAND, Y. (1994): Le Miroir du Marchand. Paris. Editions Comptables Malesherbes.

CONSEIL NATIONAL DE LA COMPTABILITE (1986): Plan comptable général. Paris. CNC.

FINANCIAL ACCOUNTING STANDARDS BOARD (1991): Discussion Memorandum No.109-A. Recognition and Measurement of Financial Instruments. Norwalk, Conn. FASB.

FORRESTER, D. (1977): Schmalenbach and after. Glasgow. Strathclyde Convergencies.

HAIN, P. (1980): Uniformity and Diversity: The Development of Classification Concepts in Double Entry Accounting. N.Y. Arno.

JOHNSON, H./KAPLAN, R. (1987): Relevance Lost: The Rise and Fall of Management Accounting. Boston. Harvard Business School.

LEMARCHAND, Y. (1993): Du dépérissement à l'amortissement. Nantes. Ouest Editions.

MOMMEN, M. (1957): Le Plan comptable selon différentes formes d'expressions et son aboutissement international. Brussels. Cambel.

OLSON, M. (1982): The Rise and Decline of Nations: Economic Growth, Stagflation and Social Rigidities. New Haven. Yale University Press.

RICHARD, J. (1995): The evolution of accounting chart models in Europe from 1900 to 1945: Some historical elements. The European Accounting Review, 4/1. 87-124.

RICHARD, J. (1995): The evolution of the Romanian and Russian accounting charts after the collapse of the communist system. The European Accounting Review, 4/2. 305-322.

SINGER, H. (1943): Standardized Accountancy in Germany. Cambridge. University Press.

STANDISH, P. (1990): Origins of the Plan comptable général: A study in cultural intrusion and reaction. Accounting and Business Research. Autumn. 337-351.

STANDISH, P. (1996, forthcoming): The French Plan Comptable: Scope, Operation, Implications (Paris: Editions Comptables Malesherbes).

Marc Gaudry
Ulrich Blum
John McCallum

A First Gross Measure of Unexploited Single Market Integration Potential

1. Introduction: measuring single market integration failure

2. Structure of generation-distribution models

   A. Activity terms and spatial structures
   B. The ease of interaction term
   C. The gravity model proper

3. A baseline trade flow model for North America and Europe

   A. Economic specification
   B. Econometric specification and estimation procedure

4. Results

   A. Functional form: not multiplicative, but close
   B. Elasticities for Gross Domestic Product and distance; the GOM

1. Introduction: measuring single market integration failure

How could failures of single market integration be measured? One possibility is to use the very successful gravity model as the reference model of spatial interaction and define with this model a GROSS measure of unexploited opportunity, with the intent of deriving a NET measure obtained after systematic subtraction of "suitable" components. We will provide here examples of this approach, using a flexible-form generalization of the gravity model applied to interregional trade indicators for Europe and North America. They will not be complete examples of the approach, but will be sufficient to establish the strength of the proposed method by pointing out extraordinary resemblances between the results for the 40 North American regions and for the 21 European regions considered, and by providing for each group a first distance-based GROSS OPPORTUNITY MEASURE (GOM).

2. Structure of generation-distribution models

The general structure of Generation-Distribution models consists in:

(Flow indicator $_{ij}$) <—(Activities $_{i \text{ and } j}$; Socioeconomic $_{i \text{ and } j}$; Ease of interaction $_{ij}$)

where the indices i and j denote origin and destination zones, activities and socioeconomic variables denote factors such as population, or income and, following BLUM and LEIBBRAND (1994), the ease or (dis-)utility of transaction is an impedance metric that can be of many types (geographical, preference or taste, legal or regulatory in nature, or other).

A. Activity terms and spatial structures

Although we will take the level and distribution of activities as given , it is appropriate to keep in mind that the structure of the spatial distribution of activities is the normal object of trade theory, which in effect attempts to explain , partly as a function of transportation costs, both the level and the distribution of these activities. In a generation-distribution model, this is in effect the "trade potential" defined primarily by the the activity terms. There are three broad approaches to this explanation. The Neoclassical Reference Model, (summarized by the well-known Stolper-Samuelson, Heckscher-Ohlin, Rybczyski, and Factor price equalization theorems) defines a reference paradigm for *economic convergence* in real incomes, which excludes two possibilities of *economic divergence* underlined by new trade theory and polarization theory.

New trade theory (KRUGMAN 1990; HELPMAN and KRUGMAN 1985; MARTIN 1993) shows that the neoclassical convergence properties no longer hold under a situation of imperfect competition due to

- external economies and economies of scale and of scope,
- monopolistic or oligopolistic market structures,
- product differentiation resulting in monopolistic competition,
- sunk costs.

The most important results are that intra-industry trade is now explicable by the existence of product differentiation and external economies, by the inability of new suppliers working at lower costs to enter markets due to the use of monopolistic power and the advantage of the first producer: in particular, development strategies already proposed by LIST (1848) may be economically efficient and the state or nation has a role to play in trade (KRUGMAN 1990).

Polarization theory is based on the concepts of spatial economies and the existence of transaction costs. Furthermore, certain economies of scale or of scope must exist to promote agglomeration tendencies, e.g. through central markets (v. THÜNEN 1826; ALONSO 1964), technologies (LÖSCH 1942; HIRSCHMAN 1958 and MYRDAL 1956, 1957) have applied polarization theory to center-periphery problems and to problems of developing countries. More general concepts, including those of economic and geographic space, have been proposed by PERROUX (1964) and empirically validated by BOUDEVILLE (1972). The main arguments behind the polarization tendencies are existing rigidities, lacking physical and human capital at the periphery and a high speed of innovation in developed countries also exploiting economies of scale.

CHATTERJI (1992) has proposed a concept of spatial economic clubs with convergence tendencies internally and divergence with respect to other clubs (e.g. EU or the OECD vs. the former COMECON, or the Third World, etc.).

B. The ease of interaction term

The most important transaction costs relating to the problem of integration are

1. transportation costs (transaction costs in geographical space),
2. language and culture,
3. institutional setup and political norms including political borders,
4. economic barriers such as monetary systems.

C. The gravity model proper

A great advantage of the gravity model, defined as a simple multiplicative (Cobb-Douglas) form of the generation-distribution model, with or without double constraints imposed on flows originating or destinating in each zone, is that, by being conditional upon the distribution of production and consumption activities, it makes it possible to focus on the specific spatial role of impedance in determining the spatial extension of the market (its area) without simultaneously requiring an explanation of the underlying structure. It also affords the possibility of detecting irregularities in this range at the limit of which the marginal costs of controlling space are matched by the willingness to pay for the products offerred. Although some of the factors mentioned above are of direct relevance in explaining such irregularities (e.g. the *spatial* exercise of imperfect competition, whereby, for instance, identical cars can be sold at very different prices among neighbouring regions), most of them are not very likely to impound on the spatial regularity of territorial flows: they are more likely to affect the size of blanketed areas than their regularity.

The simple multiplicative gravity model has for many decades had extraordinary success in explaining such regularities in transportation flows and, more recently, in explaining trade flows as well. Similarly, transportation flow models have long included explanations of irregularitites due to linguistic and political borders, and even used flexible mathematical forms to do so (GAUDRY and WILLS 1978, BLUM and LEIBBRAND 1994). In particular, many uses of Origin or Destination dummy variables in some of these models (depending on the meaning of zones) have been observationally equivalent to border dummy variables.

3. A baseline trade flow model for North America and Europe

A. Economic specification

It is our intent to remedy this situation and to introduce flexible mathematical forms on a trade flow model. In order to bring out the structure of the problem and obtain a first estimate of a GOM, we use the simplest specification which includes only the variables *Gross Domestic Product* a *distance* impedance metric and a (gross) *border effect dummy*. Flow indicators will be the *value of shipments* for North America, (as in MCCALLUM`s model, our starting point) and the *tonnage shipped* for Europe (because value of shipment data were not available on a regional basis, but only on a national basis). In the North American case, 1988 flows are observed among the 10 Canadian provinces, as well as between them and 30 American states (but not among American states): there are 683 observations. In the European Union case, 1987 flows are observed among the 11 German provinces, as well as between them and 10 other European countries (but not among European countries): there are 316 observations.

B. Econometric specification and estimation procedure

We use Box-Cox transformations (BCT) on the dependent and independent variables (except the dummy variables) of the model. This transformation has the advantage of letting the data decide whether the usual linear-in-logarithms case (corresponding to the BCT parameter value LAMBDA=0), the linear case (corresponding to the parameter value LAMBDA =1), or a more general case (as LAMBDA can have any value), gives the best fit for the chosen list of variables. In addition, we allow for a correction of a very general nature to establish constancy of variance of the regression errors (an exponential function of a variable --in this case the product of Gross Domestic Products at the origin and destination-- itself subjected to a BCT); this transformation can yield as a special nested case the classical correction consisting in weighing all observations by the chosen heteroskedasticity variable. The estimates were obtained by the TRIO program (GAUDRY, 1993).

4. Results

Results for both data sets are shown in two tables of similar structure, *North America 1* and *European Community 1*. Column headings denote, from left to right:

- **LOG:** the usual model (LAMBDA=0);
- **BC1:** estimation of a BCT that is common to all variables;
- **BC2:** estimation of a BCT on the dependent variable, and another on the explanatory variables;
- **BC2GH1:** addition to the previous case of the heteroskedasticity variable with its own BCT.

The tables have three sections:

- In the first one, *elasticities* of the flows with respect to explanatory variables, as well as *t-statistics* of underlying regression coefficients (except the regression constants), are listed; one may note that the last variable listed is the heteroskedasticity variable.
- In the second section, values of the *estimated BCT* are found, with *two t-statistics* of interest.
- In the third section, values of the *log likelihood* and other summary statistics are listed.

A. Functional form: not multiplicative, but close

Starting with the North America table, we note that the first column is an exact replication of McCALLUM's (1993) result. Large gains in log-likelihood occur when one BCT or two are used, even though the estimated values of the LAMBDA are close to zero. Further gains are made when the heteroskedasticity correction *(product of GNP at origin and destination)*$^{-0.19}$ is estimated.

Almost identical results can be found in the European Union table, where we note that the estimated signs of the BCT, as well as their values, are strikingly close. The use of flexible forms clearly yields impressive gains, as does the chosen heteroskedasticity correction. However, had we used the classical heteroskedasticity correction *(product of GNP at origin and destination)*$^{+2.00}$ mentioned above, we would have obtained results (not shown) that are worse than making no correction at all.

B. Elasticities for Gross Domestic Product and distance; the GOM

As one would expect, elasticities of GNP are much higher for North America than Europe, as befits the difference between shipments in money values and shipments in tons. It is interesting to note that the destination elasticities are higher than the origin elasticities in both cases.

The distance elasticities are almost equal (about -1.20).

The impact of the interprovincial trade dummy variables, defined as the percentage change in the flows associated with the presence of that variable is about 3 times as large in North America than in the European Community. This measure of the GOM is derived from the mean values of the flows in the sample and calculated only with respect to the positive values of the binary variable. These high values of the GOM (respectively about 2,70 and 0,90) imply that borders matter, but do not tell us the extent to which linguistic, administrative, natural, protectionist, regulatory or even transportation money and time costs make contributions unaccounted for by the distance impedance metric.

NORTH AMERICA 1: TRADE FLOW MODELS BETWEEN 30 AMERICAN STATES AND 10 CANADIAN PROVINCES, AND AMONG THE LATTER (1988 SHIPMENTS AT PRODUCER PRICES)

I.	TYPE =	LEVEL-1	LEVEL-1	LEVEL-1	LEVEL-1
	VARIANT =	LOG	BC1	BC2	BC2GH1
ELASTICITY E(y) (EP)	VERSION =	2	0	0	0
(COND. T-STATISTIC)	DEP.VAR. =	ship	ship	ship	ship
LEVEL VARIABLES					
GROSS DOMESTIC PRODUCT AT ORIGIN	agdpm	1.062	.974	.859	.922
		(34.33)	(35.76)	(37.75)	(33.86)
		LAM 1	LAM 1	LAM 1	LAM 1
GROSS DOMESTIC PRODUCT AT DESTINATION	agdpx	1.206	1.088	.961	1.020
		(38.59)	(40.77)	(42.03)	(40.68)
		LAM 1	LAM 1	LAM 1	LAM 1
DISTANCE	dist	-1.425	-1.291	-1.216	-1.160
		(-22.66)	(-24.95)	(-25.77)	(-24.08)
		LAM 1	LAM 1	LAM 1	LAM 1
INTERPROVINCIAL TRADE DUMMY	cdummy ======	3.093	2.718	2.648	2.869
		(23.69)	(21.35)	(22.60)	(20.20)
HETEROSKEDASTICITY STRUCTURE					
DELTA COEFFICIENTS					
---	---	---	---	---	---
PRODUCT OF GDP AT ORIGIN AND DESTINATION	dpmdpx				-.056
					(-5.77)
					LAM
II. PARAMETERS	VARIANT =	LOG	BC1	BC2	BC2GH1
HETEROSKEDASTICITY STRUCTURE					
BOX-COX TRANSFORMATIONS: UNCOND: [T-STATISTIC=0] / [T-STATISTIC=1]					
---	---	---	---	---	---
LAMBDA(Z)	dpmdpx				.000
					FIXED
---	---	---	---	---	---
BOX-COX TRANSFORMATIONS: UNCOND: [T-STATISTIC=0] / [T-STATISTIC=1]					
---	---	---	---	---	---
LAMBDA(Y)	ship			.076	.051
				[9.00]	[5.41]
				-109.32]	-101.21]
LAMBDA(Y) - GROUP 1	LAM 1	.000	.066		
		FIXED	[7.74]		
			-109.37]		
LAMBDA(X) - GROUP 1	LAM 1	.000	.066	-.033	-.051
		FIXED	[7.74]	[-1.47]	[-2.13]
			-109.37]	[-46.70]	[-43.93]
III. GENERAL STATISTICS	VARIANT =	LOG	BC1	BC2	BC2GH1
LOG-LIKELIHOOD		-8089.56	-8057.10	-8043.88	-8032.77
PSEUDO-R2 : - (E)		-15.391	.577	.643	.500
- (L)		.999	.999	.999	1.000
- (E) ADJUSTED FOR D.F.		-15.487	.574	.640	.494
- (L) ADJUSTED FOR D.F.		.999	.999	.999	1.000
AVERAGE PROBABILITY (Y=LIMIT OBSERV.)		.000	.000	.000	.000
SAMPLE : - NUMBER OF OBSERVATIONS		683	683	683	683
- FIRST OBSERVATION		1	1	1	1
- LAST OBSERVATION		683	683	683	683
NUMBER OF ESTIMATED PARAMETERS :					
- FIXED PART :					
. BETAS		5	5	5	5
. BOX-COX		0	1	2	2
. ASSOCIATED DUMMIES		0	0	0	0
- AUTOCORRELATION		0	0	0	0
- HETEROSKEDASTICITY :					
. DELTAS		0	0	0	1
. BOX-COX		0	0	0	0
. ASSOCIATED DUMMIES		0	0	0	0

EUROPEAN COMMUNITY 1: TRADE FLOW MODELS BETWEEN 10 EUROPEAN COUNTRIES AND 11 GERMAN PROVINCES, AND AMONG THE LATTER (1987 SHIPMENTS IN TONS)

I.	TYPE =	LEVEL-1	LEVEL-1	LEVEL-1	LEVEL-1
	VARIANT =	LOG	BC1	BC2	BC2GH1
ELASTICITY E(y) (EP)	VERSION =	1	1	1	2
(COND. T-STATISTIC)	DEP.VAR. =	goods	goods	goods	goods
ALL LEVEL VARIABLES					
GROSS DOMESTIC PRODUCT AT ORIGIN	mecu87_o	.709	.681	.613	.668
		(14.65)	(13.85)	(14.77)	(16.64)
		LAM 1	LAM 1	LAM 1	LAM 1
GROSS DOMESTIC PRODUCT AT DESTINATION	mecu87_d	.731	.704	.635	.688
		(15.15)	(14.77)	(15.80)	(17.36)
		LAM 1	LAM 1	LAM 1	LAM 1
DISTANCE	distance	-1.298	-1.272	-1.137	-1.257
		(-15.54)	(-15.62)	(-19.00)	(-20.37)
		LAM 1	LAM 1	LAM 1	LAM 1
INTERPROVINCIAL TRADE DUMMY	gdummy ======	.990	.959	.886	.949
		(6.38)	(5.18)	(5.42)	(5.36)
HETEROSKEDASTICITY STRUCTURE					
DELTA COEFFICIENTS					
PRODUCT OF GDP AT ORIGIN AND DESTINATION	mecuprod				-.066
					(-4.28)
					LAM

II. PARAMETERS	VARIANT =	LOG	BC1	BC2	BC2GH1
HETEROSKEDASTICITY STRUCTURE					
BOX-COX TRANSFORMATIONS: UNCOND: [T-STATISTIC=0] / [T-STATISTIC=1]					
LAMBDA(Z)	mecuprod				.000
					FIXED
BOX-COX TRANSFORMATIONS: UNCOND: [T-STATISTIC=0] / [T-STATISTIC=1]					
LAMBDA(Y)	goods			.052	.014
				[2.68]	[.59]
				[-49.29]	[-41.93]
LAMBDA(Y) - GROUP 1	LAM 1	.000	.025		
		FIXED	[1.60]		
			[-61.94]		
LAMBDA(X) - GROUP 1	LAM 1	.000	.025	-.134	-.119
		FIXED	[1.60]	[-3.58]	[-3.10]
			[-61.94]	[-30.29]	[-29.16]

III.GENERAL STATISTICS	VARIANT =	LOG	BC1	BC2	BC2GH1
LOG-LIKELIHOOD		-2356.63	-2355.19	-2348.69	-2341.57
PSEUDO-R2 :	- (E)	-.271	.294	-.586	-3.747
	- (L)	.990	.990	.990	.991
	- (E) ADJUSTED FOR D.F.	-.288	.282	-.616	-3.855
	- (L) ADJUSTED FOR D.F.	.990	.990	.990	.990
AVERAGE PROBABILITY (Y=LIMIT OBSERV.)		.000	.000	.000	.000
SAMPLE :	- NUMBER OF OBSERVATIONS	316	316	316	316
	- FIRST OBSERVATION	1	1	1	1
	- LAST OBSERVATION	316	316	316	316
NUMBER OF ESTIMATED PARAMETERS :					
- FIXED PART :					
	. BETAS	5	5	5	5
	. BOX-COX	0	1	2	2
	. ASSOCIATED DUMMIES	0	0	0	0
- AUTOCORRELATION		0	0	0	0
- HETEROSKEDASTICITY :					
	. DELTAS	0	0	0	1
	. BOX-COX	0	0	0	0
	. ASSOCIATED DUMMIES	0	0	0	0

Perhaps, for different flow indicators (transportation, communications, or sectoral industrial or service flows) could one define a GOM and then derive decompositions of its components in such a way as to obtain a Net Opportunity Measure (NOM). Tracking the evolution of these indicators over time would provide a good idea of the degree of integration of single markets.

If one wanted to develop such indicators, a set of reference models could be defined (for different flow indicators). Then, work could be carried out to develop variants of these models that would break down the Gross Opportunity Measure into both an explained component (say in terms of language, currency and other factors) and a residual, unexplained, or Net Opportunity Measure. The latter is the desired measure of potential associated with institutional and nationalistic idiosyncracier ; but its exact significance is conditional upon the contents of the explained component.

The reference models themselves could give rise to different generations of models, or vintages, if for instance the distance measure were replaced by more sophisticated indicators of transportation and communications costs and services.

As in all cases the measures of interest are expressed as percentages of flows, the resulting gross and net measures are intuitively attractive. For instance, in this case the differences between the European and the American measures are clear but, as the explained flows are totally different in nature, are not directly comparable.

Résumé

Une mesure du potentiel d'intégration inexploité du marché unique

Nous montrons qu'une des formulations des modèles de Génération-Distribution, le modèle gravitaire, est utilisable pour définir une mesure brute du potentiel d'intégration du marché unique qui demeure inexploité. Nous utilisons pour la première fois des transformations Box-Cox dans le cas d'un modèle gravitaire appliqué aux flux commerciaux interrégionaux et trouvons que ces transformations donnent un ajustement aux données très supérieur à celui qui est obtenu par la forme multiplicative habituelle. Les résultats obtenus pour l'Amérique du Nord et les résultats obtenus pour l'Europe ont des ressemblances saisissantes qui établissent la robustesse et la pertinence de notre proposition de développer des indices d'intégration potentielle bruts et nets, et de suivre leur évolution.

Zusammenfassung

Rohmaß für das Integrationspotential der Europäischen Märkte

Wir zeigen, daß eine der Formulierungsmöglichkeiten des Erzeugungs-Verteilungsmodells, nämlich das Gravitationsmodell, geeignet ist, um ein Rohmaß für das Integrationspotential einheitlicher Märkte anzugeben, das bisher nicht ausgeschöpft wurde. Zum erstenmal verwenden wir hierfür Box-Cox-Transformationen in einem Gravitationsmodell für interregionale Handelsflüsse. Diese Transformationen ermöglichen eine Anpassung der Daten, die der, die mit der üblichen multiplikativen Form durchgeführt wird, überlegen ist. Die Ergebnisse für Nordamerika und Europa zeigen erstaunliche Ähnlichkeiten, die zugleich ein Nachweis für die Robustheit und die Bedeutung unseres Vorschlages sind, derartige Indikatoren des Integrationspotentials zu erarbeiten und ihre Entwicklung zu verfolgen.

References

ALONSO, W. (1964): Location and Land Use. Harvard University Press. Cambridge (Mass.).

BLUM, U./LEIBBRAND, F. (1994): A Typology of Barriers Applied to Business Trip Data. in: European Transport and Communication Networks. D. Banister/R. Capello/P. Nijkamp ed./Pion. London.

BOUDEVILLE, J.R. (1972): Problems of Regional Planning. Edinburgh.

CHATTERJI, M. (1992): Convergence Clubs and Endogenous Growth. Oxford Review of Economic Policy 8. pp. 57-69.

GAUDRY, M. (1993): Cur cum TRIO?. Publication CRT-901. Université de Montréal.

GAUDRY, M./MANDEL, B./ROTHENGATTER, W. (1994): Introducing Spatial Competition through an Autoregressive Contiguous Distributed (AR-C-D) Process in Intercity Generation-Distribution Models within a Quasi-Direct Format (QDF). Publication CRT-972. Université de Montréal.

GAUDRY, M./WILLS, M. J. (1978): Estimating the functional form of travel demand models. Transportation Research 12, 4, 257-289.

HELPMAN, E./KRUGMAN, P. R. (1990): Market Structure and Foreign Trade. MIT-Press. Cambridge (Mass.).

HIRSCHMAN, A. O. (1958): The Strategy of Economic Development. New-Haven and. London.

KRUGMAN, P. (1990): Rethinking International Trade. MIT-Press. Cambridge (Mass.).

KRUGMAN, P. (1991): Geography and Trade. MIT-Press. Cambridge (Mass.).

LIST, F. (1848): Das nationale System der politischen Ökonomie. Jena (1928).

LÖSCH, A. (1942): Die räumliche Ordnung der Wirtschaft. Gustav Fischer Verlag. Stuttgart (1962).

MARTIN, S. (1993): Advanced Industrial Economics. Blackwell. Oxford and Cambridge (Mass.).

McCALLUM, J. (1993): National Borders Matter: Regional Trade Patterns in North America. Dept. of Economics. McGill University. Forthcoming in the American Economic Review, 85, 3, 615-623 (1995).

MYRDAL, G. (1956): An International Economy, Problems and Prospects. Harper and Bros.. New York.

MYRDAL, G. (1957): Economic Theory and Underdeveloped Regions. Duckleworth and Co.. London.

OKAZAKI, F./HASEGAWA, M./IDE, M. (1987): General Verification of the Logit-Type Stochastic Trade Pattern Usin Intertemporal. Interregional Input-Output Data. Papers of the Regional Science Association. Vol. 63. pp. 1-11.

PERROUX, F. (1964): L'Économie du Xxème siècle. Paris.

von THÜNEN, J. H. (1826): Der isolierte Staat. Fischer. Stuttgart (1966).

MIX
Papier aus verantwortungsvollen Quellen
Paper from responsible sources
FSC® C105338

If you have any concerns about our products,
you can contact us on
ProductSafety@springernature.com

In case Publisher is established outside the EU,
the EU authorized representative is:
Springer Nature Customer Service Center GmbH
Europaplatz 3, 69115 Heidelberg, Germany

Printed by Libri Plureos GmbH
in Hamburg, Germany